WHY ZEBRAS DON'T
GET ULCERS

WHY ZEBRAS DON'T GET ULCERS

A Guide to Stress, Stress-Related Diseases, and Coping

Robert M. Sapolsky

W. H. Freeman and Company
New York

Library of Congress Cataloging-in-Publication Data

Sapolsky, Robert M.
    Why zebras don't get ulcers : a guide to stress, stress-related
diseases, and coping / by Robert M. Sapolsky.
        p.   cm.
    Includes bibliographical references and index.
    ISBN 0-7167-2391-3 (hard); ISBN 0-7167-2718-8 (paper)
    1. Stress (Physiology)   2. Stress (Psychology)   3. Stress
management.   I. Title.
QP82.2.S8S266   1994
616.9'8--dc20   93-27078
                                                                         CIP

Printed in the United States of America

Fourth printing 1997, VB

CONTENTS

PREFACE

Perhaps you're reading this while browsing in a bookstore. If so, glance over at the guy down the aisle when he's not looking, the one pretending to be engrossed in the Stephen Hawking book. Take a good look at him. He's probably not missing fingers from leprosy, or covered with smallpox scars, or shivering with malaria. Instead, he probably appears perfectly healthy, which is to say he has the same diseases that most of us have—cholesterol levels that are high for an ape, hearing that has become far less acute than in a hunter-gatherer of his age, a tendency to dampen his tension with Valium. We in our Westernized society now tend to get different diseases than we used to. But even more importantly, we tend to get different *kinds* of diseases now, with very different causes and consequences. A millennium ago, a young hunter-gatherer inadvertently eats a reedbuck riddled with anthrax and the consequences are clear—he's dead a few days later. Now, a young lawyer unthinkingly decides that red meat, fried foods, and a couple of beers per dinner constitute a desirable diet, and the consequences are anything but clear—a half century later, maybe he's crippled with cardiovascular disease, or maybe he's taking bike trips with his grandkids. Which outcome occurs depends on some obvious factors, like what his liver does with cholesterol, the levels of certain enzymes in his fat cells, whether he has any congenital weaknesses in the walls of his blood vessels. But the outcome will also depend heavily on such vagaries as his personality, the amount of emotional stress he experiences over the years, whether he has someone's shoulder to cry on when those stressors occur.

There has been a revolution in medicine concerning how we think about the diseases that now afflict us. It involves recognizing the interactions between the body and the mind, the ways in which emotions and personality can have a tremendous impact upon the functioning and health of virtually every cell in the body. It is about the role of stress in making some of us more vulnerable to disease, the ways in which some of us cope with stressors, and the critical notion that you cannot really understand a disease *in vacuo*, but rather only in the context of the person suffering from that disease.

This is the subject of my book. I begin by trying to clarify the meaning of the nebulous concept "stress" and to teach, with a minimum of pain, how various hormones and parts of the brain are mobilized in response to stress. I then focus on the links between stress and increased risk for certain types of disease, going chapter by chapter through the effects of stress on the circulatory system, on energy storage, on growth, reproduction, the immune system, and so on. I then examine the link between stress and the most common and arguably most crippling of psychiatric disorders, major depression, and describe how the aging process may be influenced by the amount of stress experienced over the lifetime.

Some of the news is grim—sustained or repeated stress can disrupt our bodies in seemingly endless ways. Yet most of us are not incapacitated by stress-related disease. Instead, we cope, both physiologically and psychologically, and some of us are spectacularly successful at it. For the reader who has held on until the end, the final chapter reviews what is known about stress management and how some of its principles can be applied to our everyday lives. There is much to be optimistic about.

I believe that everyone can benefit from some of these ideas and can be excited by the science on which they are based. Science provides us with some of the most elegant,

stimulating puzzles that life has to offer. It throws some of
the most provocative ideas into our arenas of moral debate.
And occasionally, it improves our lives. I love science, and it
pains me to think that so many are terrified of the subject or
feel that choosing science means that you cannot also choose
compassion, or the arts, or being awed by nature. Science is
not meant to cure us of mystery, but to reinvent and
reinvigorate it.

Thus I think that any science book for nonscientists
should attempt to convey that excitement, to make the subject
interesting and accessible even to those who would normally
not be caught dead near the subject. That has been a
particular goal of mine in this book. Often, that has meant
simplifying complex ideas, and as a counterbalance to this, I
include copious references at the end of the book, often with
annotations concerning controversies and subtleties about
material presented in the main text. These references are an
excellent entrée for those readers who want something more
detailed on the subject.

Many sections of this book contain material about which
I am far from expert, and over the course of the writing, a
large number of savants have been called for advice,
clarification, and verification of facts. I thank them all for
their generosity with their time and expertise: Robert Axelrod,
Alan Baldrich, Marcia Barinaga, Alan Basbaum, Justo Bautisto,
Tom Belva, Anat Biegon, Vic Boff (whose brand of vitamins
graces the cupboards of my parents' home), Carlos Camargo,
Matt Cartmill, M. Linette Casey, Richard Chapman, Cynthia
Clinkingbeard, Felix Conte, George Daniels, Regio DeSilva,
Irven DeVore, James Doherty, John Dolph, Leroi DuBeck,
Richard Estes, Michael Fanselow, David Feldman, Caleb
"Tuck" Finch, Paul Fitzgerald, Rose Frisch, Roger Gosden,
Ray Hintz, Allan Hobson, Robert Kessler, Bruce Knauft, Mary
Jeanne Kreek, Stephen Laberge, Emmit Lam, Jim Latcher,
Richard Lazarus, Helen Leroy, Jon Levine, Seymour Levine,
John Liebeskind, Ted Macolvena, Jodi Maxmin, Peter Milner,
Gary Moberg, Terry Muilenburg, Ronald Myers, Carol Otis,
Daniel Pearl, Ciran Phibbs, Jenny Pierce, Gerald Reaven, Sam

Ridgeway, Carolyn Ristau, Paul Rosch, Ron Rosenfeld, Aryeh Routtenberg, Paul Saenger, Saul Schanburg, Kurt Schmidt-Nielson, Carol Shively, J. David Singer, David Spiegel, Ed Spielman, Dennis Styne, Steve Suomi, Jerry Tally, Carl Thoresen, Peter Tyak, David Wake, Michelle Warren, Owen Wolkowitz, Carol Worthman, and Richard Wurtman.

I am particularly grateful to the handful of people — friends, collaborators, colleagues, and ex-teachers — who took time out of their immensely busy schedules to read chapters. I shudder to think of the errors and distortions that would have remained had they not tactfully told me I didn't know what I was writing about. I thank them all sincerely: Robert Ader of the University of Rochester, Marvin Brown of the University of California, San Diego, Laurence Frank at the University of California, Berkeley, Jay Kaplan of Bowman Gray Medical School, Charles Nemeroff of Emory University, Seymour Reichlin of Tufts/New England Medical Center, Robert Rose of the MacArthur Foundation, Wylie Vale of the Salk Institute, Jay Weiss of Emory University, and Redford Williams of Duke University.

A number of individuals were instrumental in getting this book off the ground and into its final shape. Much of the material in these pages was developed in continuing medical education lectures I have given for health professionals over the years. These have been presented under the auspices of the Institute for Cortex Research and Development, and its director, Will Gordon, who has given me much freedom and support in exploring this material. Bruce Goldman of the Portable Stanford series first planted the idea for this book in my head, and Kirk Jensen recruited me for W. H. Freeman and Company; both helped in the initial shaping of the book. Finally, my secretary Patsy Gardner has been of tremendous help in all the logistical aspects of pulling this book together. I thank you all, and look forward to working with you in the future.

I received tremendous help with organizing and editing the book, and for that I thank Audrey Herbst, Tina Hastings, Amy Johnson, and Meredyth Rawlins of Freeman. Liz

Meryman, who selects the art for *The Sciences*, helping to merge the two cultures in that beautiful publication, graciously consented to read the manuscript and gave splendid advice on appropriate artwork. In addition, I thank Alice Fernandes-Brown of Freeman, who was responsible for making my idea for the cover such a pleasing reality.

This book has been, for the most part, a pleasure to write and I think it reflects one of the things in my life for which I am most grateful — that I take so much joy in the science that is both my vocation and avocation. I thank the mentors who taught me to do science and, even more so, taught me to enjoy science: the late Howard Klar, Howard Eichenbaum, Mel Konner, Lewis Krey, Bruce McEwen, Paul Plotsky, and Wylie Vale.

Above all, four people have been indispensable to the writing of this book. Michelle Pearl, Serena Spudich, and Steve Balt served as research assistants, wandering the basements of archival libraries, calling strangers all over the world with questions, distilling arcane articles into coherency. In the line of duty, they have sought out drawings of opera castrati, the daily menu at Japanese-American internment camps, the causes of voodoo death, and the history of firing squads. All of it was done with spectacular competence, speed, and humor. I am fairly certain this book could not have been completed without their help and am absolutely certain its writing would have been much less enjoyable. And finally, I thank my editor at Freeman, Jonathan Cobb. He has taught me about writing style, reminded me that commas cannot be randomly distributed, and has supplied a clear and correct vision of what is needed, whether on the scale of fixing a single awkward phrase or an awkward concept permeating the entire book. And, somewhere amid this process, he has also become a friend.

Parts of the book describe work carried out in my own laboratory, and these studies have been made possible by funding from the National Institutes of Health, the National Institute of Mental Health, the National Science Foundation, the Sloan Foundation, the Klingenstein Fund, the Alzheimer's

Association, and the Adler Foundation. The African fieldwork described herein has been made possible by the long-standing generosity of the Harry Frank Guggenheim Foundation. Finally, I heartily thank the MacArthur Foundation for supporting all aspects of my work.

There is a tradition among stress physiologists who dedicate their books to their spouses or significant others. It seems an unwritten rule that you are supposed to incorporate something cutesy about stress in the dedication: "To Madge, who attenuates my stressors"; "For Arturo, the source of my eustress"; "For my wife who, over the course of the last umpteen years, has put up with my stress-induced hypertension, ulcerative colitis, loss of libido, and displaced aggression." I will forgo that style here in dedicating this book to my wife; I have something simpler to say.

ROBERT M. SAPOLSKY
July 1993

For Lisa, my best friend,
who has made my life complete.

1

WHY DON'T ZEBRAS GET ULCERS?

It's two o'clock in the morning and you're lying in bed. You have something immensely important and challenging to do that next day—a critical meeting, a presentation, an exam. You have to get a decent night's rest, but you're still wide awake. You try different strategies for relaxing—take deep, slow breaths, try to imagine restful mountain scenery—but instead you keep thinking that unless you fall asleep in the next minute, your career is finished. Thus you lie there, more tense by the second.

If you do this on a regular basis, somewhere around two-thirty, when you're lying there clammy and hyperventilating, an entirely new, disruptive chain of thoughts will no doubt intrude. Suddenly, amid all your other worries, you begin to contemplate that nonspecific pain you've been having in your side, that sense of exhaustion lately, that frequent headache. The realization hits you—I'm sick, fatally sick! Oh, why didn't I recognize the symptoms, why did I have to deny it, why didn't I go to the doctor?

When it's two-thirty on those mornings, I always have a brain tumor. They're very useful for that sort of terror, because you can attribute every conceivable nonspecific symptom to a brain tumor and convince yourself it's time to panic. Perhaps you do, too; or maybe you lie there thinking that you have cancer, or an ulcer, or you've just had a stroke.

Even though I don't know you, I feel confident in predicting that you don't lie there thinking, "I just know it, I have leprosy." True? You are exceedingly unlikely to obsess about getting a serious case of dysentery if it starts pouring. And few of us lie there feeling convinced that our bodies are teeming with intestinal parasites or liver flukes.

Of course not. Our nights are not filled with worries about smallpox, scarlet fever, malaria, or bubonic plague. Cholera doesn't run rampant through our communities; river blindness, black water fever, and elephantiasis are third world exotica. Few female readers will die in childbirth, and even fewer of those reading this page are likely to be malnourished.

Thanks to revolutionary advances in medicine and public health, our patterns of disease have changed, and we are no longer kept awake at night worrying about infectious diseases (except, of course, AIDS) or the diseases of poor nutrition or hygiene. As a measure of this, consider the leading causes of death in the United States at the turn of the century, a mere nine decades ago: pneumonia, tuberculosis, and influenza. When is the last time you heard of someone under age seventy dying of the flu? Yet in 1918, one of the most barbaric years of World War I, a soldier was far more likely to die of the flu or pneumonia than of battle wounds.

Our current patterns of disease would be unrecognizable to our great-grandparents or, for that matter, to most mammals. Put succinctly, we get different diseases and are likely to die in different ways from most of our ancestors (or most humans currently living in the less privileged areas of this planet). Our nights are filled with worries about a different class of diseases; we are now living well enough and long enough to slowly fall apart.

Influenza pandemic, 1918.

The diseases that plague us now are ones of slow accumulation of damage—heart disease, cancer, cerebrovascular disorders. While none of these diseases is particularly pleasant, they certainly mark a big improvement over succumbing at age twenty after a week of sepsis or dengue fever. Along with this relatively recent shift in the patterns of disease have come changes in the way we perceive the disease process. We have come to recognize the vastly complex intertwining of our biology and our emotions, the endless ways in which our personalities, feelings, and thoughts both reflect and influence the events in our bodies. One of the most interesting manifestations of this recognition is understanding that extreme emotional disturbances can adversely affect us. Put in the parlance with which we have grown familiar, *stress can make us sick*, and a critical shift in medicine has been the recognition that many of the damaging diseases of slow accumulation can either be caused or made far worse by stress.

In some respects this is nothing new. Centuries ago, sensitive clinicians intuitively recognized the role of individual differences in vulnerability to disease. Two individuals could get the same disease, yet the courses of their illness could be quite different and in vague, subjective ways might reflect the personal characteristics of the individuals. Or a clinician might have sensed that certain types of people were more likely to contract certain types of disease. But what has made stress physiology—the study of how the body responds to stressful events—a real discipline since early in this century has been the addition of rigorous science to these vague clinical perceptions. As a result, there is today an extraordinary amount of physiological, biochemical, and molecular information available as to how all sorts of intangibles in our lives—emotional turmoil, psychological characteristics, our place in society, and the sort of society in which we live—can affect very real bodily events: whether cholesterol gums up our blood vessels or is safely cleared from the circulation, whether a cell that has become cancerous will be detected in time by the immune system, whether neurons in our brain will survive five minutes without oxygen during a cardiac arrest.

This book is a primer about stress, stress-related disease, and the mechanisms of coping with stress. How is it that our bodies can adapt to some stressful emergencies, while other ones make us sick? Why are some of us especially vulnerable to stress-related diseases? How can purely psychological stressors make us sick? What might stress have to do with our vulnerability to depression, or with the speed at which we age? Finally, how can we increase the effectiveness with which we cope with the stressors that surround us?

Perhaps the best way to begin is by making a mental list of the sorts of things that we find stressful. No doubt you would immediately come up with some obvious examples—traffic, deadlines, family relationships, money worries. But what if I said, "You're thinking like a speciocentric human. Think like a zebra for a second." Suddenly, new items might appear at the top of your list—serious physical injury, predators, starvation. The need for that prompting illustrates something critical—you and I are more likely to get an ulcer than a zebra is. For animals like zebras, the most upsetting things in life are *acute physical stressors*. You are that zebra, a lion has just leapt out and ripped your stomach open, you've managed to get away, and now you have to spend the next hour evading the lion as it continues to stalk you. Or, perhaps just as stressfully, you are that lion, half starved, and you had better be able to sprint across the savanna at top speed and grab something to eat or you won't survive. These are extremely stressful events, and they demand immediate physiological adaptations if you are going to live. Your body's responses are brilliantly adapted for handling this sort of emergency.

An organism can also be plagued by *chronic physical stressors*. The locusts have come and eaten your crops; for the next six months, you have to wander a dozen miles a day to get enough food. Drought, famine, parasites, that sort of unpleasantness—not the sort of experience we have often, but central events in the lives of non-Westernized humans and most other mammals. The body's stress-responses are reasonably good at handling these sustained disasters.

Critical to this book is a third category of ways to get upset—*psychological and social stressors*. Regardless of how poorly we are getting along with a family member or how incensed we are about losing a parking spot, we rarely settle that sort of thing with a fistfight. Likewise, it is a rare event when we have to stalk and personally wrestle down our dinner. Essentially, we humans live well enough and long enough, and are smart enough, to generate all sorts of stressful events purely in our heads. How many hippos worry about whether Social Security is going to last as long as they will, or even what they are going to say on a first date? Viewed from the perspective of the evolution of the animal kingdom, psychological stress is a recent invention. We humans can experience wildly strong emotions (provoking our bodies into an accompanying uproar) linked to mere thoughts. Two people can sit facing each other,

Robert Longo, 1981: untitled work on paper. (Two yuppies contesting the last double latte at a restaurant?)

doing nothing more physically strenuous than moving little pieces of wood now and then, yet this can be an emotionally taxing event: chess grand masters, during their tournaments, can place metabolic demands on their bodies that begin to approach those of athletes during the peak of a competitive event. (Perhaps journalists are aware of this fact; consider this description of the Kasparov/Karpov tournament of 1990: "Kasparov kept pressing for a murderous attack. Toward the end, Karpov had to oppose threats of violence with more of the same and the game became a melee.") Or a person can do nothing more exciting than sign a piece of paper: if she has just signed the order to fire a hated rival after months of plotting and maneuvering, her physiological responses might be shockingly similar to those of a savanna baboon who has just lunged and slashed the face of a competitor. And if someone spends months on end twisting his innards in anxiety, anger, and tension over some emotional problem, this might very well lead to illness.

This is the critical point of this book. If you are that zebra running for your life, or that lion sprinting for your meal, your body's physiological response mechanisms are superbly adapted for dealing with such short-term physical emergencies. When we sit around and worry about stressful things, we turn on the same physiological responses — and they are potentially a disaster when provoked chronically for psychological or other reasons. A large body of convergent evidence suggests that stress-related disease emerges, predominantly, out of the fact that we so often activate a physiological system that has evolved for responding to acute physical emergencies, but we turn it on for months on end, worrying about mortgages, relationships, and promotions.

This difference between the ways that we get stressed and the ways a zebra does lets us begin to wrestle with some definitions. To start, I must call forth a concept that you were tortured with in ninth-grade biology and probably have not had to think about since — homeostasis. Ah, that dimly remembered concept, the idea that the body has an ideal level of oxygen that it needs, an ideal degree of acidity, an ideal temperature, and so on. All of these different variables are maintained in homeostatic balance, the state of all sorts of physiological measures being kept at the optimal level for that time of day, season, age of organism, and so on. A stressor can be defined as anything that throws your body out of homeostatic balance — for example, an injury, an illness, subjection to great heat or cold. The stress-response, in turn, is your body's attempt to restore homeostatic balance. This consists of the secretion of certain hormones, the inhibition of others, the activation of particular parts of the nervous system, and other physiological changes that will be described in subsequent chapters. These are definitions that would suffice for that lion or zebra — if being half dead with hunger or half dead from blood loss doesn't qualify as being out of homeostatic balance, then what does?

But when we consider ourselves and our human propensity to worry ourselves sick, we have to expand on the notion of stressors merely being things that knock you out of homeostasis. A stressor can also be the *anticipation* of that happening. Sometimes we are smart enough to see things coming and can turn on just as robust a stress-response merely based on anticipation.

Some aspects of anticipatory stress are not unique to humans—
whether you are a human surrounded by a bunch of threatening
teenagers on a deserted subway station or a zebra face to face
with a lion, your heart is probably racing, even though nothing
physically damaging has occurred (yet). But unlike less cognitively sophisticated species, we can turn on the stress-response
by thinking about potential stressors that may throw us out of
homeostatic balance far in the future. For example, think of the
African farmer watching a swarm of locusts descend on his
crops. There is some food stored away; he is not about to suffer
the homeostatic imbalance of starving for months, but that
man will still be undergoing a stress-response. Zebras and lions
may see trouble coming and mobilize a stress-response in anticipation, but they can't get stressed about things so far in advance.

And sometimes we humans can be stressed by things that
simply make no sense to zebras or lions. It is not a general
mammalian trait to become anxious about mortgages or the
Internal Revenue Service, about public speaking or fears of what
you will say in a job interview, about the inevitability of death.
Our human experience is replete with psychological stressors, a
far cry from the physical world of hunger, injury, blood loss, or
temperature extremes. When we activate the stress-response out
of fear of something that turns out to be real, we congratulate
ourselves that this cognitive skill allows us to mobilize our
defenses early. And when we get into a physiological uproar for
no reason at all, or over something we cannot do anything
about, we call it things like anxiety, neurosis, paranoia, or need-
less hostility.

Thus, the stress-response can be mobilized not only in
response to physical or psychological insults, but also in expec-
tation of them. It is this generality of the stress-response that is
the most surprising—a physiological system activated not only
by all sorts of physical disasters but by just thinking about them
as well. This generality was first appreciated about sixty years
ago by one of the godfathers of stress physiology, Hans Selye.
To be only a bit facetious, stress physiology exists as a discipline

because this man was both a very insightful scientist and somewhat inept at handling laboratory rats.

In the 1930s, Selye was just beginning his work in endocrinology, the study of hormonal communication in the body. Naturally, as a young, unheard-of assistant professor, he was fishing around for something with which to start his research career. A biochemist down the hall had just isolated some sort of extract from the ovary, and colleagues were wondering what this ovarian extract did to the body. So Selye obtained some of the stuff from the biochemist and set about studying its effects. He attempted to inject his rats daily, but apparently with not a great display of dexterity. Selye would try to inject the rats, miss them, drop them, spend half the morning chasing the rats around the room or vice versa, flailing with a broom to get them out from behind the sink, and so on. At the end of a number of months of this, Selye examined the rats and discovered something extraordinary: the rats had peptic ulcers, greatly enlarged adrenal glands, and shrunken immune tissues. He was delighted; he had discovered the effects of the mysterious ovarian extract.

Being a good scientist, he ran a control group: rats injected daily with saline alone, instead of the ovarian extract. And thus every day they, too, were injected, dropped, chased, and chased back. At the end, lo and behold, the control rats had the same peptic ulcers, enlarged adrenal glands, and atrophy of tissues of the immune system.

Now your average budding scientist, at this point, might throw up his or her hands and furtively apply to business school. But Selye, instead, reasoned through what he had observed. The physiological changes couldn't be due to the ovarian extract after all, since the same changes occurred in both the control and the experimental groups. What did the two groups of rats have in common? Selye reasoned that it was his less-than-trauma-free injections. Perhaps, he thought, these changes in the rats' bodies were some sort of nonspecific responses of the body to generic unpleasantness. To test this idea, he put some on the roof of the research building in the winter, others down in the boiler room. Still others were exposed to forced exercise, or to surgical procedures. In all cases, he found increased incidences of peptic ulcers, adrenal enlargement, and atrophy of immune tissues.

We know now exactly what Selye was observing. He had just discovered the tip of the iceberg of stress-related disease. Legend (mostly promulgated by Selye himself) has it that Selye was the person who, searching for a way to describe the nonspecificity of the unpleasantness to which the rats were responding, borrowed a term from engineering and proclaimed that the rats were undergoing "stress." But in fact, the term had already been introduced to medicine in roughly the sense that we understand it today by a physiologist named Walter Cannon. What Selye did was to formalize the concept with two ideas:

- The body has a surprisingly similar set of responses (which he called the General Adaptation Syndrome) to a broad array of stressors.

- Under certain conditions, stressors will make you sick.

It is this generality that is puzzling. If you are trained in physiology, it makes no sense at first glance. In physiology, one is typically taught that *specific* challenges to the body trigger *specific* responses and adaptations. Warming a body causes sweating and dilation of blood vessels in the skin. Chilling a body causes just the opposite—constriction of those vessels and shivering. Being too hot seems to be a very specific and different physiologic challenge from being too cold, and it would seem logical that the body's responses to these two very different states should be extremely different. Instead, what kind of crazy bodily system is this that is turned on whether you are too hot or too cold, whether you are the zebra, the lion, or a terrified adolescent going to a high-school dance? Why should your body have such a generalized and convergent stress-response, regardless of the predicament you find yourself in?

On further reflection, it makes some physiological sense, given the adaptations brought about by the stress-response. Regardless of whether you are that zebra or that lion, you need energy if you are going to survive a demanding emergency. And you need it immediately, in the most readily utilizable form, rather than stored away somewhere in your fat cells. One of the hallmarks of the stress-response is the rapid mobilization of energy from storage sites and the inhibition of further storage. Glucose and the simplest forms of proteins and fats come pouring out of your fat cells, liver, and muscles, all to stoke whichever muscles are struggling to save your neck.

If your body has mobilized all that glucose, it needs also to deliver it to the critical muscles as rapidly as possible. Heart rate, blood pressure, and breathing rate increase, all to transport nutrients and oxygen at greater rates.

Equally logical is another feature of the stress-response. During an emergency, it makes sense that your body halts long-term, expensive building projects. If there is a tornado bearing down on the house, this isn't the day to repaint the kitchen. Hold off until you've weathered the disaster. Thus, during stress, digestion is inhibited—there isn't enough time to derive the energetic benefits of the slow process of digestion, so why waste energy on it? You have better things to do than digest breakfast when you are trying to avoid being someone's lunch. Similarly, growth is inhibited during stress, and the logic is just as clear. You're sprinting for your life: grow antlers or extend your long bones some other day. Along with that, reproduction, probably the most energy-expensive, optimistic thing that you can do with your body (especially if you are female) is curtailed —worry about eggs and sperm and that sort of thing some other time; keep your mind and your energies on the problem at hand. During stress, sexual drive decreases in both sexes; females are less likely to ovulate or to carry pregnancies to term, while males begin to have trouble with erections and secrete less testosterone.

Along with these changes, the immune system is also inhibited, and at least some argument can be made that this fits into the same general picture of suppressing long-term processes during an emergency. The immune system, which defends against infections and illness, is ideal for spotting the tumor cell that will kill you in a year, or making enough antibodies to protect you in a few weeks. The logic here appears to be the same—look for tumors some other time; expend the energy more wisely now.

Another feature of the stress-response becomes apparent during times of extreme physical pain. With sufficiently sustained stress, our perception of pain can become blunted. It's the middle of a battle; soldiers are storming a stronghold with wild abandon and intensity. A soldier is shot, grievously injured, and the man doesn't even notice it. He'll see blood on his clothes and worry that one of his buddies near him has been wounded, or he'll wonder why his innards feel numb. As the battle fades, someone will point with amazement at his injury—didn't it hurt like hell? It didn't. Such stress-induced analgesia is highly adaptive and well documented. If you are that zebra and injured, you still have to escape. Now would not be a particularly clever time to go into shock from extreme pain.

Finally, during stress shifts occur in cognitive and sensory skills. Suddenly certain aspects of memory improve, which is always helpful if you're trying to figure out how to get out of an emergency (has this happened before? is there a good hiding place?). Moreover, your senses become sharper. Think about watching a terrifying movie on television, on the edge of your seat at the tensest part. The slightest noise—a creaking door, a car backfiring three blocks away—and you nearly jump out of your chair. Better memory, sharper detection of sensations—all quite adaptive and helpful.

Collectively, the stress-response is ideally adapted for that zebra or lion. Energy is mobilized and delivered to the tissues that need them; long-term building and repair projects are deferred until the disaster has passed. Pain is blunted, cognition sharpened. Walter Cannon, the physiologist who, at the beginning of the century, paved the way for much of Selye's work and is generally considered the other godfather of the field, concentrated on the adaptive aspect of the stress-response in dealing with emergencies such as these. He formulated the well-known "fight or flight" syndrome to describe the stress-response, and he viewed it in a very positive light. His books, with titles such as *The Wisdom of the Body*, were suffused with a pleasing optimism about the ability of the body to weather all sorts of stressors.

Yet stressful events can sometimes make us sick. Why?

Selye, with his ulcerated rats, wrestled with this puzzle and came up with what is now generally thought to be the wrong answer. He developed a three-part view of how the stress-response worked. In the initial (Alarm) stage a stressor is noted —metaphorical alarms go off in your head, telling you that you are hemorrhaging, too cold, low on blood sugar, or whatever. The second stage (Adaptation, or Resistance) comes with the successful mobilization of the stress-response system and the reattainment of homeostatic balance.

It is with prolonged stress that one enters the third stage, which Selye termed Exhaustion, where stress-related diseases emerge. Many researchers at the time believed that one became sick at that point because stores of the hormones secreted during the stress-response are depleted. Like an army that runs out of bullets, suddenly we have no defenses left against the threatening stressor.

It is very rare, however, as we will see, that any of the crucial hormones are actually depleted during even the most sustained of stressors. The army does not run out of bullets. Instead, spending so much on bullets causes the rest of the body's economy to collapse. It is not so much that the stress-response runs out; rather, with sufficient activation, *the stress-response itself can become damaging.* This is a critical concept, because it underlies the emergence of much stress-related disease.

That the stress-response itself can become harmful makes a certain sense when you examine the things that occur in reaction to stress. They are generally shortsighted, inefficient, and penny-wise and dollar-foolish, but they are the sorts of costly things your body has to do to respond effectively in an emergency. If you experience every day as an emergency, you will pay the price.

If you constantly mobilize energy at the cost of energy storage, you will never store any surplus energy. You will fatigue more rapidly, and your risk of developing a form of diabetes will even increase. The consequences of chronically over-activating your cardiovascular system are similarly damaging: if your blood pressure rises to 180/140 when you are sprinting away from a lion, you are being adaptive, but if it is 180/140 every time you see the mess in your teenager's bedroom, you could be heading for cardiovascular disease (a surprising fact that will be discussed in Chapter 3; periods of stress-induced high blood pressure are more likely to get you into trouble by causing the formation of atherosclerotic plaques in your blood vessels rather than is permanent high blood pressure). If you constantly turn off long-term building projects, nothing is ever repaired. For paradoxical reasons that will be explained in later chapters, you become more at risk for peptic ulcers. In kids, growth can be inhibited to the point of a rare but recognized pediatric endocrine disorder—stress dwarfism—and in adults, repair and remodeling of bone and other tissues can be disrupted. If you are constantly under stress, a variety of reproductive disorders may ensue. In females, cycles can become irregular or cease entirely; in males, sperm count and testosterone levels may decline. In both sexes, interest in sexual behavior decreases.

But that is only the start of your problems in response to chronic or repeated stressors. If you suppress immune function too long, trouble will surely follow. The tragedy of those who have AIDS has taught us that we become susceptible to all sorts of horrendous diseases if we are grossly immunodeficient. In a less dramatic way, the immune suppression brought about by chronic stress may exact a price: individuals are less likely to resist any of a variety of diseases including, some believe, cancer.

Finally, the same systems of the brain that function more cleverly during stress can also be damaged by one class of hormones secreted during stress. As will be discussed, this may have something to do with how rapidly the brain loses cells during aging, and how much memory loss occurs with old age.

All of this is pretty grim. In the face of repeated stressors, we may be able to precariously reattain homeostasis, but it doesn't come cheap, and the efforts to reestablish that balance will eventually wear us down. Here's a way to think about it: the Two Elephants on a Seesaw Model of stress-related disease. Put two little kids on a seesaw, and they can pretty readily balance themselves on it. This is homeostatic balance when nothing stressful is going on, the children representing the low levels of the various stress hormones that will be introduced in coming chapters. In contrast, the torrents of those same stress hormones released by a stressor can be thought of as two massive elephants on the seesaw. With great effort, they can balance themselves as well. But if you constantly try to balance a seesaw with two elephants instead of two little kids, all sorts of problems will emerge:

- First, the enormous potential energies of the two elephants are consumed balancing the seesaw, instead of put to some more useful task, like having the elephants mow the lawn or paint the house. This is equivalent to diverting energy from various long-term building projects in order to solve short-term stressful emergencies.

- By using two elephants to do the job, damage will occur just because of how large, lumbering, and unsubtle elephants are. They squash the flowers in the process of entering the playground, they strew copious amounts of leftovers and garbage all over the place from the snacks they must eat while balancing the seesaw, they wear out the seesaw faster, and so on. This is equivalent to a pattern of stress-related disease that will run through many of the subsequent chapters: it is hard to fix one major problem in the body without knocking something else out of balance. Thus, you may be able to solve one bit of homeostatic imbalance brought on during stress with your elephants (your massive levels of various stress hormones), but such great quantities of those hormones can make a mess of something else in the process.

- A final, subtle problem: When two elephants are balanced on a seesaw, it's tough for them to get off. Either one hops off and the other comes crashing to the ground, or there's the extremely delicate task of coordinating their jumping off lithely at the same time. This is a metaphor for another theme that will run through subsequent chapters—sometimes stress-related disease can arise from turning off the stress-response too slowly, or turning off the different components of the stress-response at different speeds. When the secretion rate of one of the hormones of the stress-response returns to normal yet another of the hormones is still being secreted like mad, that can be the equivalent of one of the elephants suddenly left alone on the seesaw, crashing to earth.*

The preceding pages should allow you to begin to appreciate the two punch lines of this book:

- If you are faced with a physical stressor and you cannot appropriately *turn on* the stress-response, you are in big trouble. To see this, all you have to do is examine someone who cannot activate the stress-response. As will be explained in the coming chapters, two critical classes of hormones are secreted during stress. In one disorder, Addison's disease, you are unable to secrete one class of these hormones, called glucocorticoids. In another, called Shy-Drager syndrome, it is the secretion of the second class, the hormones epinephrine and norepinephrine (also called adrenaline and noradrenaline), that is impaired. People with Addison's disease or Shy-Drager syndrome are not more at risk for cancer or heart disease or any other such disorders of slow accumulation of damage. Individuals with untreated Addison's disease, however, when faced with a major stressor such as a car accident or an infectious illness, fall into an "Addisonian" crisis—their blood pressure drops, they cannot maintain circulation, they go into shock. In Shy-Drager's syndrome, it is hard enough simply to stand up, let alone go sprinting after a zebra for dinner—mere standing causes a severe drop in blood pressure, involuntary twitching and rippling of muscles, dizziness, all sorts of unpleasantness.

*If you find this analogy silly, imagine what it is like to have a bunch of scientists locked up together at a stress conference working with it. I was at a meeting where this analogy was first introduced, and in no time at all there were factions pushing analogies about elephants on pogo sticks, elephants on monkey bars and merry-go-rounds, Sumo wrestlers on seesaws, and so on.

These two diseases teach something important, namely, that you need the stress-response during physical challenges.

- That first punch line is obviously critical, especially for the zebra who occasionally has to run for its life. But the second punch line is far more relevant to us, sitting frustrated in traffic jams, worrying about expenses, mulling over tense interactions with colleagues. If you *repeatedly turn on* the stress-response, or if you cannot appropriately *turn off* the stress-response at the end of a stressful event, the stress-response can eventually become nearly as damaging as some stressors themselves. A large percentage of what we think of when we talk about stress-related diseases are disorders of excessive stress-response.

A few important qualifications are necessary concerning that last statement, which is one of the central ones of this book. On a superficial level, the message it imparts might seem to be that stressors make you sick or, as emphasized in the last few pages, that chronic or repeated stressors make you sick. It is actually more accurate to say that chronic or repeated stressors can *potentially* make you sick or can increase your *risk* of being sick. Stressors, even if massive, repetitive, or chronic in nature, do not automatically lead to illness, and most of us are free of stress-related diseases at any given time. Just how particular patterns of stressors lead to disease is far from clear, but the link is not inevitable. Much of the final chapter will concentrate on this good piece of news.

There is an additional point that has to be emphasized. To state that "chronic or repeated stressors can increase your risk of being sick" is actually incorrect, but in a subtle way that will initially seem like semantic nit-picking. It is never really the case that stress makes you sick, or even increases your risk of being sick. Stress increases your risk of getting *diseases* that make you sick, or if you have such a disease, stress increases the risk of your defenses being overwhelmed by the disease. This distinction is important in a few ways. First, by putting more steps between a stressor and getting sick, there are more explanations for individual differences—why only some people wind up actually getting sick. Moreover, by clarifying the progression between stressors and illness, it becomes easier to design ways to intervene in the process. Finally, it begins to explain why the stress concept often seems so suspect or slippery to many practitioners of more mainstream medicine — clinical medicine is traditionally quite good at being able to make statements like "You feel sick because you have Disease X," but is traditionally quite bad at being able to explain how you got Disease X in the first place. Thus, mainstream medical practitioners often say, in effect, "You feel sick because you have Disease X, not because of some nonsense having to do with stress," which ignores the stressors' role in where the disease came from.

With this framework in mind, we can now begin the task of understanding the individual steps in this system. Chapter 2 introduces the hormones and brain systems involved in the stress-response: which ones are activated during stress, which ones are inhibited? This leads the way to chapters 3 through 9, which examine the individual parts of your body that are affected. How do those hormones enhance cardiovascular tone during stress, and how does chronic stress cause heart disease (chapter 3)? How do those hormones and neural systems mobilize energy during stress, and how does too much stress cause energetic diseases (chapter 4)? And so on. As will be seen, these processes are often more complicated and subtle than they may seem from the simple picture presented in this chapter.

Chapter 10 ushers in a topic obviously of central importance to understanding our own propensity toward stress-related disease: why is psychological stress stressful? This serves as a prelude to chapter 11, which reviews major depression, a horrible psychiatric malady that afflicts vast numbers of us and that is often closely related to psychological stress. Chapter 12 examines the role of stress in the aging process and the disturbing recent findings that sustained exposure to certain of the hormones secreted during stress may actually accelerate the aging of the brain.

In many ways, the ground to be covered up until that point is all bad news, as we are regaled with the evidence about new and unlikely parts of our bodies and minds that are made miserable by stress. The final chapter is meant to give some hope. Given the same external stressors, certain bodies and certain psyches deal with stress better than others. What are those folks doing right, and what can the rest of us learn from them? We'll look at the main principles of stress management, and some surprising and exciting realms in which they have been applied with stunning success. While the intervening chapters document our considerable vulnerabilities to stress-related disease, the final chapter shows that we have an enormous potential to protect ourselves from many of them. Most certainly, all is not lost.

2

GLANDS, GOOSEFLESH, AND HORMONES

In order to begin the process of learning how stress can make us sick, there is something about the workings of the brain that we have to appreciate. It is perhaps best illustrated in the following rather technical paragraph from an early investigator in the field:

> As she melted small and wonderful in his arms, she became infinitely desirable to him, all his blood-vessels seemed to scald with intense yet tender desire, for her, for her softness, for the penetrating beauty of her in his arms, passing into his blood. And softly, with that marvellous swoon-like caress of his hand in pure soft desire, softly he stroked the silky slope of her loins, down, down between her soft, warm buttocks, coming nearer and nearer to the very quick of her. And she felt him like a flame of desire, yet tender, and she felt herself melting in the flame. She let herself go. She felt his penis risen against her with silent amazing force and assertion, and

she let herself go to him. She yielded with a quiver that was like death, she went all open to him.

Now think about this. If D. H. Lawrence is to your taste, there may be some interesting changes occurring in your body. You haven't just run up a flight of stairs, but maybe your heart is beating faster. The temperature has not changed in the room, but you may have just activated a sweat gland or two. And even though certain rather sensitive parts of your body are not being overtly stimulated by touch, you are suddenly very aware of them.

You sit in your chair not moving a muscle, and simply think a thought, a thought having to do with your feeling angry or sad or euphoric or lustful, and suddenly your pancreas secretes some hormone. Your *pancreas?* How did you manage to do that with your pancreas? You don't even know where your pancreas is. Your liver is making an enzyme that wasn't there before, your spleen is faxing a message to your thymus gland, blood flow in little capillaries in your ankles has just changed. All from thinking a thought.

We all understand intellectually that the brain can regulate functions throughout the rest of the body, but it is still surprising to be reminded of how far-reaching those effects can be. The purpose of this chapter is to learn a bit about the lines of communication between the brain and elsewhere, in order to see which sites are activated and which quieted when you are sitting in your chair and feeling severely stressed. This is a prerequisite for seeing how the stress-response can save your neck during a sprint across the savanna, but make you sick during months of worry.

STRESS AND THE AUTONOMIC NERVOUS SYSTEM

The principal way in which your brain can tell the rest of the body what to do is to send messages through the projections—

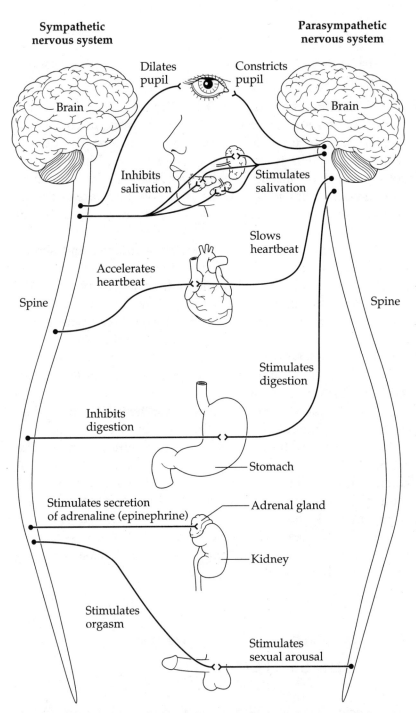

Sympathetic nervous system

Parasympathetic nervous system

Dilates pupil

Constricts pupil

Brain

Brain

Inhibits salivation

Stimulates salivation

Slows heartbeat

Accelerates heartbeat

Spine

Spine

Stimulates digestion

Inhibits digestion

Stomach

Stimulates secretion of adrenaline (epinephrine)

Adrenal gland

Kidney

Stimulates orgasm

Stimulates sexual arousal

Outline of some of the effects of the sympathetic and parasympathetic nervous systems on various organs and glands.

nerves—that branch from your brain down your spine and out to the periphery of your body. One dimension of this communication system is pretty straightforward and familiar. The voluntary nervous system is a conscious one. You decide to move a muscle and it happens. This part of the nervous system allows you to shake hands or fill out your tax forms or scratch behind your ear or do a polka. It is another branch of the nervous system that projects to organs besides skeletal muscle, and this part controls the other interesting things your body does— blushing, getting gooseflesh, having an orgasm. In general, we have less control over what our brain says to our sweat glands, for example, than to our thigh muscles. (The workings of this autonomic nervous system are not entirely out of our control, however; biofeedback, for example, consists of learning to alter autonomic nervous system function consciously. On a more mundane level, we are doing the same thing when we repress a loud burp during a wedding ceremony.) The set of nerve projections to places like sweat glands carry messages that are relatively involuntary and automatic. It is thus termed the autonomic nervous system, and it has everything to do with your response to stress. One half of this system is activated in response to stress, one half is suppressed.

The half of the autonomic nervous system that is turned on is called the sympathetic nervous system. Originating in the brain, sympathetic projections exit your spine and branch out to nearly every organ, every blood vessel, and every sweat gland in your body. They even project to the scads of tiny little muscles attached to hairs on your body. If you are truly terrified by something and activate those projections, your hair stands on end; you get gooseflesh on the parts of your body where those muscles exist but lack hairs attached to them.

The sympathetic nervous system kicks into action during emergencies, or what you think are emergencies. It helps mediate vigilance, arousal, activation, mobilization. To generations of first-year medical students, it is described through the feeble but obligatory joke of mediating the four F's of behavior—flight, fight, fright, and sex. It is the archetypal system that is turned on at times when life gets exciting or alarming—such as during stress. The nerve endings of this system release adrenaline. When someone jumps out from behind a door and startles you, it's your sympathetic nervous system releasing adrenaline that causes your stomach to clutch. Sympathetic nerve endings also release the closely related substance noradrenaline (adrenaline and noradrenaline are actually British designations; the American terms, which will be used from now on, are epinephrine and norepinephrine). Epinephrine is secreted by the sympathetic nerve endings in your adrenal glands (located just above your kidneys); norepinephrine is secreted by all of the other sympathetic nerve endings throughout the body. These are the chemical messengers that kick various organs into gear, within seconds.

The other half of the autonomic nervous system plays an opposing role. This parasympathetic component mediates calm, vegetative activities—everything but the four F's. If you are a growing kid and you have gone to sleep, your parasympathetic system is activated. It promotes growth, energy storage, and other optimistic processes. Have a huge meal, sit there bloated and deliciously drowsy, and the parasympathetic is going like gangbusters. Sprint for your life across the savanna, gasping and trying to control the panic, and you've turned the parasympathetic component down. Thus, the autonomic system works in opposition: sympathetic and parasympathetic projections from the brain course their way out to a particular organ where, when activated, they bring about opposite results. The sympathetic speeds up the heart, the parasympathetic slows it down. The sympathetic diverts blood flow to your muscles, the parasympathetic does the opposite. It's no surprise that it would be a disaster if both branches were very active at the same time, kind of like putting your foot on the gas and brake simultaneously. Lots of safety features exist to make sure that does not happen. For example, the parts of the brain that activate the sympathetic component during a stressful emergency, or when you are anticipating one, typically inhibit the parasympathetic at the same time.

THE BRAIN AS AN ENDOCRINE STRUCTURE

The neural route represented by the sympathetic system is a first means by which the brain can mobilize waves of activity in response to a stressor. There is another way as well—through the secretion of hormones. If a neuron (a cell of the nervous system) secretes a chemical messenger that travels a thousandth of an inch and causes the next neuron (or other type of cell) in line to do something different, that messenger is called a neurotransmitter. Thus, when the sympathetic nerve endings in your heart secrete norepinephrine, which causes heart muscle to work differently, norepinephrine is playing a neurotransmitter role. If a neuron (or any cell) secretes a messenger that, instead, percolates into the bloodstream and affects events far and wide, that messenger is a hormone. All sorts of glands secrete hormones; the secretion of some of them is turned on during stress, and the secretion of others is turned off.

What does the brain have to do with all of these glands secreting hormones? People used to think, nothing. The assumption was that the peripheral glands of the body—your pancreas, your adrenal, your ovaries, your testes, and so on—in some mysterious way "knew" what they were doing, had "minds of their own." They would "decide" when to secrete their messengers, without directions from any other organ. This erroneous idea gave rise to a rather silly fad during the first decades of this century. Scientists noted that men's sexual drive declined with age, and assumed that this occurs because the testicles of aging men secrete less male sex hormone, testosterone. (In fact, testosterone levels do not plummet with age, there is a moderate and highly variable decline in a population of aging males, and even a decline in testosterone down to perhaps 5 percent of normal levels does not have much of an effect on sexual behavior.) Making another leap, they then ascribed aging to diminishing sexual drive, to less testosterone. (One may then wonder why females, without testes, manage to grow old,

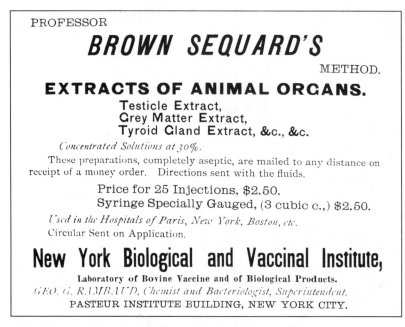

Advertisement, New York Therapeutic Review, 1893.

but the female half of the population didn't figure much in these ideas back then.) How, then, to reverse aging? Give the aging males some testosterone. Thus, a craze developed of aged, monied gentlemen checking into impeccable Swiss sanitariums and getting injected daily in their rears with testicular extracts from dogs, from roosters, from monkeys. By the 1920s, captains of industry, heads of state, famous religious leaders—all were doing it, and reporting wondrous results. Not because the science was accurate, but because if you're paying a fortune for painful daily injections of extracts of a dog's testicles, there's a certain incentive to decide you feel like a young bull. One big placebo effect.

Once scientists figured out that the extracts did not really work, the next fad arose, namely, of transplanting pieces of animal testes themselves. This was nonsense as well—if aging testes are secreting less testosterone, it is not because the testes are failing, but because another organ (stay tuned) is no longer telling them to do so. Put in a brand-new set of testes and they should fail also, for lack of a stimulatory signal. Nevertheless, placebo effects being what they are, the transplantation technique was also wondrously popular for a while.

With time scientists figured out that the peripheral hormone-secreting glands were not autonomous, but were under the control of something else. Attention turned to the pituitary gland, sitting just underneath the brain. It was known that when the pituitary was damaged or diseased, hormone secretion throughout the body became disordered. In the early part of the century, careful experiments showed that a peripheral gland released its hormone only if the pituitary first released a hormone that kicked that gland into action. The pituitary contained a whole array of hormones that ran the show throughout the rest of the body; it was the pituitary that actually "knew" the game plan and regulated what all the other glands did. This realization gave rise to the memorable statement that the pituitary is the "master gland" of the body.

This understanding was disseminated far and wide, mostly in the *Reader's Digest* in the 1960s, which ran the "I Am Joe's ————series of articles. ("I Am Joe's Pancreas," "I Am Joe's Shinbone," "I Am Joe's Ovaries," and so on. By the third paragraph of "I Am Joe's Pituitary," out comes that master gland business.) By the 1950s, however, scientists were already learning that the pituitary wasn't really the master gland after all.

The simplest evidence was that if you removed the pituitary from a body and put it in a little bowl filled with pituitary nutrients, the pituitary would act abnormally. Various hormones that it would normally secrete were no longer secreted. Sure, you might say, remove any organ and throw it in some nutrient soup and it isn't going to be good for much of anything. But, interestingly, while this "explanted" pituitary stopped secreting certain hormones, it did secrete others at immensely high rates. It wasn't just that the pituitary was traumatized. It was acting erratically because, it turned out, the pituitary didn't really have the whole hormonal game plan. It was following orders from the brain.

The evidence for this was relatively easy to obtain. Destroy the part of the brain right near the pituitary and the pituitary stops secreting some hormones and oversecretes others. This tells you that the brain controls certain pituitary hormones by stimulating their release and controls others by inhibiting them. The problem was to figure out how the brain did this. By all logic, you would look for nerves projecting from the brain to the pituitary (like the nerve projections to the heart and elsewhere), and for releasing neurotransmitters that called the shots. But no one could find these projections. In 1944, the physiologist Geoffrey Harris proposed that the brain was also a hormonal gland, that it released hormones that traveled to the pituitary and directed the pituitary's actions. In principle, this was not a crazy idea; a quarter century before, one of the godfathers of the field, Ernst Scharrer, had shown that some other hormones, thought to originate from a peripheral gland, were actually made in the brain. Nevertheless, lots of scientists thought this idea of Harris's was bonkers. You can get hormones from peripheral glands like ovaries, testes, pancreas—but your *brain* oozing hormones? Preposterous.

Two scientists, Roger Guillemin and Andrew Schally, began looking for these brain hormones. This was a stupendously difficult task. The brain communicates with the pituitary by a minuscule circulatory system, only slightly larger than the period at the end of this sentence. You couldn't search for these hypothetical brain "releasing hormones" and "inhibiting hormones" in the general circulation of blood; if the hormones existed, by the time they reached the voluminous general circulation, they would be diluted beyond detection. Instead, you would have to search in the tiny bits of tissue at the base of the brain containing those blood vessels going from the brain to the pituitary.

Not a trivial task, but these two scientists were up to it. They were highly motivated by the abstract intellectual puzzle of these hormones, by their potential clinical applications, by the acclaim waiting at the end of this scientific rainbow. Plus the two of them loathed each other, which invigorated the quest. Initially, in the late 1950s, Guillemin and Schally collaborated in the search for these brain hormones. Perhaps one tired evening over the test tube rack, one of them made a snide remark to the other—the actual events have sunk into historical obscurity; in any case a notorious animosity resulted, one enshrined in the annals of science at least on a par with the Greeks versus the Trojans, maybe even with Coke versus Pepsi. Guillemin and Schally went their separate ways, each intent on isolating the putative brain hormones first.

How do you isolate a hormone that may not exist or that, even if it does, occurs in tiny amounts in a minuscule circulation system to which you can't gain access? Both Guillemin and Schally hit on the same strategy. They started collecting animal brains from slaughterhouses. Cut out the part at the base of the brain, near the pituitary. Throw a bunch of those in a blender,

Mounds of frozen sheep hypothalami used by Guillemin's laboratory. Five million such fragments, dissected from 500 tons of sheep brain, were utilized in the lab's research over four years.

pour the resulting brain mash into a giant test tube filled with chemicals that purify the mash, collect the droplets that come out the other end. Then inject those droplets into a rat and see if the rat's pituitary changes its pattern of hormone release. If it does, maybe those brain droplets contain one of those imagined releasing or inhibiting hormones. Try to purify what's in the droplets, figure out their chemical structure, make an artificial version of it, and see if that regulates pituitary function. Pretty straightforward in theory. But it took them years.

One factor in this Augean task was the scale. There was at best a minuscule amount of these hormones in any one brain, so the scientists wound up dealing with thousands of brains at a time. The great Slaughterhouse War was on. Truckloads of pig or sheep brains were collected, chemists poured cauldrons of brain into monumental chemical-separation columns, while others pondered the thimblefuls of liquid that dribbled out the bottom, purifying it further in the next column and the next column. . . . But it wasn't just mindless assembly-line work either. New types of chemistry had to be invented, completely novel ways of testing the effects in the living body of hormones that might or might not actually exist. An enormously difficult scientific problem, made worse by the fact that lots of influential people in the field didn't believe there were any such hormones and these two guys were expending a lot of time and money.

Guillemin and Schally pioneered a whole new corporate approach to doing science. One of our clichés is the lone scientist, sitting there at two in the morning, trying to figure out the meaning of a result. Here there were whole teams of chemists, biochemists, physiologists, and so on, coordinated into isolating these putative hormones. And it worked. A "mere" fourteen years into the venture, the structure of the first releasing hormone was published.* Two years after that, in 1971, Schally got

*So, asks the breathless sports fan, who won the race? It depends on how you define getting there first. The first hormone isolated indirectly regulates the release of thyroid hormone (that is, it controls the way in which the pituitary regulates the thyroid). Schally and crew were the first to submit a paper for publication saying, in effect, "There really does exist a hormone in the brain which regulates thyroid hormone release, and its chemical structure is X." In a photofinish, Guillemin's team submitted a

there with the sequence for the next hypothalamic hormone, and Guillemin published two months later. Guillemin took the next round in 1972, beating Schally to the next hormone by a solid three years. Everyone was delighted, the by-then-deceased Geoffrey Harris was proved correct, and Guillemin and Schally got the Nobel Prize in 1976. One, urbane and knowing what would sound right, proclaimed that he was motivated only by science and the impulse to help mankind; he noted how stimulating and productive his interactions with his co-winner had been. The other, less polished but more honest, said the competition was all that drove him for decades and described his relationship with his co-winner as "many years of vicious attacks and bitter retaliation."

So hooray for Guillemin and Schally; the brain turned out to be *the* master gland. It is now recognized that the base of the brain, the hypothalamus, contains a huge array of those releasing and inhibiting hormones, which instruct the pituitary, which in turn regulates the secretions of the peripheral glands. In some

---

paper reaching the identical conclusion *five weeks* later. But as a complication, a number of months before, Guillemin and friends had been the first to publish a paper saying, in effect, "If you synthesize a chemical with structure X, it regulates thyroid hormone release and does so in a way similar to the way hypothalamic brain mash does; we don't know yet if whatever it is in the hypothalamus also has structure X, but we wouldn't be one bit surprised if it did." So Guillemin was the first to say, "This structure works like the real thing," and Schally was the first to say, "This structure is the real thing." As I have discovered firsthand, nearly a quarter of a century afterward, the battle-scarred veterans of the Guillemin/Schally prizefight years are still willing to get worked up as to which counts as the knockout.

One might wonder why something obvious wasn't done a few years into this insane competition, like the National Institutes of Health sitting the two down and saying, "Instead of us giving you all of this extra taxpayers' money to work separately, why don't you two work together?" Surprisingly, this wouldn't necessarily be all that great for scientific progress. The competition served an important purpose. Independent replication of results is essential in science. Years into a chase, a scientist triumphs and publishes the structure of a new hormone or brain chemical. Two weeks later the other guy comes forward. He has *every* incentive on earth to prove that the first guy was wrong. Instead, he is forced to say, "I hate that son of a bitch, but I have to admit he's right. We get the identical structure." That is how you know that your evidence is really solid, from independent confirmation by a hostile competitor. When everyone works together, things usually do go faster, but everyone winds up sharing the same assumptions, leaving them vulnerable to small, unexamined mistakes that can grow into big ones.

cases, the brain triggers the release of pituitary hormone X through the action of a single releasing hormone. Sometimes it halts the release of pituitary hormone Y by releasing a single inhibiting hormone. In some cases, a pituitary hormone is controlled by the coordination of both a releasing and inhibiting hormone from the brain — dual control. To make matters worse, in some cases (for example, the miserably confusing system that I study) there is a whole array of hypothalamic hormones that collectively regulate the pituitary, some as releasers, others as inhibitors.

HORMONES OF THE STRESS-RESPONSE

Thus, the brain can experience or think of something stressful and activate components of the stress-response through this hormonal route. Some of the hypothalamus-pituitary-peripheral gland links are activated during stress, some inhibited.

Two hormones vital to the stress-response, as noted already, are epinephrine and norepinephrine, released by the sympathetic nervous system. Another important class of hormones in the response to stress are called glucocorticoids. By the end of this book you will be astonishingly informed about glucocorticoid trivia, since I am in love with these hormones. Glucocorticoids are steroid hormones. ("Steroid" is used to describe the general chemical structure of five classes of hormones: androgens — the famed "anabolic" steroids like testosterone that get you thrown out of the Olympics — estrogens, progestins, mineralocorticoids, and glucocorticoids.) Secreted by the

---

Outline of the control of glucocorticoid secretion. A stressor is sensed or anticipated in the brain, triggering the release of CRF (and related hormones) by the hypothalamus. These hormones enter the private circulatory system linking the hypothalamus and the anterior pituitary, causing the release of ACTH by the anterior pituitary. ACTH enters the general circulation and triggers the release of glucocorticoids by the adrenal gland.

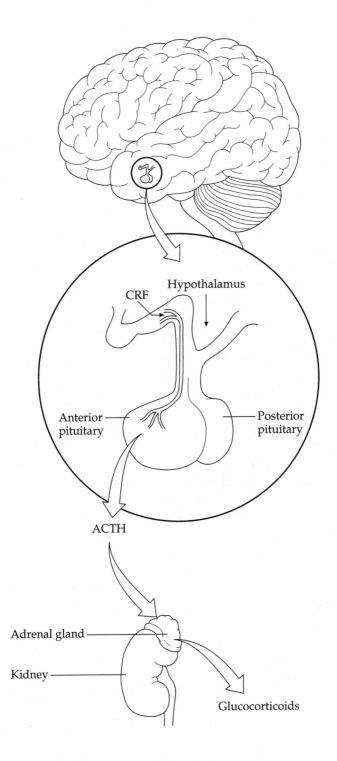

adrenal gland, they often act, as we will see, in ways similar to epinephrine. Epinephrine acts within seconds; glucocorticoids back this activity up over the course of minutes or hours.

Because the adrenal gland is basically witless, glucocorticoid release must ultimately be under the control of the hormones of the brain. When something stressful happens or you think a stressful thought, the hypothalamus secretes the critical initiating releasing hormone, CRF (corticotropin releasing factor) into the hypothalamus-pituitary circulatory system. Within fifteen seconds or so, CRF triggers the pituitary to release the hormone ACTH (also known as corticotropin). After ACTH is released into the bloodstream, it reaches the adrenal gland and, within a few minutes, triggers glucocorticoid release. Together, glucocorticoids and the secretions of the sympathetic nervous system (epinephrine and norepinephrine) account for a large percentage of what happens in your body during stress. These are the workhorses of the stress-response.

In addition, in times of stress your pancreas is stimulated to release a hormone called glucagon. Glucocorticoids, glucagon, and the sympathetic nervous system raise circulating levels of the sugar glucose — as we will see, these hormones are essential for mobilizing energy during stress. Other hormones are activated as well. The pituitary secretes prolactin, which among other effects, plays a role in suppressing reproduction during stress. Both the pituitary and the brain also secrete a class of endogenous morphine-like substances called endorphins and enkephalins, which help blunt pain perception, among other things. Finally, the pituitary also secretes vasopressin, also known as antidiuretic hormone, which plays a role in the cardiovascular stress-response.

Just as some glands are activated in response to stress, various hormonal systems are inhibited during stress. The secretion of various reproductive hormones such as estrogen, progesterone, and testosterone is inhibited. Hormones related to growth (such as growth hormone) are also inhibited, as is the secretion of insulin, a pancreatic hormone that normally tells your body to store energy for later use.

A FEW COMPLICATIONS

This, then, is an outline of our current understanding of the neural and hormonal messengers that carry the brain's news that something awful is happening. Cannon was the first to recognize the role of epinephrine, norepinephrine, and the sympathetic nervous system. Selye pioneered the glucocorticoid component of the story. Since then the roles of the other hormones and neural systems have been recognized. Collectively, these shifts in secretion and activation form the primary stress-response.

Naturally there are complications in the simple endocrine story outlined in this chapter. One concerns variability among species; not all the features of the stress-response work quite the same way in different species. For example, while stress causes a prompt decline in the secretion of growth hormone in rats, it causes a transient increase in growth hormone secretion in humans (this puzzle and its implication for humans are discussed in the chapter about growth).

Another complication concerns consistency of the stress-response. Central to Selye's conceptualization of the stress-response was the belief that whether you are too hot or too cold, that zebra or that lion, or simply stressed by the repetitiveness of that phrase, you activate the same pattern of secretion of glucocorticoids, epinephrine, growth hormone, estrogen, and so forth for each of those stressors.

It turns out that the pattern of response is not quite that consistent, however. In general, stressors of all kinds particularly massive physical stressors, involve the hormonal changes outlined in this chapter, with the glucocorticoid and sympathetic components being the most reliable. But the speed and the magnitude with which the secretion of some particular hormone changes may vary according to the stressor, especially for more subtle ones. The orchestration, the patterning of hormone release tends to vary from stressor to stressor, and a hot topic in stress research these days is figuring out the hormonal "signature" of a particular stressor.

One example concerns the relative magnitude of the gluco-corticoid versus the sympathetic stress-responses. James Henry, who has done important work on the ability of social stressors such as subordinacy to cause heart disease in rodents, has found that the sympathetic nervous system is particularly activated in a socially subordinate rodent that is vigilant and trying to cope with a challenge. In contrast, it is the glucocorticoid system that is relatively more activated in a subordinate rodent that has basically given up on coping. Studies of stressed or depressed humans have shown what may be a human analogue of that dichotomy. Sympathetic arousal is a relative marker of anxiety and vigilance, while heavy secretion of glucocorticoids is more a marker of depression (as glucocorticoid levels are elevated in about half of depressives).

Furthermore, all stressors do not cause secretion of both epinephrine and norepinephrine, nor of norepinephrine from all branches of the sympathetic system. Finally, as will be the topic of chapter 10, two identical stressors can cause very different stress signatures depending on the psychological context of the stressors.

Thus, every stressor does not generate exactly the same stress-response. This is hardly surprising. Despite the dimensions common to various stressors, it is still a very different physiological challenge to be too hot or too cold, to be extremely anxious or deeply depressed. Despite this, the hormonal changes outlined in this chapter, which occur pretty reliably in the face of impressively different stressors, still constitute the superstructure of the neural and endocrine stress-response. We are now in a position to see how these responses collectively save our skins during acute emergencies but can make us sick in the long run.

3

STROKE, HEART ATTACKS, AND VOODOO DEATH

It's one of those unexpected emergencies: you're walking down the street, on your way to meet a friend for dinner. You're already thinking about what you'd like to eat, savoring your hunger. Come around the corner and—oh, no, a lion! Immediately, activities throughout your body shift to meet the crisis: your digestive tract shuts down and your breathing rate skyrockets. Secretion of sex hormones is inhibited, while epinephrine, norepinephrine, and glucocorticoids pour into the bloodstream. Your leg muscles are doing their best to save you, and if that is going to happen, your cardiovascular output must increase enough to deliver oxygen and energy to those exercising muscles.

THE CARDIOVASCULAR STRESS-RESPONSE

Activating your cardiovascular system is relatively easy, so long as you have a sympathetic nervous system and don't bother with too many details. The first thing you do is shift your heart into higher gear, get it to beat faster and harder. Such effects are accomplished by turning up sympathetic, turning down para-sympathetic, activity. We all know this effect. The actual process is extremely complex and beyond the scope of this book — some of the changes in the functioning of the heart, for example, are secondary to changes elsewhere and rely upon some fancy con-tractile features of heart muscle. The net result, however, is that blood is now moving faster and with more force. In the face of a maximum stressor, this produces about five times the output of the heart during rest.

A second set of changes occurs in the blood vessels. To appreciate this, one needs a detailed familiarity with garden hoses, because the principles are the same. Suppose there is a water tap at one end of your house; you want to attach a hose to it and spray some water on a fire that has just started at the other end of the house. There's a problem, however. You have two hoses of different diameters to choose from, but each is ten feet too short to reach the fire. You want to pick the hose that will allow you to spray the water with the most force across those last ten feet. The first hose, admittedly unlikely for the garden variety, has a diameter of three feet, and its walls are made of a soft expandable material with about as much rigidity as a marshmallow. The second hose has a diameter of one inch and is made of a tough, rigid material. Which hose do you choose?

Obviously if you go for the first one, it is going to take forever to fill, because of its huge diameter; once pressure does begin to build up, it will simply distend the hose outward, because of the soft walls. Eventually, a puddle will form at your feet while your house burns down. If you pick the second hose, however, the water from the tap is going to come streaming out with a lot of force, because of the narrowness and rigidity of the hose. Hoses like that make for increased water pressure. And arteries like that make for increased blood pressure. As the second general step in response to the stressor, your sympathetic nervous system constricts some of your major arteries. Astonishingly, each of these arteries is wrapped in tiny circular muscles, and their sympathetic innervation now causes them to tighten. Up goes blood pressure.

A third change also occurs in your blood flow. The arteries of the mesenteric system, which supply blood to your digestive tract, constrict, as do vessels supplying your kidneys and skin. This increases blood flow to muscles and to your brain, to help you out of this mess. This was first noted in 1833, in an extended study of a Canadian Native American who had a tube placed in his abdomen after a gunshot wound there. When the man sat quietly, his gut tissues were bright pink, well supplied with blood. Whenever he became anxious or angry, the gut mucosa would blanch, because of decreased blood flow. (Pure speculation perhaps, but one suspects that his transients of anxiety and anger might have been related to those white folks sitting around experimenting on him, instead of doing something useful — like sewing him up.)

There's one final cardiovascular trick in response to stress, involving the kidneys. As that zebra with its belly ripped open, you've lost a lot of blood. Furthermore, you may have to sprint across the veld and go into an hour of evasive maneuvers. It's hot, normally a time you would drink; but that is out of the question now. It makes sense to conserve water. If blood volume goes down because of dehydration or hemorrhage, it doesn't matter what your heart and veins are doing; your ability to deliver glucose and oxygen to your muscles will be impaired. What's the most likely place to be losing water? Urine formation, and the source of the water in urine is the bloodstream. Thus your brain sends a message to the kidneys: stop the process, reabsorb the water into the circulation. This is accomplished by the hormone vasopressin (known as "antidiuretic hormone" for its ability to block diuresis, or urine formation), as well as a host of related hormones that regulate water balance.

A question no doubt at the forefront of every reader's mind at this point: If one of the features of the cardiovascular stress-response is to conserve water in the circulation, and this is accomplished by inhibition of urine formation in the kidneys, why is it that when we are *really* terrified, we wet our pants? I congratulate the reader for honing in on one of the remaining unanswered questions of modern science. In trying to answer it, we run into a larger one. Why do we have bladders? They are dandy if you are a hamster or a dog, because species like those fill their bladders up until they are just about to burst and then run around their territories, demarcating the boundaries— odoriferous little "keep-out" signs to the neighbors. A bladder is logical for scent-marking species, but I presume that you don't do that sort of thing on a regular basis. For humans, it is a mystery, just a boring storage site. The kidneys, now those are

THE FAR SIDE   By GARY LARSON

"So! Planning on roaming the neighborhood
with some of your buddies today?"

something else. Kidneys are reabsorptive, bidirectional organs, which means you can spend your whole afternoon happily putting water in from the circulation and getting some back and regulating the whole thing with a collection of hormones. But once the urine leaves the kidneys and heads south to the bladder, you can kiss that stuff good-bye; the bladder is unidirectional. When it comes to a stressful emergency, a bladder means a lot of sloshy dead weight to carry in your sprint across the savanna. The answer is obvious: empty that bladder.

Everything is great now—you have kept your blood volume up, it is roaring through the body with more force and speed, delivered where it is most needed. This is just what you want when running away from a lion. Interestingly, Marvin Brown of the University of California at San Diego and Laurel Fisher of the University of Arizona have shown that a different picture emerges when one is being vigilant—a gazelle crouching in the grass, absolutely quiet, as a lion passes nearby. The sight of a lion is obviously a stressor, but of a very subtle sort; while having to remain as still as possible, you must also be prepared, physiologically, for a wild sprint across the grasslands with the briefest of warnings. During such vigilance, heart rate and blood flow tend to slow down, and vascular resistance throughout the body increases, including at the muscle. Another example of the complicating point brought up at the end of chapter 2 about stress signatures—you don't turn on the identical stress-response for every type of stressor.

CHRONIC STRESS AND CARDIOVASCULAR DISEASE

You've escaped the lion, thanks to your cardiovascular system. But if you put your heart, blood vessels, and kidneys to work in this way every time your teenager agitates you, you increase your risk of heart disease. Never is the maladaptiveness of the stress-response during psychological stress clearer than in the case of the cardiovascular system. You sprint through the restaurant district terrified, and you alter cardiovascular functions to divert more blood flow to your thigh muscles. In such cases, there's a wonderful match between blood flow and metabolic demand. In contrast, if you sit and think about the consequences of giving your adolescent the car keys, driving yourself into a hyperventilating panic, you still alter cardiovascular function to divert more blood flow to your limb muscles. Crazy. And, potentially, eventually damaging. But how does stress-induced elevation of blood pressure during chronic psychological stress wind up causing cardiovascular disease?

The short of it is that your heart is just a dumb, simple mechanical pump, and your blood vessels are nothing more exciting than hoses. The cardiovascular stress-response basically consists of making them work harder for a while, and if you do that on a regular basis, they will wear out, just like any pump or hoses you could buy at Sears. The long of it is the rest of this chapter.

Part of the problem is the way that blood vessels wear out. You get in trouble here because of a combination of what is described in this chapter and what you do with your energy stores (described in the next chapter). A general feature of the circulatory system is that, at various points, large blood vessels (your descending aorta, for example) branch into smaller vessels, then even smaller ones, and so on, down to tiny beds of thousands of capillaries. This process of splitting into smaller and smaller units is called "bifurcation." (As a measure of how extraordinarily efficient this repeated bifurcation is in the circulatory system, no cell in your body is more than five cells away from a blood vessel—yet the circulatory system takes up only 3 percent of the body mass.) One of the features of systems that bifurcate in this way is that points of bifurcation, or branching, are particularly vulnerable to injury. The branch points in the vessel wall where bifurcation occurs bear the brunt of the fluid pressure slamming into them. Thus, a simple rule: when you increase the force with which the fluid is moving through the system, turbulence increases and those outposts of wall are more likely to wear down (simple fluid mechanics, which applies as readily to bodies as it does to the city's water supply).

With the chronic increase in blood pressure that accompanies repeated stress, damage begins to occur at branch points in arteries throughout the body. The smooth inner lining of the vessel begins to tear, scar, and pit. Once this layer is damaged, the fatty acids and glucose that are mobilized into your bloodstream by the onset of the metabolic stress-response begin to work their way underneath this layer and stick there, thickening the lining. There is also some evidence that during stress, epinephrine makes circulating platelets (a type of blood cell that promotes clotting) more likely to clump together underneath the torn lining, adding to the problem. In addition, cells full of fatty nutrients, called foam cells, begin to form there too. Before you know it, you are beginning to clog your vessels, and blood flow through them decreases.

Thus, chronic stress causes atherosclerosis — the accumulation of plugs called "plaques" made of fats, starches, foam cells, calcium, and so on underneath the inner lining of blood vessels. One of the clearest demonstrations of this, with great application to our own lives, is to be found in the work of the

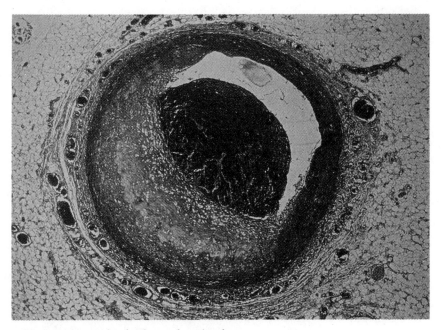

Photomicrograph of atherosclerotic plaque.

physiologist Jay Kaplan at Bowman Grey Medical School. Kaplan built on the landmark work of an earlier physiologist, James P. Henry, who showed that purely social stress caused atherosclerosis (as well as high blood pressure) in mice. Kaplan and colleagues have shown a similar phenomenon in primates, bringing the story much closer home to us humans. Establish monkeys in a social group and over the course of days to months they figure out where they stand with respect to one another. Once a stable dominance hierarchy has emerged, the last place you want to be is on the bottom: you have little opportunity to predict what will happen to you, no control over what does, and few outlets when something stressful does occur. Such subordinate animals show a lot of the physiological indices of chronically turning on their stress-responses. Often, these animals wind up with atherosclerotic plaques.

Kaplan showed that another group of animals is also at risk. Suppose you keep the dominance system *un*stable by shifting the monkeys into new groups every month, so that all the animals are perpetually in the tense, uncertain stage of figuring out where they stand with respect to everyone else. Under those circumstances, it is generally the animals precariously holding on to their places at the top of the shifting dominance hierarchy who do the most fighting and who show the most behavioral and hormonal indices of stress. They have tons of atherosclerosis; some of the monkeys even have heart attacks (abrupt blockages of one or more of the coronary arteries).

In general, the monkeys under the most social stress were most at risk for plaque formation. Kaplan showed that this can even occur with a low-fat diet, which makes sense, since, as will be described in the next chapter, a lot of the fat that forms plaques is being mobilized from stores in the body, rather than coming from the cheeseburger the monkey ate just before the tense conference. But if you couple the social stress with a high-fat diet, the effects synergize, and plaque formation goes through the roof.

The atherosclerotic plaques are probably formed because the sympathetic nervous system is continuously activated in the stressed monkeys. First, the monkeys who developed the most

atherosclerosis were what Kaplan termed "hot" reactors: they responded to stress with the greatest degree of sympathetic nervous system activity. Elevating heart rate and blood pressure, as the sympathetic nervous system does, makes atherosclerosis more likely to occur. Finally, give the monkeys at risk drugs that prevent sympathetic activity ("beta-blockers"), and they don't form plaques. This makes sense, given what we have already learned about the actions of norepinephrine and epinephrine, as do Kaplan's findings that glucocorticoids make the atherosclerosis worse.

Secretion of large amounts of these stress hormones on a regular basis is a prescription for trouble. Form enough atherosclerotic plaques to seriously obstruct flow to the lower half of the body and you get "claudication," which means that your legs and chest hurt like hell for lack of oxygen and glucose whenever you walk; you are then a candidate for bypass surgery. If the same thing happens to the arteries going to your heart, you can get coronary heart disease, myocardial ischemia, all sorts of horrible things. Try the same trick with the blood vessels going to your brain and you can get a stroke—a brain hemorrhage.

If chronic stress has made a mess of your blood vessels, each individual new stressor is even more damaging, for a very insidious reason. This has to do with myocardial ischemia—a condition that arises when the arteries feeding your heart have become sufficiently clogged that your heart itself is partially deprived of blood flow and thus of oxygen and glucose. (It may initially seem illogical for the heart to need special arteries feeding it. When the walls of the heart—the heart muscle—require the energy and oxygen stores in the blood, you might imagine that these could simply be absorbed from the vast amounts of blood passing through the chambers of the heart. But instead it has evolved that heart muscle is fed by arteries coursing from the main aorta. As an analogy, consider people working at a city's water reservoir. Every time they get thirsty, they might go over to the edge of the reservoir with a bucket and pull up some water to drink. Instead, the usual solution is to have a water fountain in the office, fed indirectly by that reservoir just outside.)

Suppose something acutely stressful is happening, and your cardiovascular system is in great shape. You get excited, the sympathetic nervous system kicks into action. Your heart speeds up in a strong, coordinated fashion, and its contractive force increases. As a result of working harder, the heart muscle consumes more energy and oxygen and, conveniently, the arteries going to your heart dilate in order to deliver more nutrients and oxygen to the muscle. Everything is fine.

But if you encounter an acute stressor with a heart that has been suffering from chronic myocardial ischemia, you're in trouble. The coronary arteries, instead of vasodilating in response to the sympathetic nervous system, vaso*constrict*. Just when your heart needs more oxygen and glucose delivered

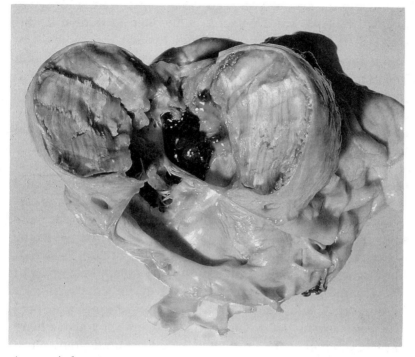

A necrotic heart.

through these already clogged vessels, acute stress shuts them down even more—exactly the opposite of what you need.* Your chest is going to hurt like crazy—angina pectoris.

Chronic myocardial ischemia from atherosclerosis, therefore, sets you up for, at the least, terrible chest pain whenever anything physically stressful occurs. When cardiology tech-

---

*Cardiologists are beginning to get some sense of what causes this paradoxical vasoconstriction. In healthy tissue, when the heart starts working hard, hormones called EDRF (endothelium-derived relaxant factors) and prostacyclin are secreted, which causes the vasodilation. When cardiac tissue is made ischemic on a regular basis, it loses the capacity to release EDRF and prostacyclin for some reason. In addition, hormones called endothelin and serotonin, which cause vasoconstriction, seem to be released. As a result, epinephrine and norepinephrine now cause constriction instead of dilation. Interestingly, this paradoxical vasoconstriction is also observed in the socially stressed monkeys, discussed above, who developed atherosclerosis. One way to dilate coronary arteries during angina pectoris is to take a synthetic version of EDRF—nitroglycerin.

niques improved a few years ago, cardiologists were surprised to discover that we are even more vulnerable to trouble in this realm than had been guessed. With the old techniques, you would take someone with myocardial ischemia and wire him (men are more prone to heart disease than are women) up to some massive ECG machine (same as EKG), focus a huge X-ray camera on his chest, and then send him running on a treadmill until he was ready to collapse. Just as one would expect, blood flow to the heart would decrease and his chest would hurt.

Some engineers invented a miniature ECG machine that can be strapped on while you go about your daily business, and "ambulatory electrocardiography" was invented. Suddenly cardiologists could see how the whole thing worked at a far more subtle level. And everyone got a rude surprise. There were little ischemic crises occurring all over the place in people at risk. Most ischemic episodes turned out to be "silent"—they didn't give a warning signal of pain. Moreover, all sorts of psychological stressors could trigger them—public speaking, pressured interviews, exams. According to the old dogma, if you had heart disease, you had better worry when you were undergoing physical stress and getting chest pains. Now it appears that, for someone at risk, trouble is occurring under all sorts of circumstances of psychological stress in everyday life; one may not even know it. This evidence fits well with animal studies showing that fibrillation—uncoordinated heart beats—occurs in dogs when they are angry or fearful. Once the cardiovascular system is damaged, it appears to be immensely sensitive to acute stressors, whether physical or psychological.

SUDDEN CARDIAC DEATH

The preceding sections demonstrate how chronic stress will hammer away at the cardiovascular system, with each succeeding stressor making the system even more vulnerable. Ultimately, this greatly increases the risk of cardiac catastrophe—the scenario of the man sitting there, finishing his breakfast, who is struck down by a fatal heart attack, the number one killer in the United States.

But one of the most striking and best-known features of heart disease is how often that cardiac catastrophe hits during a stressor. A man gets shocking news: his wife has died; he's lost his job; a child long thought to be dead appears at the door; he wins the lottery. The man weeps, rants, exults, staggers about gasping and hyperventilating with the force of the news. Five minutes or five hours later, he suddenly grasps at his chest, goes into ventricular fibrillation, and he falls over dead from sudden cardiac arrest.

The phenomenon is quite well documented. (An early report of what was possibly sudden cardiac death can be found in the New Testament, Acts 5:1–11, in which Ananias and Sapphira die after being caught in a lie by Peter.) In one study, a physician collected newspaper clippings on sudden cardiac death in 170 individuals. He identified a number of events that seemed to be associated with such deaths: the death, collapse, or threat of loss of someone close; acute grief; loss of status or self-esteem; mourning, on an anniversary; personal danger; threat of an injury, or recovery from such a threat; triumph or extreme joy. Other studies have shown the same. As a measure of the phenomenon, during the 1991 Persian Gulf War fewer deaths in Israel were due to SCUD missile damage than to sudden cardiac death among frightened elderly people. The actual causes are obviously tough to study (since you can't predict what is going to happen, and you can't interview the persons afterward to find out what they were feeling), but the general consensus among cardiologists is that sudden cardiac death is simply an extreme version of acute stress causing ventricular fibrillation* and severe ischemia in the heart. As you would guess, it involves the sympathetic nervous system, and it is more likely to happen in damaged heart tissue than in healthy

*Don't panic. Ventricular fibrillation: the half of your heart called the ventricles begins to contract in a rapid, disorganized way that accomplishes nothing at all in terms of pumping blood. This is in contrast to arrhythmia, in which the overall heartbeat becomes irregular.

tissue. People can suffer sudden cardiac death without a history of heart disease; autopsies have generally shown, however, that these people had a fair amount of atherosclerosis. Mysterious cases still occur, however, of seemingly healthy thirty-year-olds, victims of sudden cardiac death, who show little evidence of atherosclerosis on autopsy.

Fibrillation seems to be the critical event in sudden cardiac death. As one cause, the muscle of a diseased heart becomes more electrically excitable, making it prone to fibrillation. In addition, activation of stimulatory inputs *to* the heart becomes disorganized during a massive stressor. The sympathetic nervous system sends two symmetrical nervous projections to the heart; it is theorized that during extreme emotional arousal, the two inputs are activated to such an extent that they become uncoordinated—major fibrillation, clutch your chest, fall over dead.

FATAL PLEASURES

Embedded in the list of categories of precipitants of sudden cardiac death is a particularly interesting one: triumph or extreme joy. Consider the scenario of the man dying in the aftermath of the news of his winning the lottery; or the proverbial "at least he died happy" instance of someone dying during sex (when these circumstances apparently claimed the life of an ex-Vice President, the medical minutiae of the incident received especially careful examination because he was not with his wife at the time).

The possibility of being killed by pleasure seems crazy. Isn't stress-related disease supposed to arise from stress? How can joyful experiences kill you in the same way that sudden grief does? Clearly, because they share some similar traits. Extreme anger and extreme joy have different effects on reproductive physiology, on growth, most probably on the immune system as well; but with regard to the cardiovascular system, they have fairly similar effects. Once again, we deal with the central concept of stress physiology in explaining similar responses to being too hot or too cold, a prey or a predator: some parts of our body, including the heart, do not care in which direction we are knocked out of homeostasis, but rather simply how much. Thus wailing and pounding the walls in grief or leaping about and shouting in ecstasy can place similarly large demands on a diseased heart. Put another way, your sympathetic nervous system probably has roughly the same effect on your coronary arteries whether you are in the middle of a murderous rage or a thrilling orgasm. In that vein, anthropologist Irven DeVore has said that if two people look into each other's eyes for more than about six seconds, they are either preparing to kill each other or to make love. Diametrically opposite emotions can have surprisingly similar physiological underpinnings. When it comes to the cardiovascular system, rage and ecstasy, grief and triumph all represent challenges to homeostasis.

VOODOO DEATH

The time has come to examine a subject far too rarely discussed in our public schools. Well-documented examples of voodoo death have emerged from all sorts of traditional non-Westernized cultures. Someone eats a forbidden food, insults the chief, sleeps with someone he or she shouldn't have, does something unacceptably violent or blasphemous. The outraged village calls in a shaman who waves some ritualistic hideous gewgaw at the transgressor, makes a voodoo doll, or in some other way puts a hex on the person. Convincingly soon, the hexed one drops dead.

The Harvard team of ethnobotanist Wade Davis and cardiologist Regis DeSilva recently reviewed the subject.* Davis and

*Wade Davis is the favorite ethnobotanist of horror movie fans far and wide. As detailed in the reference section, his prior research uncovered a possible pharmacological basis of how zombies (people in a deathlike trance with no will of their own) are made in Haiti. Davis's Harvard doctoral dissertation about zombification was first turned into a book, *The Serpent and the Rainbow* (Warner Books, Inc. 1985), and then a grade-B horror movie of the same name—a dream come true for every graduate student whose thesis is destined to be skimmed briefly by a distracted committee member or two.

DeSilva object to the use of the term "voodoo death," since it reeks of Western condescension toward non-Western societies —grass skirts, bones in the nose, and all that. Instead, they prefer the term "psychophysiological death," noting that in many cases even psychophysiological death is probably a misnomer. In some instances, the shaman may spot people who are already very sick and, by claiming to have hexed them, gain brownie points when the person kicks off. Or the shaman may simply poison them and gain kudos for his cursing powers. In the confound (that is, the source of confusion) that I found most amusing, the shaman puts a visible curse on someone, and the community says, in effect, "Voodoo cursing works; this person is a goner, so don't waste good food and water on him." The individual, denied food and water, starves to death; another voodoo curse come true.

Nevertheless, instances of psychophysiological death do occur and, oddly, they have been the focus of interest of some great physiologists in this century. In a great face-off, Walter Cannon (the man who came up with the fight or flight concept) and Curt Richter (a grand old man of psychosomatic medicine) differed in their postulated mechanisms of psychophysiological death. Cannon thought it was due to overactivity of the sympathetic nervous system; in that scheme, the person becomes so nervous at being cursed that the sympathetic system kicks into gear and vasoconstricts blood vessels to the point of rupturing them, causing a fatal drop in blood pressure. Richter thought death was due to too much *para*sympathetic activity; in this surprising formulation the individual, realizing the gravity of the curse, gives up on some level. The parasympathetic projection to the heart (the vagus nerve) becomes very active, slowing the heart down to the point of stopping—death due to a "vagal storm," as it was called. Both Cannon and Richter kept their theories unsullied by never examining anyone who had died of psychophysiological death, voodoo or otherwise. It turns out that Cannon was probably right. Hearts almost never stop outright in a vagal storm. Instead, Davis and DeSilva suggest that these cases are simply dramatic versions of sudden cardiac death, with too much sympathetic tone driving the heart into ischemia and fibrillation.

All very interesting, in that it explains why psychophysiological death might occur in individuals who already have some degree of cardiac damage. But a puzzling feature about psychophysiological death in traditional societies is that it can also occur in young people who are extremely unlikely to have any latent cardiac disease. This mystery remains unexplained, perhaps implying more silent cardiac risk lurking within us than we ever would have guessed, perhaps testifying to the power of cultural belief. As Davis and DeSilva note, if faith can heal, faith can also kill.

PERSONALITY AND CARDIAC DISEASE

If two people both run like crazy on a treadmill to an equal state of exhaustion, they will not be equally vulnerable to cardiovascular trouble at that point. If those two people experience a more subtle, but still stressful, social situation, they are not equally likely to develop arrhythmia and severe ischemia. Finally, if those two people go through a decade's worth of life's ups and downs, only one of them may get a heart attack.

These individual differences could be due to one person already having a damaged cardiovascular system—for example, decreased coronary blood flow. They could also be due to genetic factors that influence the mechanics of the system—the elasticity of blood vessels, the numbers of norepinephrine receptors, and so on. They could be the result of differences in how many risk factors each individual experiences—does the person smoke, have high blood pressure, high circulating fatty acid (triglyceride) levels? (Interestingly, individual differences in these risk factors explain less than half the variability in patterns of heart disease.)

Faced with similar stressors, whether large or small, two people may also differ in their risk for cardiovascular disease as a function of their personalities. As will be described in greater detail in later chapters, our lives are filled with events that are ambiguous in meaning. If you are the type of person who habitually decides that those ambiguous events always mean something stressful, you will be at greater risk for various stress-related diseases, including heart disease.

In some cardiology circles, personality types that are atypically prone to viewing life's ambiguities as stressful have been given certain labels. One label refers to the mythic king of Corinth who, angering Zeus and being an all-around wise guy, was sentenced to spend the rest of time rolling the same boulder up the side of a mountain; it always rolled back just before reaching the top. Persons of the "Sisyphus pattern" view life as a joyless struggle — the workaholic executive whose only pleasure in life appears to be checking off items on a "to do" list. One researcher has found that such individuals appear to be at special risk for sudden cardiac death. Other researchers have noted a connection between certain depressive personality types and cardiac disease. The best-known connection proposed between personality and heart disease is, of course, that of the famed "Type A" personality.

Two cardiologists, Meyer Friedman and Ray Rosenman, coined the term Type A in the early 1960s to describe a collection of traits that they found in some individuals. They didn't describe these traits in terms related to stress (for example, defining Type A people as those who responded to neutral or ambiguous situations as if they were stressful). Instead, they characterized Type A people as immensely competitive, over-achieving, time-pressured, impatient, and hostile. As we will see in the chapter on psychological stress, those personality traits are one way of describing some variables that increase the likelihood of perceiving ambiguous events as stressful: if someone sees a two-minute wait in a bank line as a major infringement on her time, that will constitute a stressor; if someone responds angrily to every offhand remark, those will constitute stressors.

Initially Friedman and Rosenman observed that many of their coronary patients had what they ultimately termed Type A personalities. Thus, a connection between personality and disease appeared to exist, but there was no way to know from that observation how the two traits were related. For example, getting heart disease might make some people act in a more Type A manner. Then the pair did what is called a "prospective" study;

they looked at healthy people, examining whether being Type A increased the risk of eventually getting heart disease — which is precisely what they found. The finding made a huge splash, and by the early 1980s, a panel of some of the biggest guns in cardiology convened, checked the evidence, and concluded that being Type A carries at least as much cardiac risk as does smoking or having high cholesterol levels.

Everyone was delighted, and "Type A" entered common parlance. The trouble was, soon thereafter a bunch of very carefully done studies failed to replicate the basic findings of Friedman and Rosenman. Suddenly, Type A wasn't looking predictive of coronary heart disease after all. Then, to add insult to injury, a pair of careful studies came out showing that, once you had coronary heart disease, being Type A was associated with *better* survivorship — being Type A was seemingly good for you (in the endnotes, I discuss some of the subtle ways this finding might have occurred).

In recent years, scientists are finally beginning to make some sense of this confusion. The problem appears to be that the original Type A characterization incorporated some relevant and some irrelevant traits. Being time-pressured, impatient, and overachieving probably have little to do with heart disease risk. But work by Redford Williams, a Duke University physician, has paved the way to showing that hostility seems to have a great deal to do with it. For example, when scientists reanalyzed some of the original Type A studies and broke the constellation of traits into individual ones, hostility popped out as the only significant predictor of heart disease. The same result was found in studies of middle-aged doctors who had taken personality inventory tests 25 years earlier as an exercise in medical school. And the same thing was found when looking at American lawyers, Finnish twins, Western Electric employees — a whole range of populations. These various studies have suggested that a high degree of hostility predicts coronary heart disease, atherosclerosis, and higher rates of mortality with these diseases. Many of these studies, moreover, controlled for important variables like age, weight, and smoking. Thus, it is unlikely that the hostility/heart disease connection could be due to some other factor (for example, that hostile people are more likely to smoke, and the heart disease arises from the smoking, not the hostility).

Given the recency of these findings, it is not surprising that there is some confusion as to what aspects of hostility are bad news for your heart. For example, the study of lawyers suggested that overt aggressiveness and cynical mistrust were critical — in other words, frequent open expression of the anger that you feel predicts heart disease. By contrast, in the reanalysis of the original Type A data a particularly powerful predictor of heart disease was not only high degrees of hostility, but the tendency *not* to express it when annoyed. The latter finding makes more intuitive sense to me; it has always seemed as if feeling anger and bottling it up is more stressful than expressing it.

Why would great hostility (of whatever variant) be bad for your heart? Subjectively, we can describe hostile persons as those who get all worked up and angry over incidents that the rest of us would find only mildly provocative, if at all. Similarly, their stress-responses switch into high gear in circumstances that fail to perturb everyone else's. Give both hostile and non-hostile people a nonsocial stressor (like some math problems) and nothing exciting happens; everyone has roughly the same degree of mild cardiovascular activation. But if you generate a situation with a social provocation, the hostile individuals dump more epinephrine and norepinephrine into their bloodstreams and wind up with higher blood pressures. All sorts of social provocations have been used in studies: the subjects may be requested to take a test and, during it, be repeatedly interrupted; or they may play a video game in which the opponent not only is rigged to win but acts like a disparaging smart aleck. Or the subjects may be asked to role-play a scene involving social conflict, or may be given useless instructions for an unsolvable task. In all of these cases, the cardiovascular stress-responses of the nonhostile are relatively mild. But blood pressure goes through the roof in the hostile people. (There are striking similarities between these hostile people, prone toward cardiac disease, and Kaplan's "hot" reactor monkeys, who are the most aggressive, tend to have exaggerated sympathetic responses to stressors, and are most at risk for atherosclerosis.) This is probably representative of the rest of their lives. If each day is filled with cardiovascular provocations that everyone else responds to as no big deal, life will slowly hammer away at the hearts of the hostile. An increased risk of cardiovascular disease is no surprise.

When scientists do studies, they aim to control variables. They study rats that are genetically inbred; they try to study people of similar ages, races, and health profiles—all so they can get clear-cut answers (it helps, for example, if all of your study subjects have similar cardiovascular function if you are still trying to learn what exactly that function is).

But far too frequently, after the scientist has carefully controlled as many variables as possible, different individuals in the same experimental group still wind up with dramatically different outcomes. For example, put two people in the same situation and only one of them has blood pressure that soars; observe two people in similar conditions over years, and only one of them suffers congestion of blood vessels to the heart. This kind of variability usually drives scientists up the wall. But in reality, such variability is anything but bad news. If two people go through similar lives but only one gets a heart attack, and you can identify what it is about him that puts him at risk—free-floating hostility, for example—you've made an important first step. Now you know what you have to try to change. And, critically, some very recent work suggests that if you can reduce the hostility component in Type A people through therapy, you reduce the risk for further heart disease.

This style of thinking extends beyond the cardiovascular system. Examine the range of variability among people in the workings of all of their various physiologic systems that respond to stress. From the same stressful sorts of lives, identify who emerges in the best shape. Figure out what is special about those people, and then determine how everyone else can become more like that—a theme of the final chapter of this book.

This discussion has served as the first example of the style of analysis that will dominate the coming chapters. In the face of a short-term physical emergency, the cardiovascular stress-response is vital. In the face of chronic stress, those same changes are terrible news. These adverse effects are particularly deleterious when they interact with the adverse consequences of too much of a metabolic stress-response, the subject of the next chapter.

4

STRESS, METABOLISM, AND LIQUIDATING YOUR ASSETS

So you're sprinting down the street with the lion after you. Things looked grim for a moment there, but—your good luck —your cardiovascular system kicked into gear, and now it is delivering oxygen and energy to your exercising muscles. But what energy? There's not enough time to consume a candy bar and derive its benefits as you sprint along; there's not even enough time to digest food already in the gut. Your body must get energy from its places of storage, like fat or liver or muscle. To understand how you mobilize energy in this circumstance, and how that can make you sick at times, we need to learn how the body stores energy in the first place.

PUTTING ENERGY IN THE BANK

The basic process of digestion consists of breaking down chunks of animals and vegetables so that they can then be transformed into chunks of human. We can't make use of the chunks exactly as they are; we can't, for example, make our leg muscles stronger by grafting on the piece of chicken muscle we ate. Instead, complex food matter is broken down into its simplest parts (molecules): amino acids (the building blocks of protein),

THE FOUR MAJOR FOOD GROUPS

Regular:

Hamburger, cola, French fries, fruit pie.

Company:

Cracker variety, canapé, "interesting" cheese, mint.

Remorse:

Plain yogurt, soybeans, mineral water, tofu.

Silly:

Space-food sticks, gelatine mold with fruit salad in it, grasshopper pie.

R. Chast

simple sugars like glucose (the building blocks of more complex sugars and of starches [carbohydrates]), and free fatty acids and glycerol (the constituent parts of fat). This is accomplished in the gastrointestinal tract by enzymes, chemicals that can degrade more complex molecules. The simple building blocks thus produced are absorbed into the bloodstream for delivery to whichever cells in the body need them. Once you've done that, the cells have the ability to use those building blocks to construct the proteins, fats, and carbohydrates needed to stay in business. And just as importantly, those simple building blocks (especially the fatty acids and sugars) can also be burned by the body to provide the energy to do all that construction.

It's Thanksgiving, and you've eaten with porcine abandon. Your bloodstream is teeming with amino acids, fatty acids, glucose. It's far more than you need to power you over to the couch in a postprandial daze. What does your body do with the excess?

To answer this question, it's time we talked finances. The works: savings accounts, change for a dollar, stocks and bonds, negative amortization of interest rates, shaking coins out of piggy banks—because the process of transporting energy through the body bears some striking similarities to the movement of money. It is rare today for the grotesquely wealthy to walk around with their fortunes in their pockets, or to hoard their wealth as cash stuffed inside mattresses. Instead, surplus wealth is stored elsewhere, in forms more complex than cash: mutual funds, tax-free government bonds, Swiss bank accounts. In the same way, surplus energy is not kept in the body's form of cash—circulating amino acids, glucose, and fatty acids—but stored in more complex forms. Enzymes in fat cells can combine fatty acids and glycerol to form triglycerides (see the illustration on the next page). Accumulate enough of these in the fat cells and you grow plump. Meanwhile, enzymes in cells throughout the body can cause a succession of molecules of glucose to stick together. These long chains, sometimes thousands of glucose molecules long, are called glycogen. Glycogen gets stuck away in your muscles or liver. Similarly, enzymes in cells throughout the body can combine long strings of amino acids, forming them into proteins.

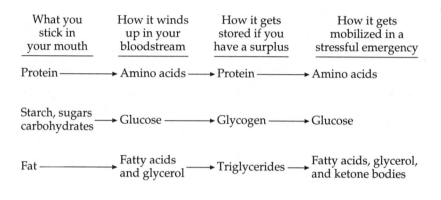

What you stick in your mouth	How it winds up in your bloodstream	How it gets stored if you have a surplus	How it gets mobilized in a stressful emergency
Protein ⟶	Amino acids ⟶	Protein ⟶	Amino acids
Starch, sugars carbohydrates ⟶	Glucose ⟶	Glycogen ⟶	Glucose
Fat ⟶	Fatty acids and glycerol ⟶	Triglycerides ⟶	Fatty acids, glycerol, and ketone bodies

The hormone that stimulates the transport and storage of these building blocks into target cells is insulin. In a sense, insulin plans for your metabolic future. Eat a huge meal and insulin pours out of the pancreas into the bloodstream, stimulating the transport of fatty acids into fat cells, stimulating glycogen and protein synthesis. It's insulin that's filling out the deposit slips at your fat banks. We even secrete insulin when we are *about* to fill our bloodstream with all those nutritive building blocks: if you eat dinner each day at six o'clock, by five forty-five your parasympathetic nervous system is already stimulating insulin secretion in anticipation.

Energy mobilization during a stressor

This grand strategy of breaking your food down into its simplest parts and reconverting it into complex storage forms is precisely what your body should do when you've eaten plenty. And it is precisely what your body should *not* do in the face of an immediate physical emergency. Then, you want to stop energy storage. Turn up the activity of the sympathetic nervous system, turn down the parasympathetic, and down goes insulin secretion: step one in meeting an emergency accomplished.

The body makes sure that energy storage is stopped in a second way as well. With the onset of the stressful emergency, you secrete glucocorticoids, which block the transport of nutrients into fat cells. This counteracts the effects of any insulin still floating around.

In addition to halting the storage of energy, you want your body to get access to the energy *already* stored. You want to dip into your bank account, liquidate some of your assets, turn stored nutrients into your body's equivalent of cash to get you through this crisis. Your body reverses all of the storage steps, through the release of the stress hormones glucocorticoids, glucagon, epinephrine, and norepinephrine. These cause triglycerides to be broken down in the fat cells and, as a result, free fatty acids and glycerol pour into the circulatory system. The same hormones trigger the degradation of glycogen to glucose in cells throughout the body, and the glucose is then flushed into the bloodstream. These hormones also cause protein in nonexercising muscle to be converted back to individual amino acids.

The stored nutrients have now been converted into simpler forms. Your body makes another simplifying move. Amino acids are not a very good source of energy, but glucose is. Your body shunts the circulating amino acids to the liver, where they are converted to glucose. The liver can also generate new glucose, a process called gluconeogenesis, and this glucose is now readily available for energy during the disaster.

As a result of these processes, lots of energy is available to your leg muscles. There's a burst of activity, you leave the lion in the dust, and arrive at the restaurant only a smidgen late for your five forty-five anticipatory insulin secretion. (The scenario I've been outlining is basically a strategy to shunt energy from storage sites like fat to muscle during an emergency. But it doesn't make adaptive sense to automatically fuel, say, your arm muscles while you're running away from a predator. It turns out that the body has solved this problem. Glucocorticoids and the other hormones of the stress-response also act to block energy uptake into muscles and into fat tissue. Somehow the individual muscles that are exercising during the emergency have a means to override this blockade and to grab all the nutrients floating around in the circulation. No one knows what the local signal is, but the net result is that you shunt energy from fat and from nonexercising muscle to the exercising ones.)

So WHY DO WE GET SICK?

If the mobilization of energy in response to stress works so wonderfully, why should the process make us sick when we turn on the same stress-response for months on end? For many of the same reasons that constantly running to the bank and drawing on your account is a foolish way to handle your finances.

On the most basic level, it's inefficient. Another financial metaphor helps. Suppose you have some extra money and decide to put it away for a while in a high-interest account. If you agree not to touch the money for a certain period (six months, two years, whatever), the bank agrees to give you a higher than normal rate of interest. And typically, you also agree that if you request the money earlier, you will pay a penalty for the early withdrawal. Suppose, then, that you happily deposit your money with that agreement. The next day you develop the financial jitters, withdraw your money, and pay the penalty. The day after, you change your mind again, put the money back in, and sign a new agreement, only to change your mind again that afternoon, withdraw the money, and pay another penalty. Soon you've squandered half your money on penalties.

In the same way, every time you store energy away from the circulation and then return it, you lose a fair chunk of the potential energy. It takes energy to shuttle those nutrients in and out of the bloodstream, to power the enzymes that glue them together (into proteins, triglycerides, and glycogen) and the other enzymes that then break them apart, to fuel the liver during that gluconeogenesis trick. In effect, you are penalized if you activate the stress-response too often: you wind up expending so much energy that, as a first consequence, you tire more readily—just plain old, everyday fatigue.

As a second consequence, your muscles can waste away, although this rarely happens to a significant degree. Muscle is chock-full of proteins. If you are stressed chronically, constantly triggering the breakdown of proteins, your muscles never get the chance to rebuild. While they atrophy ever so slightly each time your body activates this component of the stress-response, it requires a really extraordinary amount of stress for this to happen to a serious extent. However, such myopathy of muscle can occur when massive amounts of glucocorticoids are given to a patient to control any of a variety of diseases; in such cases, the wasting away is typically known as "steroid myopathy."

Finally, with enough stress, you become at added risk for developing adult-onset diabetes, one of the most common diseases of older people in Western societies. This takes some explaining. We are all familiar with juvenile diabetes, in which there is hardly any insulin secreted by the pancreas and therefore little ability to promote the uptake of glucose into target cells (thus the disease is also known as insulin-dependent diabetes, or type 1 diabetes). Cells starve: big trouble.

In adult-onset diabetes (type 2, or non-insulin-dependent diabetes), the trouble is not too little insulin, but the failure of the cells to respond to insulin. Another name for the disorder is thus insulin-resistant diabetes. The problem here arises with the tendency of many people to put on weight as they age. (Some recent work shows that, to the extent that people do not put on weight with age, they show no increased risk of this disease. For example, people in non-Westernized populations typically show no incidence of adult-onset diabetes. This disease is not, therefore, a normal feature of aging; instead, it is a disease of inactivity and fat surplus, conditions that just happen to be more common with age in some societies.) With enough fat stored away, the fat cells essentially get full; once you are an adolescent, the number of fat cells that you have is fixed, so if you put on weight, the individual fat cells are distended. Yet another

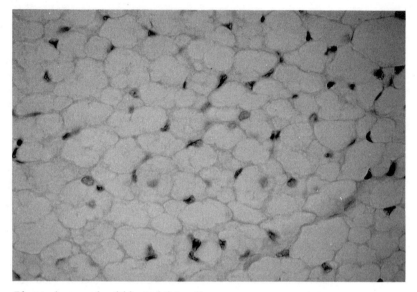

Photomicrograph of bloated fat cells.

heavy meal, a burst of insulin trying to promote more fat storage by the fat cells, and the fat cells refuse: Tough luck, I don't care if you are insulin, we're completely full. The fat cells become less responsive to insulin trying to promote more fat storage, and less glucose is taken up by these cells.

This decreased sensitivity is mostly due to the cells losing their specialized receptors for insulin, in response to the constant insulin signal—a process called receptor "down-regulation." (The careful reader may be confused at this point—if insulin regulates *glucose* uptake, why does it influence the amount of *fat* being stored in fat cells [since triglyceride storage is a function of the uptake of fatty acids and glycerol, not of glucose]? For immensely complex reasons, the storage of free fatty acids and glycerol as triglycerides requires glucose uptake.)

Do the cells now starve? Certainly not; the amount of fat stored in them was the source of the trouble in the first place. Why, then, is this a dangerous state? Because now there's all that extra glucose and those free fatty acids circulating in the bloodstream—oleaginous hoodlums with no place to go, and soon you are in trouble. They gum up the blood vessels in the kidneys, making it harder for these organs to do their job. They form atherosclerotic plaques in arteries and make it impossible for oxygen and glucose to be delivered to the tissues depending on those blood vessels, causing little strokes in those tissues and, often, chronic pain. They also link proteins together in the eyes to make cataracts. Trouble on all fronts.

How does chronic stress affect this process? First, the hormones of the stress-response cause even more glucose and fatty acids to be mobilized into the bloodstream. And there is another, more subtle effect: when something stressful happens, it makes sense for the body to block insulin secretion. Basically, the brain doesn't quite trust that the pancreas won't still secrete a little insulin. So a second step occurs—during stress, glucocorticoids act on fat cells throughout the body to make them less sensitive to insulin, just in case there's some still floating around.

Suppose that you're in your fifties, overweight, and just on the edge of adult-onset diabetes. Along comes a period of chronic stress; even more glucose and fatty acids in the bloodstream, plus those glucocorticoids repeatedly urging cells to listen to insulin even less. Enough of this and you pass the threshold for becoming overtly diabetic, set up for more atherosclerotic trouble. Given the role of the glucocorticoids (which are of the "steroid" class of hormones) in bringing about this state, this type of diabetes is called "steroid diabetes" when it refers to the development of type 2 diabetes from taking synthetic glucocorticoids (to control any of a variety of diseases that will be discussed later in this book)—in other words, as a side effect of taking the medication. (I have not seen the term used to describe the increased tendency toward type 2 diabetes when a person's own glucocorticoids are secreted during chronic stress.)

For convenience, physicians usually use an absolute cutoff to decide when someone has type 2 diabetes (that is to say, once you demonstrate a certain level of glucose in the bloodstream during a glucose tolerance test, you get labeled as having the disorder). However, the disease really represents a continuum —there is no hard and fast point of insulin resistance and hyperglycemia (elevated blood glucose levels) at which the body suddenly begins to get into trouble. Instead, for every bit of insulin resistance and hyperglycemia, there is a bit more risk of the types of damage discussed. And this is no trivial problem.

Adult-onset diabetes is nearly epidemic in the United States, afflicting more than 15 percent of people sixty-five and over. The disease more than doubles mortality, and nearly triples the rate of heart disease in men. Furthermore, it is a leading cause of blindness, and the seventh leading cause of death. It is one thing to have too great a metabolic stress-response causing you to feel fatigued, but quite another for it to increase the risk or severity of adult-onset diabetes. This chapter serves as a second example of the double-edged nature of the stress-response and the pathogenic consequences when it is prolonged.

ULCERS, COLITIS, AND THE RUNS

When it comes to your gut, there's no such thing as a free lunch. You've just finished some feast, eaten like a hog — slabs of turkey, somebody's grandma's famous mashed potatoes and gravy, a bare minimum of vegetables to give a semblance of healthiness, and — oh, why not — another drumstick and some corn on the cob, a slice or two of pie for dessert, ad nauseam. You expect your gut to magically convert all that into a filtrate of nutrients in your bloodstream? It takes energy, huge amounts of it. Muscular work. Your stomach not only breaks down food chemically, it does so mechanically as well. It undergoes systolic contractions: the muscle walls contract violently on one side of your stomach and hunks of food are flung against the far wall, breaking them down in a cauldron of acids and enzymes. Your small intestines do a snake dance of peristalsis (directional contraction), contracting the muscular walls at the top end in order to squeeze the food downstream in time for the next stretch of muscle to contract. After that your bowels do the same, and you're destined for the bathroom soon. Circular muscles called sphincters located at the beginning and end of each organ open and close, serving as locks to make sure that things don't move to the next level in the system until that stage of digestion is complete, a process no less complicated than shuttling boats through the locks of the Panama Canal. At your mouth, stomach, and small intestines, water has to be poured into the system to keep everything in solution, to make sure that the sweet potato pie, or what's left of it, doesn't turn into a dry plug. By this time, the action has moved to your large intestines, which have to extract the water and return it to your bloodstream so that you don't inadvertently excrete all that fluid and desiccate like a prune. All this takes energy, and we haven't even considered jaw fatigue.

So our by now familiar drama on the savanna: If you are that zebra, you can't waste energy on your stomach walls doing a rumba; there isn't time to get any nutritional benefits from digestion. And if you are that lion, by definition, you haven't just roused yourself from a heavy meal.

Digestion is quickly shut down during stress. We all know the first step in that process. If you get nervous, you stop secreting saliva and your mouth gets dry. Your stomach grinds to a halt, contractions stop, enzymes and digestive acids are no longer secreted, your small intestines stop peristalsis, nothing is absorbed. The rest of your body even knows that the digestive tract has been shut down—blood flow to your stomach and gut is decreased so that the bloodborne oxygen and glucose can be delivered elsewhere, where it's needed. The parasympathetic nervous system, perfect for all that calm, vegetative physiology, normally mediates the actions of digestion. Along comes stress: turn off the parasympathetic, turn on the sympathetic, and forget about digestion. End of stress; switch gears again, and the digestive process resumes.

As usual, this all makes wonderful sense for the zebra or the lion. And as usual, it is in the face of chronic stress that diseases emerge instead. The remainder of the chapter is concerned with four pressing questions:

• How do ulcers originate during stress?

• Why, when we're truly terrified, do we soil our pants (and why is it so frequently diarrhea under those charming circumstances)?

- What about colitis and irritable bowel syndrome?

- Why, if the logic of the stress-response is to inhibit digestion during stress, do so many of us overeat during periods of emotional turmoil?

ULCER FORMATION

An ulcer is a hole in the wall of an organ, and ulcers originating in the stomach or in the organs immediately bordering it are termed peptic ulcers. The ones within the stomach are called gastric ulcers; those a bit higher up than the stomach are esoph-

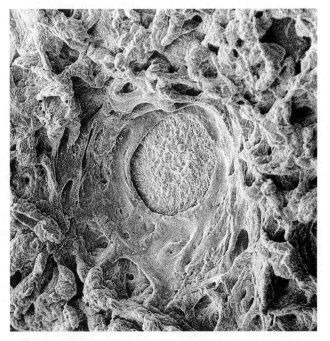

Photomicrograph of a stomach ulcer.

ageal, and those at the border of the stomach and the intestine
are duodenal (the most common of peptic ulcers).

As will be recalled, peptic ulcers were among the trio of
symptoms Selye noted more than fifty years ago when he exposed his rats to nonspecific unpleasantness. Since then, stomach ulcers have emerged as the disorder most recognized by the
lay public as a stress-related disease: in this view, you have
upsetting thoughts for a long period of time and holes appear in
the walls of your stomach. Most clinicians agree that there is a
subtype of ulcers that forms relatively rapidly (sometimes over
the course of days) in humans who are exposed to immensely
stressful crises — hemorrhage, massive infection, trauma due to
accident or surgery, and so on. Such stress ulcers can be life-
threatening in severe cases. Recent studies have shown that
even the gradually emerging kinds of ulcers tend to appear
during times of stressful life events.

Just what percentage of human ulcers are caused by stress
remains highly controversial. It is probably safest to say that
stress is not at the top of the list of causes, but near the top, with
the capacity to worsen the effects of some of the more common
causes (such as genetics or diet). Surprisingly enough, it's also
not yet clear *how* stress causes ulcers. Here are six different
possible routes to ulcer formation, starting with my favorite. (In
general, the first two mechanisms are thought to account for
most ulcer formation, although it is quite possible that more
than one of these mechanisms go on simultaneously.)

- Acid-rebound. To understand this mechanism of ulcer formation, we once again have to grapple with the grim reality of
  what bizarre things we are willing to eat and expect our stomachs to digest. The only way that the stomach is going to be
  able to handle some of this stuff is if it has powerful degrada-
  tive weapons. The systolic contractions certainly help, but the
  main weapon is the hydrochloric acid that pours into your
  stomach from the cells lining it. Hydrochloric acid is immensely
  acidic; all well and good, but it raises the obvious question of
  why your stomach is not itself digested by the digestive acids.
  Eat somebody else's stomach and your stomach disintegrates it.
  How do your own stomach walls remain unscathed? Basically,

your stomach has to spend a fortune protecting itself. It builds many layers of stomach wall and coats them with thick, soothing mucus that buffers the acid. In addition, bicarbonate is secreted into the stomach to neutralize the acid. This is a wonderful solution, and you happily go about digestion.

Along comes a stressful period lasting months. Your body cuts down on the acid secretion—there are now frequently times where digestion is being inhibited. During this period, your stomach essentially decides to save itself some energy by cutting corners. It cuts back a bit on the constant thickening of the stomach walls, undersecretes mucus and bicarbonate, and pockets the difference. Why not? There isn't much acid around during this stressful period anyway.

End of stressful period; you decide to celebrate by eating a large chocolate cake inscribed for the occasion, stimulate your parasympathetic nervous system, start secreting hydrochloric acid, and . . . your defenses are down. The walls have thinned, there isn't as thick a protective mucous layer as there used to be, the bicarbonate is overwhelmed, and before you know it, the hydrochloric acid has damaged a few cells. You are secreting normal amounts of hydrochloric acid, but your stomach walls aren't as able to defend against it. If you repeatedly go through this cycle of sustained periods of decreased hydrochloric acid secretion followed by periods of normal secretion, an ulcer can eventually emerge.

Suppose you are in the middle of a very stressful period, and you worry that you are at risk for an ulcer. What's the solution? You could make sure that you remain under stress every second for the rest of your life. You definitely will avoid ulcers caused by hydrochloric acid secretion, but of course you'll die for a zillion other reasons. The paradox is that, in this scenario, ulcers are not formed so much during the stressor as during the recovery. This idea predicts that several periods of transient stress should be more ulcerative than one long, continuous period, and animal experiments have generally shown this to be the case.

• Acid overproduction. When some people eat a meal, their hydrochloric acid secretion is abnormally large for the amount of food consumed: clearly, bad news for stomach walls. Normally, the cells in the stomach that secrete acid keep close track of just how acidic they have made the neighborhood, and if the level rises too high, they stop secreting acid. For some reason this regulatory system appears to fail in some people, putting them at greater risk for forming an ulcer. While this defect is thought to have a strong genetic component, stress is hypothesized to exaggerate this problem of failing to curb acid secretion.

- Dramatic decrease in blood flow. This probably occurs only in certain types of stressful emergencies. In an emergency, you want to deliver as much blood as possible to the muscles that are exercising. In response to stress, your sympathetic nervous system diverts blood from the gut to more important places— remember the man with a gunshot wound in the stomach, whose guts would blanch from decreased blood flow everytime he became angry or anxious. If your stressor is one that involves a dramatic decrease in blood flow to the gut (for example, following a hemorrhage), it begins to cause little infarcts— small strokes—in your stomach walls, because of lack of oxygen. You develop small lesions of necrotic (dead) tissue, which are the building blocks of ulcers.

This condition probably arises for at least two reasons. First, with decreased blood flow, less of the acid that accumulates is being flushed away. The second reason involves another paradoxical piece of biology. We all obviously need oxygen and would turn an unsightly blue without it. However, running your cells on oxygen occasionally produces an odd, dangerous class of compounds called oxygen radicals. Normally, we have no trouble disposing of oxygen radicals. There is some evidence that during periods of chronic stress, when blood flow (and thus oxygen delivery) to the gut decreases, your stomach stops making the compounds (so-called free-radical quenchers or scavengers) that protect you from the oxygen radicals. Fine for the period of stress; it is a clever way to save energy during a crisis. At the end of stress, however, when blood flow chock-full of oxygen resumes and the normal amount of oxygen radicals is generated, the stomach has its oxidative pants down. Without sufficient scavengers, the oxygen radicals start killing cells in the stomach walls, setting you up for an ulcer. Note how similar this scenario is to the acid-rebound mechanism: in both cases, the damage occurs not during the period of stress but in its aftermath, and not so much because stress increases the size of an insult (for example, the amount of acid secreted or the amount of oxygen radicals produced), but because, during the stressful emergency, the gut scrimps on defenses against such insults.*

- The bacterial scenario. There are all sorts of bacteria in your stomach that can potentially attack your stomach walls and cause ulcers. Under normal circumstances, your immune system can usually take care of the bacteria and protect you. However, in the face of chronic stress your immune system provides less protection (the subject of chapter 8), and bacteria run amok. This mechanism is getting a tremendous amount of attention; researchers are particularly excited about the theory that bacteria cause ulcers because one bacterium, *Helicobacter pylori*, tends to occur in stomachs with ulcers. No one has been able to show yet that this bacterium, or any other, actually *causes* ulcers; however, recent studies suggest that treating an ulcer with antibiotics that kill bacteria of this sort works much better than treating with antacids.

- Insufficient amounts of prostaglandins. In this scenario, micro-ulcers begin now and then in your gut, as part of the expected wear and tear on the system. Normally your body can repair the damage by secreting a class of chemicals called prostaglandins, thought to aid the healing process by increasing blood flow through the stomach walls. During stress, however, the

---

*Oxygen radicals also probably have something to do with why brain cells die after a stroke. When blood flow to a neuron ceases, either because of cardiac arrest or because a blood vessel in the neighborhood has clogged up, the neuron is deprived of both glucose and oxygen. Trying to function in these coming minutes without either is difficult enough to kill some neurons. But evidence suggests that at least some of the damage comes in the aftermath when, for example, the heart has started up again. Oxygenated blood begins to be delivered, the brain cells leap at the opportunity to go back to normal, and oxygen radicals are generated in the process. But the neuron is caught short, since the oxygen deprivation depleted it of oxygen-radical scavengers. Oxygen radicals may also play a role in how heart muscle is damaged during cardiac arrest.

synthesis of these prostaglandins is inhibited by the actions of glucocorticoids. In the case of this mechanism, stress does not so much cause the formation of ulcers as impair your ability to catch them early and repair them. It is not yet well established how often this is the route for ulcer formation during stress. (Aspirin also inhibits prostaglandin synthesis, which is why aspirin can aggravate a bleeding ulcer.)

• Stomach contractions. For unknown reasons, stress causes the stomach to initiate slow, rhythmic contractions (about one per minute); and for unknown reasons, these seem to add to ulcer risk. One idea is that during the contractions, blood flow to the stomach is disrupted, causing little bursts of ischemia; there's not much evidence for this, however. Another idea is that the contractions mechanically damage the stomach walls. The jury is still out on that mechanism as well.

Most of these mechanisms are pretty well-documented routes by which ulcers can form; of those credible mechanisms, most can occur during at least certain types of stressors. More than one mechanism may occur simultaneously, and people seemingly differ as to how likely each mechanism is to occur in their gut during stress. Duodenal ulcers are most likely to involve too much acid, whereas gastric ulcers are most likely to involve impaired defenses against acid. Additional mechanisms for ulcer formation will no doubt be discovered, but for the moment, these six should be quite sufficient to make anyone sick.

BOWELS IN AN UPROAR

Regardless of how stressful that board meeting or examination is, we're not likely to soil our pants. Nevertheless, we are all aware of the tendency of immensely terrified people — convicts about to be executed, soldiers amid horrifying battle — to defecate spontaneously. No doubt they are intensely curious at such times as to why that is happening, and modern science can finally supply us with answers.

The logic is similar to why we lose control of our bladders if we are very frightened, as reviewed in chapter 3. Most of digestion is a strategy to get your mouth, stomach, bile ducts, and so forth, to work together to break your food down into its constituent parts by the time it reaches the small intestines. The small intestines, in turn, are responsible for absorbing nutrients out of this mess and delivering them to the bloodstream. As is apparent to most of us, not much of what we eat is actually nutritious, and a large percentage of what we consume is left over after the small intestines pick through it. In the large intestines, the leftovers are converted to feces and eventually exit stage left.

Yet again, you sprint across the veld. All that stuff sitting in your large intestines, from which the nutritive potential has already been absorbed, is just dead weight. You have the choice of sprinting for your life with or without a couple of pounds of excess baggage in your bowels. Empty them.

The biology of this is quite well understood. The sympathetic nervous system is responsible. At the same time that it is sending a signal to your stomach to stop its contractions and to your small intestine to stop peristalsis, your sympathetic nervous system is actually stimulating muscular movement in your large intestine. Inject into a rat's brain the chemicals that turn on the sympathetic nervous system, and suddenly the small intestine stops contracting and the large intestine starts contracting like crazy.

But why, to add insult to injury, is it so frequently diarrhea when you are truly frightened? Relatively large amounts of water are needed for digestion, to keep your food in solution as you break it down so that it will be easy to absorb into the circulation when digestion is done. The job of the large intestine is to get that water back, and that's why your bowels have to be so long—the leftovers slowly inch their way through the large intestine, starting as a soupy gruel and ending up, ideally, as reasonably dry stool. Disaster strikes, run for your life, increase that large intestinal motility, and everything gets pushed through too fast for the water to be absorbed optimally. Diarrhea, simple as that.

Thus, because of the ability of stress to increase large intestinal motility, being executed can often lead to socially embarrassing gastrointestinal consequences. But similar problems, writ small, may occur among people who are less dramatically stressed. Colitis, irritable colon, and spastic colon are all ways of describing bowel disturbances that can occur in response to more common stressors. Collectively, irritable bowel syndromes are the most common gastrointestinal diseases and are probably the most common of stress-related disorders: estimates are that 75 percent of us will have some sort of irritable bowel syndrome related to stress at some point in our lives. Personally, all of the major rites of passage in my life have been marked by pretty impressive cases of the runs a few days before—my bar mitzvah, going away to college, my doctoral defense, proposing marriage, my wedding. (Finally, that confessional tone obligatory to successful books these days. Now if I can only name some famous Hollywood starlets with whom I've taken diuretics, this may become a best-seller.)

Irritable bowel syndrome is a hodgepodge of disorders. Colitis is inflammation of the colon (also known as the bowels); as the most common consequence, the colon can become irritable. Spastic colon is another way of describing irritable colon. Finally, irritable bowel syndrome is a way of describing the collectivity of the inflammation and the subsequent consequences. Some folks suffer frequent stomach pain and gas, particularly right after a meal. In others, diarrhea predominates, while others are chronically constipated. There seem any number of reasons why these disorders should cause discomfort—malabsorption of nutrients, loss of water, distention of your bowels.

The disorder seems to arise not only from being under a lot of stress, but also from having a gastrointestinal system that is abnormally sensitive to such stress. The first component—being exposed to too many stressors—can probably best be thought of as a problem of different parts of the gastrointestinal tract getting desynchronized in their function. A scenario in a perfect world: the small and large intestines are doing their jobs correctly; something stressful occurs, and both organs respond promptly (with motility decreasing in the small intestines and increasing in the large). End of the stressor, and both organs promptly resume their normal level of activity.

Instead of this ideal, however, with repeated stressors the responses of the small and large intestines may become uncoordinated—one of the organs may have a relatively larger stress-response than the other, or a more rapid recovery of function after the stressor ends. If the relative net result of this uncoordination is small intestinal motility being too inhibited, the result is constipation. If the result is large intestinal motility being too stimulated, the result is diarrhea.

In addition, these are not only disorders of too much stress, but of too much gastrointestinal sensitivity to stress. This can be shown in experimental situations, where a person with irritable bowel syndrome is subjected to a stressor (keeping his hand in ice water for a while, trying to make sense of two recorded conversations at once, participating in a pressured interview). These individuals show a greater gastrointestinal response than do healthy controls. Those who tend toward chronic diarrhea are the ones who show the greatest large intestinal responses, while those who tend toward constipation show the greatest small intestinal ones.

STRESS AND APPETITE

Clearly, regulation of the gastrointestinal tract during stress involves some component of eating patterns and appetite. Just as clearly, it is pretty confusing what exactly happens. Our everyday experiences are contradictory. You get upset over something, become agitated and anxious, and find yourself mechanically chewing away at some junk food without even tasting it. You get nervous and upset over something, and find you have no appetite for dinner. Dogs lose their beloved masters and pine away, refusing to eat. People go through a traumatic divorce and balloon up. People go through a traumatic divorce and waste away, claiming that they feel queasy every time they eat anything. I could conclude that "stress influences appetite," but that wouldn't tell us anything about why it does so in opposite directions in different cases.

Mark Daughhetee 1985: The Sin of Gluttony, *oil on silver print.*

Initially, when you study the biology of the effect of stress on appetite, the picture is no clearer. At least one of the critical hormones of the stress-response stimulates appetite, while another inhibits it. You might recall from earlier chapters that this hormone (CRF) is released by the hypothalamus and, by stimulating the pituitary to release ACTH, starts the cascade of events that culminates in adrenal release of glucocorticoids. Evolution has allowed the development of efficient use of the body's chemical messengers, and CRF is no exception. It is also used in parts of the brain to regulate other features of the stress-response. It helps to turn on the sympathetic nervous system, and it plays a role in increasing vigilance and arousal during stress. It also suppresses appetite. This might lead us to the conclusion that stress inhibits food intake. (Unsuccessful dieters should be warned against running to the neighborhood pharmacist for a bottle of CRF. It will probably help you lose weight, but you'll feel awful—as if you were always in the middle of an anxiety-provoking emergency: heart racing, jumpy, hyposexual, irritable. Opt for a few more sit-ups.)

On the other side of the picture are glucocorticoids. In addition to the actions already outlined in response to stress, they appear to stimulate appetite. This is typically demonstrated in rats: glucocorticoids make these animals more willing to run mazes looking for food, more willing to press a lever for a food pellet, and so on. To my knowledge, the equivalent has not been tested in humans — stoking people up on adrenal steroids to see how many times they are willing to scurry up and down supermarket aisles in order to find the apricot fruit rolls or the pickled onions that they've been craving. Nevertheless, scientists have a reasonably good idea where in the brain glucocorticoids stimulate appetite, which type of glucocorticoid receptors are involved, and so on.

Thus, the CRF literature leads to the conclusion that stress will decrease food intake, while the glucocorticoid literature predicts that stress will do just the opposite. How do you reconcile these opposite effects of CRF and glucocorticoids? Time may have something to do with it. When a stressful event occurs, there is a burst of CRF secretion within a few seconds. ACTH levels take about half a minute to go up, while it takes, perhaps, half an hour for glucocorticoid levels to surge in the bloodstream (depending on the species). In any case, CRF is the fastest wave of the adrenal cascade, glucocorticoids the slowest. This difference in what experimenters call "timecourse" is also seen in the speed at which these hormones work on various parts of the body. CRF makes its effects felt within seconds, while glucocorticoids take hours to exert some of their actions. Finally, when the stressful event is over, it takes mere seconds for CRF and ACTH to be cleared from the bloodstream, while it can take hours for glucocorticoids.

These differences enable us to make some pretty confident predictions. If there are large amounts of CRF and ACTH in your bloodstream, yet almost no glucocorticoids, it is a pretty safe bet that you are in the first few minutes of a stressful event. If there are large amounts of CRF, ACTH, *and* glucocorticoids in the bloodstream, you are probably right in the middle of a

sustained stressor. And if there are substantial amounts of glucocorticoids in the circulation but little CRF or ACTH, you have
probably started the recovery period.

The conflicting effects of CRF and glucocorticoids on appetite begin to make some sense. At the very beginning of a
stress-response, it is logical to shut down digestion, turn off
activity in the gut, mobilize energy from sites of storage in your
body. If your salivary glands have stopped secreting and your
stomach is asleep, this is a reasonable time to lose your appetite,
and the burst of CRF release helps bring that about. Then, when
the stressful event is finished, digestion starts up again and your
body can begin to replenish those stores of energy consumed in
that mad dash across the savanna. Appetite is stimulated. In this
case, glucocorticoids would not so much serve as the mediator of
the stress-response, but as the means of *recovering* from the
stress-response.

These processes may even begin to explain why some of us
lose our appetites during stress and others get the munchies. It
may be related to the pattern, the duration of our stressors.
Something truly stressful occurs, and a maximal signal to secrete
CRF, ACTH, and glucocorticoids is initiated. If the stressor ends
after, for example, ten minutes, there will cumulatively be perhaps a twelve-minute burst of CRF exposure (ten minutes during the stressor, plus the two minutes or so it takes to clear the
CRF afterward) and a two-hour burst of exposure to glucocorticoids (the ten minutes of secretion during the stressor plus the
much longer time to clear). This may be a case where the net
result of the stressor is stimulation of appetite. By contrast, the
longer the stressor lasts, the longer the cumulative time of exposure to CRF, causing inhibition of appetite. (This model assumes
what is generally the case: that the inhibitory effects of CRF on
appetite are stronger than the stimulatory effects of glucocorticoids, if they reach hunger centers in the brain at the same time.)
Thus, lots of short stressful events should lead to overeating,
while one long, continuous stressor should lead to appetite loss.
I do not think this idea has been tested, but in considering
individual responses, one would also have to factor in the precise quantities of CRF and glucocorticoids secreted in a particu-

lar person, just how effectively they influence hunger centers in the brain, what their half-lives are, and so on. In other words, there are likely to be many complex, individual differences in how people respond. Moreover, there are a large number of other hormones that are probably relevant to the regulation of appetite during stress—in some cases, scientists know these hormones are involved in the stress-response and are less sure of their effects on hunger, and in others, they are certain the hormones are involved in the regulation of appetite but are less sure that they are sensitive to stress.

Eating and digesting are fundamental ways in which a body plans for the future, while sprinting across the veld in panicked abandon represents one of the most fundamental ways in which a body responds to an immediate crisis. The central lesson of this chapter is how incompatible it is to plan for the future and simultaneously deal with a current emergency. This idea will dominate the coming two chapters, which review two of the most optimistic projects your body can undertake in planning ahead—growth and reproduction.

6

DWARFISM AND THE IMPORTANCE OF MOTHERS

It still surprises me that organisms grow. Maybe I don't believe in biology as much as I should. Eating and digesting a meal seems very real. You put a massive amount of something or other in your mouth, and as a result all sorts of very tangible things happen—your jaw gets tired, your stomach distends, and eventually something comes out the other end. The results of growth seem pretty tangible, too. Long bones get longer, kids weigh more when you heft them, your squirrelly little nephew starts towering over you. Pretty concrete.

My difficulty is with the intervening steps. I know theoretically what happens in the blood after a meal; my university even allows me to teach impressionable students about it. A lot more glucose, fatty acids, and amino acids wind up in the circulation, and I know that this stuff is nutritive. But you can't look with the naked eye at a vial of blood and tell if it's chock-full of nutrients. Someone ate a mountain of spaghetti, salad, garlic bread, *and* two slices of cake for dessert—and that has been transformed and is now in this test tube of blood? Hard to believe. And somehow it's going to be reconstructed into bone? Just think, your femur is made up of tiny pieces of your mother's chicken pot pie that you ate throughout your youth. Ha! You see, you don't really believe in the process either. Maybe we're too primitive to comprehend the transmogrification of material. Perhaps it would make more sense if we could actually observe globs of bread pudding moving directly from our stomachs and welding themselves onto the ends of our bones to make them longer.

Nevertheless, growth does occur. And in a kid, it's not a trivial process. The brain gets bigger, the shape of the head changes. Cells divide, grow in size, and synthesize new proteins. Long bones lengthen as cartilaginous cells called chondrocytes at the ends of bones migrate into the shaft and solidify into bone. Baby fat melts away and is replaced by muscle. The larynx thickens and the voice deepens, hair grows in all sorts of unlikely places on the body, breasts develop, testes enlarge—the works.

From the standpoint of understanding the effects of stress on growth, the most important feature of the growth process is that, of course, growth doesn't come cheap. Calcium must be obtained to build bones, amino acids are needed for all that protein synthesis, fatty acids build cell walls, glucose pays for the building costs. Appetite soars, and nutrients pour in from the intestines. A large part of what various hormones do is to mobilize the energy and the material needed for all of these civic expansion projects. Growth hormone dominates the process. Sometimes it works directly on cells in the body—for example, growth hormone helps to break down fat cells, depleting them of their fatty acids so that these stored nutrients can be diverted to the growing cells. Alternatively, sometimes growth hormone must first trigger the release of another class of hormones called somatomedins, which actually do the job—for example, promoting cell division. Thyroid hormone plays a role, promoting growth hormone release, making bones more responsive to somatomedins. Insulin does something similar as well. The reproductive hormones come into play around puberty. Estrogen promotes the growth of long bones, both by acting directly at bone and by increasing growth hormone secretion. Testosterone does similar things to long bones and, in addition, enhances muscle growth.

The differential effects of estrogen and of testosterone on growth are the reasons why at puberty girls get taller, whereas boys get taller and more muscular. Testosterone increases muscle mass in adults as well, which is why various football players and weightlifters abuse "anabolic" (growth-enhancing) steroids, of which testosterone is the prime example, as part of their muscle-building programs. Adolescents stop growing when the ends of the long bones meet and begin to fuse, but for complex reasons, testosterone, by accelerating the growth of the ends of long bones, can actually speed the cessation of growth. Thus, pubescent boys given particularly high concentrations of testosterone will, paradoxically, wind up having their adult stature blunted a bit. Conversely, boys castrated before puberty grow to be quite tall, with lanky bodies and particularly long limbs. Opera history buffs will recognize this morphology: castrati were famed for this body shape.

GROWTH INHIBITION DURING STRESS

Growth is great when you are a ten-year-old lying in bed at night with a full belly. However, it wouldn't make sense to spend much energy on this sort of thing during a stressful event. You're sprinting for your life, trying to evade the lion, that whole scenario. If there is no time to derive any advantages from digesting your meal at that point, there certainly isn't time to get any benefit from growth.

To understand the process by which stress inhibits growth, it helps to begin with extreme cases. A child of, say, eight years, is brought to a doctor because she has stopped growing. There are none of the typical problems—the kid is getting enough food, there is no apparent disease, she has no intestinal parasites that compete for nutrients. No one can identify an *organic* cause of her problem; yet she doesn't grow. In many such cases, there turns out to be something dreadfully stressful in her life—emotional neglect or psychological abuse. In such circumstances, the syndrome is called stress dwarfism, psychosocial, or *psychogenic* dwarfism.

Perhaps right now a question is running through the minds of the half of you who are below average height. If you are short, yet didn't have any obvious chronic diseases as a kid and can recall an unpleasant period in your childhood, are you a product of mild stress dwarfism? Suppose one of your parents had a job necessitating frequent moves, and every year or two throughout childhood you were uprooted, forced to leave your friends, off to a strange school. Is this the sort of situation associated with psychogenic dwarfism? Definitely not. How about something more severe? Suppose that your parents divorced when you were a kid; it was very acrimonious, and at some point it became horrifyingly clear that neither of them particularly wanted you to live with them afterward. Stress dwarfism? Probably not.

The syndrome is extremely rare, and physicians fall over themselves to see the occasional cases. These are the kids who are incessantly harassed and psychologically terrorized by the crazy stepfather. These are the kids who, when the police and the social workers break down the door, are discovered to have been locked in a dark closet for months, fed a tray of food slipped under the door. These are the products of vast, grotesque family psychopathology. And they pop up in every endocrinology textbook, standing nude in front of a growth chart. Stunted little kids, years behind their expected growth rate, years behind in mental development, bruised and with distorted, flinching postures, haunted, slack facial expressions, eyes masked by the obligatory rectangles that accompany all naked people in medical texts. And invariably with stories to take your breath away and make you wonder at the potential sickness of the human mind.

And, invariably, on the same page in the text is a surprising second photo—the same child a few years later, after having been placed in a different environment (or, as one pediatric endocrinologist drolly termed it, having undergone a "parentec-

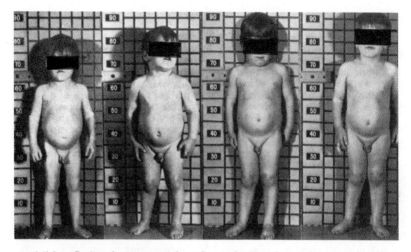

*A child suffering from stress dwarfism: changes in appearance during
hospitalization (left to right).*

tomy"). No bruises, maybe a tentative smile. And a lot taller. As
long as the stressor is removed before the child is far into
puberty (when the ends of the long bones fuse together and
growth ceases), there is the potential for some degree of "catch-
up" growth, although shortness of stature and some degree of
stunting of personality and intellect usually persist into
adulthood.

Despite the clinical rarity of stress dwarfism, instances pop
up throughout history. One possible case arose during the thir-
teenth century as the result of an experiment by that noted
endocrinologist, King Frederick II of Sicily. It seems that his
court was engrossed in philosophic disputation over the natural
language of humans. In an attempt to resolve the question,
Frederick (who was apparently betting on Hebrew, Greek, or
Latin) came up with a surprisingly sophisticated idea for an
experiment. He commandeered a bunch of infants and had each
one raised in a room by itself. Every day someone would bring
the child food, fresh blankets, and clean clothes, all of the best
quality. But they wouldn't stay and play with the infant, or hold
it—too much of a chance that the person would speak in the

child's presence. The infants would be raised without human language, and everyone would get to see what was actually the natural language of humans.

Of course, the kids did not spontaneously burst out of the door one day reciting poetry in Italian or singing opera. The kids didn't burst out of the door at all. None of them survived. The lesson is obvious to us now — optimal growth and development do not merely depend upon being fed the right number of calories and being kept warm. Frederick "laboured in vain, for the children could not live without clappings of hands and gestures and gladness of countenance and blandishments," reported the contemporary historian Salimbene. It seems quite plausible that these kids, all healthy and well fed, died of stress dwarfism.*

A recent study makes the same point, if more subtly. This one winds up in half the textbooks, and if it had been planned intentionally, it could not have produced a cleaner result. The subjects of the "experiment" were children raised in two different orphanages in Germany just after World War II. Both orphanages were run by the government; thus there were important controls in place — the kids in both had the same general diet, the same frequency of doctors' visits, and so on. The main identifiable difference in their care was the two women who ran the orphanages. The scientists even checked them, and their description sounds like a parable. In one orphanage was Fraulein Grun, the warm, nurturant mother who played with the children, comforted them, and spent all day singing and laughing. In the other was Fraulein Schwarz, a woman who was clearly in the wrong profession. She discharged her professional obligations, but minimized her contact with the children; she frequently criticized and berated them, typically among their assembled peers. The growth rates at the two orphanages were

*Some clinical nomenclature. "Maternal deprivation syndrome," "deprivation syndrome," and "nonorganic failure to thrive" usually refer to infants and invariably to the loss of the mother. "Stress dwarfism," "psychogenic dwarfism," and "psychosocial dwarfism" usually refer to children aged three years or older. However, some papers do not follow this age dichotomy; during the nineteenth century, infants dying of failure to thrive in orphanages were said to suffer from "marasmus," Greek for "wasting away."

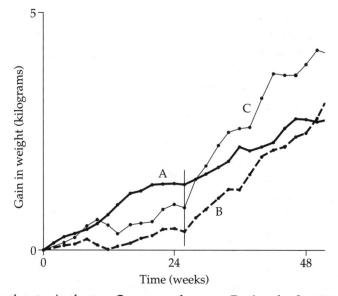

Growth rates in the two German orphanages. During the first 26 weeks of the study, growth rates in Orphanage A, under the administration of the warm Fraulein Grun, were much greater than those in Orphanage B, with the stern Fraulein Schwarz. At 26 weeks (vertical line), Fraulein Grun left Orphanage A and was replaced by Fraulein Schwarz. The rate of growth in that orphanage promptly slowed; growth in Orphanage B, now minus the stern Fraulein Schwarz, accelerated and soon surpassed that of Orphanage A. A fascinating elaboration emerges from the fact that Schwarz was not completely heartless, but had a subset of children who were her favorites (Curve C), whom she had transferred with her.

entirely different. Fraulein Schwarz's kids grew in height and weight at a slower pace than the kids in the other orphanage. Then, in an elaboration that couldn't have been more useful if it had been planned by a scientist, Fraulein Grun moved on to greener pastures and, for some bureaucratic reason, Fraulein Schwarz was transferred to the other orphanage. Growth rates in her former orphanage promptly increased; those in her new one decreased.

Until recent decades, being placed in an orphanage was one of the most dangerous events that could happen to a child. In 1915, despite adequate food and health care, the majority of orphanages in the United States had close to 100 percent mortality rates. Even some thirty years later, a third of infants in orphanages were still dying, "in spite of good food and meticulous medical care." It should be noted that this was a period when child-rearing practices were intensely Spartan, and the leading expert, Dr. Luther Holt of Columbia University, warned parents of the adverse effects of the "vicious practice" of using a cradle, picking up the child when it cried, or handling it too often. Ironically, in the less wealthy orphanages, where the staff was often not up-to-date on the advice of this savant, mortality rates were lower than in the "better" orphanages.

A final and truly disturbing example comes to mind. If you ever find yourself reading chapter after chapter about growth endocrinology (which I don't recommend), you will note an occasional odd reference to Peter Pan — perhaps a quotation from the play, or a snide comment about Tinker Bell. For a long time, I couldn't make sense of this phenomenon. Finally, buried in a chapter in one textbook, I found the explanation.

The chapter reviewed the regulation of growth in children and the capacity for severe psychological stress to trigger psychogenic dwarfism. It gave an example that occurred in a British Victorian family. A son, age thirteen, the beloved favorite of the mother, is killed in a skating accident. The mother, despairing and bereaved, takes to her bed in grief for years afterward, utterly ignoring her other, six-year-old son. Horrible scenes ensue. The boy, on one occasion, enters her darkened room; the mother, in her delusional state, briefly believes it is the dead son — "David, is that you? Could that be you?" — before realizing: "Oh, it is only you." On the rare instances when the mother interacts with the younger son, she repeatedly expresses the same obsessive thought: the only solace that she feels is that David died when he was still perfect, still a boy, never to be ruined by growing up and growing away from his mother.

The younger boy, ignored (the rather stern and distant father appears to have had no interactions with any of the children), seizes upon this idea; by remaining a boy forever, by not growing up, he will at least have some chance of pleasing his mother, winning her love. Although there is no evidence of disease or malnutrition in his well-to-do family, he ceases grow-ing. As an adult, he is just barely five feet in height, and his marriage is unconsummated.

The forlorn boy became the author of the much-beloved children's classic, *Peter Pan*. J. M. Barrie's plays and novels are filled with children who didn't grow up, who were fortunate enough to die in childhood, who came back as ghosts to visit their mothers.

THE MECHANISMS UNDERLYING STRESS DWARFISM

Despite the rarity of stress dwarfism, it is known that these children tend to have extremely low growth hormone levels in their circulation, which would certainly account for the dwarf-ism. Why do growth hormone levels decline in these kids? Growth hormone is secreted by the pituitary gland, which in turn is regulated by the hypothalamus in the brain (see chapter 2). The hypothalamus controls growth secretion through the release of two hormones—one that stimulates growth hormone release ("growth hormone releasing hormone," or GHRH) and one that inhibits release ("growth hormone inhibiting hor-mone," GHIH, or as it is more commonly termed, "somato-statin"). The normal fluctuation in growth hormone levels rep-resents the integration of the brain's stimulatory GHRH signal and inhibitory GHIH signal.

If growth hormone levels are suppressed in kids with stress dwarfism, it could be because of a problem at the level of the hypothalamus, perhaps secretion of too little GHRH and/or too much GHIH. This has been tough to study in humans, but animal studies indicate that it is probably too much GHIH that drives down growth hormone levels. In addition, the pituitary might be responding strangely to the hypothalamic hormones. If it becomes overly sensitive to GHIH, or insensitive to GHRH, that could account for the declining growth hormone levels as well.

Once growth hormone is secreted it binds, along with the related somatomedins, to receptors in target cells and causes these cells to begin growing and dividing. There is some indication that psychogenic dwarfism results not only from too little growth hormone being secreted, but also from target cells becoming insensitive to growth hormone and somatomedins. Cynthia Kuhn and Saul Schanberg at Duke University have studied an enzyme called ornithine decarboxylase (ODC), which is critical for cell division during growth. If infant rats are deprived of their mothers, growth hormone levels and ODC activity both rapidly decline. That may suggest that ODC activity declines because there is no longer growth hormone around to stimulate it. However, if you inject those infant rats with growth hormone, ODC activity still does not return to normal—the cells no longer respond to the growth hormone signal.

There are hints that other hormones may also mediate the decline in growth hormone concentrations associated with dwarfism. The sympathetic nervous system may be overactive in these children, which would block growth hormone secretion. As evidence for the sympathetic overactivity hypothesis, scientists have found that giving a drug that blocked one branch of the sympathetic system to a child with stress dwarfism caused his growth hormone levels to return to normal. This certainly would fit a picture of kids under stress and the lesson of the four F's from chapter 2.

Glucocorticoids may also be involved. While in most studies kids with stress dwarfism are found to have normal to low levels of these stress hormones, a few report elevated levels; moreover, when infant rats are separated from their mothers, their glucocorticoid levels soar. Glucocorticoids disrupt growth in many ways. They block the secretion of growth hormone, the sensitivity of target cells to growth hormone, and the synthesis of new proteins and of new DNA in dividing cells. In human children, levels of glucocorticoids need only be two to three times higher than normal to arrest growth.

In addition to hormonal problems, kids with stress dwarfism appear to have gastrointestinal problems as well. With perfectly adequate diets, they fail to absorb the nutrients out of their guts. This is probably due to the enhanced activity of their sympathetic nervous systems producing excessive levels of epinephrine and norepinephrine. As discussed in the last chapter, these sympathetic hormones will halt the release of various digestive enzymes, stop the muscular contractions of the stomach and intestinal walls, and block nutrient absorption. (Stress/psychogenic dwarfism, the kind that hits kids three and older, seems to involve the growth hormone shortage more than gastrointestinal malabsorption problems, whereas the failure-to-thrive syndrome of infants seems to involve gastrointestinal problems more than hormonal ones.)

One study repeats some of the lessons of the German orphanage report and, in addition, shows how dramatically the hormones involved in growth respond to environmental subtleties. The paper follows a single child with stress dwarfism; when brought to the hospital, he was assigned to a special nurse who spent a great deal of time with him and to whom he became emotionally attached. Item A in the table below shows his physiological profile upon entering the hospital: extremely low growth hormone levels and a low rate of growth. Item B shows his profile a few months later, while still in the hospital: his growth hormone levels have more than doubled (without his having received any synthetic hormones) and there has been a

CONDITION	GROWTH HORMONE	GROWTH	FOOD INTAKE
A. Entry into hospital	5.9	0.5	1663
B. 100 days later	13.0	1.7	1514
C. Favorite nurse on vacation	6.9	0.6	1504
D. Nurse returns	15.0	1.5	1521

Source: From Saenger and colleagues, 1977. Growth hormone is measured in terms of nanograms of the hormone per milliliter of blood following insulin stimulation; growth is expressed as centimeters per 20 days. Food intake is expressed as calories consumed per day.

A demonstration of the sensitivity of growth to the emotional state of a child.

vast increase in his growth rate. These data graphically demonstrate that stress dwarfism is not a problem of insufficient food
—the boy was eating more at the time he entered the hospital
than a few months later, when his growth resumed.

Item C in the table profiles the period during which the
nurse, to whom the boy was attached, went on a three-week
vacation. Despite the same food intake, growth hormone levels
and growth rates plummeted back to the minimal values seen
when the boy first came into the hospital. Finally, item D shows
the boy's profile after the nurse returned from vacation.

What is the critical element missing for a child raised in
pathologic isolation, for a rat separated from its mother? There
are obviously all sorts of possibilities. Kuhn and Schanberg—
and in separate studies, Myron Hofer of the New York State
Psychiatric Institute—have studied that question in infant rats.
Is it the absence of the smell of mom? Is it something in her milk
that stimulates growth? Do the rats get chilly without her? Is it
the rat lullabies that she sings? You can imagine the various
ways scientists test for these possibilities—playing recordings of
mom's vocalizations, pumping her odor into the cage, seeing
what substitutes for the real thing.

It turns out to be touch, and it has to be active touching.
Separate a baby rat from its mother and its growth hormone
levels plummet; growth stops. Allow it contact with its mother
while she is anesthetized, and growth hormone is still low.
Mimic active licking by the mother by stroking the rat pup in the
proper pattern, and growth normalizes. In a similar set of findings, other investigators have observed that handling neonatal
rats causes them to grow faster and larger.

The same seems to apply in humans, as was demonstrated
in an extremely important study. Tiffany Field of the University
of Miami School of Medicine, along with Schanberg, Kuhn, and
others, performed an incredibly simple experiment, inspired by
the rat work just described. Studying premature infants in neonatology wards, they noted that the premature kids, while pam-
pered and fretted over and maintained in near-sterile conditions, were hardly ever touched. So Field and crew went in and
started touching them: fifteen-minute periods, three times a day,
stroking their bodies, moving their limbs. It worked wonders.

Pigtailed macaque mother and infant.

The kids grew nearly 50 percent faster, were more active and alert, matured faster behaviorally, and were released from the hospital nearly a week earlier than the premature infants who weren't touched. Months later, they were still doing better than infants who hadn't been touched. If these studies turn out to be generally replicable, their implications are enormous. Given the cost of hospitalization for these infants and the number who wind up in neonatology wards, by reducing the length of the hospital stay, daily touching would save approximately one billion dollars a year—and perhaps make for healthier kids for years afterward. It's rare that the highest technology of medical instrumentation—MRI machines, artificial organs, pacemakers—has the potential for as much impact as this simple intervention.

Touch is one of the central experiences of an infant, whether rodent, primate, or human. We readily think of stressors as consisting of various unpleasant things that can be done to an organism. Sometimes a stressor can be the *failure* to provide something for an organism, and the absence of touch is seemingly one of the most marked of developmental stressors that we can suffer.

GROWTH AND GROWTH HORMONE IN ADULTS

Personally I don't grow much anymore, except wider. According to the textbooks, another dozen Groundhog Days or so and I'm going to start shrinking. Yet I, like other adults, still secrete growth hormone into my circulation (although much less frequently than when I was an adolescent). What good is it in a nongrowing adult?

Like the Red Queen in *Alice in Wonderland*, the bodies of adults have to work harder and harder just to keep standing in the same place. Once the growth period of youth is finished and the edifice is complete, the hormones of growth mostly work at rebuilding and remodeling—carrying out the paint job, plastering the cracks that appear here and there.

Much of this repair work takes place in bone. Most of us probably view our bones as pretty boring, phlegmatic—they just sit there, inert. In reality, they are dynamic outposts of activity. They are filled with blood vessels, with little fluid-filled canals, with all sorts of cell types that are actively growing and dividing. New bone is constantly being formed, in much the same way as in a teenager. Old bone is being broken down, disintegrated by ravenous enzymes (a process called "resorption"). New calcium is shuttled in from the bloodstream, old calcium is flushed away. Growth hormone, somatomedins, parathyroid hormone, and vitamin D stand around in hard hats, supervising the project.

Why all the tumult? Some of this bustle is because bones serve as the Federal Reserve for the body's calcium, constantly giving and collecting loans of calcium to and from other organs. And part is for the sake of bone itself, allowing it to gradually rebuild and change its shape in response to need. How else do cowboys' legs get bowed from too much time on a horse? The process has to be kept well balanced. If the bones sequester too much of the body's calcium, much of the rest of the body shuts down; if the bones dump too much of their calcium into the bloodstream, they become fragile and prone to fracture, and that excess circulating calcium can start forming calcified kidney stones.

Predictably, the hormones of stress wreak havoc with the trafficking of calcium, biasing bone toward disintegrating, rather than growth. The main culprits are glucocorticoids. They inhibit the growth of new bone by disrupting the division of the bone-precursor cells in the ends of bones. Furthermore, they reduce the calcium supply to bone. Glucocorticoids block the uptake of dietary calcium in the intestines (uptake normally stimulated by vitamin D), increase the excretion of calcium by the kidney, and accelerate the resorption of bone.

If your body secretes excessively large amounts of gluco-corticoids, your bones are likely to give you problems. This is seen in people with Cushing's syndrome (in which glucocorti-coids are secreted at immensely high levels because of a tumor), and in people being treated with high doses of glucocorticoids to control some disease. In those cases, bone mass decreases mark-edly, and patients are at greater risk for osteoporosis (softening and weakening of bone and fractures). Any situation that greatly elevates glucocorticoid concentrations in the blood-stream is a particular problem for older people, in whom bone resorption is already predominant (in contrast to adolescents, in whom bone growth predominates, or young adults, in which the two processes are balanced). This is especially a problem in older women. Tremendous attention is now being paid to the need for calcium supplements to prevent osteoporosis in post-menopausal women. Estrogen potently inhibits bone resorption, and as estrogen levels drop after menopause, the bones suddenly begin to degenerate. A hefty regimen of glucocorticoids on top of that is the last thing you need.

These findings suggest that chronic stress can increase the risk of osteoporosis and cause skeletal atrophy. Most clinicians would probably say that the glucocorticoid effects on bone are "pharmacological" rather than "physiological." This means that normal levels of glucocorticoids in the bloodstream, even those in response to normal stressful events, are not enough to damage bone. Instead, it takes pharmacological levels of the hormone (far higher than the body can normally generate), due to a tumor or to taking prescribed glucocorticoids, to cause these effects. However, some recent work from Jay Kaplan's group has shown that chronic social stress leads to loss of bone mass in female monkeys. While these are among the first reports of this kind, they raise the possibility that stress can damage bone.

STRESS AND GROWTH HORMONE SECRETION IN HUMANS

The pattern of growth hormone secretion during stress differs in humans from rodents, and the implications can be fascinating. But the subject is a tough one, not meant for the fainthearted.

When a rat is first stressed, growth hormone levels begin to go down in the circulation almost immediately. If the stressor continues, growth hormone levels remain depressed. And as we have seen, in humans major and prolonged stressors cause a decrease in growth hormone levels as well. The weird thing is that during the period immediately following the onset of stress, growth hormone levels actually go up in humans and some other species. In these species, in other words, short-term stress actually *stimulates* growth hormone secretion for a time.

Why? As we have seen, growth hormone stimulates the secretion of somatomedins that, in turn, stimulate bone growth, cell division, and other processes. But growth hormone does something else as well to promote growth—it helps supply the energy needed to fuel physical development. During growth, nutrients are taken out of fat cells and other storage sites and shipped to the growing tissue. Makes sense—this is why kids suddenly lose their baby fat when they start their pubescent growth spurt. Growth hormone is partially responsible for this. It works directly at fat cells to break down stored fats (triglycerides); the building blocks of fat, as we saw in chapter 4, are then dumped into the bloodstream in the form of fatty acids and glycerol, where they can be utilized by the growing muscle. In effect, growth hormone not only runs the construction site for the new building, but arranges financing for the work as well.

Thus, during growth, growth hormone causes the breakdown of nutrients tucked away in storage sites and diverts them to *growing tissue*. As we saw in chapter 4, the main thing that your body does metabolically with glucocorticoids, epinephrine, norepinephrine, and glucagon during stress is to break down nutrients tucked away in storage sites and divert them to *exercising muscle*. Similar first steps, very dissimilar second steps. During stress, therefore, it is adaptive to secrete growth hormone insofar as it helps to mobilize energy, but a bad move to secrete growth hormone insofar as it stimulates an expensive, long-term project like growth.

As discussed, the bulk of growth hormone's actions on tissue growth and division are mediated by somatomedins. If you block somatomedin release or action, growth hormone will not have its growth-promoting effects, while still free to have its energy-mobilizing actions. And as we have seen, somatomedin levels and tissue sensitivity to somatomedin indeed decline during stress. This winds up being a clever mechanism for taking advantage of some of growth hormone's skills while blocking others. To extend the metaphor used earlier, growth hormone has just taken out cash from the bank, aiming to fund the next six months of construction; instead, the cash is used to solve the body's immediate emergency.

As long as somatomedin release or action is blocked, your body can secrete growth hormone forever, enjoying the advantages of energy mobilization without causing undue growth during a stressor. Why, then, do growth hormone levels decline at all during stress (whether immediately, as in the rat, or after a while, as in humans)? It is probably because the system does not work perfectly — somatomedin action is not completely shut down during stress. In practice, your body can use the energy-mobilizing effects of growth hormone for only so long before causing growth. Perhaps the timing of the decline of growth hormone levels represents a compromise between the trait triggered by the hormone that is good news during stress and the trait that is undesirable.

What impresses me is how careful and calculating the body has to be during stress in order to coordinate hormonal activities just right. It must perfectly balance the costs and benefits, knowing exactly when to stop secreting the hormone. If the body miscalculates in one direction and growth hormone secretion is blocked too early, there is relatively less mobilization of energy for dealing with the stressor. If it miscalculates in the other direction and growth hormone secretion goes on too long, stress may actually enhance growth. One oft-quoted study suggests that the second type of error occurs during some stressors.

In the early 1960s, Thomas Landauer of Dartmouth and John Whiting of Harvard methodically studied the rites of passages found in various non-Westernized societies around the world; they wanted to know whether the stressfulness of the ritual was related to how tall the kids wound up being as adults. Landauer and Whiting classified cultures according to whether and when they subjected their children to physically stressful development rites. Stressful rites included piercing the nose, lips, or ears; circumcision, innoculation, scarification, or cauterization; stretching or binding of limbs, or shaping the head; exposure to hot baths, fire, or intense sunlight; exposure to cold baths, snow, or cold air; emetics, irritants, and enemas; rubbing with sand, or scraping with a shell or other sharp object. (And you thought having to play the piano for your hirsute aunts when you were ten was stressful.)

Reflecting some of the anthropological tunnel vision of the time, Landauer and Whiting only studied males. They examined 80 cultures around the world and controlled their study in an important way—they collected examples from cultures from the same gene pools, with and without those stressful rituals. For example, they compared the West African tribes of Yoruba (stressful rituals) and Ashanti (nonstressful), and similarly matched Native American tribes. With this approach, they attempted to control for genetic contributions to stature (as well as nutrition, since related ethnic groups were likely to have similar diets) and to examine cultural differences instead.

Given the effects of stress on growth, it was not surprising that among cultures where kids of ages six to fifteen went through stressful maturational rituals, growth was inhibited (relative to cultures without such rituals—the difference was about 1.5 inches). Surprisingly, going through such rituals at ages two to six had no effect on growth. And most surprising, in cultures in which those rituals took place with kids under two years of age, growth was stimulated—adults were about 2.5 inches taller than in cultures without stressful rituals.

There are some possible confounds that could explain the results. One is fairly silly—maybe tall tribes like to put their young children through stressful rituals. One is more plausible —maybe putting very young children through these stressful rituals kills a certain percentage of them, and you inadvertently select survivors who are more robust and likely to wind up as tall adults. Landauer and Whiting noted that possibility and could not rule it out. In addition, even though they attempted to pair similar groups, there may have been differences other than just the stressfulness of the rites of passage—perhaps in diet or child-rearing practices. Not surprisingly, no one has ever measured levels of growth hormone, somatomedins, and so on, in Shilluk or Hausa kids while they are undergoing some grueling ritual, so there is no direct endocrine evidence that such stressors actually stimulate growth hormone secretion in a way that increases growth. Despite these problems, these cross-cultural studies have been interpreted by many biological anthropologists as evidence that some types of stressors in humans can actually stimulate growth.

THE "L" WORD

In looking at research on how stress and/or understimulation can disrupt growth, a theme pops up repeatedly: an infant human or animal can be well fed, maintained at an adequate temperature, peered at nervously, and ministered to by the best of neonatologists, yet still not thrive. Something is still missing. Perhaps we can even risk scientific credibility and detachment and mention the word "love" here, because that most ephemeral of phenomena lurks between the lines of this chapter; something roughly akin to love is needed for proper biological development, and its absence is among the most aching, distorting stressors that we can suffer. Scientists, physicians, and other caregivers have often been dim at recognizing its importance in the mundane biological processes of organs and tissues growing and developing. Yet young organisms were able to teach this fact to surprised scientists in a classic set of studies conducted in the 1950s through the 1970s, studies that are, in my opinion, among the most haunting and troubling of all the pages of science.

The work was carried out by Harry Harlow of the University of Wisconsin, a renowned and controversial scientist. Harlow helped to answer a seemingly obvious question in a nonobvious way. Why do infants become attached to their mothers? Psychology at that time was dominated by a rather extreme school of thought called behaviorism, in which behavior (of an animal or a human) was thought to operate according to rather simple rules: an organism does something more frequently because it has been positively reinforced (rewarded) for it in the past; an organism does something less frequently because it has been negatively reinforced (punished) for that behavior. In this view, there are just a few basic things that lie at the basis of reinforcement—primary drives like hunger, pain, sex. Look at the behaviors, view organisms as machines responding to stimuli, and develop a predictive mathematics built around the idea of rewards and punishments. Naturally, behaviorists had a theory as to why babies get attached to their mothers. Mothers are good at relieving the state of hunger; and that's why kids like their moms.

Harlow smelled a rat and decided to test what everyone considered obvious. He raised infant rhesus monkeys without mothers. Instead, he gave them a choice of two types of artificial "surrogate" mothers. One pseudo-mother had a monkey head constructed of wood and a wire-mesh tube resembling a torso.

Infant monkey and cloth mother, in a Harlow study.

In the middle of the torso was a bottle of milk. This surrogate mother gave nutrition. The other surrogate mother had a similar head and wire-mesh torso. But instead of containing a milk bottle, this one's torso was wrapped in terry cloth. We know exactly what the behaviorists would say. Aha, the first surrogate mother supplies food and thus is more positively reinforcing. But the baby monkeys chose the terry-cloth mothers. Kids don't love their mothers because mom balances their nutritive intake, these results suggested. They love them because, usually, mom loves them back, or at least is someone soft to cling to. "Man cannot live by milk alone. Love is an emotion that does not need to be bottle- or spoon-fed, and we may be sure that there is nothing to be gained by giving lip service to love," wrote Harlow.

Harlow's work remains controversial because of the nature of these experiments, and variations upon them (for example, raising monkeys in complete social isolation, never seeing another living animal). These were brutal studies, and they are often among the primary ones cited by those opposed to animal experimentation. Moreover, Harlow's scientific writing displayed a striking callousness to the suffering of these animals, and that is often cited by animal rights activists as well. Why were these experiments necessary? they ask; everyone knows that love is important. Why torture baby monkeys to prove the obvious? The other side retorts, oh yeah, everyone predicted just the opposite back then; it wasn't obvious at all. Then the rejoinder, but wasn't the point made? Why has this experimentation gone on for decades with endless elaborations? And the answer typically given is that such studies have enabled us to generate animal models of childhood trauma and abuse, in order to understand why, for example, humans and monkeys abused in childhood are likely to be abusive parents someday; other variants on Harlow's work have taught us how repeated separations of infants from their mothers can predispose those individuals to depression when they are adults.

Personally, I am torn on this one. To animal rights activists who would ban all animal experimentation, I unapologetically say that I am in favor of the use of animals in research, and much good has come out of this particular type of research. To the scientist who would deny the brutality of some types of animal research, I unapologetically say that things can go too far. It is sad and pathetic when we must experiment on infant animals in order to be taught the importance of love. But it is sadder and more pathetic to consider that we have learned about love so poorly and still have to be reminded of its importance at every possible opportunity.

7

SEX AND REPRODUCTION

Sure, we all care deeply about what our kidneys do during stress, and heart disease is a drag, but what we really want to know is why, when we are being stressed, our menstrual cycles become irregular, erections are more difficult to achieve, and we lose our interest in sex. There are an astonishing number of ways in which reproductive mechanisms may go awry when we are upset.

MALES: TESTOSTERONE AND LOSS OF ERECTIONS

It makes sense to start simple, so let's initially consider the easier reproductive system, that of males. In the male, the brain releases the hormone LHRH (luteinizing hormone releasing hormone), which stimulates the pituitary to release LH (luteinizing hormone) and FSH (follicle-stimulating hormone). LH, in turn,

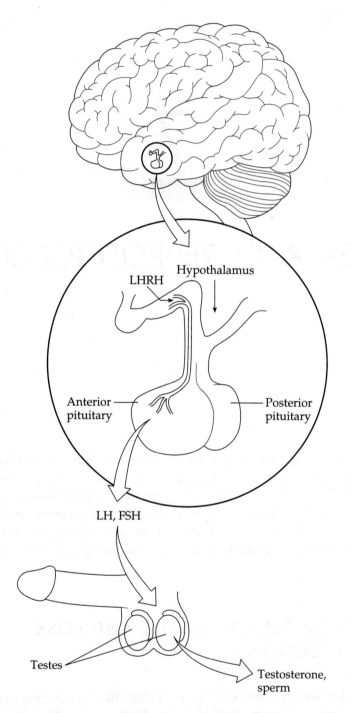

A simplified version of male reproductive endocrinology. The hypothalamus releases LHRH into the private circulatory system that it shares with the anterior pituitary. LHRH triggers the release by the pituitary of LH and FSH, which work at the testes to cause testosterone secretion and sperm production.

stimulates the testes to release testosterone. Since men don't have follicles to be stimulated by follicle-stimulating hormone, FSH instead stimulates sperm production. This is the reproductive system of your basic off-the-rack male.

With the onset of a stressor, the whole system is inhibited. LHRH concentrations decline, followed shortly thereafter by declines in LH and FSH, and then the testes close for lunch. The result is a decline in circulating testosterone levels. The most vivid demonstrations of this occur during physical stress. If a male goes through surgery, within seconds of the first slice through his skin, the reproductive axis begins to shut down. Injury, illness, starvation, surgery—all of these drive down testosterone levels. But subtle psychological stressors are just as disruptive. Lower the dominance rank of a social primate and down go his testosterone levels. Put a person or a monkey through a stressful learning task and the same occurs. In a celebrated study several decades ago, Officer Candidate School trainees who underwent an enormous amount of physical and psychological stress were subjected to the further indignity of having to pee into Dixie cups so that military psychiatrists could measure their hormone levels. Lo and behold, testosterone levels were down; maybe not to the levels found in cherubic babies, but still it's worth keeping in mind the next time you see some leatherneck at a bar bragging about his circulating steroid concentrations.

Why do testosterone concentrations plunge with the onset of a stressor? For a variety of reasons. The first occurs at the brain. With the onset of stress, two important classes of hormones, the endorphins and enkephalins (mostly the former), act to block the release of LHRH from the hypothalamus. As will be reviewed in chapter 9, endorphins play a role in blocking pain perception and are secreted in response to exercise (helping to account for the famed "runner's high" or "endorphin high" that hits many hardy joggers around the thirty-minute mark). If males secrete endorphins when they are experiencing runner's high, and these compounds inhibit testosterone release, will exercise suppress male reproduction? Sometimes. Males who do extreme amounts of exercise (for example, professional soccer players, runners who run more than 40 or 50 miles a week) have less LHRH, LH, and testosterone in their circulation, smaller testes, less mobile sperm. (A similar decline in reproductive function is found in men who are addicted to opiate drugs.) To jump ahead to the female section, reproductive dysfunction is also seen in women athletes, and this is at least partially due to endorphin release as well. Serious runners often stop having menstrual cycles, and highly athletic girls reach puberty later than usual.

This brings up a broader issue important to our era of lookin' good. Obviously if you don't exercise at all, it is not good for you. A little exercise helps all sorts of physiological systems to function well. More exercise helps more. But at some point, too much begins to damage various physiological systems. Everything in physiology follows this rule — just because more of something is better, a lot more of something isn't necessarily a lot better. Too much can be as bad as too little. There are optimal points of homeostasis. In our age of jogging mania, thirty-year-old athletes who run more than 40 or 50 miles a week are showing up with dramatically decalcified bones, decreased bone mass, increased risk of stress fractures and scoliosis (sideways curvature of the spine) — their skeletons look like those of seventy-year-olds. In general, a moderate amount of exercise leads to an increase in bone mass, particularly in the bones that are bearing the greatest brunt of the exercise (for example, the ankle bones of runners). But too much causes trouble, and it appears that these very serious athletes have passed the optimal point in the exercise/bone mass curve and are beginning to damage themselves.

To put exercise in perspective, imagine this: sit with a group of hunter-gatherers from the African grasslands and explain to them that in our world we have so much food and so much free time that some of us run 26 miles a day simply to exercise. They are likely to say, "Are you crazy? That's stressful." Throughout history, hominids who run 26 miles in a day have generally been pretty intent on finding food, or about to be eaten by someone. Not all that normal.

Thus, we have a first step. With the onset of stress, LHRH secretion declines. In addition, prolactin, another pituitary hormone that is released during major stressors, decreases the sensitivity of the pituitary to LHRH. A double whammy—less of the hormone dribbling out of the brain, and the pituitary no longer responding as effectively to it. Finally, glucocorticoids block the response of the testes to LH, just in case any of that hormone manages to reach them during the stressor (and serious athletes tend to have pretty dramatic elevations of glucocorticoids in their circulation, no doubt adding to the reproductive problems just discussed).

Decline in testosterone secretion is only half the story of what goes wrong with male reproduction during stress. The other half concerns the nervous system and erections. Getting an erection to work properly is so incredibly complicated physiologically that if men ever actually had to understand it, none of us would be here. Fortunately, it runs automatically. In order for a male to have an erection, his parasympathetic nervous system must be turned on. In some species, including humans, the parasympathetic causes hemodynamic erections—blood flow into the penis is increased, the exit route for the blood via the veins is blocked, and the penis fills with blood and stiffens. In other species, such as rodents, erections are muscular—a particular muscle contracts, yanks on a penile bone, and up goes the penis. Hemodynamic erections take a longer time to occur, but last longer. In either case, erections are mediated by the parasympathetic system. Calm, vegetative, relaxed.

What happens next for males? You are having a terrific time with someone. Maybe you are breathing faster, your heart rate has increased. Your body is taking on a sympathetic tone— remember the four F's of sympathetic function introduced in chapter 2. Your autonomic nervous system is functioning in an oddly compartmentalized state. After awhile, most your body is screaming sympathetic while, heroically, you are trying to hold on to parasympathetic tone in that one lone outpost as long as possible. Finally, when you can't take it any more, the parasympathetic shuts off at the penis, the sympathetic comes roaring on, and you ejaculate. (Incredibly complicated choreography of these two systems; don't try this unsupervised.) This new understanding generates tricks that sexual therapists advise—if you are close to ejaculating and don't want to yet, take a deep breath. Expanding the chest muscles briefly triggers a parasympathetic volley that defers the shift from parasympathetic to sympathetic.

What, then, changes during stress? First, it becomes difficult to establish parasympathetic activity if you are nervous or anxious. You have trouble having an erection. Impotency. And if you already have the erection, you get in trouble as well. You're rolling along, parasympathetic to your penis, having a wonderful time. You suddenly get worried, nervous, and—shazaam—you switch from parasympathetic to sympathetic far faster than you wanted. Premature ejaculation.

It is extremely common for problems with impotency and premature ejaculation to arise during stressful times. A number of studies have shown that more than half the visits to doctors by males complaining of reproductive dysfunction turn out to be due to "psychogenic" impotency rather than "organic" impotency (there's no disease there, just too much stress). How do you tell if it is organic or psychogenic impotency? This is actually diagnosed with surprising ease, because of a quirky thing about human males. As soon as they go to sleep and enter REM (rapid eye-movement) dream sleep, they get erections. No one has a clue why, but that's how they work. So a man comes in complaining that he hasn't been able to have an erection in six months. Is he just under stress? Does he have some neurological disease? Take a handy little penile cuff with an electronic pressure transducer attached to it. Have him put it on just before he goes to sleep. By the next morning you may have your answer —if this guy gets an erection when he goes into REM sleep, his problem is likely to be psychogenic. (I was recently told about an advance on this technology. Instead of having to use one of these fancy electronic cuffs, you simply tape a few postage stamps to the penis just before going to sleep. By the morning, if the stamps have been pulled loose on one side or torn, you had a REM-stage erection during the night.)

Thus, stress will knock out male sexual responses quite readily. In general, the problems with erections are more disruptive than problems with testosterone secretion. Testosterone and sperm production have to shut down almost entirely to affect performance. A little testosterone and a couple of sperm wandering around and most males can muddle through. But no erection, and forget about it. The erectile component is exquisitely sensitive to stress in an incredible array of species. To put this in context, it might be worth describing here the one species that constitutes an exception, a species that breaks all the rules in terms of the effects of stress on erectile function. It is time we had a little talk about hyenas.

OUR FRIEND, THE HYENA

The spotted hyena is a vastly unappreciated, misrepresented beast. I know this because over the years, in my work in East Africa, I have shared my campsite with the hyena biologist Laurence Frank of the University of California at Berkeley. For lack of distracting televisions, books, or telephones, he has devoted his time there to singing the hyena's praises to me. They are wondrous animals who have gotten a bad rap from the press.

We all know the scenario. It's dawn on the savanna. Marlin Perkins of Mutual of Omaha's "Wild Kingdom" is there filming lions eating something dead. We are delighted, craning to get a good view of the blood and guts. Suddenly, on the edge of our field of vision, we spot them—skulky, filthy, untrustworthy hyenas looking to dart in and steal some of the food. Scavengers! We are invited to heap our contempt on them (a surprising bias, given how few of the carnivorous among us ever wrestle down our meals with our canines). It wasn't until the Pentagon purchased a new line of infrared night viewing scopes and decided to unload its old ones on various university zoologists that, suddenly, researchers could watch hyenas at night (important, given that hyenas mostly sleep during the day). Turns out that they are fabulous hunters. And you know what happens? Lions, who are not particularly effective hunters, because they are big and slow and conspicuous, spend most of their time keying in on hyenas and ripping off their kills. No wonder when it's dawn on the savanna the hyenas on the periphery are looking cranky, with circles under their eyes. They stayed up all night hunting that thing, and who's having breakfast now?

Having established a thread of sympathy for these beasts, let me explain what is really strange about them. Among hyenas, females are socially dominant. They are more muscular, more aggressive, and have more of a male sex hormone (a close relative of testosterone called androstenedione) in their bloodstreams than males. It's also almost impossible to tell the sex of a hyena by looking at its external genitals.

More than two thousand years ago, Aristotle, for reasons obscure to even the most learned, dissected some dead hyenas, discussing them in his treatise *Historia Animalium*, VI, XXX. The conclusion among hyena savants at the time was that these animals were hermaphrodites—animals that possess all the machinery of both sexes. Hyenas are actually what gynecologists would call pseudohermaphrodites (they just look that way). The female has a fake scrotal sac made of compacted fat cells; she doesn't really have a penis but, instead, an enlarged clitoris that can become erect. The same clitoris, I might add, with which she has sex and through which she gives birth. It's pretty wild. Laurence Frank, who is one of earth's experts on hyena genitals, will dart some animal and haul it, anesthetized, into camp. Excitement; we go to check it out, and maybe twenty minutes into examining it, he kind of thinks he knows what sex this particular one is. (Yes, the hyenas themselves know exactly who is which sex, most probably by smell.)

Perhaps the most interesting thing about hyenas is that there is a fairly plausible theory as to why they evolved this way, a theory complicated enough for me to mercifully relegate it to the endnotes. For our purposes here, what is important is that hyenas have not only evolved genitals that look unique, but also unique ways to use these organs for social communication. This is where stress comes into play.

Among many social mammals, males have erections during competitive situations as a sign of dominance. If you are having a dominance display with another male, you get an erection and wave it around in his face to show what a tough guy you are. Social primates do this all the time. In hyenas, an erection is, instead, a sign of social *subordinance*. When a male is menaced by a terrifying female, he gets an erection—"Look, I'm just some poor no-account male, don't hit me, I was just leaving." Low-ranking females do the same thing; if a low-ranking female is about to get trounced by a high-ranking one, she gets a conspicuous clitoral erection—"Look, I'm just like one of those males, don't attack me, you know you are dominant, why bother?" If you're a hyena, you get an erection *when you are stressed.* Among male hyenas, the autonomic wiring has got to be completely reversed in order to account for the fact that stress causes erections. This has not been demonstrated yet, but as I write, Berkeley scientists are slaving away at the study of issues like this, consuming tax dollars that could otherwise be spent on Cruise missiles.

Thus the hyena stands as the exception to the rule about erectile function being adversely affected by stress, a broader

Behold, the female hyena.

demonstration of the importance of looking at a zoologic oddity as a means of better seeing the context of our own normative physiology, and a friendly word of warning before you go out on a date with a hyena.

FEMALES: LENGTHENED CYCLES AND AMENORRHEA

We now turn to female reproduction. Its basic outline is similar to that of the male. LHRH is released by the brain, which releases LH and FSH from the pituitary. The latter stimulates the ovaries to release eggs; the former stimulates ovaries to synthesize estrogen. During the first half of the menstrual cycle, the "follicular" stage, levels of LHRH, LH, FSH, and estrogen build up, heading toward the climax of ovulation. This ushers in the second half of the cycle, the "luteal" phase. Progesterone, made in the corpus luteum of the ovary, now becomes the dominant hormone on the scene, stimulating the uterine walls to mature so that an egg, if fertilized just after ovulation, can implant there and develop into an embryo. Because the release of hormones fluctuates rhythmically over the menstrual cycle, the part of the hypothalamus that regulates the release of these hormones is generally more structurally complicated in females than in males.

The first way in which stress disrupts female reproduction concerns a surprising facet of the system. There is a small amount of male sex hormone in the bloodstream of females, even nonhyena females. In human beings, this doesn't come from the ovaries (as in the hyenas), but from the adrenals. The amount of these "adrenal androgens" is only about 5 percent of that in males, but enough to cause trouble. (Point of information: the adrenal androgens are usually not testosterone, the principal male sex steroid hormone, but a related hormone, androstenedione.) An enzyme in the fat cells of females usually eliminates these androgens by converting them to estrogens. Problem solved. But what if you are starving because the crops

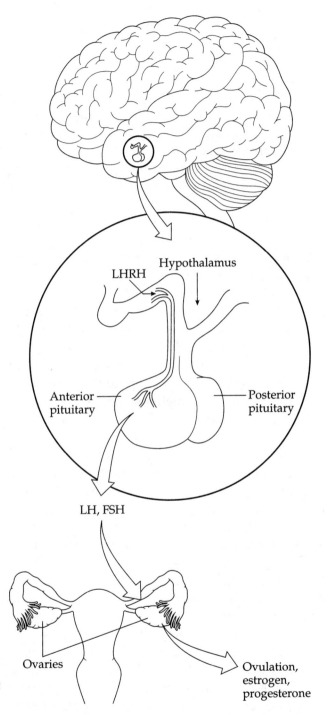

A simplified version of female reproductive endocrinology. The hypothalamus releases LHRH into the private circulatory system that it shares with the anterior pituitary. LHRH triggers the release by the pituitary of LH and FSH, which in turn bring about ovulation and hormone release from the ovaries.

failed this year, or there is a drought? Body weight drops, fat stores drop, and suddenly there isn't enough fat around to convert all of the androgen to estrogen. Less estrogen, therefore, is produced. More important, androgen concentrations build up, which inhibits numerous steps in the reproductive system.

Reproduction is similarly inhibited if you starve voluntarily. One of the hallmarks of anorexia nervosa is disruption of reproduction in the (typically) young women who are starving themselves. And loss of body fat leading to androgen buildup is one of the mechanisms by which reproduction is impaired in females who are extremely active physically. This has been best documented in young girls who are very serious dancers or runners, in whom puberty can be delayed for years, and in women who exercise enormous amounts, in whom cycles can become irregular or cease entirely. Overall this is a very logical mechanism. In the human, an average pregnancy costs approximately 50,000 calories, and nursing costs about a thousand calories a day; neither is something that should be gone into without a reasonable amount of fat tucked away.

Stress also can inhibit reproduction in ways other than shrinkage of fat cells. Many of the same mechanisms apply as in the male. Endorphins and enkephalins will inhibit LHRH release (as discussed, this occurs in female athletes as readily as in males), prolactin and the glucocorticoids will block pituitary sensitivity to LHRH, and glucocorticoids will also affect the ovaries to inhibit responsiveness to LH. The net result is lowered secretion of LH, FSH, and estrogen, making the likelihood of ovulating decrease. As a result, the follicular stage is extended, making the entire cycle longer and less regular. At an extreme, the entire ovulatory machinery is not merely delayed, but shut down, a condition termed anovulatory amenorrhea.

Stress can also cause other reproductive problems. Progesterone levels are often inhibited, which disrupts maturation of the uterine walls. The release of prolactin during stress adds to this effect, interfering with the activity of progesterone. Thus even if there is still enough hormonal action during the follicular period to cause ovulation, and the egg has become fertilized, it is now much less likely to implant normally.

The loss of estrogen with sustained stress has some consequences beyond the reproductive realm. As noted earlier, athletes who exercise very heavily can begin to decalcify their bones, decreasing bone mass and increasing the risk of fractures and osteoporosis. Studies of these effects are predominantly of women, in whom the consequences are most severe, and it is amenorrheic women in whom the problems are most likely to occur. As noted in the chapter on growth, estrogen helps recalcify bone (a reason why osteoporosis becomes so serious in postmenopausal women). Furthermore, as noted in chapter 3, estrogen helps protect the heart against atherosclerosis, and stress can endanger the cardiovascular system by lowering estrogen levels. For example, Jay Kaplan and colleagues have shown that social subordinance in monkeys suppresses estrogen to levels as low as those seen in females with their ovaries removed, and that such subordinance increases the risk for atherosclerosis.

Of all the hormones that inhibit the reproductive system during stress, prolactin is probably the most interesting. It is extremely powerful and versatile; if you don't want to ovulate, this is the hormone to have lots of in your bloodstream. It not only plays a major role in the suppression of reproduction during stress and exercise, but is also the main reason that breast-feeding is such an effective form of contraception.

Oh, you are shaking your head smugly, everyone knows that's an old wives' tale; nursing isn't an effective contraceptive. On the contrary; nursing works fabulously. It probably prevents more pregnancies than any other type of contraception. All you have to do is do it right.

Breast-feeding causes prolactin secretion. There is a reflex loop that goes straight from the nipples to the hypothalamus. If there is nipple stimulation for any reason (in males as well as females), the hypothalamus signals the pituitary to secrete prolactin. And as we now know, prolactin in sufficient quantities causes reproduction to cease.

The problem with nursing as a contraceptive is how it is done in Western societies. During the six months or so that she breast-feeds, the average mother in the West allows perhaps half a dozen periods of nursing a day, each for 30 or 60 minutes. Each time she nurses, prolactin levels go up in the bloodstream within seconds, and at the end of the feeding, prolactin settles back to prenursing levels fairly quickly. This most likely produces a scalloping sort of pattern in prolactin release.

This is not how most women on earth nurse. A prime example emerged a few years ago in a study of hunter-gatherer Bushmen in the Kalahari Desert of southern Africa (the folks depicted in the movie *The Gods Must Be Crazy*). Bushman men and women have plenty of intercourse, and no one uses contraceptives, but the women have a child only about every four years. Initially, this seemed easy to explain. Western scientists looked at this pattern and said, "They're hunter-gatherers: life for them must be short, nasty, and brutish; they must all be starving." Malnutrition-induced cessation of ovulation.

However, when anthropologists looked more closely, they found that the Bushmen were anything but suffering. If you are going to be non-Westernized, choose being a hunter-gatherer over being a nomadic pastoralist or an agriculturalist. The Bushmen hunt and gather only a few hours a day, and spend much of the rest of their time sitting around chewing the fat. Scientists have called them the original affluent society. Out goes the idea that the four-year birth interval is due to malnutrition.

Instead, the lengthy interval is probably due to their nursing pattern. This was discovered by a pair of scientists, Melvin Konner and Carol Worthman. When a hunter-gatherer woman gives birth, she begins to breast-feed her child for a minute or two approximately every fifteen minutes. Around the clock. For the next three years. (Suddenly this doesn't seem like such a hot idea after all, does it?) The young child is carried in a sling on the mother's hip so he can nurse easily and frequently. At night, he sleeps with his parents and will nurse every so often without even waking the parents (as Konner and Worthman, no doubt with their infrared night viewing goggles and stopwatches, scribble away on their clipboards at two in the morning). Once the kid can walk, he'll come running in from playing every hour or so to nurse for a minute.

A Kalahari Bushman mother with her child in a hip sling.

When you breast-feed in this way, the endocrine story is going to be very different. At the first nursing period, prolactin levels rise. And with the frequency and timing of the thousands of subsequent nursings, prolactin stays high for years. Estrogen and progesterone levels are suppressed, and you don't ovulate.

This pattern has a fascinating implication. Consider the life history of a hunter-gatherer woman. She reaches puberty at about age 13 or 14 (a bit later than in our society). Soon she is pregnant. She nurses for three years, weans her child, has a few menstrual cycles, becomes pregnant again, and repeats the pattern until she reaches menopause, or dies (an event unlikely to wait for her eighth decade of life). Think about it: over the course of her life span, she has perhaps two dozen periods. Contrast that with modern Western women, who average perhaps 500 periods over their lifetime. Huge difference. The hunter-gatherer pattern, the one that has occurred throughout most of human history, is what you see in nonhuman primates. Perhaps some of the gynecological diseases that plague modern Westernized women have something to do with this activation of a major piece of physiological machinery 500 times when it may have evolved to be used only 20 times; an example of this is probably endometriosis, which is more common among women with fewer pregnancies and who start at a later age.

FEMALES: DISRUPTION OF LIBIDO

The preceding section describes how stress disrupts the nuts and bolts of female reproduction — uterine walls, eggs, ovarian hormones, and so on. But what about its effects upon sexual behavior? Just as stress does not do wonders for erections or for the desire of a male to do something with his erections, stress disrupts female libido. This is a commonplace experience among women stressed by any of a number of circumstances, as well as among laboratory animals undergoing stress.

It is relatively easy to document a loss of sexual desire among women when they are stressed — just hand out a questionnaire on the subject and hope it is answered honestly. But how is sexual drive studied in a laboratory animal? How can one possibly infer a libidinous itch on the part of a female rat, for example, as she gazes into the next cage at the male with the limpid eyes and cute incisors? The answer is surprisingly simple — how often would she be willing to press a lever in order to gain access to that male? This is science's quantitative way of measuring rodent desire (or, to use the jargon of the trade, "proceptivity").* A similar experimental design can be used to measure proceptive behavior in primates. Proceptive and receptive behaviors fluctuate among animals as a function of factors like the point in the reproductive cycle (both of these measures of sexual behavior generally peak around ovulation), the recency of sex, the time of year, or vagaries of the heart (who is the male in question). In general, stress suppresses both proceptive and receptive behaviors.

This effect of stress is probably rooted in its suppression of the secretion of various sex hormones. Among rodents, both proceptive and receptive behaviors disappear when a female's ovaries are removed, and the absence of estrogen after the ovariectomy is responsible; as evidence, injection of overiectomized females with estrogen reinstates these sexual behaviors. Moreover, the peak in estrogen levels around ovulation explains why sexual behavior is almost entirely restricted to that period. A similar pattern holds in primates, but it is not as dramatic as in rodents. A decline in sexual behavior, although to a lesser extent, follows ovarectomy in a primate. For humans, estrogen plays a role in sexuality, but a still weaker one—social and interpersonal factors are far more important.

Estrogen exerts these effects both in the brain and peripheral tissue. Genitals and other parts of the body contain ample amounts of estrogen receptors and are made more sensitive to stimulation by the hormone. Within the brain, estrogen receptors occur in areas that play a role in sexual behavior; through one of the more poorly understood mechanisms of neuroendocrinology, when estrogen floods those parts of the brain, salacious thoughts follow.

---

*Quick primer on how to describe animal sex the way professionals do: "Attractivity" refers to how much the subject animal interests another animal. This can be operationally defined as how many times the other animal is willing to press a lever, for example, to gain access to the subject. "Receptivity" describes how readily the subject responds to the entreaties of the other animal. Among rats, this can be defined by the occurrence of the "lordosis" reflex, a receptive stance by the female in which she arches her back, making it easier for the male to mount. Female primates show a variety of receptive reflexes that facilitate male mounting, depending on the species. "Proceptivity" refers to how actively the subject pursues the other animal.

Surprisingly, adrenal androgens also play a role in proceptive and receptive behaviors; as evidence, sex drive goes down
following removal of the adrenals and can be reinstated by
administration of synthetic androgens. This appears to be more
of a factor in primates and humans than in rodents. While the
subject has not been studied in great detail, there are some
reports that stress suppresses the levels of adrenal androgens in
the bloodstream. And stress certainly suppresses estrogen secretion; as noted in chapter 3, Jay Kaplan has shown that the
stressor of social subordinance in a monkey can suppress estrogen levels as effectively as removing her ovaries. Given these
findings, it is relatively easy to see how stress disrupts sexual
behavior in a female.

MISCARRIAGE AND PSYCHOGENIC ABORTIONS*

The link between stress and spontaneous abortion in humans
prompted Hippocrates to caution pregnant women to avoid
unnecessary emotional disturbances. Since then, it is a thread
that runs through some of our most florid and romantic inter-
pretations of the biology of pregnancy, whether it is Anne Boleyn attributing her miscarriage to the shock of seeing Jane
Seymour sitting on King Henry's lap, or Rosamond Vincy losing
her baby when frightened by a horse in *Middlemarch*. In the
movie *Pacific Heights* (which took the Reagan-Bush era to its
logical extreme, encouraging us to root for the poor landlords
being menaced by a predatory tenant), the homeowner played
by Melanie Griffiths has a miscarriage in response to psychological harassment by the Machiavellian renter.

---

*"Miscarriage" and "abortion" are used interchangably in medical texts and will be
throughout this section. In everyday clinical usage, however, spontaneous termination
of a pregnancy when the fetus is close to being viable is more likely to be termed
miscarriage than abortion.

Stress can cause miscarriages in other animals as well. This may occur, for example, when pregnant animals in the wild or in a corral have to be captured for some reason (a veterinary exam) or are stressed by being transported. It has been well documented in animals in the wild under the following set of conditions. In many social species, not all males do equivalent amounts of reproducing. Sometimes the group contains only a single male (typically called a "harem male") who does all the mating; sometimes there are a number of males, but only the one or few most dominant reproduce. Suppose the harem male is killed or driven out by an intruding male, or a new male migrates into the multimale group and moves to the top of the dominance hierarchy. Typically, the now-dominant male goes about trying to increase his own reproductive success, at the expense of the prior male.

What does the new guy do? In some species, males will systematically try to kill the infants in the group (a pattern called "competitive infanticide" and observed in a number of monkey species and lions, among others), thus reducing the reproductive success of the preceding male. Following the killing, moreover, the female ceases to nurse and, as a result, is soon ovulating and ready for mating, to the convenient advantage of the newly resident male. Grim stuff — and a pretty strong demonstration of something well recognized by most evolutionists these days — contrary to what Marlin Perkins taught us, animals very rarely behave "for the good of the species." Instead, they typically act for the good of their own genetic legacy and that of their close relatives. Among some species — wild horses, for example, and baboons — the male will also systematically harass any pregnant females to the point of miscarriage, by the same logic.

This pattern is seen in a particularly subtle way among rodents. A group of females resides with a single harem male. If he is driven out by an intruder male who takes up residence, within days, among females who have recently become pregnant, the fertilized egg fails to implant. Remarkably, this termination of pregnancy does not require physical harassment on the part of the male. It is his new, strange odor that causes the failed pregnancies by triggering a disruptive rise in prolactin levels. As proof of this, researchers can trigger this phenomenon (called the "Bruce-Parkes effect") with merely the odor of a novel male. Why is it adaptive for females to terminate pregnancy just because a new male has arrived on the scene? If the female completes her pregnancy, the kids will promptly be killed by this new guy. So, making the best of a bad situation, it is seemingly more adaptive to at least save the further calories that would be devoted to the futile pregnancy, terminate it, and ovulate a few days later. (Not surprisingly, females have evolved many strategies of their own to salvage reproductive success from these battling males. One is to go into a fake heat [in primates called "pseudo-estrus"] to sucker the new guy into thinking he's the father of the offspring she is already carrying. Touché.)

Despite the drama of the Bruce-Parkes effect, stress-induced miscarriages are relatively rare among animals, particularly among humans. It is not uncommon to decide retrospectively that when something bad happens (such as a miscarriage), there was significant stress beforehand. To add to the confusion, there is a tendency to attribute miscarriages to stressful events occurring in the *day* or so preceding them. In actuality, most miscarriages involve the expelling of a dead fetus, which has typically died quite a while before. If there was a stressful cause, it is likely to have come days or even weeks before the miscarriage, not immediately preceding it.

When a stress-induced miscarriage does occur, however, there is a fairly plausible explanation of how it happens. The delivery of blood to the fetus is exquisitely sensitive to blood flow in the mother, and anything that decreases uterine blood flow will be disruptive to the fetal blood supply. Moreover, fetal heart rate closely tracks that of the mother, and various psychologic stimuli that stimulate or slow down the heart rate of the mother will cause a similar change a minute or so later in the fetus. This has been shown in a number of studies of both humans and primates.

Trouble seems to occur during stress as a result of repeated powerful activation of the sympathetic nervous system, causing increased secretion of norepinephrine and epinephrine. Studies of a large number of different species show that these two hormones will decrease blood flow through the uterus—dramatically, in some cases. Exposing animals to something psychologically stressful (for example, a loud noise in the case of pregnant sheep, or the entrance of a strange person into the room in which a pregnant rhesus monkey is housed) will cause a similar reduction in blood flow. As a result, fetuses rapidly become "hypoxic" and "bradycardic" (their blood pressure drops and their heart rate slows down). The general assumption in the field is that a few of these events cause little problem, but that repeated episodes of fetal hypoxia will eventually cause asphyxiation.

This may well be a mechanism by which a sudden stressful crisis could be disastrous for a human fetus. In recent decades, there has been a shift from studying the physiological mechanisms of stress-induced abortions toward studying the characteristics of women who repeatedly miscarry for no obvious medical reason (these are often characterized as "psychogenic abortions"). The goal in these studies has been to determine whether women with certain personalities or temperaments are at greater risk for psychogenic abortions; this is analogous to the studies of Type A personalities and the slow emergence of cardiovascular disease (see chapter 3). Some researchers have identified one subgroup of women with repeated psychogenic abortions, accounting for about half the cases, as being "retarded in their psychological development." They are characterized as emotionally immature women, highly dependent on their husbands, who on some unconscious level view the impending arrival of the child as a threat to their own childlike relationship with the husband. Another personality type, at the opposite extreme, has also been linked in studies to psychogenic abortions. These are women who are characterized as being assertive and independent, who really don't want to have a child.

Not surprisingly, many scientists are skeptical about these studies for a number of reasons. First, a diagnosis of "psychogenic" anything (impotency, amenorrhea, abortion, and so on) is usually a diagnosis by exclusion. In other words, the physician can't find any disease or organic cause, and until one is discovered the disorder gets tossed into the psychogenic bucket. This may mean that in truth it is psychologically based, or it may simply mean that the relevant hormone, neurotransmitter, or genetic abnormality has not yet been discovered. Once that occurs, the psychogenic disease is magically transformed into an organic problem.

Another difficulty is that these studies are all retrospective in design, which means that the researchers examine the personalities of women *after* they have had repeated abortions. A study may thus cite the case of a woman who has had three miscarriages in a row, noting that she is emotionally withdrawn and dependent on her husband. But because of the nature of the research design, one can't tell whether these traits are a cause of the miscarriages or a response to them — it seems quite reasonable that three successive miscarriages would exact an emotional price, perhaps making the subject withdrawn and more dependent on her husband. In order to properly study the phenomenon, one would need to look at personality profiles of women *before* they become pregnant, to see if these traits predict who is going to have repeated miscarriages. This kind of study has not yet been carried out.

As a final problem, none of the studies provides any sort of reasonable speculation as to how a particular personality type may lead to a tendency not to carry fetuses to term. What are the mediating physiological mechanisms? What hormones and organ functions are disrupted? Psychological stressors can increase the risk of a miscarriage, but although there is precedent in the medical literature for thinking that having a certain type of personality is associated with an increased risk for miscarriages, scientists are far from being able to agree on *what* personality is associated, let alone whether the personality is a cause or consequence of the miscarriages.

How detrimental to female reproduction is stress?

As we have seen, there is an extraordinary array of mechanisms by which reproduction can be disrupted in stressed females — fat depletion; secretion of endorphins, prolactin, and glucocorticoids acting on the brain, pituitary, and ovaries; lack of progesterone; excessive prolactin acting on the uterus. Moreover, possible blockage of implantation of the fertilized egg and changes in blood flow to the fetus generate numerous ways in which stress can make it less likely that a pregnancy will be carried to term. With all these different mechanisms implicated, it seems as if even the mildest of stressors would shut down the reproductive system completely. Surprisingly, however, this is not the case; collectively, these mechanisms are not all that effective.

One way of appreciating this is to examine the effects of chronic low-grade stress on reproduction. Consider traditional non-Westernized agriculturalists with a fair amount of background disease (seasonal malaria, for example), a high incidence of parasites, and some seasonal malnutrition thrown in — farmers in Kenya, for example. Before family planning came into vogue, the average number of children born to a Kenyan woman was about eight. Compare this to the Hutterites, non-mechanized farmers who live a life similar to that of the Amish. Hutterites experience none of the chronic stressors of the Kenyan farmers, use no contraceptives, and have essentially the identical reproductive rate — an average of nine children per woman. (It is difficult to make a close quantitative comparison of these two populations. The Hutterites, for example, delay marriage, decreasing their reproductive rate, whereas Kenyan agriculturalists traditionally do not. Conversely, Kenyan agriculturalists typically breast-feed for at least a year, decreasing their reproductive rate, in contrast to the Hutterites, who typically nurse far less. The main point, however, is that even with such different life styles, the two reproductive rates are nearly equal.)

How about reproduction during extreme stress? This has been studied in a literature that always poses problems for those discussing it: how to cite a scientific finding without crediting the monsters who did the research? These are the studies of women in the Third Reich's concentration camps, conducted by Nazi doctors. (The convention has evolved never to credit the names of the doctors, and always to note the criminality of their collaboration.) In a study of the women in the Theresienstadt concentration camp, 54 percent of the reproductive-age women were found to have stopped menstruating. This is hardly surprising; starvation, slave labor, unspeakable psychological terror are going to disrupt reproduction. The point typically made is that, of the women who stopped menstruating, the majority stopped within their first month in the camps — before starvation and labor had pushed fat levels down to the decisive point. Many researchers cite this as a demonstration of how disruptive even psychological stress can be to reproduction.

To me, the surprising fact is just the opposite. *Despite* starvation, exhausting labor, and the daily terror that each day would be your last, *only* 54 percent of those women ceased menstruating. Reproductive mechanisms were still working in nearly half the women (although a certain number may have been having anovulatory cycles). And I would wager that despite the horrors of their situation, there were still many men who were reproductively intact. That reproductive physiology still operated in any individual to any extent, under those circumstances, strikes me as extraordinary.

Reproduction represents a vast hierarchy of behavioral and physiological events that differ considerably in subtlety. Some steps are basic and massive — the eruption of an egg, the diverting of rivers of blood to a penis. Others are as delicate as whether the line of a poem awakens your heart or the whiff of a person's scent awakens your loins. Not all the steps are equally sensitive to stress. The basic machinery of reproduction can be astoundingly resistant to stress in a subset of individuals, as evidence from the Holocaust shows. Reproduction is one of the strongest of biological reflexes — just ask a salmon leaping upstream to spawn, or males of various species risking life and limb for access to females, or any adolescent with that steroid-crazed look. But when it comes to the pirouettes and filigrees of sexuality, stress can wreak havoc with subtleties. That may not be of enormous consequence to a starving refugee or a wilde-beest in the middle of a drought. But it matters to us, with our culture of multiple orgasms and minuscule refractory periods and oceans of libido. And while it is easy to make fun of those obsessions of ours, the *Cosmos* and *GQs* and other indices of our indulged lives, those nuances of sexuality matter to us. They provide us with some of our greatest, if also our most fragile and evanescent, joys.

IMMUNITY, STRESS, AND DISEASE

The halls of academe are filling with a newly evolved species of scientist — the psychoneuroimmunologist — who makes a living studying the extraordinary fact that what goes on in your head can affect how well your immune system functions. Those two realms were once thought to be fairly separate — your immune system kills bacteria, makes antibodies, hunts for tumors; your brain thinks up poetry, invents the wheel, has favorite TV shows. Yet the dogma of the separation of the immune and nervous systems has fallen by the wayside. The autonomic nervous system sends nerves into the tissues that form or store the cells of the immune system that wind up in the circulation. Furthermore, tissue of the immune system turns out to be sensitive to (that is, it has receptors for) all the interesting hormones released by the pituitary under the control of the brain. The result is that the brain has a vast potential for sticking its nose into the immune system's business.

The evidence for the brain's influence on the immune system goes back at least a century, dating to the first demonstrations that an artificial rose could trigger an allergic response in a patient. But the study of the link between brain and immune system has really solidified only in the last decade or two. Probably the most convincing demonstrations are experiments using a paradigm called "conditioned immunosuppression."

Give an animal a drug that suppresses the immune system. Along with it, provide, à la Pavlov's experiments, a "conditioned stimulus"—for example, an artificially flavored drink, something that the animal will associate with the suppressive drug. A few days later, present the conditioned stimulus by itself—and down goes immune function. In 1982 the report of an experiment using a variant of this paradigm carried out by two pioneers in this field, Robert Ader and Nicholas Cohen, stunned scientists. The two researchers experimented with a strain of mice that spontaneously develop disease because of overactivity of their immune systems. Normally, the disease is controlled by treating the mice with an immunosuppressive drug. Ader and Cohen showed that by using their conditioning techniques, they could substitute the conditioned stimulus for the actual drug—and sufficiently alter immunity in these animals to extend their lifespans.

Studies such as these convinced scientists that there is a strong link between the nervous system and the immune system. It should come as no surprise that if the sight of an artificial rose, or the taste of an artificially flavored drink, can alter immune function, then stress can too. In the first half of this chapter, I discuss how stress tends to suppress immune function, and consider why it might be useful to suppress immunity during a stressful emergency. In the second half, we'll examine whether sustained stress, by way of chronic suppression of immunity, can impair the ability of a body to fight off infectious disease. This is a fascinating question, which can only be answered with a great deal of caution and many caveats. Although evidence is emerging that stress-induced immunosuppression can indeed increase the risk and severity of disease, the connection is probably relatively weak and its importance often exaggerated.

In order to evaluate the results of this confusing but important field, we need to start with a primer about how the immune
system works.

IMMUNE SYSTEM BASICS

The primary job of the immune system is to defend the body
against infectious agents such as viruses, bacteria, and parasites.
The process is dauntingly complex. For one thing, the immune
system must tell the difference between cells that are normal
parts of the body and cells that are invaders; the immunologic
jargon for this is the process of distinguishing between "self"
and "nonself." Somehow, the immune system can remember
what every cell in your body looks like, and any cells (for
example, bacteria) that lack your distinctive cellular signature
are attacked. Moreover, when your immune system does encounter a novel invader, it can even form an immunologic memory of what the infectious agent looks like, to better prepare for
the next invasion—a process which is exploited when you are
vaccinated with a mild version of an infectious agent in order to
prime your immune system for a real attack.

Such immune defenses are brought about by a complex
array of circulating cells called lymphocytes and monocytes
(which are collectively known as white blood cells). There are
two classes of lymphocytes: T cells and B cells. Both originate in
the bone marrow, but T cells migrate to mature in the thymus
(hence the "T"), while B cells mature in the bone marrow. B cells
principally produce antibodies, but there are several kinds of T
cells (T helper and T suppressor cells, cytotoxic killer cells, and
so on).

The T and B cells attack infectious agents in very different
ways. T cells bring about cell-mediated immunity (see the illustration on the facing page). When an infectious agent invades
the body, it is recognized by a type of monocyte called a macrophage, which presents the foreign particle to a T helper cell. A
metaphorical alarm is now sounded, and T cells begin to prolif-

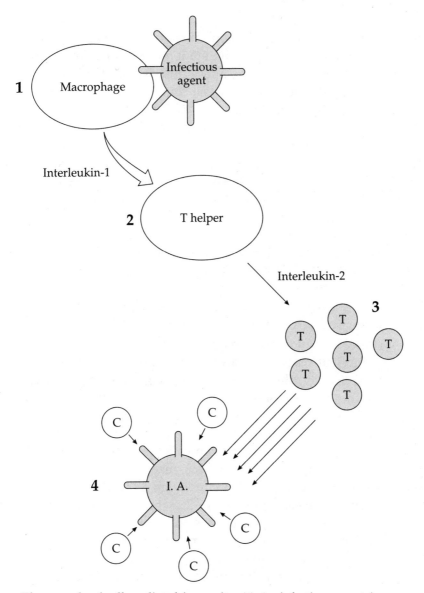

The cascade of cell-mediated immunity. (1) An infectious agent is encountered by a type of monocyte called a macrophage. (2) This stimulates the macrophage to present the infectious agent to a T helper cell (a type of white blood cell) and to release interleukin-1 (IL-1), which stimulates T helper cell activity. (3) The T helper cell, as a result, releases interleukin-2 (IL-2), which triggers T-cell proliferation. (4) This eventually causes another type of white blood cell, cytotoxic killer cells, to proliferate and destroy the infectious agent.

erate in response to the invasion. This alarm system ultimately results in the activation and proliferation of cytotoxic killer cells, which, as their name implies, attack and destroy the infectious agent. As orientation, it is the T-cell component of the immune system that is knocked out by the AIDS virus.

By contrast, B cells cause antibody-mediated immunity (see the illustration on the facing page). Once the macrophage/T helper cell combination has become alarmed, the latter will also stimulate B-cell proliferation. The main task of the B cells is to differentiate and generate antibodies, large proteins that will recognize and bind to some specific feature of the invading infectious agent (typically, a distinctive surface protein). This specificity is critical — the antibody formed has a fairly unique shape, which will conform perfectly to the shape of the distinctive feature of the invader, like the fit between a lock and key. In binding to the specific feature, antibodies immobilize the infectious agent and target it for destruction.

There is an additional complex feature of the immune system. If different parts of the liver, for example, need to coordinate some activity, they have the advantage of sitting adjacent to each other. But the immune system is distributed throughout the circulation. In order to sound immune alarms throughout this far-flung system, there must be bloodborne chemical messengers that communicate between different cell types. For example, when macrophages first recognize an infectious agent, they release a messenger called interleukin-1. This triggers the T helper cell to release interleukin-2, which stimulates T-cell growth (to make life complicated, there are at least half a dozen additional interleukins with more specialized roles). On the antibody front, T cells also secrete B-cell growth factor. Other classes of messengers, such as interferons, activate broad classes of lymphocytes.

The process of the immune system sorting self and nonself usually works well (although truly insidious tropical parasites like those that cause schistosomiasis have evolved to evade your immune system by pirating the signature of your own cells). Your immune system happily spends its time sorting out self from nonself: "Red blood cells. Part of us. Eyebrows. Our side. Virus. No good, attack. Muscle cell. Good guy. . . ."

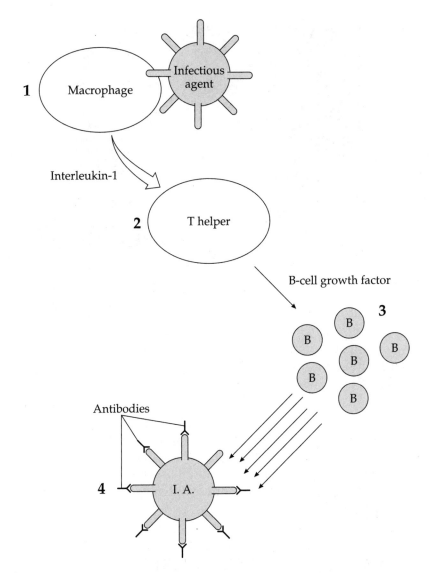

The cascade of antibody-mediated immunity. (1) An infectious agent is encountered by a macrophage. (2) This encounter stimulates it to present the infectious agent to a T helper cell and to release interleukin-1 (IL-1), which stimulates T helper cell activity. (3) The T helper cell then secretes B-cell growth factor, triggering differentiation and proliferation of another white blood cell, B cells. (4) The B cells make and release specific antibodies that bind to surface proteins on the infectious agent, targeting it for destruction by a large group of circulating proteins known as complement.

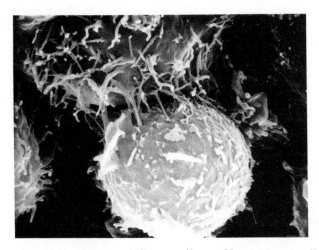

Photomicrograph of a killer T cell attacking a tumor cell.

What if something goes wrong with the immune system's sorting? One obvious kind of error could be that the immune system misses an infectious invader; clearly, bad news. Equally bad is the opposite sort of mistake, where the immune system mistakes a normal part of the body for an infectious agent and attacks it. When the immune system erroneously attacks a normal part of the body (autoimmunity), a variety of horrendous autoimmune diseases may result. In multiple sclerosis, for example, part of your nervous system is attacked; in juvenile diabetes, the cells in the pancreas that normally secrete insulin. As we'll see shortly, stress has some rather confusing effects on autoimmune diseases.

HOW DOES STRESS INHIBIT IMMUNE FUNCTION?

It's been almost sixty years since Selye discovered the first evidence of stress-induced immunosuppression, noting that immune tissues like the thymus gland atrophied among rats subjected to nonspecific unpleasantness. Scientists have learned more about the subtleties of the immune system since then, and it turns out that a period of stress will disrupt a wide variety of immune functions—the formation of new lymphocytes and their release into the circulation, the manufacture of antibodies in response to an infectious agent, and communication among lymphocytes through the release of relevant messengers, to name just a few of these actions.

The best-documented way in which such immune-system suppression occurs is via glucocorticoids. Glucocorticoids, for example, can cause shrinking of the thymus gland; this is such a reliable effect that in the olden days (circa 1960), before it was possible to easily and directly measure the amount of glucocorticoids in the bloodstream, one indirect way of doing so was to see how much the thymus gland in an animal had shrunk. The smaller the thymus, the more glucocorticoids in the circulation. Glucocorticoids halt the formation of new lymphocytes in the thymus, and most of thymic tissue is made up of these new cells, ready to be secreted into the bloodstream. Because glucocorticoids inhibit the release of messengers like interleukins and interferons, they also make circulating lymphocytes less responsive to an infectious alarm. Glucocorticoids, moreover, cause lymphocytes to be yanked out of the circulation. And most impressively, glucocorticoids can actually kill lymphocytes. This occurs through a mechanism that cell biologists are wild about: glucocorticoids can enter a lymphocyte and cause it to synthesize a suicide protein that chops the DNA in the lymphocyte into thousands of tiny pieces. (Then the lymphocyte is dead as a doorknob, since you need DNA to generate the proteins that keep you in business.)

Scientists are less sure, though, what immune-system role is played by sympathetic nervous system hormones or beta-endorphin during stress. These hormones definitely regulate the immune system, but it is not clear whether they stimulate or inhibit immunity. You would think that this would be easy to answer, but it's not. For example, results vary with how much beta-endorphin is used in an experiment, for how long, and in what species. Some types of immune cells inhibit the activity of other types, and the net result of a hormone blocking these "suppressor" cells could be enhanced overall immunity. Thus, the percentage of these suppressor cells can change the results, as can whether you study immune cells in test tubes (in vitro) or intact organisms (in vivo).

WHY IS IMMUNITY SUPPRESSED DURING STRESS?

In the first chapter, I offered an explanation of why it makes adaptive sense to suppress immunity during stress; now that the process of stress-induced immunosuppression has been explained in a little more detail, it should be obvious that my early explanation makes no sense. I suggested that during stress it is logical for the body to shut down long-term building projects in order to divert energy for more immediate needs — this inhibition includes the immune system, which, while fabulous at spotting a tumor that will kill you in six months or making antibodies that will help you in a week, is not vital in the next few moments' emergency. That explanation would make sense only if stress froze the immune system right where it was — no more immune expenditures until the emergency is finished. However, that is not what happens. Instead, stress *actively* disassembles the system — tissues are shrunk, cells are destroyed. This cannot be explained by a mere halt to expenditures — so out goes this extension of the long-term versus short-term theory.

Why should evolution set us up to do something as apparently stupid as disassembling our immune system during stress? Many answers have been proposed over the years.

Hypothesis 1. *Stress actually stimulates the immune system, by aiding the release of antibodies.* This idea, first put forward in the 1940s, focused on the ability of glucocorticoids to burst white blood cells. When lymphocytes make antibodies, some-one theorized, the cells have no means to release them; gluco-corticoids, by bursting the cells, liberate these antibodies. Thus, in this scenario, immunosuppression is actually boosting im-mune competence. That idea went down the drain when it became apparent that white blood cells were capable of secret-ing antibodies on their own.

Hypothesis 2. *During stress, the cells of the immune system are destroyed so that the remnants of these cells can be used for energy.* In principle, this hypothesis makes some adaptive sense, given the energetic demands of a physical stressor. Neverthe-less, this idea didn't last long. In a stressful emergency, energy comes from the liver and fat cells, not the immune system. Besides, if you were at the point of needing so much energy that you were cannibalizing your cells (rather than the energy stored within the cells), the immune system would be an unlikely place to start.

Hypothesis 3. *Stress actually boosts immunity by selectively suppressing the inhibitory elements of the immune system.* Earlier I noted that one class of immune cells suppresses the activity of the primary defense cells, keeping them under control. Suppose that stress preferentially destroys the activity of these secondary "suppressor" cells, rather than the primary defense cells. The net result would be enhanced immune activity — while destroy-ing most parts of a car will make it less likely to move, destroy-ing its brakes makes the car *more* likely to move at some point. Thus, this is another scenario in which apparent immunosup-pression during stress is actually a means of enhancing immu-nity. Nice idea, but at present little support for it.

Hypothesis 4. *Stress fine-tunes the immune response by sup-pressing most of the (inessential) components and enhancing the parts that you really need.* In chapter 4 I noted that as part of the metabolic stress-response, muscle tends to stop absorbing en-ergy. How is the subset of muscles that will save your life going to function now? The solution appears to be a mechanism that enables the muscles that really need the energy (the ones exer-cising) to override the generalized blockade and receive plentiful amounts of nutrients from the bloodstream.

The immune-response idea here is somewhat similar. In this view, stress will, in a general way, suppress immunity, but the immune system has an override mechanism that can produce the specific antibodies needed to combat whatever the specific infectious stressor is. Nice idea, in that you then save energy by running only the part of the immune system that is essential under those circumstances. There is even some evidence for this. Massive doses of glucocorticoids will suppress every component of the immune system. But the lower (though still large) levels seen during stressful events are not as uniformly suppressive. They suppress certain immune measures, but some aspects of the immune system are buffered from these glucocorticoid actions, and some facets are even stimulated. Some sort of selective patterning that no one yet understands is taking place.

A problem with this idea, however, is one that we have already come across. This explanation would be great if stress caused most of immune function simply to halt while it facilitated the tiny subset of immune responses needed for this particular crisis. As noted, however, the immune system is not merely suspended; instead, the body begins to disassemble what is already there.

Hypothesis 5. *Suppression of the immune system occurs during stress to avoid the danger of developing autoimmune diseases.* This is a very influential idea proposed by Allan Munck (one of the giants of glucocorticoid endocrinology) and his colleagues at Dartmouth Medical School. When something stressful happens, alarms go off throughout the body—just the sort of circumstance where the immune system might, amid all the excitement, get *too* active and accidentally initiate autoimmune disease. Immunosuppression during stress would then make sense in that it would limit the extent of immune activation and protect us from autoimmunity. In this view, immunosuppression is not so much a piece of the stress-response as a piece of the *recovery* from the stress-response. (A variant of this idea, offered by the same authors recently, is that the danger is not so much that the immune system will be so overactive as to cause

autoimmunity, but that some of the immune messengers triggered by the stressor can cause damage when released in excess.
Once again, immunosuppression serves to keep the stress-response from overshooting to a damaging extent.)

Although the general idea that immunosuppression is part
of the recovery from the stress-response, rather than part of the
stress-response itself, has attracted many adherents, I find it has
some difficulties. First, there is no indication that there is a wild
burst of immune activity during the early minutes of exposure to
various psychological or physical stressors. Only if there were
such an outburst would it make sense that sometime later glucocorticoids come in and save us from this dangerously overactive immune system.

Munck has recently proposed a possible response to that
problem. If stressors are usually the short-term type common to
most mammals (that lion and zebra again), the stress-induced
immunosuppression brought about by glucocorticoids is likely
to be of little consequence: the crisis is over before there is any
chance of compromising the immune system to any serious
extent. Where immunosuppression really helps the recovery of
the stress-response is following one specialized type of stressor
—infection. In those instances, there are convincing data that
the immune system really does become excited and overactive,
and you do need the glucocorticoids to calm things down a bit.
For example, in one strain of rats that are unable to secrete
glucocorticoids, normal inflammatory responses spiral out of
control to the point of causing arthritis. In this reasonable view,
stress-induced immunosuppression is helpful for reining in the
stress-response after infectious stressors, and is of little consequence for short-term physical stressors.

Hypothesis 6. *During a stressor, the immune system is suppressed so that it does not inadvertently make you appear vulnerable and sick to competitors and predators.* Most terrestrial mammals live in ecosystems in which they are somewhat visible.
What is it that an animal most fears in such a situation? Looking
conspicuously vulnerable, either to predators or to competitors
of one's own species. A wildebeest injures itself by tripping in

Henri Rousseau, 1910 detail from Horse Attacked by a Jaguar, *oil on canvas.*

an aardvark hole, shows a limp, and is a goner that evening— the hyenas will cue in on it. A male lion in a pride gets an obvious illness, and some other male will make the move on him. A number of early field biologists discovered this principle the hard way—they would manage to get a distinctive paint mark on the flank of some zebra, in order to make identifying it easier, and the zebra would be eaten that night by predators. It didn't have to be sick, just conspicuously different, and various carnivores decide that it is the one in a thousand that will be an easy target. You don't want to look different or weak out in the savanna bloody in tooth and claw. What makes you look conspicuous? When you get an injury, it's the inflammatory response — it makes that knee swell up and causes you to limp. When you are sick, it is the immune system. Benjamin Hart, a scientist at the University of California at Davis, has written extensively on how the immune system makes animals and humans look like hell when they have an infection. Suddenly it makes sense to suppress immunity during stress. Stressful events for an animal in the savanna are often a fight with a competitor or flight from a predator, and those are the last possible times that you want to look conspicuously weak. Suppress the overt signs of it and you have the "stress-induced immunosuppression evolved because ill zebra don't want to have pallid complexions when they are being checked out by a hungry lion" hypothesis. The reader will note that while this hypothesis may have a certain charm, it has the same problem as some of the other hypotheses already cited — it doesn't explain why it makes sense for the body to actively disassemble the immune system. Back to the drawing board.

It appears that no one knows just yet why it makes sense to suppress immunity during stress. One further possibility is that there is no direct evolutionary explanation for the suppression. Some scientists, for example the paleontologist Stephen Jay Gould, believe that not everything in the body has to have an explanation in terms of evolutionary adaptiveness. Maybe stress-induced immunosuppression is a by-product of something else; it just happened.

This is probably not the case. During infections, the immune system releases the chemical messenger interleukin-1, which among other activities stimulates the hypothalamus to release CRF. As noted in chapter 2, CRF stimulates the pituitary to release ACTH, which then causes adrenal release of glucocorticoids. These in turn suppress the immune system. In other words, under some circumstances, the immune system will *ask* the body to secrete hormones that will ultimately suppress the immune system. This fits well with the variant on Munck's idea (#5) — the specialized stressor of infection is particularly good at turning on glucocorticoid secretion, and it is that specialized stressor that is otherwise most likely to overstimulate the immune system. For whatever reason the immunosuppression occurs, the immune system sometimes encourages it. It is probably not just an accident.*

CHRONIC STRESS AND DISEASE RISK

Numerous chapters in this book have followed the structure: "X happens during stress, which is good for you in the face of short-term stressors, but is a disaster in the long run." We've already seen that it is far from clear what good it does to suppress the immune system during a short-term stressor. Now for the even harder question—how damaging is stress-induced immunosuppression, if it occurs chronically? As the AIDS virus has taught us, if you suppress the immune system sufficiently, a 30-year-old will fester with cancers and pneumonias that doctors used to see once in fifty-year careers. But can chronic stress suppress the immune system to the point of making you more susceptible to diseases you wouldn't otherwise get? Once you have a disease, are you less capable of fighting it off? If we ignore major stressors, what effect does more subtle stress have on the capacity to resist disease? When college students take examinations, the effectiveness of their immune systems declines slightly, but is this enough to matter? When we get up in the morning, there is a mild increase in our glucocorticoid con-

---

*My tiny footnote in science: I was the discoverer of the fact that interleukin-1 stimulates CRF release. Or at least I thought I was. It was a few years ago, the idea made some sense, the lab I was in jumped on it under my prompting. We worked like maniacs and at two o'clock one morning I had one of those moments of euphoria that scientists die for: looking at the printout from one of the machines and realizing, aha, I was right, it does work that way. Interleukin-1 released CRF. We wrote up the findings, they were accepted by the prestigious journal *Science*, everyone was very excited, I called up my parents, and so on. Paper gets published, and right next to it was an *identical!* study from a group in Switzerland, sent in to the journal the same exact week. So I became *a* discoverer of this obscure fact. (To hark back to a theme of chapter 2, if you are a mature, confident individual—which unfortunately I am only rarely—you take pleasure in this sort of thing: two labs, working independently on opposite sides of the globe, come up with the same novel observation. It must be true. Scientific progress lurches forward an inch.)

centrations. (If getting up in the morning isn't a mild stressor, then what is?) Relatively subtle changes in glucocorticoid levels such as these are enough to change some immune parameters. As a result, are we more likely to let some infectious bug slip by our immune defenses as we stagger half-comatose into the shower?

Evidence pouring in from many quarters suggests that stress may indeed impair our immune systems and increase the risk of illness. Both massive stressors—death of a spouse or a child, divorce, marital discord, a major depression, chronic care-giving for a family member with Alzheimer's disease—and everyday stressors, such as taking a set of examinations, have been linked with decreased immune function and, in the case of the more extreme stressors, increased mortality. Stressful periods have been shown to precede the onset of immune-related disorders such as multiple sclerosis, post-polio syndrome, and juvenile diabetes. People who are more psychologically stressed are less resistant to respiratory infections that cause the common cold. Stress also appears to play a role in the development of cancer: stress, including social stress, will cause tumors to grow faster in laboratory rodents, and render the rodents' bodies less capable of rejecting a tumor. In humans, stressors such as major depressions are associated with increased risks of cancer years after the depression. Cancer victims in support groups live longer, while people with few social relationships—a situation associated with greater stress—have shorter life expectancies and are at greater risk for a variety of diseases.

Despite these fascinating findings, it remains far from clear just how much chronic stress makes you more vulnerable to diseases that would normally be fought off by the immune system. In order to appreciate the current disarray of the research, let us try to break down the findings above into their component parts.

Essentially, all of these studies show a link between something that increases or decreases stress and some disease/mortality outcome. The approach of many psychoneuroimmunologists is based on the assumption that this link is established through the following steps:

1. We differ as to the pattern and frequency of stressors to which we are exposed.

2. These variations will determine the magnitude and frequency with which we turn on the stress-response (glucocorticoids, epinephrine, and so on).

3. The magnitude and frequency of the stress-response regulates immune competence.

4. Our level of immune competence, in turn, determines what diseases we get and how readily we resist them.

Now, let's begin to analyze the separate steps.

First, how much stress are you exposed to? In studies of nonhuman animals, general consensus is that stress can lead to Steps 2 through 4. But a problem in extrapolating to humans is that the experimental stressors used in animal studies are usually more awful than would be considered ethical to subject humans to. The stressors used in human experiments are mostly milder, and some mild, short-term stressors have been shown to actually *stimulate* components of the immune system. Not only that, but we differ tremendously among ourselves as to what we experience as truly stressful—that whole realm of individual differences that will be the focus of the last chapter of this book. Therefore, if you try to study the effects of everyday, natural stressors on people's immune systems, you must wrestle with the problem of whether these things actually seem stressful to a given individual or not.

There is another problem with Step #1: it is often not clear whether humans are really exposed to the stressors they claim they are. We tend to be notoriously bad reporters of what goes on in our lives. An imaginary experiment: Take 100 lucky people and slip them a drug that will give them a bad stomachache for a few days. Then send them to a doctor participating in this experiment, who tells them that they have developed stomach ulcers. The doctor asks innocently, "Have things been particularly stressful for you recently?" At least 90 of those individuals will come up with something or other putatively stressful to which they will now attribute the ulcer. In *retrospective* studies like this, people confronted with an illness are extremely likely to decide there were stressful events going on. When you rely heavily on retrospective studies with humans, you are likely to get a falsely strong link between stress and disease; and the trouble is, most studies in this field are retrospective. The very expensive and lengthy *prospective* studies are just becoming more common — pick a bunch of healthy people and follow them for decades to come, recording as an objective outsider when they are being exposed to stressors and whether they are becoming sick.

We move to the next step: from the stressor to the stress-response (#1 to #2). Again, if you give an organism a massive stressor, it will reliably have a strong stress-response. With more subtle stressors, we have more subtle stress-responses.

The same thing holds for the step from #2 to #3. In experimental animal studies, large amounts of glucocorticoids will cause the immune system to hit the floor. The same occurs if a human has a tumor that causes massive amounts of glucocorticoids to be secreted (Cushing's syndrome), or if a person is taking huge doses of synthetic glucocorticoids to control some other disease. But most stressors cause only moderate stress-responses, prompting only moderate reductions in immune profiles. And, as noted, there is some indication that small amounts of glucocorticoids can even stimulate the immune system.

We now move from Step #3 to #4. How much does a change in immune profile alter patterns of disease? The odd thing is that immunologists are not sure about this. If your immune system is massively suppressed, you are more likely to get sick, no doubt about that. People taking high doses of glucocorticoids as medication, who are thus highly immunocompromised, are vulnerable to all sorts of infectious diseases, as are people with Cushing's syndrome. Or AIDS.

The more subtle fluctuations in immunity are less clear in their implications, however. Few immunologists would be likely to assert that "for every tiny decrease in some measure of immune function, there is a tiny increase in disease risk." Their hesitancy is because the relationship between immune competence and disease may be *nonlinear*. In other words, once you pass a certain threshold of immunosuppression you are up the creek without a paddle; but before that, immune fluctuations may not really matter much. The immune system is so complex that being able to measure a change in one little piece of it in response to stress may mean nothing about the system as a whole. Thus, the link between relatively minor immune fluctuation and patterns of disease in humans winds up being relatively weak.

There is another reason why it may be difficult to generalize from findings in the laboratory to the real world. In the laboratory, you might be studying the effects of Step #1, #2, or #3 on disease outcome #4. It is inconvenient for most scientists to manipulate a rat's levels of stress/glucocorticoids/immunity and then wait for the rest of the rat's lifetime to see if it is more likely to become ill than is a control rat. That's slow and expensive. Typically, instead, scientists study *induced* diseases. Manipulate Step #1, #2, or #3 in a rat that has been exposed to a certain virus; then see what happens. When you do that, you get information about the links to #4 when dealing with severe, artificially induced disease challenges—but that approach unfortunately misses the point that we don't get sick because some scientist deliberately exposes us to disease. Instead, we spend our lives passing through a world filled with scattered carcinogenic substances, occasional epidemics, someone sneezing from across the room. Relatively few experimental animal studies have looked at *spontaneous* diseases, rather than induced ones.

Finally, many scientists assume that if there is a link between stress (Step #1) and disease (Step #4), it occurs by way of a stress-response (Step #2) causing suppression of immunity (Step #3). But there may be other ways to get from Step #1 to Step #4. Suppose an elderly man loses his wife. It is a well-documented scientific fact that his risk of dying rises in the next year. An obvious interpretation: because of the stressor of bereavement (#1), he activates his stress-response (#2), causing enough immunosuppression (#3) to make him sick (#4). But Steps 2 and 3 aren't the only possible things going on in that man. Perhaps the widower is too depressed to take his daily hypertension medicine or to eat regular, healthy meals. Some-

times the confound is more subtle. It is known that the fewer
social relationships a person has, the more she is at risk for a
variety of diseases. Is this because this woman, lacking support
networks, is less buffered from stressors and thus more immunosuppressed? Perhaps. But how about the possibility that un-
healthy people are less likely to establish and maintain social
relationships? Here's an even more subtle confound: Losing a
spouse increases disease risk (as well as risk of dying) in the
years afterward—maybe because of the stress. But people tend
to marry people who are ethnically and genetically quite similar
to themselves. Intrinsic in this trend toward "homogamy" is a
tendency of married couples to have higher-than-random
chances of sharing certain genetic disease tendencies, which
makes it more likely that they will get sick around the same
time.

Amid all these confounds and caveats and problems and
"not so fast's," how likely are we to get in trouble because stress
suppresses immunity? Some very careful studies are showing
impressive links among stress, immune function, disease outcome, and longevity; in general, they have done a good job of
controlling for age, health, socioeconomic status, smoking, alco-
hol consumption, physical activity, obesity, and use of preven-
tive health services. A sampling:

• The fewer social relationships, the shorter the life expectancy.
  Medically "protective" relationships can take the form of marriage, contact with friends and extended family, church mem-
  bership, or other group affiliations. This finding is based on
  some careful prospective studies and is seen in both sexes and
  in different races, in American and European populations living
  in both urban and rural areas. The impact of social relationships on life expectancy, moreover, appears to be at least as
  large as that of variables such as cigarette smoking, hypertension, obesity, and level of physical activity. People with the
  fewest social connections had approximately two-and-a-half
  times as much chance of dying as those with the most connections, after controlling for such variables as age, gender, and
  health status. Possibly linked to that finding is the observation
  that people who score high on loneliness scales have been

found to have relatively depressed immune function. In a similar vein, young monkeys separated from their mothers show depressed immune function, which is somewhat reversible if, after separation, they are housed with other animals.

- In another carefully controlled prospective study, the parents of young men who had died in war or in accidents were followed for ten years afterward. Loss of a son did not affect mortality rate in the population of grieving parents in general; however, significantly higher mortality rates occurred among parents who were already widowed or divorced. In other words, this stressor is associated with increased mortality in the subset of parents with the least social support.

- Having a major depression at some point in life increases the risk of dying of cancer up to twenty years later.

- In a recent study that has attracted an enormous amount of attention, David Spiegel and his colleagues at Stanford Medical School showed that group therapy will increase survivorship for cancer patients. Women being treated for metastatic breast cancer were randomly assigned to cohorts that either did or did not have weekly supportive group therapy sessions. As expected, the women in group therapy experienced improved mood and reduced pain. But what shocked Spiegel and colleagues was the discovery that the women in group therapy lived twice as long as those in the control group. Spiegel himself points out that the extended lifespan may not be due to the fact that the women in the group therapy were less stressed. Perhaps being in a supportive group makes patients more likely to comply with medication schedules, perform the therapeutic exercises required of them, follow difficult diets more strictly, and so on. Nevertheless, the effect is striking, and similar findings have since emerged for lymphoma and leukemia patients in some, but not all, studies.

Collectively, these are impressive findings. It is worth exploring two facets of this literature in greater detail, both because of their potential importance and because of current confusion surrounding them. The first regards the effects of stress on autoimmune diseases. One can generate a plausible prediction: if stress causes the secretion of glucocorticoids, which suppress the activity of the immune system, then stress should *decrease* the severity of autoimmune diseases, since those are diseases of overactive immunity. On the other hand, some papers report that stress *worsens* the symptoms of autoimmune diseases, including multiple sclerosis and juvenile diabetes. There have only been a handful of such reports, and they suffer from the weakness of reliance on self (patient)-reported retrospective data, rather than prospective data. Nevertheless, they suggest that, somehow, stress makes an already overly active immune system even more active.

This is obviously confusing. It is absolutely clear that massive amounts of glucocorticoids will help people with autoimmune disorders—in fact, prescribing high-dose glucocorticoids is typically the first thing a doctor does for someone diagnosed with an autoimmune disease. (The goal of "putting someone on steroids," as the treatment is often called, is to give glucocorticoids in a dose that will damp the autoimmune component of the immune system without wiping out the rest of the immune response or causing hypertension, diabetes, reproductive problems, and so on. Unfortunately, this strategy rarely works—the side effects of glucocorticoid treatment for autoimmune disease are typically enormous.)

Why, then, should stress be associated with a worsening of autoimmune symptoms in some cases? One possible explanation involves the fact that stress does not equal massive glucocorticoid exposure per se—other hormones are secreted as well, and many of them influence the immune system. In addition, stressors do not necessarily cause *massive* glucocorticoid secretion. As already cited, mild elevations of glucocorticoid levels have been reported to actually stimulate the immune system,* and this may be what is going on in the cases where stress seems

---

*Perhaps this occurs through a mechanism already discussed—if low levels of glucocorticoids selectively disrupt the activity of inhibitory suppressor cells, the net result may be activation of the rest of the immune system.

to worsen autoimmune disorders. Clearly, a lot more careful research is needed on this important topic before firm conclusions can be reached.

The second issue to be explored in detail is the link between stress and cancer risk, both because of the powerful effects that were seen in some of those reports and because we are all so terrified of cancer. There is, by now, a reasonably convincing animal-experimentation literature showing that stress affects the course of some types of cancer. For example, the rate at which some tumors grow in mice can be affected merely by what sort of cages the animals are housed in—the more noisy and stressful, the faster the tumors grow. Other studies show that if you expose rats to electric shocks from which they can eventually escape, they reject transplanted tumors at a normal rate. Take away the capacity to escape, yet give the same total number of shocks, and the rats lose their capacity to reject tumors. Stress mice by putting their cages on a rotating platform (basically, a record player) and there is a tight relationship between the number of rotations and the rate of tumor growth. Substitute glucocorticoids for the rotation stressor, and tumor growth is accelerated, as well. These are the results of very careful studies performed by some of the best scientists in the field.

How might stress make tumors grow faster? Probably through a number of mechanisms. The first is probably immunologic. The immune system contains a specialized class of cells (most notably, natural killer cells) which prevent the spread of tumors. Stress suppresses the numbers of circulating natural killer cells. A second route is probably nonimmunologic. Once a tumor starts growing, it needs enormous amounts of energy, and one of the first things that tumors do is to send a signal to the nearest blood vessel to grow a bush of capillaries into the tumor. Such "angiogenesis" allows for the delivery of blood and nutrients to the hungry tumor. Glucocorticoids, at the concentration generated during stress, aid angiogenesis. A final route may involve glucose delivery. Tumor cells are very good at absorbing glucose out of the bloodstream. Recall the zebra sprinting away from the lion: Energy storage has stopped, in order to increase concentrations of circulating glucose, to be used by the muscles. But, as my own lab recently discovered, when circulating glucose concentrations are elevated in rats during stress, at least one kind of experimental tumor can grab the glucose before the muscle does. Your storehouses of energy, intended for your muscles, are being emptied and inadvertently transferred to the ravenous tumor instead.

These findings are potentially unnerving to us all. As a source of some comfort, it appears that stress has little to do with whether a tumor gets started in the first place — it seems to have greater impact on the rate of growth of tumors once they are established. Moreover, stress appears to have its most pronounced effect on the growth of tumors that are caused by viruses;* in humans, most cancers are currently thought to arise from carcinogens like chemicals or radiation, rather than viruses. Finally, most of the studies showing this stress/cancer link are experimental ones with the unique features I've already noted — the animals are exposed to major stressors while fighting off induced tumors. With more normal stressors and spontaneous incidences of cancer, the stress/cancer link is likely to be weaker.

CANCER AND MIRACLES

To summarize these various studies, prolonged stress does appear to have an impact on the immune system and on disease processes, and this probably includes cancer. Conversely, interventions that provide social support and reduce stress appear to strengthen resistance to diseases that involve challenges to immunity. However, it is rare that these effects are very large. (In science, it is quite possible to have an observation that is correct but not of great importance.) If you have cancer, for example,

---

*In such cases, viruses take over the replicative machinery of a cell and cause it to start dividing — and growing — out of control.

developing or maintaining active social relationships and joining a cancer support group appear to be significantly helpful adjuncts to mainstream cancer treatment. It would be utterly foolish, however, to do those things *instead* of mainstream cancer treatment. There are many traditional forms of cancer treatment that will cause tumors to shrink in size, and there is simply no scientific evidence at present that any known stress reduction technique will accomplish the same.

This leads to a tirade. Once we recognize that psychological factors, stress-reducing interventions, and so on can *influence* something like cancer, it is often a hopeful, desperate leap to the conclusion that such factors can *control* cancer. And when that proves to be false, there is a corrosive, poisonous flip side: if you falsely believe you had the power to prevent or cure cancer through positive thinking, you may then come to believe that it is your own fault if you are dying of the disease.

The advocates of a rather damaging overstatement of these psychology/health relationships are not always addled voices from the lunatic fringe. They include influential health practitioners whose medical degrees appear to lend credence to their extravagant claims. I will focus my attention here on the claims of Bernie S. Siegel, a Yale University surgeon who has been wildly effective at disseminating his ideas to the public as the author of a best-seller.

The premise of Seigel's magnum opus, *Love, Medicine and Miracles* (New York: Harper & Row, 1986), is that the most effective way of stimulating the immune system is through love, and that miraculous healing happens to patients who are brave enough to love. Siegel purports to demonstrate this.

As the book unfolds, you note that it is a strange world that Siegel inhabits. When operating on anesthetized patients, "I also do not hesitate to ask the [anesthetized] patient not to bleed if circumstances call for it" (p. 49), he asserts. In his world, deceased patients come back as birds (p. 222), there are unnamed countries in which individuals consistently live for a century (p. 140), and best of all, people who have the right spirituality not only successfully fight cancer, but can drive cars that consistently break down for other people (p. 137).

This is relatively benign gibberish, and history buffs may even feel comforted by those among us who live the belief system of medieval peasants. Where the problems become appallingly serious is when Siegel concentrates on the main point of his book. No matter how often he puts in disclaimers saying that he's *not* trying to make people feel guilty, the book's premise is that cancer (or any other disease) is curable if the patient has sufficient courage, love, and spirit; if the patient is not cured, it is because of insufficient amounts of those admirable traits. The problem with Siegel's view is that very few scientists would consider there to be any scientific justification for these claims. This is not how disease works, and a physician simply should not go about telling seriously ill people otherwise.

His book is full of people who get cancer because of their uptightness and lack of spirituality. He speaks of one woman who was repressed in her feelings about her breasts: "*Naturally,* [my emphasis] Jan got breast cancer" (p. 85). Of another patient: "She held all her feelings inside and developed leukemia" (p. 164). Or, in an extraordinary statement: "Cancer generally seems to appear in response to loss. . . . I believe that, if a person avoids emotional growth at this time, the impulse behind it becomes misdirected into malignant physical growth" (p. 123).

Naturally, individuals who do have enough courage, love, and spirit can defeat cancer. Sometimes it takes a little prodding from Siegel. He advises on page 108 that people with serious diseases consider the ways in which they may have wanted their illness because we are trained to associate sickness with reward (Siegel cites our receiving cards and flowers—p. 110). Sometimes Siegel has to be a bit more forceful with a recalcitrant cancer patient. One woman was apparently inhibited about drawing something Siegel requested her to, being embarrassed about her poor drawing skills. "I asked [her] how she expected to get over cancer if she didn't even have the courage to do a picture" (p. 81). You know whose fault it was if she eventually died.

But once the good patients overcome their attitude problems and get with the program, miracles just start popping up everywhere you look. One patient with the proper visualizing techniques cured his cancer, his arthritis and, as long as he was at it, his 20-year problem with impotency as well (p. 153). Of another: "She chose the path of life, and as she grew, her cancer shrank" (p. 113). Consider the following exchange (p. 175):

> I came in, and he said, "Her cancer's gone."
> "Phyllis," I said, "Tell them what happened."
> She said, "Oh, you know what happened."
> "I know that I know," I said, "But I'd like the others to know."
> Phyllis replied, "I decided to live to be a hundred and leave my troubles to God."
> I really could end the book here, because this peace of mind can heal anything.

According to Siegel, cancer is curable with the right combination of attributes, and those people without them may get cancer and die of it. An incurable disease is the fault of the victim. He tries to soften his message now and then: "Cancer's complex causes aren't all in the mind," he says (p. 103), and on page 75 he tells us he's interested in a person gaining understanding of his role in a disease rather than in creating guilt. But when he gets past his anecdotes about individual patients and states his premise in its broadest terms, its poisonousness appears unmistakable: "The fundamental problem most patients face is an inability to love themselves" (p. 4); "I feel that all disease is ultimately related to a lack of love" (p. 180).

Siegel has a special place in his book for children with cancer and for the parents of those children trying to understand why it has occurred. After noting that developmental psychologists have learned that infants have considerably greater perceptual capacities than previously believed, Siegel says he "wouldn't be surprised if cancer in early childhood was linked to messages of parental conflict or disapproval perceived even in the womb" (p. 75). In other words, if your child gets cancer, consider the possibility that you caused it.

And perhaps most directly: "There are no incurable diseases, only incurable people" (p. 99). (Compare the statement by the psychiatrist and stress researcher Herbert Weiner: "Diseases are mere abstractions; they cannot be understood without appreciating the person who is ill." Superficially, Weiner's and Siegel's notions bear some resemblance to each other. The former, however, is a scientifically sound statement of the interactions between diseases and individual makeups of sick people; the latter seems to me an unscientific distortion of those interactions.)

Since at least the Middle Ages, there has been a philosophical view of disease that is "lapsarian" in nature, characterizing illness as the punishment meted out by God for sin (all deriving from humankind's lapse in the Garden of Eden). Its adherents obviously predated any knowledge about germs, infection, the workings of the body. This view has mostly passed (although see the endnotes for an extraordinary example of this thinking that festered in the Reagan administration), but as you read through Siegel's book, you unconsciously wait for its reemergence, knowing that disease has to be more than just not having enough groovy New Age spirituality, that God is going to be yanked into Siegel's world of blame as well. Finally, it bubbles to the surface on page 179: "I suggest that patients think of illness not as God's will but as our deviation from God's will. To me it is the absence of spirituality that leads to difficulties." Cancer, thus, is what you get when you deviate from God's will, a view likely to be enormously offensive to many who are religiously inclined, to say nothing of those who have some understanding of actual disease processes.

Oh, and one other thing about Siegel's views. He runs a cancer program called Exceptional Cancer Patients, which incorporates his many ideas about the nature of life, spirit, and disease. To my knowledge there has been only a single published study of his program and its effects on survival time, and this is its conclusion: "Preliminary findings suggest a strong beneficial effect of the program on survival, which is statistically significant. However, this observed effect is due largely to a selection bias caused by the failure to match on the duration of the lag period between cancer diagnosis and program entry.* Correcting for this bias in the analysis results in a small, nonsignificant program effect." In other words, by the rules of statistical analysis that biomedical science uses to tell the difference between a real effect and one due merely to a random blip in the data, the program has no effect on survivorship. One last word from Siegel, on pages 185–186 of his book, washing his hands of that inconvenient study: "I prefer to deal with individuals and effective techniques, and let others take care of the statistics."

Siegel is certainly not alone in this style of thinking; I analyze his ideas at length simply because he is such an effective and credentialed promulgator of these potentially damaging and ill-conceived ideas. Stress can influence immune resistance and the likelihood of getting certain diseases. It appears that, at least in the laboratory setting, stress can influence some aspects of tumor growth. However, these influences are simply not all that strong. It is bad enough to have cancer without being led by some perversion of psychoneuroimmunology into thinking that it is your fault that you have it and that it is within your power to cure it.

This topic is one that I will return to in the final chapter of the book when I discuss stress management theories. Obviously, a theme of this book is just how many things can go wrong in the body because of stress and how important it is for everyone to recognize this. However, it would be utterly negligent to exaggerate the implications of this idea. Every child cannot grow up to be President; it turned out that merely by holding hands and singing folk songs we couldn't end all war, and hunger does not disappear just by visualizing a world without it. Everything bad in human health now is not caused by stress, nor is it in our

---

*This is a technical way of saying that the scientists who conducted the study compared patients in Siegel's program with a random collection of cancer patients as the control group and, for some unknown reason, Siegel's patients tend to join his program atypically early after their cancer diagnosis. Thus, even if Siegel's program has no special benefits for prolonging survival, his patients will seemingly have survived their cancer a longer time.

power to cure ourselves of all our worst medical nightmares merely by reducing stress and thinking healthy thoughts full of courage and spirit and love. Would that it were so. And shame on those who would sell this view.

POSTSCRIPT: A GROTESQUE PIECE OF MEDICAL HISTORY

The notion that the mind can influence the immune system, that emotional distress can change resistance to certain diseases, is fascinating; psychoneuroimmunology exerts a powerful pull. Nevertheless, it sometimes amazes me just how many psychoneuroimmunologists are popping up. They are even beginning to speciate into subspecialties. Some study the issue only in humans, others in animals; some analyze epidemiological patterns in large populations, others study single cells. During breaks at scientific conferences, you can even get teams of psychoneuroimmunological pediatricians playing volleyball against the psychoneuroimmunological gerontologists. I am old enough, I admit frankly, to remember a time when there were no such things as psychoneuroimmunologists. Now, like an aging Cretaceous-era dinosaur, I watch these new mammals proliferating; yet there was even a time when it was not common knowledge that stress caused immune tissues to shrink — and as a result, one medical researcher carried out an influential study and misinterpreted his findings, which indirectly led to the deaths of thousands of people.

By the nineteenth century, scientists and doctors were becoming concerned with a new pediatric disorder. On certain occasions parents would place their apparently perfectly healthy infant in bed, tuck the blankets in securely, leave for a peaceful night's sleep — and return in the morning to find the child dead. "Crib death," or sudden infant death syndrome (SIDS), came to be recognized during that time. When it happened, one initially had to explore the unsettling possibility that there was foul play or parental abuse, but that was usually eliminated, and one was left with the mystery of healthy infants dying in their sleep for no discernible reason.

Today, scientists have made some progress in understanding SIDS. It seems to arise in infants who, during the third trimester of fetal life, have some sort of crisis where their brains do not get enough oxygen, causing certain neurons in the brain stem that control respiration to become especially vulnerable. But in the nineteenth century, no one had a clue as to what was going on.

One pathologist began a logical course of research in the 1890s. He would carefully autopsy SIDS infants and compare them to the normal infant autopsy material. Here is where the subtle, fatal mistake occurred. "Normal infant autopsy material." Who gets autopsied? Who gets practiced on by interns in teaching hospitals? Whose bodies wind up being dissected in gross anatomy by first-year medical students? Usually, it has been poor people.

The nineteenth century was the time when men with strong backs and a nocturnal bent could opt for a career as "resurrectionists" — grave robbers, body snatchers, who would sell corpses to anatomists at the medical schools for use in study and teaching. Overwhelmingly, the bodies of the poor, buried without coffins in shallow mass graves in potter's fields, were taken; the wealthy, by contrast, would be buried in triple coffins. As body-snatching anxiety spread, adaptations evolved for the wealthy. The "patent coffin" of 1818 was explicitly and expensively marketed to be resurrectionist-proof, and cemeteries of the gentry would offer a turn in the dead-house, where the well-guarded body could genteelly putrify past the point of interest to the dissectors, at which time it could be safely buried. This period, moreover, gave rise to the verb "burking," after the aging resurrectionist who pioneered the practice of luring beggars in for a charitable meal and then strangling them for a quick sale to the anatomists. (Ironic-ending department: William Burke and his sidekick, after their execution, were handed over to the anatomists. Their dissection included particular attention to their skulls, with an attempt to find phrenological causes of their heinous crimes.)

All very helpful for the biomedical community, but with some drawbacks. The poor tended to express a riotous displeasure with the medico–body-snatcher complex (to coin a phrase). Frenzied crowds lynched resurrectionists who were caught, attacked the homes of anatomists, burned hospitals. Concerned about the mayhem caused by unregulated preying on the bodies of the poor, governments moved decisively to supervise the preying. In the early nineteenth century, various European governments acted to supply adequate bodies to the anatomists, put the burkers and resurrectionists out of business, and keep the poor in line — all with one handy little law: anyone who died destitute in a poorhouse or a paupers' hospital would now be turned over to the dissectors.

Doctors were thus trained in what the normal human body looked like by studying the bodies and tissues of the poor. Yet the bodies of poor people are changed by the stressful circumstances of their poverty. In the "normal" six-month-old autopsy population, the infants had typically died of chronic diarrheal disorders, malnutrition, tuberculosis. Prolonged, stressful diseases. Their thymus glands had shrunk.

We now return to our pathologist, comparing the bodies of SIDS infants with those of "normal" dead infants. By definition, if children had been labeled as having died of SIDS, there was nothing else wrong with them. No prior stressors. No shrinking of the thymus gland. The researcher begins his study and discovers something striking: SIDS kids had thymuses much larger than those of "normal" dead infants. This is where he got things backward. Not knowing that stress shrinks the thymus gland, he assumed that the thymuses in the "normal" autopsy population were normal. He concluded that some children have an *abnormally* large thymus gland, and that SIDS is caused by that large thymus pressing down on the trachea and one night suffocating the child. The pathologist and those practitioners who read his work soon came up with what seemed like a logical way of preventing this from happening: parents, if you want to avoid SIDS in your infants, have their throats irradiated to shrink the thymus gland. The imaginary disorder of large thymuses soon had a fancy name, "status thymicolymphaticus," and irradiation became a standard practice. Estimates are that in the ensuing decades it caused tens of thousands of cases of cancers in the thyroid gland, which sits near the thymus.

What recommendations does one offer from the history of status thymicolymphaticus? I could try for some big ones. That so long as all people are not born equal and certainly don't get to live equally, we should at least be dissected equally. How about something even more grandiose, such as that something should be done about infants getting small thymuses from economic inequality.

Okay, I'll aim for something on a more manageable scientific scale. For example, while we expend a great deal of effort trying to do extraordinary things in medical research — sequencing the human genome, transplanting neurons, building artificial organs — we still need smart people to study some of the moronically simple problems, like "how big is a normal thymus?" Because they are often not so simple. Maybe another lesson is that confounds can come from unexpected quarters — bands of very smart, very subtle public health researchers wrestle with that idea for a living. Perhaps the best moral is that when doing science (or perhaps when doing anything at all in a society as judgmental as our own), be very careful and very certain before pronouncing something to be the norm — because at that instant, you have made it supremely difficult to ever again look objectively at an exception to that supposed norm.

STRESS-INDUCED
ANALGESIA

In Joseph Heller's classic novel about World War II, *Catch-22*, the anti-hero, Yossarian, is in bed with a woman with whom he has an unlikely argument about the nature of God. Unlikely, because they are both atheists, which would presumably lead to agreement about the subject. However, it turns out that while he merely does not believe in the existence of a God and is rather angry about the whole concept, the God that she does not believe in is one who is good and warm and loving, and thus she is offended by the vehemence of his attacks.

> "How much reverence can you have for a Supreme Being who finds it necessary to include such phenomena as phlegm and tooth decay in His divine system of creation? What in the world was running through that warped, evil, scatological mind of His when He robbed old people of the power to control their bowel movements? Why in the world did He ever create pain?"
>
> "Pain?" Lieutenant Scheisskopf's wife pounced upon the word victoriously. "Pain is a useful symptom. Pain is a warning to us of bodily dangers."

"And who created the dangers?" Yossarian demanded.
He laughed caustically. "Oh, He was really being charitable to
us when He gave us pain! Why couldn't He have used a
doorbell instead to notify us, or one of his celestial choirs? Or
a system of blue-and-red neon tubes right in the middle of
each person's forehead. Any jukebox manufacturer worth his
salt could have done that. Why couldn't He?"

"People would certainly look silly walking around with
red neon tubes in the middle of their foreheads."

"They certainly look beautiful now writhing in agony or
stupefied with morphine, don't they?"

Unfortunately, we lack neon lights in the middle of our
foreheads, and in the absence of such innocuous signs, we
probably do need pain perception. Pain can hurt like hell, but it
can inform us that we are sitting too close to the fire, or that we
should never again eat the novel item that just gave us food
poisoning. It effectively discourages us from trying to walk on
an injured limb that is better left immobilized until it heals. And
in our Westernized lives, it is often a good signal that we had
better see a doctor before it is too late. People who congenitally
lack the ability to feel pain (a condition known as "pain asymbolia") are a mess; their feet may ulcerate, their knee joints may
disintegrate, and their long bones may crack because they don't
know how much force to step down with; they burn themselves
unawares; in some cases, they've even lost a toe without knowing it.

Pain is useful to the extent that it motivates us to modify
our behaviors in order to reduce whatever insult is causing the
pain, because invariably that insult is damaging our tissues. Pain
is useless and debilitating, however, when it is telling us that
there is something dreadfully wrong that we can do nothing
about. We must praise evolution or God for providing us with a
physiological system that lets us know when our stomachs are
empty. Yet at the same time we must deeply rue evolution or
God for providing us with a physiological system that can wrack
an untreatable, terminal cancer patient with unrelenting pain.

Pain, until we get the lights on our foreheads, will remain a
necessary but highly problematic part of our natural physiology.
What is surprising is how malleable pain signals are—how

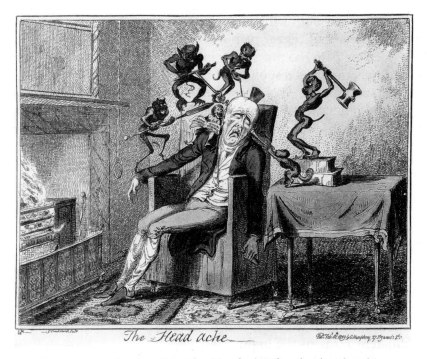

George Cruikshank, 1819: The Headache, *hand-colored etching.*

readily the intensity of a pain signal is changed by the sensations, feelings, and thoughts that coincide with the pain. One example of this modulation, the blunting of pain perception during some circumstances of stress, is the subject of this chapter.

THE BASICS OF PAIN PERCEPTION

The sensation of pain originates in receptors located throughout our body. Some are deep within the body, telling us about muscle aches, tendon pulls, fluid-filled, swollen joints. Others, in our skin, can tell us that we have been cut, burned, abraded, poked. Often, these skin receptors respond to the signal of local tissue damage. Cut yourself with a paring knife, and you will slice open various cells of microscopic size that then spill out their proverbial guts; and typically, within this cellular soup now flooding out of the area of injury is a variety of chemical messengers that trigger pain receptors into action.

Some pain receptors carry information only about pain (for example, the ones responding to cuts); others carry information both about pain and also everyday sensations. For example, by way of various tactile receptors on my back, I am greatly pleased to have my back scratched and rubbed by my wife. However, as evidence that there are limits to all good things, I would not at all enjoy it if she vigorously scratched with coarse sandpaper, instead of more languidly with her fingers. In much the same way, we often are pleased to have our thermal receptors stimulated by warm sunlight, but are rarely so when scalded by boiling water. Sometimes pain consists of everyday sensations writ large.

Regardless of the particular type of pain and the particular receptor activated, all these receptors send nervous projections to the spinal cord. There they funnel their information to other specialized pain neurons, which in turn send the information to different areas of the brain.

Activate these pathways, for example, by stomping on a tack with your bare foot. One part of your cortex receives information that something painful has happened; another part figures out what part of the body has been insulted. While they are communicating about this, a far more rapid part of the system effects the reflexive withdrawal of your foot (this part is mostly based in the spinal cord rather than the brain, which allows the withdrawal reflex to be faster). Other regions of your brain are activating your autonomic nervous system and speeding up your heart, and another part signals the hypothalamus to start secreting CRF, which ultimately triggers glucocorticoid secretion from the adrenals.

MODULATION OF PAIN PERCEPTION

A striking aspect of the pain system is how readily it can be modulated by other factors. The strength of a pain signal, for example, can depend on what other sensory information is funneled to the spine at the same time. This is why it feels great to have a massage when you have sore muscles. Chronic, throbbing pain can be inhibited by certain types of sharp, brief sensory stimulation.

The physiology behind this is one of the most elegant bits of wiring that I know of in the nervous system, a circuit sorted out some decades ago by the pain physiologists Patrick Wall and Ronald Melzack. It turns out that the nervous projections — the fibers carrying pain information from your periphery to the spinal cord — are not all of one kind. Instead, they come in different classes. Probably the most relevant dichotomy is between fibers that carry information about acute, sharp, sudden pain and those that carry information about slow, diffuse, constant, throbbing pain. Both project to spinal cord neurons and activate them, but in different ways (see part A of the illustration on page 170).

Two types of neurons found in the spinal cord are being affected by painful information (see part B of the illustration on page 170). The first ("X") is the same neuron diagrammed before, which relays pain information to the brain. The second neuron ("Y") is a local one called an "interneuron." When Y is stimulated, it inhibits the activity of X.

As things are wired up, when a sharp, painful stimulus is felt, the information is sent on the fast fiber. This stimulates both neurons X and Y. As a result, X sends a painful signal up the spinal cord and, an instant later, Y kicks in and shuts X off. Thus the brain senses a brief, sharp burst of pain, such as after stepping on a tack.

By contrast, when a dull, throbbing pain is felt, the information is sent on the slow fiber. It communicates with both neurons X and Y, but differently from the way it does on the fast fiber. Once again the X neuron is stimulated and lets the brain know that something painful has occurred. This time, however, the slow fiber *inhibits* the Y neuron from firing. Y remains silent, X keeps firing, and your brain senses a slow, throbbing pain, such as after you've burned yourself.

Suppose that you have some sort of continuous, throbbing pain — sore muscles, an insect bite, a painful blister. How can you stop the throbbing? Briefly stimulate the fast fiber. This adds to the pain for an instant, but by stimulating the Y inter-

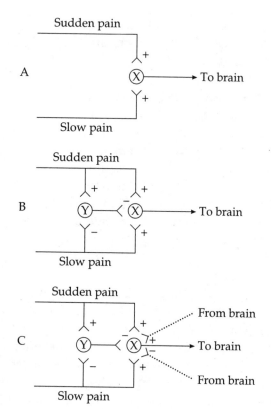

A schematic diagram of how pain information is passed to the brain,
and how it can be modulated by the brain. (A) A neuron (X) in the
spinal cord sends a signal to the brain that something painful has
happened, once it is stimulated by a pain fiber. Such pain fibers can
carry information about sudden pain or slow, diffuse pain. (B) A more
realistic version of how the system actually works, showing why sudden
and slow pain information is differentiated. In the case of sudden pain,
the sudden pain fiber stimulates neuron X, causing a pain signal to be
relayed to the brain. The sudden pain fiber also stimulates an
interneuron (Y) that inhibits neuron X, after a brief delay. Thus, neuron
X sends a pain signal to the brain for only a short time. In contrast, the
slow pain fiber stimulates neuron X and inhibits interneuron Y. Thus, Y
does not inhibit X, and X continues to send a pain signal to the brain,
producing a slow, diffuse pain. (C) Both stimulatory and inhibitory
fibers come from the brain and send information to neuron X,
modulating its sensitivity to incoming pain information. Thus, the brain
can sensitize neuron X to a painful signal, or blunt its sensitivity.

neuron, the system is then shut down for awhile. And that is precisely what we often do in all of those circumstances. Experiencing a good vigorous mauling massage inhibits the dull throbbing pain of sore muscles for awhile. An insect bite throbs and itches unbearably, and we often scratch hard right around it to dull the pain. Or we'll pinch ourselves. In all of these cases, the slow chronic pain pathway is shut down for awhile.

This model has had important clinical implications. For one thing, it has allowed scientists to design treatments for people with severe chronic pain syndromes (for example, a patient who has had a nerve root crushed in his back). By implanting a little electrode into the fast pain pathway and attaching it to a stimulator on the person's hip, they enable the patient to buzz that pathway now and then to turn off the chronic pain; works wonders in many cases.

This dual pathway also explains a clinical feature of severe diabetes. In cases when energy delivery is disrupted for lack of insulin, nerves may become damaged. In general it is the fast fibers, which take more energy to operate than the lower-maintenance slow fibers, that are damaged. Thus, the person loses the ability to ever shut down the Y interneuron in that pathway, and what would be a mild chronic pain for anyone else becomes a constant throbbing one for a diabetic.

The Wall and Melzack model explains how sensory information can modulate how much pain you feel. The vagaries of your thoughts and feelings can influence pain sensitivity as well. At one extreme, people will have sex in all sorts of unlikely places, happily abrading their rear ends on all sorts of rough surfaces, and hardly notice a thing. Or consider that most paradoxically euphoric of pains, childbirth. At the other extreme, if you are skittish enough about dentists, you're going to decide it hurts the instant your teeth are so much as touched with a pick.

A study conducted in the 1980s provides a particularly striking example of the modulation of pain sensitivity by other sensory information. The scientist examined a decade's worth of records at a suburban hospital, noting how many painkillers were requested by patients who had just had gallbladder surgery; and he found that patients who had views of trees from their windows requested significantly less pain medication than those who looked out on blank walls. Other studies of chronic pain patients show that manipulating psychological variables such as the sense of control over events also dramatically changes the quantity of painkillers that they request.

Your mind's capacity to affect pain sensitivity is obviously going to be important in the effects of stress on pain perception. How can the brain create these effects? We complicate our wiring diagram, shown on page 170 even further. Descending projections from the brain, terminating in the spinal cord, influence how sensitive neuron X is to a painful signal. Look at a blank wall out of your hospital window, sit in the dentist's chair in terror of every move, and these descending pathways make neuron X very jumpy. Look at a stand of trees out your window, think about sex instead of the bristly carpet you're lying on while having sex, and your brain makes neuron X less responsive to an incoming pain signal.

STRESS-INDUCED ANALGESIA

Thus, both "ascending" and "descending" influences modulate the workings of the pain pathway in the spine. The descending projections help mediate stress-induced analgesia, the phenomenon that, when you experience stress in just the right way, you don't feel much pain.

Chapter 1 recounted anecdotal cases of people who, highly aroused during battle, did not notice a severe injury. One of the first to note this phenomenon of stress-induced analgesia was the Harvard anesthesiologist Henry Beecher, who examined injured soldiers as a battlefront medic in World War II and compared them to civilian populations. He found that for injuries of similar severity, approximately 80 percent of civilians requested morphine, while only a third of the soldiers did. He cited the French physician Dupuytren, who, more than a century earlier, noted the same pattern and pointed out that for the wounded soldier facing a medic in a field tent, the news of an injury is almost a relief — things could easily have been worse; there might have been no medic; at least I'm out of the battle now; and so on.

Few of us experience stress-induced analgesia in the midst of battle. For us, it is more likely to happen during some sporting event where, if we are sufficiently excited and involved in what we are doing, we can easily ignore an injury. On a more every-day level, stress-induced analgesia is experienced by the droves who exercise. Invariably the first stretch is agony, as you search for every possible excuse to stop before you suffer the coronary that you are now fearing. Then suddenly, about half an hour into this self-flagellation, the pain melts away. You even start feeling oddly euphoric. The whole venture seems like the most wonderful self-improvement conceivable, and you plan to work out like this daily until your hundredth birthday. (All vows, of course, are forgotten the next day when you start the painful process all over again.)

Traditionally many hard-nosed laboratory scientists, when encountering something like stress-induced analgesia, would relegate it to the "psychosomatic" realm, dismissing it as some fuzzy aspect of "mind over matter." The analgesia, however, is an extremely concrete phenomenon, as real as how your brain distinguishes between light and dark.

One bit of evidence is that stress-induced analgesia occurs in other animals as well, not just in humans emotionally in-vested in the success of their nation's army or their office's softball team. This can be shown in animals with the "hot-plate test." Put a rat on a hot plate; then turn it on. Carefully time how long it takes for the rat to feel the first smidgen of discom-fort, when it picks up its foot for the first time (at which point the rat is removed from the hot plate). Now do the same thing to a rat that has been stressed — forced to swim in a tank of water, put in a cage with a threatening rat, whatever. It will take longer for this rat to notice the heat of the plate: stress-induced analgesia.

The best evidence that such analgesia is a real phenome-non is the neurochemistry that has been discovered to underlie it. The tale begins in the 1970s, with the subject in which every

ambitious, cutting-edge neurochemist of the time was interested — the various opiate drugs that were being used recre-
ationally in vast numbers: heroin, morphine, opium. All those
compounds have similar chemical structures and are made in
certain plants in similar ways. In the early 1970s, three different
groups of neurochemists almost simultaneously demonstrated
that these opiate drugs bound to specific opiate receptors in the
brain. And these receptors tended to be located in the parts of
the brain that process pain perception. This turned out to solve
the problem of how opiate drugs block pain — they activate
those descending pathways that blunt the sensitivity of the X
neuron shown in the illustration on page 170.

Terrific; but two beats later, something puzzling hits you.
Why should the brain make receptors for a class of compounds
synthesized in poppy plants? The realization rushes in; there
must be some chemical — neurotransmitter? hormone? — made
in the body that is structurally very similar to opiates. Some kind
of endogenous morphine must occur naturally in the brain.

Neurochemists went wild at this point looking for endogenous morphine. It was a great chemistry problem in the abstract.
It was a fascinating applied problem to find the brain's natural
painkillers. And if one could modify these putative compounds
to make synthetic versions that blocked pain without being
addictive, there was a pot of gold to be earned.

In the ensuing years, competing teams of scientists found
exactly what they were looking for: endogenous compounds
with chemical structures reminiscent of the opiate drugs. They
turned out to come in three different classes — enkephalins,
dynorphins, and the most famous of them all, endorphins (a
contraction for "endogenous morphines"). The opiate receptors
were discovered to bind these endogenous opioid compounds,
just as predicted. Furthermore, the opioids were synthesized
and released in parts of the brain that regulated pain perception.
("Opiate" refers to analgesics not normally made by the body,
such as heroin or morphine. "Opioid" refers to those made by
the body itself. Because the field began with the study of the
opiates — since no one had discovered the opioids as yet — the
receptors found then were called opiate receptors. But clearly,
what their real job is is to bind the opioids.)

Chapter 7 introduced the finding that the endorphins and enkephalins also regulate sex hormone release. An additional intriguing finding concerning opioid action emerged: Release of these compounds explained how acupuncture worked. Until the 1970s, many Western scientists had heard about the phenomenon, but most had written it off, dumping it into a bucket of anthropological oddities—inscrutable Chinese herbalists sticking needles into people, Haitian witch doctors killing with voodoo curses, Jewish mothers curing any and all diseases with their secret-recipe chicken soup. Then, right around the time of the explosion in opiate research, Nixon opened China to the West, and documentation started coming out about the reality of acupuncture. Furthermore, scientists noted that Chinese veterinarians used acupuncture to do surgery on animals, thereby refuting the argument that the painkilling characteristic of acupuncture was one big placebo effect ascribable to cultural conditioning (no cow on earth will go along with unanesthetized surgery just because it has a heavy investment in the cultural mores of the society in which it dwells). Then, as the corker, a prominent Western journalist (James Reston of *The New York Times*) got appendicitis in China, underwent surgery using acupuncture as anesthesia, and he survived just fine.

Acupuncture stimulates the release of large quantities of endogenous opioids, for reasons no one really understands. The best demonstration of this is what is called a "subtraction" experiment. Employ a synthetic drug that blocks opiate receptors, cancelling out the activity of any endogenous opioids that are released: when such a receptor blocker (called naloxone) is active, acupuncture no longer effectively dulls the perception of pain.

All of this is a prelude to the discovery that stress releases opioids as well. This finding was first reported in 1977 by Roger Guillemin. Fresh from winning the Nobel Prize for the discoveries described in chapter 2, he demonstrated that stress triggers the release of one type of endorphin, beta-endorphin, from the pituitary gland.

The rest is history. We all know about the famed runner's high that kicks in after about half an hour and creates that glowing, irrational euphoria as you edge closer to collapse, just because the pain has gone away. During exercise, beta-endorphin pours out of the pituitary gland, finally building up to levels in the bloodstream around the thirty-minute mark that will cause analgesia. The other opiates, especially the enkephalins, are mobilized as well, mostly within the brain and spine. They activate the descending pathway originating in the brain to shut off the X neurons in the spinal cord, and they work directly at the spinal cord to accomplish the same thing. All sorts of other stressors produce similar effects. Surgery, low blood sugar, exposure to cold, examinations, spinal taps, giving birth —all do it.

Vic Boff, New York Polar Bear Club member known as "Mr. Iceberg," sitting in the snow after a swim during the blizzard of 1978.

Wonderful, very useful. Exactly the sort of stress-response needed to keep that zebra functioning when it is injured yet still must get away from the lion. To follow the structure laid out in previous chapters, this represents the good news. So what's the bad news? How does an excess of opioid release make us sick in the face of the chronic psychologic stressors that we specialize in? Does chronic stress make you an endogenous opioid addict? Does it cause so much of the stuff to be released that you can't detect useful pain anymore? What's the downside in the face of chronic stress?

Here the answer is puzzling, because it differs from all the other physiological systems examined in this book. When Hans Selye first began to note that chronic stress causes illness, he thought that illness occurs because an organism runs out of the stress-response — that the various hormones and neurotransmitters are depleted, and the organism is left vulnerable to the pummelings of the stressor, undefended. As we've seen in previous chapters, the modern answer is that the stress-response doesn't become depleted; instead, one gets sick because the stress-response itself eventually becomes damaging.

Opioids turn out to be the exception to the rule. Stress-induced analgesia does not go on forever, and the best evidence ascribes this to diminishing secretion of the particular opioids that are effective at blocking pain perception. You are not permanently out of business, but it takes a while for supply to catch up with demand.

To my knowledge, there is no stress-related disease that results from too much opioid release during sustained stressors. From the standpoint of this book and our propensity toward chronic psychologic stressors, that is good news — one less stress-related disease to worry about. From the standpoint of pain perception and the world of real physical stressors, the eventual depletion of the opioids means that the soothing effects of stress-induced analgesia are just a short-term fix. And for the elderly woman agonizing through terminal cancer, the soldier badly injured in combat, the zebra ripped to shreds but still alive, the consequence is obvious. The pain will soon return.

WHY IS PSYCHOLOGICAL STRESS STRESSFUL?

Some people are born to biology. You can spot them instantly as kids—they're the ones comfortably lugging around the toy microscopes, stowing dead squirrels in the freezer, ostracized at school for their obsession with geckos.* But all sorts of folks migrate to biology from other fields—chemists, psychologists, physicists, mathematicians.

Several decades after stress physiology began, the discipline was inundated by people who had spent their formative years as engineers. Like physiologists, they thought there was a

---

*Personally, I used to collect the leftover chicken bones from everyone at the Friday-night dinner table, clean them with my knife, and proudly display an articulated skeleton by the end of dessert. In retrospect, I think this was more to irritate my sister than to begin an anatomical quest. A biography of Teddy Roosevelt, however, recently helped me to appreciate that the world lost one of its great potential zoologists when he lapsed into politics. At age eighteen, he had already published professionally in ornithology; when he was half that age, he reacted to the news that his mother had thrown out his collection of field mice, stored in the family icebox, by moping around the house, proclaiming, "The loss to science! The loss to science!"

ferocious logic to how the body worked, but for bioengineers, that tended to mean viewing the body a bit like the circuitry diagram that you get with a new tape recorder: input-output ratios, impedance, feedback loops, servomechanisms. I shudder to even write such words, as I barely understand them; but the bioengineers did wonders for the field, adding a tremendous vigor.

Suppose you wonder how the brain knows when to stop glucocorticoid secretion—when enough is enough. In a vague sort of way, everyone knew that somehow the brain must be able to measure the amount of glucocorticoids in the circulation, compare that to some desired setpoint, and then decide whether to continue secreting CRF or turn off the faucet. The bioengineers came in and showed that the process was vastly more interesting and complicated than anyone had imagined. There are "multiple feedback domains"; some of the time the brain measures the *quantity* of glucocorticoids in the bloodstream, and sometimes how *fast* the level is changing. The bioengineers solved another critical issue: is the stress-response linear, or all-or-nothing? Epinephrine, glucocorticoids, prolactin, and other substances are all secreted during stress; but are they secreted to the same extent regardless of the intensity of the stressor (all-or-nothing responsiveness)? The system turns out, on the contrary, to be incredibly sensitive to the size of the stressor, demonstrating a linear relationship between the extent of blood pressure drop and the extent of epinephrine secretion, between the degree of hypoglycemia (drop in blood sugar) and glucagon release. The body not only can sense something stressful, but is amazingly accurate at measuring just how far and how fast that stressor is throwing the body out of homeostatic balance.

Beautiful stuff, and important. Selye loved the bioengineers, which makes perfect sense, since at his time the whole stress field must have still seemed a bit soft-headed to some mainstream physiologists. Those physiologists knew that the body does one set of things when it is too cold, and a diametrically opposite set when it is too hot, but here were Selye and his crew insisting that there were physiological mechanisms that . . . respond equally to cold *and* hot? *And* to injury *and* hypoglycemia *and* hypotension? The beleaguered stress experts welcomed the bioengineers with open arms. You see, it's for real; you can do math about stress, construct flow charts, feedback loops, formulas. . . . Golden days for the business. The system was turning out to be far more complicated than ever anticipated, but complicated in a way that was precise, logical, mechanistic. Soon it would be possible to model the body as one big input-output relationship: you tell me exactly to what degree a stressor impinges on an organism (how much it disrupts the homeostasis of blood sugar, fluid volume, optimal temperature,

FREE-FLOATING ANXIETY
(MAGNIFIED 200,000,000 TIMES)

and so on), and I'll tell you exactly how much of a stress-response is going to occur.

This approach, fine for most of the ground that we've covered up until now, will probably allow us to estimate quite accurately what the pancreas of that zebra is doing when the organism is sprinting from a lion. But the approach is not going to tell us which of us will get an ulcer when the factory closes down. Starting in the late 1950s, a new style of experiments in stress physiology began to be conducted that burst that lucid, mechanistic bioengineering bubble. A single example will suffice. An organism is subjected to a painful stimulus, and you are interested in how great a stress-response will be triggered. The bioengineers had been all over that one, mapping the relationship between the intensity and duration of the stimulus and the response. But this time, when the painful stimulus occurs, the organism under study can reach out for its Mommy and cry in her arms. And under these circumstances, this organism shows less of a stress-response.

Nothing in that clean, mechanistic world of the bioengineers could explain this phenomenon. The input was still the same; the same number of pain receptors should have been firing while the child underwent some painful procedure. Yet the output was completely different. A critical realization roared through the research community: the physiological stress-response can be modulated by psychological factors. Two identical stressors with the same extent of homeostatic disruption can be *perceived* differently, and the whole show changes from there.

Suddenly the stress-response could be made bigger or smaller, depending on psychological factors. In other words, psychological variables could *modulate* the stress-response. Inevitably, the next step was shown: in the absence of any change in physiological reality—any actual disruption of homeostasis—psychological variables alone could *trigger* the stress-response. Flushed with excitement, Yale physiologist John Mason, one of the leaders in this approach, even went so far as to proclaim that all stress-responses were psychological stress-responses.

The old guard was not amused. Just when the conception of stress was becoming systematized, rigorous, credible, along came this rabble of psychologists muddying up the picture. In a series of published exchanges in which they first praised each other's achievements and ancestors, Selye and Mason attempted to shred each other's work. Mason smugly pointed to the growing literature on psychological initiation and modulation of the stress-response. Selye, facing defeat, insisted that *all* stress-responses couldn't be psychological and perceptual: if an organism is anesthetized, it still gets a stress-response when a surgical incision is made.

The psychologists succeeded in getting a place at the table, and as they have acquired some table manners and a few gray hairs, they have been treated less like barbarians. We now have to consider which psychological variables are critical. Why is psychological stress stressful?

PSYCHOLOGICAL STRESSORS

You would expect key psychological variables to be mushy concepts to uncover, but in a series of elegant experiments, a physiologist at Rockefeller University named Jay Weiss demonstrated exactly what is involved. The subject of one experiment is a rat that receives mild electric shocks (roughly equivalent to the static shock you might get from scuffing your foot on a carpet). Over a series of these, the rat develops a prolonged stress-response: its heart rate and glucocorticoid secretion rate go up, for example. For convenience, we can express the long-term consequences by how likely the rat is to get an ulcer, and in this situation, the probability soars. In the next room, a different rat gets the same series of shocks—identical pattern and intensity; its homeostasis is challenged to exactly the same extent. But this time, whenever the rat gets a shock it can run over to a bar of wood and gnaw on it. The rat in this situation is far less likely to get an ulcer. You have given it an *outlet for its frustration*. Other types of outlets work as well—let the stressed rat eat something, drink water, or sprint on a running wheel, and it is less likely to develop an ulcer.

We humans also deal better with stressors when we have outlets for frustration—punch a wall, take a run, find solace in a hobby. We are even cerebral enough to *imagine* those outlets and derive some relief: consider the prisoner of war who spends hours imagining a golf game in tremendous detail. I have a friend who passed a prolonged and very stressful illness lying in bed with a mechanical pencil and a notepad, drawing topographic maps of imaginary mountain ranges and taking hikes through them.

A variant of Weiss's experiment uncovers a special feature of the outlet-for-frustration reaction. This time, when the rat gets the identical series of electric shocks and is upset, it can run across the cage, sit next to another rat and . . . bite the hell out of it. Stress-induced displacement of aggression: the practice works wonders at minimizing the stressfulness of a stressor. It's a real primate specialty as well. A male baboon loses a fight. Frustrated, he spins around and attacks a subordinate male who was minding his own business. The subadult lunges at an adult female, who bites a juvenile, who knocks an infant out of a tree. An extremely high percentage of primate aggression represents frustration displaced onto innocent bystanders. Humans are pretty good at it, too, and we have a technical way of describing the phenomenon in the context of stress-related disease: "He's one of those guys who doesn't get ulcers, he gives them." Taking it out on someone else—how well it works at minimizing the impact of a stressor.

There is an additional way in which we can interact with another organism to minimize the impact of a stressor on us, a way that is considerably more encouraging for the future of our planet than is displacement aggression. Rats rarely use it, but primates are great at it. Put an infant primate through something unpleasant: it gets a stress-response. Put it through the same stressor while in a room full of other primates and . . . it depends. If those primates are strangers, the stress-response gets worse. But if they are friends, the stress-response is decreased. *Social support networks*—it helps to have a shoulder to cry on, a hand to hold, an ear to listen to you, someone to cradle you and to tell you it will be okay.

Tooker, 1966: Landscape with Figures, *egg tempera on gesso.*

Sometimes remarkably little social contact is sufficient. In one subtle demonstration, the hormonal stress-response was studied in people who were undergoing a painful and frightening cardiac catheterization. Those who talked to their doctors about their fear during the procedure had smaller glucocorticoid stress-responses than the stoics.

Some of my work has uncovered the importance of these social support networks. While I mostly do laboratory research on how stress and glucocorticoids affect the brain, I spend my summers in Kenya studying patterns of stress-related physiology and disease among wild baboons living in a national park. The social life of a male baboon can be pretty stressful—you get beaten up as a victim of displaced aggression; you carefully search for some tuber to eat and clean it off, only to have it stolen by someone of higher rank; and so on. Glucocorticoid levels are elevated among low-ranking baboons, and among the entire group if the dominance hierarchy is unstable or after a new, aggressive male has joined the troop. But if you are a male baboon with a lot of friends—you play with kids, or you have frequent nonsexual grooming bouts with females, for example —you have lower glucocorticoid concentrations than males of the same general rank who lack these outlets. (In a similar vein, for both primates and humans, holding hands or making physical contact lowers cardiovascular response to stress.)

As noted in the chapter on immunity, people with spouses and/or close friends have longer life expectancies. When the spouse dies, the risk of dying skyrockets. Recall also from that chapter the study of parents of Israeli soldiers killed in the Yom Kippur War: In the aftermath of this stressor, there was no notable increase in risk of diseases or mortality—except among those who were already divorced or widowed. A final example: in a study of patients with severe coronary heart disease, Redford Williams of Duke University and colleagues found that half of those lacking social supports were dead within five years—a rate three times higher than was seen in patients who had a spouse or close friend.

The rat studies also uncovered another variable modulating the stress-response. The rat gets the same pattern of electric shocks, but this time, just before each shock, it hears a warning bell. Fewer ulcers. *Unpredictability* makes stressors much more stressful. The rat with the warning gets two pieces of information. It learns when something dreadful is about to happen. And the rest of the time, it learns that something dreadful is *not* about to happen. It can relax. The rat without a warning always feels as if it is a half-second away from the shock. In effect, information that increases predictability tells you that there is bad news, but comforts you that it's not going to be worse—you are going to get shocked soon, but it's never going to be sprung on you without warning. As another variant on the helpfulness of predictability, organisms will eventually habituate to a stressor if it is applied over and over; it may knock physiological homeostasis equally out of balance the umpteenth time that it happens, but it is a familiar, predictable stressor by then and a smaller stress-response is triggered. I've never appreciated the importance of predictability as much as after living through the 1989 San Francisco earthquake. Now I think, "Those lucky people elsewhere, they know what time of year you don't have to worry much about tornadoes or hurricanes. But an earthquake, now that could be any second, maybe even while I'm sitting bumper-to-bumper beneath this highway overpass."

The power of loss of predictability as a psychological stressor is shown in an elegant, subtle study. A rat is going about its business in its cage, and at measured intervals the experimenter delivers a piece of food down a chute into the cage; rat eats happily. This is called an intermittent reinforcement schedule. Change the pattern of food delivery so that the rat gets *exactly* the same total amount of food over the course of an hour, but at a random rate. The rat receives just as much reward, but less predictably; and up go glucocorticoid levels. There is not a single physically stressful thing going on in the rat's world. It's not hungry, pained, running for its life—nothing is out of homeostatic balance. In the absence of any stressor, loss of predictability triggers a stress-response.

There are even circumstances in which stress-related disease can be *more* likely to occur among individuals with the lower rate of stressors. You can easily imagine how to design a rat experiment to demonstrate this, but the human version has already been done. During the onset of the Nazi blitzkrieg bombings of England, London was hit every night like clockwork. Lots of stressful negative reinforcement. In the suburbs the bombings were far more sporadic, occurring perhaps once a week. Fewer stressful negative reinforcers, but much less predictability. There was a significant increase in the incidence of ulcers during that time. Who developed more ulcers? The suburban population. (Another measure of the importance of unpredictability: by the third month of the bombing, ulcer rates in all the hospitals had dropped back to normal.) A similar anxious state has often been described by individuals awaiting execution at an uncertain date. For example Gary Gilmore, the multiple murderer who was executed in 1977 amid a media circus in Utah, expressed relief bordering on euphoria when all the appeals through various courts and the stays of execution were finally exhausted. In such cases, uncertainty can eventually appear even worse than death.

Rat studies also demonstrate a related facet of psychological stress. Give the rat the same series of shocks. This time, however, you study a rat that has been trained to press a lever to avoid electric shocks. Take away the lever, shock it, and it develops a massive stress-response. It's as if the rat were thinking, "I can't believe this. I know what to do about electric shocks; give me a goddamn lever and I could handle this. This isn't fair." Ulceration city. Give the trained rat a lever to press; even if it is disconnected from the shock mechanism, it still helps: down goes the stress-response. So long as the rat has been exposed to a higher rate of shocks previously, it will think that the lower rate now is due to it having control over the situation. This is an extraordinarily powerful variable in modulating the stress-response.

The identical style of experiment with humans yields the same results. Place a person in each of two adjoining rooms, and expose both to intermittent noxious, loud noises; the person who has a button and believes that pressing it decreases the likelihood of more noise is less hypertensive. In one variant on this experiment, subjects with the button who did not bother to press it did just as well as those who actually pressed the button —the *exercise* of control is not critical; rather, it is the *belief* that you have it. An everyday example: airplanes are safer than cars, yet more of us are phobic about flying. Why? Because, despite the fact that we're at greater risk in a car, most of us in our heart of hearts believe that we are above-average drivers, thus more in control. In an airplane, we have no control at all. My wife and I, neither of us happy fliers, tease each other on flights, exchanging control: "Okay, you rest for awhile, I'll take over concentrating on keeping the pilot from having a stroke."

The variable of control is extremely important; controlling the rewards that you get can be more desirable than getting them for nothing. As an extraordinary example, both pigeons and rats prefer to press a lever in order to obtain food (so long as the task is not too difficult) over having the food delivered freely—a theme found in the activities and statements of many scions of great fortunes, who regret the contingency-free nature of their lives, without purpose or striving.

Some researchers have emphasized that the stressfulness of loss of control and of loss of predictability share a common element. They subject an organism to novelty. You thought you knew how to manage things, you thought you knew what would happen next, and it turns out you are wrong in this novel situation. Others have emphasized that these types of stressors cause arousal and vigilance, as you search for the new rules of control and prediction. Both views are different aspects of the same issue.

Yet another critical psychological variable has been uncovered. A hypothetical example: two rats get a series of electric shocks. On the first day, one gets 10 shocks an hour, the other 50. Next day, both get 25 shocks an hour. Who becomes hypertensive? Obviously, the one going from 10 to 25. The other rat is thinking, "25!? Piece of cheese, no problem, I can handle that." Given the same degree of disruption of homeostasis, a perception that events are improving helps tremendously. I recently observed a version of this among the baboons I study in Kenya. In general, when dominance hierarchies are unstable, resting glucocorticoid levels rise. This makes sense, because such instabilities make for stressful times. Looking at individual baboons, however, shows a more subtle pattern: given the same degree of instability, males whose ranks are *dropping* have elevated glucocorticoid levels, while males whose ranks are *rising* amid the tumult don't show this endocrine trait. Similarly, in one classic human study, parents who were told that their children had, for example, a 25 percent chance of dying from cancer showed only a moderate rise in glucocorticoid levels in the bloodstream. How could that be? Because the children were all in remission after a period where the odds of death had been far higher. Twenty-five percent must have seemed like a miracle. Twenty-five shocks an hour, a certain degree of social instability, a one in four chance of your child dying—each can imply either good news or bad, and only the latter seems to stimulate a stress-response.

Thus there are some powerful psychologic factors that can trigger a stress-response on their own or make another stressor seem more stressful: loss of control or predictability, loss of outlets for frustration or sources of support, a perception that things are getting worse. These factors play a major role in explaining how we all go through lives full of stressors, yet differ so dramatically in our vulnerability to them. The final chapter of this book examines the bases of these individual differences in greater detail, serving as a blueprint so that we can analyze how to learn to exploit these psychological variables — how in effect, to manage stress better. As we'll see, many ideas about stress management revolve around issues of control and predictability. However, the answer will not be simply "Maximize control. Maximize predictability. Maximize outlets for frustration." It is considerably more complicated than that.

SOME SUBTLETIES OF PREDICTABILITY

We have already seen how predictability can ameliorate the consequences of stress: one rat gets a series of shocks and develops a higher risk for an ulcer than the rat who gets warnings beforehand. Predictability doesn't always help, however. The experimental literature on this is pretty dense; some human examples of this point make it more accessible.

You're in the dentist's chair, no novocaine; the dentist drills away. Ten seconds of nerve-curling pain, some rinsing, five seconds of drilling, a pause while the dentist fumbles a bit, fifteen seconds of drilling, and so on. In one of the pauses, frazzled and trying not to whimper, you gasp, "Almost done?" "Hard to say," the dentist mumbles, returning to the intermittent drilling. Think how grateful we are for the dentist who, instead, says, "Two more and we're done." The instant the second burst of drilling ends, down goes blood pressure. By being given news about the stressor to come, you are also implicitly being comforted by now knowing what stressors are not coming.

But here are several scenarios, organized by the salient issues, where foreknowledge doesn't help. (Remember, the stressor is inevitable; the warning cannot change the stressor, just the perception of it.)

How predictable is the stressor, in the absence of a warning? What if, one morning, an omnipotent voice says, "There is

no way out of it; a meteor is going to crush your car while you're at work today (but it's the only time it will happen this year)." Not soothing. There's the good news that it's not going to happen again tomorrow, but that's hardly comforting; this is not an event that you anxiously fret over often. At the other extreme, what if one morning an omnipotent voice whispers, "Today it's going to be stressful on the rush hour subway — crowded, noisy, and impersonal. Tomorrow, too. In fact, every day this year, except November 9, when the subway will be clean and quiet, your fellow passengers polite, and the brakeman will insist you split his coffeecake with him." Who needs predictive information about the obvious fact that the subway is going to be stressful? Thus, warnings are less effective for very rare stressors (you don't usually worry much about meteors) and very frequent ones (they approach being predictable even without the warning).

How far in advance of the stressor does the warning come? Each day, you go for a mysterious appointment: you are led into a room with your eyes closed and are seated in a deep, comfortable chair. Then, with roughly even probabilities but no warning, either a rich, avuncular voice reads you to sleep with your favorite childhood stories, or a bucket of ice water is sloshed over your head. Not a pleasing prospect, I would bet. Would the whole thing be any less unsettling if you were told which treatment you were going to get five seconds before the event? Probably not — there is not enough time to derive any psychological benefits from the information. At the other extreme, would you wish for an omnipotent voice to tell you, "Eleven years and twenty-seven days from now your ice-water bath will last 10 full minutes"? Information either just before or long before the stressor does little good to alleviate the psychological anticipation.

Some types of predictive information can even increase the cumulative anticipatory stressor — vague information, for example. How about, "Attention all shoppers. Someone in this supermarket is going to be mugged soon (but only one person — good news) by a man who looks menacing." Won't every man now look menacing to every person there? Or if the stressor is terrible enough, no degree of warning is likely to be welcome. Would you be comforted by the omnipotent message, "Tomorrow an unavoidable accident will mangle your left leg, although your right leg will remain in great shape"?

Collectively, these scenarios tell us that predictability does not always work to protect us from stress. The much more systematic studies with animals suggest that it only works in a midrange of frequencies and intensities of stressors, and with certain lag times and levels of accurate information.

INTERNAL STRATEGIES FOR COPING

These ideas suggest to me that predictability, when it is working as a buffer from stress, helps humans differently from the way it does rats. The warning of impending shocks to the rat has little effect on the size of the stress-response *during* the shocks; instead, by allowing the rat to feel more confident about when it *doesn't* have to worry, it reduces the rat's anticipatory stress-response the rest of the time. Analogously, when the dentist says, "Only two more times and then we're done," it allows us to relax *at the end* of the second burst of drilling. But I suggest, although I cannot prove it, that unlike with the rat, proper information will also lower our stress-response *during* the pain. If you were told "only two times more" versus "only ten times more," wouldn't you use different mental strategies to try to cope? With each scenario, you would pull out the comforting thought of "only one more and then it's the last one" at different times; you would save your most distracting fantasy for a different point; you would try counting to zero from different numbers. Predictive information lets us know what internal coping strategy is likely to work best during a stressor.

SUBTLETIES OF CONTROL

To understand the subtleties of control, we need to return to the paradigm of the rat being shocked. It has been previously trained to press a lever to avoid shocks, and now it's pounding away like crazy on a lever. The lever does nothing; the rat is still getting shocked, but with less chance of an ulcer because the rat thinks it has control. To introduce a sense of control into the experimental design decreases the stress-response because, in effect, the rat is thinking, "Ten shocks an hour. Not bad; just imagine how bad it would be if I wasn't on top of it with my lever here." But what if things backfire, and adding a sense of control makes the rat think, "Ten shocks an hour, what's wrong with me?! I have a lever here, I should have avoided the shocks, it's my fault." If you believe you have control over inevitable stressors, you may consider it somehow to be your fault that the inevitable occurred.

An inappropriate sense of control in the face of awful events can make us feel terrible. Some of our most compassionate words to people experiencing tragedy involve minimizing their perceived sense of control. "It's not your fault, no one could have stopped in time, she just darted out from between the cars." "It's not something you could have done anything about, you tried your best, the economy's just lousy now." "Honey, getting him the best doctor in the world couldn't have cured him." And some of the most brutally callous of society's attempts to shift blame attribute more personal control during a stressor than exists. "She was asking for it" (rape victims have the control to prevent the rape). "It's your fault that your child is schizophrenic" (schizophrenia is generated by poor mothering —a destructive belief that dominated psychiatry for decades before the disease was recognized to be neurochemical). "If they'd only made the effort to assimilate, they wouldn't have these problems" (minorities have the power to prevent their persecution).

The effects of the sense of control on stress are highly dependent on context. In general, if the stressor is of a sort where it is easy to imagine how much worse it could have been, inserting an artificial sense of control helps. "That was awful, but think of how bad it would have been if I hadn't done X." But when the stressor is truly awful, an artificial sense of control is damaging—it is difficult to conceive a yet-worse scenario that you managed to avoid, but easy to be appalled by the disaster you didn't prevent.

These subtleties about control and predictability help to explain a confusing feature of the stress literature. In general, the less control and/or predictability, the more at risk you are for a stress-induced disease. Yet an experiment conducted by Joseph Brady in 1958 with monkeys gave rise to the view that more control and more predictability cause ulcers. Half of the animals could press a bar to delay shocks ("executive" monkeys); the other half were passively yoked to one of the "executives" such that they received a shock whenever the first one did. In this widely reported study, the executive monkeys were more likely to develop ulcers. Out of these studies came the popular concept of the "executive stress syndrome" and associated images of executive humans weighed down with the stressful burdens of control, leadership, and responsibility. Ben Natelson, of the V.A. Medical Center in East Orange, N.J., along with Jay Weiss, noted some problems with that study. First, it was conducted with parameters where control and predictability are bad news. Second, the "executive" and "nonexecutive" monkeys were not chosen randomly; instead, the monkeys that tended to press the bar first in pilot studies were selected to be executives. Monkeys that press sooner have since been shown to be more emotionally reactive animals, so Brady was inadvertently stacking the executive side with the more reactive, ulcer-prone monkeys. In general, executives of all species are more likely to be giving ulcers than to be getting them.

To summarize, stress-responses can be modulated or even caused by psychological factors, including loss of outlets for frustration and of social support, a perception of things worsening, and under some circumstances, a loss of control and of predictability. These ideas have vastly expanded our ability to answer the question, "Why do only some of us get stress-related diseases?" Obviously we differ as to the number of stressors that befall us. And after all the chapters on physiology, you can guess that we differ in how fast our adrenals make glucocorticoids, how many insulin receptors we have in our fat cells, the thickness of our stomach walls, and so on. But in addition to those physiological differences, we can now add another dimension. We differ in the psychological filters through which we perceive the stressors in our world. Two people participating in the same event—a long wait at the supermarket checkout, public speaking, parachuting out of an airplane—may differ dramatically in their psychological perception of the event. "Oh, I'll just read a magazine while I wait" (control for frustration); "I'm nervous as hell, but by giving this after-dinner talk, I'm a shoo-in for that promotion" (things are getting better); "This is great—I always wanted to try sky-diving" (this is something I'm in control of).

In the next chapter we will consider depression as, in part, a failure of some psychological defenses against stress. And in the final chapter we will examine how stress-management techniques can aid us by teaching how to exploit these psychological defenses.

STRESS AND DEPRESSION

We are morbidly fascinated with the exotica of disease. They fill our made-for-television movies, our tabloids, and the book reports of adolescents thinking about entering medical school someday. Victorians with Elephant Man's disease, murderers with multiple personality disorders, ten-year-olds with progeria, idiot savants with autism, cannibals with kuru. Who could resist? But when it comes to the bread and butter of human misery, try a major depression. It can be life-threatening, it can sabotage careers for years on end, it can demolish the families of sufferers. And it is dizzyingly common — the psychologist Martin Seligman has called it the common cold of psychopathology. Best estimates are that from 5 to 20 percent of us will suffer a major, incapacitating depression at some point in our lives, causing us to be hospitalized or medicated or nonfunctional for a significant length of time.

This chapter differs a bit from those that preceded it, in which the concept of "stress" was at the very forefront. Initially, that may not seem to be the case in our focus on depression. The two appear to be inextricably linked, however, and the concept of stress will run through every page of this chapter. It is impossible to understand either the biology or psychology of major depressions without recognizing the critical role played in the disease by stress.

To begin to understand this connection, it is necessary to get some sense of the disorder's characteristics. We have first to wrestle with a semantic problem. "Depression" is a term that we all use in an everyday sense. Something mildly or fairly upsetting happens to us, and we get "the blues" for awhile; then we recover. This is not what psychologists and psychiatrists mean when referring to a major depression. Instead, this vastly crippling disorder leads people to attempt suicide; its victims may lose their jobs, family, and all social contact because they cannot force themselves to get out of bed, or refuse to go to a psychiatrist because they feel they don't deserve to get better. It is a horrific disease, and throughout this chapter I will be referring to this major, devastating form of depression, rather than the transient blues that we may casually signify with the term "feeling depressed."

THE SYMPTOMS

The defining feature of a major depression is loss of pleasure. If I had to define a major depression in a single sentence, I would describe it as a "genetic/neurochemical disorder requiring a strong environmental trigger whose characteristic manifestation is an inability to appreciate sunsets." Depression can be as tragic as cancer or a spinal cord injury. Think about what our lives are about. None of us will live forever, and on occasion we actually believe that; our days are filled with disappointments, failures, unrequited loves. Despite this, almost inconceivably, we not only cope but even feel vast pleasures. I, for example, am resoundingly mediocre at soccer, but nothing keeps me from my game with other faculty members each week. Invariably there comes a moment when I manage to gum up someone more

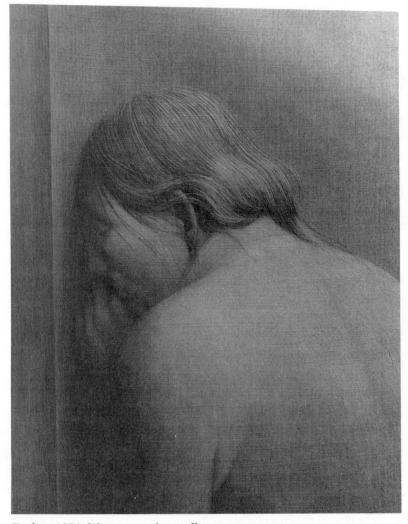

Tooker, 1974: Woman at the wall, *egg tempera on gesso.*

adept than I; I'm panting and heaving and pleased and there's still plenty more time to play and a breeze and I suddenly feel dizzy with gratitude for my animal existence. What could be more tragic than a disease which, as its defining symptom, robs us of that capacity?

This trait is called "anhedonia." Hedonism, the pursuit of pleasure; anhedonia, the inability to feel pleasure. Anhedonia is consistent among depressives. A woman has just received the long-sought promotion; a man has just become engaged to the woman of his dreams — and, amid their depression, they will tell you how they feel nothing, how it really doesn't count, how they don't deserve it.

Accompanying major depression are great grief and great guilt. We often feel grief and guilt in the everyday sadnesses that we refer to as depression. But this occurs to an incapacitating degree in a major depression. In a subset of such patients, such thinking can take on the quality of a delusion. By this, I do not mean the thought-disordered delusions of schizophrenics; instead, delusional thinking in depressives is of the sort where facts are distorted, over- or underinterpreted to the point where one must conclude that things are terrible and getting worse, hopeless.

An example: A middle-aged man, out of the blue, has a crippling heart attack. Overwhelmed by his implied mortality, the transformation of his life, he slips into a major depression. Despite this, he is recovering from the attack reasonably well, and there is every chance that he will resume a normal life. But each day he's sure he's getting worse.

The hospital in which he is staying is circular in construction, with a corridor that forms a loop. One day, the nurses walk him once around the hospital before he collapses back in bed. The next day, he does two laps; he is getting stronger. That evening, when his family visits, he explains to them that he is sinking. "What are you talking about? The nurses said that you did two loops today; yesterday you only did one." No, no, he shakes his head sadly, you don't understand. He explains that the hospital is being renovated and, um, well, last night they closed off the old corridor and opened a newer, smaller one. And, you see, the distance around the new loop is less than half the distance of the old one, so twice on that is still less than I could do yesterday.

This particular incident occurred with the father of a friend, an engineer who lucidly described radii and circumferences, expecting his family to believe that the hospital had opened up a new corridor through the core of the building in one day. This is delusional thinking; the emotional energies behind the analysis and evaluation are disordered so that the everyday world is interpreted in a way that leads to depressive conclusions—it's awful, getting worse, and this is what I deserve.

Cognitive therapists—like Aaron Beck of the University of Pennsylvania—even consider depression to be primarily a disorder of thought, rather than emotion, in that sufferers tend to see the world in a distorted, negative way. Beck and colleagues have conducted striking studies that provide evidence for this. For example, they might show an individual two pictures. In the first, a group of people are gathered happily around a dinner table, feasting. In the second, the same people are gathered around a coffin. Show the two pictures rapidly or simultaneously; which one is remembered? Depressives see the funeral scene at rates higher than chance. They are not only depressed about something, but see the goings-on around them in a distorted way that always reinforces that feeling. Their glasses are always half empty.

Another feature of a major depression is called psychomotor retardation. The person moves and speaks slowly. Everything requires tremendous effort and concentration. She finds the act of merely arranging a doctor's appointment exhausting. Soon it is too much to even get out of bed and get dressed. (It should be noted that not all depressives show psychomotor retardation; some may show the opposite pattern, termed psychomotor agitation.) People suffering from major depression also lose interest in sex. If anhedonia is a defining feature of the disorder, what is more likely to be affected than one of the most pleasurable things you can do with your body and mind?

Many of us tend to think of depressives as people who get the same everyday blahs as you and I, but that for them it just spirals out of control. We may also have the sense, whispered out of earshot, that these are people who just can't handle normal ups and downs, who are indulging themselves. (Why can't they just get themselves together?) A major depression, however, is as real a disease as diabetes. Another set of depressive symptoms supports that view. Basically, many things in the bodies of depressives work peculiarly; these are generally called "vegetative symptoms." You and I get an everyday depression. What do we do? Typically, we sleep more than usual, probably eat more than usual, convinced in some way that such comforts will make us feel better. These traits are just the opposite of the vegetative symptoms seen in most people with major depressions. Eating declines. Sleeping does as well, and in a distinctive manner. While depressives have the trouble falling asleep that one might expect, they also have the problem of "early morning wakening," spending months on end sleepless and exhausted from three-thirty or so each morning. "Do you tend to wake up very early in the morning?" is, in fact, one of the most likely questions you would be asked by an admitting doctor if you arrived at an emergency room severely depressed. Not only is sleep shortened, but the "architecture" of sleep is different as well — the normal pattern of shifting between deep and shallow sleep, the rhythm of the onset of dream states, are disturbed.

As additional vegetative symptoms, major depressives often experience elevated levels of glucocorticoids. This is critical. When looking at a depressive sitting on the edge of the bed, barely able to move, it is easy to think of the person as energyless, enervated. A more accurate picture is of the depressive as a tightly coiled spool of wire, tense, straining, active — but all inside. As we will see, a psychodynamic view of depression shows the person fighting an enormous, aggressive mental battle. In that regard, depressives bear some resemblance to an animal sprinting across the savanna — no wonder they have elevated levels of stress hormones.

Another feature of depression also confirms that it is a real disease, rather than merely the situation of someone who simply cannot handle everyday ups and downs. There are multiple *types* of depressions, and they can look quite different. In one variant, unipolar depression, the sufferer fluctuates from feeling extremely depressed to feeling reasonably normal. In another form, the individual fluctuates between deep depression and wild, disorganized hyperactivity. This is called bipolar depression or, more familiarly, manic depression (to complicate things further, there are even subtypes of manic depression). Here we run into another complication because, just as we use "depression" in an everyday sense that is different from the medical sense, "mania" has an everyday connotation as well. We may use the term distortively to refer to madness, as in made-for-television homicidal maniacs. Or we could describe someone as being in a manic state when he is buoyed by some unexpected good news—talking quickly, laughing, gesticulating. But the mania found in manic depression is of a completely different magnitude. Let me give an example of the disorder: A woman comes into the emergency room. She's bipolar, florid, completely manic, hasn't been taking her medication. She's on welfare, doesn't have a cent to her name, and in the last week she's bought *three* Cadillacs with money from loan sharks. And, get this, she doesn't even know how to drive. People in manic states will go for days on three hours of sleep a night and feel rested, will talk nonstop for hours at a time, will be vastly distractible, unable to concentrate amid their racing thoughts. Mainly, in outbursts of irrational grandiosity, they will behave in ways that are foolhardy or dangerous to themselves and others—poisoning themselves in attempting to prove their immortality, burning down their homes, giving away their life savings to strangers. It is a profoundly destructive disease.

The strikingly different subtypes of depression and their variability suggest not just a single disease, but a heterogeneity of diseases. Another feature of the disorder also indicates a biological abnormality. A patient comes to a doctor in the tropics. The patient is running a high fever that abates, only to come back a day or two later, abate again, return again, and so on every 48 to 72 hours. The doctor will recognize this instantly as malaria, because of the rhythmicity of the disorder. It has to do with the life cycle of the malarial parasite as it moves from red blood cells to the liver and spleen. The rhythmicity screams biology. In the same way, certain subtypes of depression have a rhythm. A manic-depressive may be manic for five days, followed by a week of severe depression, half a week or so of mild depression, and then a few weeks symptom-free. Then the pattern starts up again—and has been doing so for a decade.

Good things, bad things happen, but the same cyclic rhythm continues—which suggests just as much deterministic biology as in the life cycle of the malarial parasite. In another subset of depression, only recently characterized, the rhythm is annual—sufferers get depressed during the winter. Called seasonal affective disorders (SADS—"affective" is the psychiatric term for emotional responses), these are thought to be related to patterns of exposure to light. Again, the rhythmicity appears independent of external life events; there is a biological clock ticking away in there that has something to do with mood, and there is something seriously wrong with its ticking.

THE BIOLOGY OF DEPRESSION

Considerable evidence exists that something is awry with the chemistry of the brains of depressives. In order to appreciate that, it is necessary to learn a bit about how brain cells communicate with each other. The illustration on page 204 shows a schematic version of two neurons, the principal type of brain cell. If a neuron has become excited with some thought or memory (metaphorically speaking), its excitement is electrical—a wave of electricity sweeps from the dendrites over the cell body, down the axon to the axon terminals. When the wave of electrical excitation reaches the axon terminal, it releases chemical messengers that float across the synapse. These messengers —neurotransmitters—bind to specialized receptors on the adjacent dendrite, causing the second neuron to become electrically excited.

   A minor piece of housekeeping, however; what happens to the neurotransmitter molecule after it has done its job and floats off the receptor? In some cases, it is recycled—taken back up by the axon terminal of the first neuron and repackaged for future use. Or it can be degraded in the synapse and the debris flushed out to sea (the cerebrospinal fluid, then to the blood, and then the urine). If these processes of clearing neurotransmitters out of the way fail (reuptake ceases or degradation stops or both),

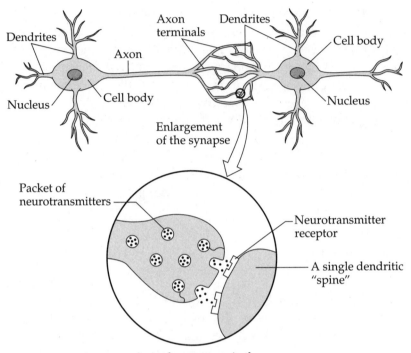

A single axon terminal

A neuron that has been excited conveys information to other neurons by means of chemical signals at synapses, the contact points between neurons. When the impulse reaches the axon terminal of the signaling neuron, it induces the release of neurotransmitter molecules. Transmitters diffuse across a narrow cleft and bind to receptors in the adjacent neuron's dendritic spine.

suddenly a lot more neurotransmitter remains in the synapse, giving a stronger signal to the second neuron than usual. Thus, the proper disposal of these powerful messengers is integral to normal neuronal communication.

There are trillions of synapses in the brain. Do we need trillions of chemically unique neurotransmitters? Certainly not. You can generate a seemingly infinite number of messages with a finite number of messengers; consider how many words we can form with the mere 26 letters in our alphabet. All you need are rules that allow for the same messenger to convey different meanings, metaphorically speaking, in different contexts. At one synapse, neurotransmitter A sends a message relevant to pancreatic regulation, while at another synapse the same neurotransmitter substance may pertain to adolescent crushes. There are many neurotransmitters, probably on the order of a few hundred, but certainly not trillions.

The best neurochemical evidence suggests that depression involves too little of one or both of a pair of neurotransmitters, norepinephrine and serotonin. We start with the former, for which the evidence of an involvement was first acquired. You are no doubt thinking, wasn't there something about norepinephrine and the sympathetic nervous system many chapters ago? Absolutely, and that proves the point about the varied roles played by any given neurotransmitter. In one part of the body (the heart, for example), norepinephrine is a messenger concerning arousal and the four F's, while in a different part of the nervous system, norepinephrine seems to have something to do with the symptoms of depression.

The best evidence for the "norepinephrine hypothesis" is that most of the drugs that lessen depression increase the amount of norepinephrine signaling in the nervous system. One class of antidepressants, called tricyclics (a reference to their biochemical structure), stops the recycling, or reuptake, of norepinephrine into the axon terminals. The result is that the neurotransmitter remains in the synapse longer, and is likely to hit the receptor a second or third time. Another class of drugs, called MAO inhibitors, blocks the degradation of norepinephrine in the synapse (by inhibiting the action of a crucial enzyme, monoamine oxidase [MAO]). The result, again, is that more of the messenger remains in the synapse to stimulate the dendrite of the receiving neuron.

As a second piece of evidence, if norepinephrine levels in axon terminals throughout the brain are decreased in normal people, they can become depressed. This often happens by accident. Suppose a person is suffering from hypertension. Aha, you conclude, too much sympathetic arousal, give the person a drug that depletes neurons in the sympathetic nervous system of norepinephrine. Terrific, blood pressure goes down. The trouble is, it is extremely difficult to design a drug that enters a person's stomach or bloodstream and targets only those norepinephrine synapses regulating blood pressure. The medication is likely to decrease the level of the neurotransmitter everywhere in the body, and along with the hypotension — and lower levels of norepinephrine — comes a depression. (The reader may now be wondering if raising norepinephrine levels in depressives with antidepressant drugs causes the side effect of high blood pressure. That indeed often occurs with some types of antidepressants, especially when ingested with certain foods.)

If too little norepinephrine plays a significant role in depression, as it appears to do, how might it affect depressive symptoms? There are two main schools of thought.

The pleasure-pathway hypothesis is my favorite, because of its charm. Several decades ago, some neuroscientists made a fundamental discovery. They had implanted electrodes into the brains of rats and stimulated areas here and there, seeing what would happen. By doing so, they found an extraordinary area of the brain. Whenever this area was stimulated, the rat became *unbelievably happy*. How can one tell when a rat is unbelievably happy? You ask the rat to tell you, by charting how many times it is willing to press a lever in order to be rewarded with stimulation in that part of the brain. It turns out that rats will work themselves to death on that lever to get stimulation. They would rather be stimulated there than get food when they are starving, or have sex, or receive drugs even when they're addicted and going through withdrawal. The region of the brain targeted in these studies was promptly called the "pleasure pathway" and has been famous since.

That humans also have a pleasure pathway was discovered shortly afterward by stimulating a similar part of the human brain during neurosurgery.* The results are pretty amazing.

---

*Because the brain is not sensitive to pain, a lot of such surgery is done on patients who are awake (with their scalps anesthetized, of course). This is helpful because prior to modern imaging techniques, surgeons often had to have the patient awake to guide what they were doing. Place an electrode in the brain, stimulate, the patient flops her arm. Go a little deeper with the electrode, stimulate, and the patient flops her leg. Quick, consult your brain road map, figure out where you are, go an inch deeper, hang a left past the third neuron, and there's the tumor. That sort of thing.

Something along the lines of "Aaaaaaah, boy, that feels good." It's kind of like getting your back rubbed but also sort of like sex or playing in the backyard in the leaves when you're a kid and Mom calling you in for hot chocolate and then you get into your pajamas with the feet. . . . Where can we sign up?

Although the neurochemistry of this pleasure pathway is not well understood, there is some indication that certain synapses along the pathway use norepinephrine. Suddenly there is a glimmer of coherence. If depressives have too little norepinephrine in this pathway, it won't communicate properly: signals don't go through, pleasures aren't perceived. Anhedonia. (A consideration for this theory: in recent years, scientists have found that a neurotransmitter called dopamine, rather than norepinephrine, is the preeminent chemical messenger of the pleasure pathway. However, it may be that as long as norepinephrine plays some role in the proper functioning of the pathway, even if not the preeminent one, a depletion of norepinephrine brings about anhedonia.)

In the competing motor-pathway hypothesis, the norepinephrine shortage in depressives does not so much affect the perception of pleasure as the ability to actually do things. Here the key symptom is not anhedonia, but the psychomotor retardation of depression — individuals become helpless, passive, unable to perform simple tasks. Critical to this scenario is norepinephrine's role as an important neurotransmitter in pathways in the brain that regulate motor function.

There are passionate adherents to each view of how norepinephrine shortage may affect the symptoms of depression; no conclusive evidence yet favors one side over the other. Recent research increasingly suggests that neither school may be correct, because there are some problems with the norepinephrine hypothesis. The first has to do with timing. Expose the brain to some tricyclic antidepressant, and norepinephrine signaling in the synapses changes within hours. However, give that same drug to a depressed person, and it takes weeks for the person to feel better. Something doesn't quite fit. Two theories have arisen in recent years that might reconcile this problem with timing, and they are both extremely complicated.

Revisionist theory #1, the "it's not too little norepineph-rine, it's actually too *much* norepinephrine" hypothesis. First, some orientation. If somebody constantly yells at you, you stop listening. Analogously, if you inundate a cell with lots of a neurotransmitter, the cell will not "listen" as carefully — it will "down-regulate" (decrease) the number of receptors for that neurotransmitter, in order to decrease its sensitivity to that mes-senger. If, for example, you double the amount of norepineph-rine reaching the dendrites of a cell and that cell down-regulates its norepinephrine receptors by 50 percent, the changes roughly cancel out. If the cell down-regulates less than 50 percent, the net result is more norepinephrine signaling in the synapse; if more than 50 percent, the result is actually less signaling in the synapse. In other words, how strong the signal is in a synapse is a function both of how loudly the first neuron yells (the amount of neurotransmitter released) and of how sensitively the second neuron listens (how many receptors it has for the neuro-transmitter).

Ok, ready. This revisionist theory states that the original problem is that there is actually too much norepinephrine in parts of the brains of depressives. What happens when you prescribe antidepressants that increase norepinephrine signaling even further? At first, that should make the depressive symp-toms worse. (Some psychiatrists argue that this actually does occur.) Over the course of a few weeks, however, the dendrites say, "This is intolerable, all this norepinephrine; let's down-reg-ulate our norepinephrine receptors a whole lot." If this occurs and, critical to the theory, more than compensates for the in-creased norepinephrine signal, the depressive problem of exces-sive norepinephrine signaling goes away: the person feels bet-ter. Note, with this theory, that we now have to explain why too much norepinephrine accounts for depressive symptoms in the first place.

Revisionist theory #2, "it really *is* too little norepinephrine after all." This theory is even more complicated than the first, and also requires orientation. Not only do dendrites contain receptors for neurotransmitters, but it turns out that on the axon terminals of the "sending" neuron, as well, there are receptors for the very neurotransmitters being released by that neuron. What possible purpose could these so-called "autoreceptors" serve? Neurotransmitters are released, float into the synapse, bind to the standard receptors on the second neuron. Some neurotransmitter molecules, however, will float back and wind up binding to the autoreceptors. They serve as some sort of feedback signal; if, say, 5 percent of the released neurotransmitter reaches the autoreceptors, the first neuron can count its metaphorical toes, multiply by 20, and figure out how much neurotransmitter it has released. Then it can make some decisions—should I release more neurotransmitter or stop now? Should I start synthesizing more? and so on. If this process lets the first neuron do its bookkeeping on neurotransmitter expenditures, what happens if the neuron down-regulates a lot of these autoreceptors? Underestimating the amount of neurotransmitter it has released, the neuron will inadvertently start increasing the amount it synthesizes and discharges.

With this as background, here's the reasoning behind the second theory (that there really is too little norepinephrine in a part of the brain of depressives). Give the antidepressant drugs that increase norepinephrine signaling. Because of the increased signaling, over the course of weeks there will be down-regulation of norepinephrine receptors. Critical to this theory is the idea that the autoreceptors on the first neuron will down-regulate to a greater extent than the receptors on the second neuron. If that happens, the second neuron may not be listening as well, but the first one will be releasing sufficient extra norepinephrine to more than overcome that. The net result is enhanced norepinephrine signaling, and depressive symptoms abate. (This mechanism may explain the efficacy of electroconvulsive therapy [ECT, or "shock therapy"]. For decades psychiatrists have used this technique to alleviate major depressions, and no one has quite known why it works. It turns out that, among its many effects, ECT decreases the number of norepinephrine autoreceptors, at least in experimental animal models.)

Aside from the problem associated with timing, there is a second major difficulty with the idea that norepinephrine (whether released in levels that are too high or too low) has something to do with depression. All of the drugs mentioned above work on norepinephrine synapses, as described, but they also work nearly as well on synapses for the neurotransmitter serotonin. The bias in the field for many years was to ignore the serotonin part of the story. In the last few years, however, a new class of antidepressants has burst on the scene and seems to be very effective. These drugs, the best known of which is marketed as Prozac, are very specific in their effects on the serotonin synapse. More problems for the norepinephrine zealots.

At this stage, most researchers in the field believe that the most likely neurochemical defects in depression involve both norepinephrine and serotonin — either in the amounts released or in the regulation of their receptors (either pre- or postsynaptic). Clearly, there is no definitive answer yet, and I suspect that the final story will involve additional neurotransmitters — perhaps ones still to be discovered.

I introduce an illustration (below) of what the brain looks

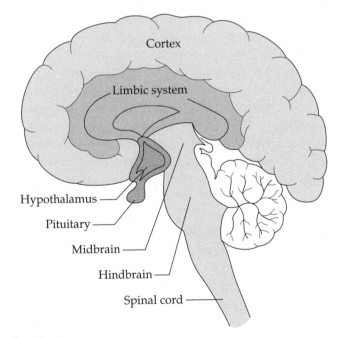

The triune brain.

like, to consider a second way in which brain function might be abnormal in depressives, in addition to the neurochemistry just discussed. One region regulates processes like your breathing and heart rate. It includes the hypothalamus, which is busy releasing hormones and instructing the autonomic nervous system. If your blood pressure drops drastically, causing a compensatory stress-response, it is the hypothalamus, midbrain, and hindbrain that kick into gear. All sorts of vertebrates have roughly the same connections here.

Layered on top of that is a region called the limbic system, the functioning of which is related to emotion. As mammals, we have large limbic systems; lizards have relatively tiny limbic systems—they are not noted for the complexity of their emotional lives. If you get a stress-response from smelling the odor of a threatening rival, it's your limbic system that is involved.

Above that is the cortex. Everyone in the animal kingdom has some, but it is a real primate specialty. The cortex does abstract cognition, invents philosophy, remembers where your car keys are.

Now think for a second. Suppose you are gored by an elephant. You may feel a certain absence of pleasure afterward, maybe a sense of grief. Throw in a little psychomotor retardation—you're not as eager for your calisthenics as usual. Sleeping and feeding may be disrupted, glucocorticoid levels may be a bit on the high side. Sex may lose its appeal for awhile. Hobbies are not as enticing; you don't jump up to go out with friends; you pass up that all-you-can-eat buffet. Sound like some of the symptoms of a depression?

Now what happens during a depression? You think a thought—about your mortality or that of a loved one; you imagine children in refugee camps; the rainforests disappearing and endless species of life evaporating; late Beethoven string quartets—and suddenly you experience some of the same symptoms as after being gored by the elephant. On an incredibly simplistic level, you can think of depression as occurring when your cortex thinks an abstract negative thought and manages to convince the rest of the brain that this is as real as a physical stressor. In this view, people with chronic depressions are those whose cortex habitually whispers sad things to the rest of the brain. Thus, an astonishingly crude prediction: *cut* the connections between the cortex and the rest of a depressive's brain and the cortex will no longer be able to get the rest of the brain depressed.

Remarkably, it actually works sometimes. The procedure is called a cingulotomy, or a cingulum bundle cut, and neurosurgeons may perform it on people with vastly crippling depressions that are resistant to drugs, other therapy, and ECT. Afterward, the flow of information from the cortex to the rest of the brain is greatly curtailed (by cutting projection pathways from the former to the latter, you are cutting axons), and depressive symptoms seem to abate. (What else changes after a cingulotomy? If the cortex can no longer send abstract thoughts to the rest of the brain, the person should not only lose the capacity for abstract misery but for abstract pleasure as well, and this is what happens; but cingulotomy is a therapy employed only in patients completely incapacitated by their illness, who spend decades on the back ward of some state hospital, rocking and clutching themselves and feebly attempting suicide with some regularity.)

So we have a few biological links in depression. There also appear to be hormonal abnormalities in many cases. Some depressives secrete abnormally high levels of glucocorticoids. This adds to the picture that depressed people, sitting on the edge of their beds without the energy to get up, are vigilant and aroused, with a hormonal profile to match—but the battle is inside them. As another hormonal feature of the story, people who secrete too little thyroid hormone can develop major depressions. This is particularly important because many people, seemingly with depressions of a purely psychiatric nature, turn out to have thyroid disease. There also may be hormonal imbalances in those who suffer from seasonal affective disorders. The evidence here points to a hormone called "melatonin" whose secretion is regulated by light (this hormone plays an important role in bringing about spring fever and synchronized matings in animals—for example, the matings of all the wildebeests on earth take place the same week of the year). Some who believe

that SAD is due to abnormal melatonin levels are trying melatonin or light therapy for depression, but it is not yet clear
whether this is effective.

There is another aspect of depression in which hormones
may play a role. The incidence rates of major depressions differ
greatly, with women suffering far more than men. Why? One
theory, from the school of cognitive therapy, concentrates on
the ways in which women and men tend to think differently.
When something upsetting happens, women are more likely to
ruminate over it—think about it or want to talk about it with
someone else. And men, terrible communicators that they so
often are, are more likely to want to think about anything but
the problem, or even better, go and *do* something—exercise, use
power tools, get drunk, start a war. A ruminative tendency, the
cognitive psychologists argue, makes you more likely to become
depressed.

Another theory about the sex difference is psychosocial in
nature. As we will see, much theorizing about the psychology of
depression suggests that it is a disorder of lack of control, and
some scientists have speculated that because women in so many
societies traditionally have less control over the circumstances of
their lives than do men, they are at greater risk for depression.
Both theories are fine, except they fail to explain why women
and men have the same rates of bipolar depressions; it is only
unipolar depressions that are more common among women.

Both these theories seem particularly weak in their failure
to explain a major feature of female depressions—namely, that
women are particularly at risk for depressions at certain reproductive points: menstruation, menopause, and most of all, the
weeks immediately after giving birth. A number of researchers
believe such increased risks are tied to the great fluctuations that
occur during menstruation, menopause, and parturition in two
main hormones: estrogen and progesterone. As evidence, they
cite the fact that women can get depressed when they artificially
change their estrogen and/or progesterone levels (for example,
when taking birth-control pills). Critically, both of these hormones can regulate neurochemical events in the brain—
including the metabolism of neurotransmitters such as norepi-

nephrine and serotonin. With massive changes in hormone levels (a thousandfold for progesterone at the time of giving birth, for example), current speculation centers on the possibility that the ratio of estrogen to progesterone can change radically enough to trigger a major depression. This is a new area of research with some seemingly contradictory findings, but there is more and more confidence among scientists that there is a hormonal contribution to the preponderance of female depressions.

Note, at this juncture, another sex difference related to depression, one that has less to do with science than with the way science is conducted. Women tend to develop more side effects from antidepressant drugs than do men, and clinical dogma has been that women are more "sensitive" to these compounds. The explanation of this is now known. Suppose you are a scientist who has discovered a new type of antidepressant. You want to test it out. Whom do you choose? Usually male rats, male monkeys, and male undergraduate volunteers. When you do that, you get a pretty good sense of what the proper dose should be for a male. It turns out that estrogen regulates the rate at which these drugs are degraded in the bloodstream, so that more of the medication reaches the female brain — that is, the same amount of drug has a greater impact (and more side effects) in females. If the bias in science were, when investigating something new and potentially helpful, to test it first in females, the clinical dogma would probably be that men, "for some reason," are rather "insensitive" to these compounds, so you have to give them more than the dosage for a "normal" person. This further underlines an important point in pharmacology: it is not only allowable, but often essential to take into account factors like age, sex, race, and ethnicity in figuring out what is appropriate dosage of a drug.

Strong evidence exists that there are biological underpinnings to major depressions — imbalances in levels of neurotransmitters, and perhaps hormonal abnormalities as well. Yet despite the modern potential for various pharmacological, hormonal, or surgical interventions, we're still dismally poor at curing depressions by taking a purely biological approach to the illness. It is time to take a look at some of the psychological features of depression and the role of stress.

THE PSYCHOLOGY OF MAJOR DEPRESSIONS

I have to begin with Freud. I know it is terribly stylish to dump on Freud these days, and I suppose some of it is deserved, but there is much that he still has to offer. There are few other scientists I can think of who, eighty years after they have completed the bulk of their work, are still considered important and correct enough for anyone to want to bother pointing out their errors instead of just consigning them to the library archives.

Freud was fascinated with depression and focused on the issue that we began with—why is it that most of us can have occasional terrible experiences, feel depressed, and then recover, while a few of us collapse into major depression ("melancholia")? In his classic essay "Mourning and Melancholia" (1917), Freud began with what the two have in common. In both cases, he felt, there is the loss of a love object. (In Freudian terms, such an "object" is usually a person, but can also be a goal or an ideal.) In Freud's formulation, in every loving relationship there is ambivalence, mixed feelings—elements of hatred as well as love. In the case of a small, reactive depression—mourning—you are able to deal with those mixed feelings in a healthy manner: you lose, you grieve, and then you recover. In the case of a major melancholic depression, you have become obsessed with the ambivalence—the simultaneity, the irreconcilable nature of the intense love alongside the intense hatred. Melancholia—a major depression—Freud theorized, is the internal conflict generated by this ambivalence.

This can begin to explain the intensity of grief experienced in a major depression. If you are obsessed with the intensely mixed feelings, you grieve doubly after a loss—for your loss of the loved individual *and* for the loss of any chance now to ever resolve the difficulties. "If only I had said the things I needed to, if only we could have worked things out"—for all of time, you have lost the chance to purge yourself of the ambivalence. For the rest of your life, you will be reaching for the door to let you into a place of pure, unsullied love, and you can never reach that door.

It also explains the intensity of the guilt often experienced in major depression. If you truly had intense anger toward the person along with the love, in the aftermath of your loss there must be some facet of you that is celebrating, alongside the grieving. "He/she is gone, that's terrible but . . . thank god, I can finally live, I can finally grow up, no more of this or that." Inevitably, a metaphorical instant later, there must come a paralyzing belief that you have become a horrible monster to feel any sense of relief or pleasure at a time like this. Incapacitating guilt.

This theory also explains the tendency of major depressives in such circumstances to, oddly, begin to take on some of the traits of the lost loved/hated one—and not just any traits, but invariably the ones that the survivor found most irritating. Psychodynamically, this is wonderfully logical. By taking on a trait, you are being loyal to your lost, beloved opponent. By picking an irritating trait, you are still trying to convince the world you were right to be irritated—you see how you hate it when I do it; can you imagine what it was like to have to put up with that for years? And by picking a trait that, most of all, *you* find irritating, you are not only still trying to score points in your argument with the departed, but you are punishing yourself for arguing as well.

Out of the Freudian school of thought has come one of the more apt descriptions of depression—"aggression turned inward." Suddenly the loss of pleasure, the psychomotor retardation, the impulse to suicide, the elevated stress-hormone levels, and increased metabolic rate all make sense. This does not describe someone too lethargic to function; it is more like the actual state of a patient in depression, exhausted from the most draining emotional conflict of his or her life—one going on entirely within.

Like other good parts of Freud, these ideas are empathic and fit many clinical traits; they just feel "right." But they are hard to assimilate into modern science, especially biologically oriented psychiatry. There is no way to study the correlation between norepinephrine receptor density and internalization of aggression, for example, or the effects of estrogen/progesterone ratios on love/hate ratios. The branch of psychological theorizing about depression that is easiest to fit into the biological branch is the one coming from experimental psychology, and work in this field has generated an extraordinarily informative model of depression.

LEARNED HELPLESSNESS: A CRITICAL LINK TO STRESS

In order to appreciate the experimental studies underlying this model, recall that in chapter 10, on psychological stress, we saw that certain features dominated as psychologically stressful: a loss of control and of predictability within certain contexts, a loss of outlets for frustration, a loss of sources of support, a perception of life worsening. In one style of experiments, pioneered by the psychologists Martin Seligman and Steven Maier, animals are exposed to pathologic amounts of these psychological stressors. The result is a condition strikingly similar to a human depression.

While the actual stressors may differ, the general approach in these studies always emphasizes repeated stressors with a complete absence of control on the part of the animal. For example, a rat may be subjected to a long series of frequent, uncontrollable, and unpredictable shocks or noises, with no outlets.

After awhile, something extraordinary happens to that rat. This can be shown with a test. Take a fresh, unstressed rat, and give it something easy to learn. Put it in a room, for example, with the floor divided into two halves. Occasionally, electricity that will cause a mild shock is delivered to one half and, just beforehand, there is a signal indicating which half of the floor is about to be electrified. Your run-of-the-mill rat can learn this "active avoidance task" easily, and within a short time it readily and calmly shifts the side of the room it sits in according to the signal. Simple. Except for a rat who has recently been exposed to repeated uncontrollable stressors. *That rat cannot learn this task.* It does not learn to cope. On the contrary, it has learned to be helpless.

This phenomenon, called "learned helplessness," is quite generalized; the animal has trouble coping with all sorts of varied tasks after its exposure to uncontrollable stressors. Such helplessness extends to tasks having to do with its ordinary life, like competing with another animal for food, or avoiding social aggression. One might wonder whether the helplessness is induced by the physical stress of receiving the shocks, or the psychological stressor of having no control over or capacity to predict the shocks. It is the latter. The clearest way to demonstrate this is to "yoke" pairs of rats—one gets shocked under conditions marked by predictability and a certain degree of control; the other rat gets the identical pattern of shocks, but without the control or predictability. Only the latter rat becomes helpless.

Seligman argues persuasively that animals suffering from learned helplessness share many psychological features with depressed humans. Such animals have a *motivational* problem —one of the reasons that they are helpless is that they often do not even attempt a coping response when they are in a new situation. This is quite similar to the depressed person who does not even try the simplest task that would improve her life. "I'm too tired, it seems overwhelming to take on something like that, it's not going to work anyway . . . "

Animals with learned helplessness also have a *cognitive* problem, something awry with how they perceive the world and think about it. When they do make the rare coping response, they can't tell whether it works or not. For example, if you tighten the association between a coping response and a reward, a normal rat's response rate increases (in other words, if the coping response works for the rat, it persists in that response). In contrast, linking rewards more closely to the rare coping responses of a helpless rat has little effect on its response rate. Seligman believes that this is a consequence, not of helpless animals somehow missing the rules of the task; instead, he thinks, they have actually *learned not to bother* paying attention. By all logic, that rat should have learned, "When I am getting shocked, there is absolutely nothing I can do, and that feels terrible, but it isn't the whole world." Instead, it has learned, "There is nothing I can do. Ever." Even when control and mastery are potentially made available to it, the rat cannot perceive them.* This is very similar to the depressed human who always sees glasses half empty, always sees people seated around a coffin. As Beck and other cognitive therapists have emphasized, much of what constitutes a depression is centered around responding to one awful thing and overgeneralizing it—cognitively distorting how the world works.

The learned helplessness paradigm produces animals with other features strikingly similar to those in humans with major depressions. There is a rat's equivalent of anhedonia—the rat stops grooming itself and loses interest in sex and food. The lack of motivation on the rat's part to even attempt coping responses suggests that it experiences an animal equivalent of psychomo-

---

*A fascinating variation: Another set of parallel experiments has shown that when an organism is *rewarded* consistently with no control or predictability (that is, no matter what the subject does, it is rewarded), it also has difficulty afterward learning coping responses. Seligman calls this a "spoiled brat" design; the investigators who discerned this phenomenon in pigeons used the much more provocative phrase, "learned laziness."

tor retardation.* In some models of learned helplessness, animals mutilate themselves, biting at themselves. Many of the vegetative symptoms appear as well — sleep loss and disorganization of sleep architecture, elevated glucocorticoid levels. Most critically, these animals tend to be depleted of norepinephrine in certain parts of the brain, while antidepressant drugs and ECT speed up their recovery from the learned helplessness state.

Learned helplessness has been induced in rodents, cats, dogs, birds, fish, insects, and primates — including humans. It takes surprisingly little in terms of uncontrollable unpleasantness to make humans give up and become helpless in a generalized way. In one study by Donald Hiroto, student volunteers were exposed to either escapable or inescapable loud noises (as in all of such studies, the two groups were paired so that they were exposed to the same amount of noise). Afterward, they were given a learning task in which a correct response turned off a loud noise; the "inescapable" group was significantly less capable of learning the task. Helplessness can even be generalized to nonaversive learning situations. Hiroto and Seligman did a follow-up study in which, again, there was either controllable or uncontrollable noise. Afterward the latter group was less capable of solving simple word puzzles. Giving up can also be induced by stressors far more subtle than uncontrollable loud noises. In another study, Hiroto and Seligman gave volunteers a

---

*One might wonder if the entire learned helplessness phenomenon is really just about psychomotor retardation. Perhaps the rat is so wiped out after the uncontrollable shocks that it simply doesn't have the energy to perform active avoidance coping tasks. This would shift the emphasis away from learned helplessness as a cognitive state ("there is nothing I can do about this") or an anhedonic emotional state ("nothing feels pleasurable") to one of psychomotor inhibition ("everything seems so exhausting that I'm just going to sit here"). Seligman and Maier strongly object to this interpretation and present data showing that rats with learned helplessness are not only as active as control rats but, more importantly, are also impaired in "passive avoidance tasks" — learning situations where the coping response involves remaining still, rather than actually *doing* something (in other words, situations where a little psychomotor retardation should *help* you). Championing the psychomotor retardation view is another major figure in this field, Jay Weiss, who presents an equal amount of data showing that "helpless" rats perform normally on passive avoidance tasks, indicating that the helplessness is a motor phenomenon and not a cognitive or emotional one. This debate has been going on for twenty years and I don't know how to resolve the conflicting views.

learning task in which they had to pick a card of a certain color according to rules that they had to discern along the way. In one group, these rules were learnable; in the other group, the rules were not (the card color was randomized). Afterward, the latter group was less capable of coping with a simple and easily solved task. Seligman and colleagues have also demonstrated that unsolvable tasks induced helplessness afterward in social coping situations.

Thus humans can be provoked into at least transient cases of learned helplessness, and with surprising ease. Naturally, there is tremendous individual variation in how readily this happens—some of us are more vulnerable than others. In the experiment involving inescapable noise, Hiroto had given the students a personality inventory beforehand. Based on that, he was able to identify the students who came into the experiment with a strongly "internalized locus of control"—a belief that they were the masters of their own destiny and had a great deal of control in their lives—and, in contrast, the markedly "externalized" volunteers who tended to attribute outcomes to chance and luck. In the aftermath of the uncontrollable stressor, the externalized students were far more vulnerable to learned helplessness.

Collectively, these studies strike me as extremely important in forming links among stress, personality, and depression. Our lives are replete with incidents in which we become irrationally helpless. Some are silly and inconsequential. Once in the African camp that I shared with Laurence Frank, the zoologist whose hyenas figured in the chapter on reproduction, we managed to make a disaster of preparing macaroni and cheese over the campfire. Inspecting the mess, we ruefully admitted that it might have helped if we had bothered to read the instructions on the box. Yet we had both avoided doing that; in fact, we both felt a formless dread about trying to make sense of such instructions. Frank summed it up: "Face it. We suffer from learned cooking helplessness."

But life is full of more significant examples. If a teacher at a critical point of our education, or a loved one at a critical point of our emotional development, frequently exposes us to his or her own specialized uncontrollable stressors, we may grow up with distorted beliefs about what we cannot learn or ways in which we are unlikely to be loved. In one chilling demonstration of this, some psychologists studied inner-city schoolkids with severe reading problems. Were they intellectually incapable of reading? Apparently not. The psychologists circumvented the students' resistance to learning to read by, instead, teaching them Chinese characters. Within hours they were capable of reading more complex symbolic sentences than they could in English. The children had apparently been previously taught all too well that reading English was beyond their ability.

A major depression, these findings suggest, can be the outcome of particularly severe lessons in uncontrollability for those of us who are already vulnerable. This may explain one of the more consistent findings in the literature on depression—loss of a parent early in life puts one at increased risk for depression years later. What could be a more severe lesson that awful things can happen that are beyond our control, a lesson coming at an age when we are first forming our impressions about the nature of the world?

"According to our model," writes Seligman, "depression is not generalized pessimism, but pessimism specific to the effects of one's own skilled actions." Subjected to enough uncontrollable stress, we learn to be helpless—we lack the motivation to try to live because we assume the worst; we lack the cognitive clarity to perceive when things are actually going fine, and we feel an aching lack of pleasure in everything.*

---

*Before we leave the issue of learned helplessness, let me acknowledge that these are brutal experiments to subject an animal to. Is there no alternative?

Painfully, I think not. You can study cancer in a petri dish—grow a tumor and then see if some drug slows the tumor's growth, and with what other toxicity; you can experiment with atherosclerotic plaque formation in a dish—grow blood-vessel cells and see if your drug removes cholesterol from their sides, and at what dosage. But you can't mimic depression in a petri dish, or with a computer. Millions of us are going to succumb to this nightmarish disorder, the treatments are still not very good, and animal models remain the best methods for seeking improvement. If you are of the school that animal research, while sad, is acceptable, your goal is to do only good science on the smallest number of animals with the least pain.

THE NEUROCHEMICAL EFFECTS OF STRESS

Psychologic approaches to depression give us some insight into the nature of the disease. According to one school, it is a state brought about by pathologic overexposure to psychologic stress, particularly loss of control and of outlets for frustration. In another psychologic view, the Freudian one, it is an internalized battle of ambivalences, aggression turned inward. These views contrast with the more biological ones—that depression is a disorder of abnormal neurotransmitter levels, abnormal communication between certain parts of the brain, abnormal hormone ratios. These are quite different ways of looking at the world, and researchers and clinicians from different orientations often don't have a word to say to one another about their mutual interest in depression. Sometimes they seem to be talking radically different languages—psychodynamic ambivalence versus neurotransmitter autoreceptors, cognitive overgeneralization versus steroid-hormone ratios in the bloodstream. Are there ways in which these very different approaches can be integrated? A crucial link has emerged with the understanding of the effects of stress upon the chemistry of the brain.

Critically, stress depletes norepinephrine in parts of the brain's limbic system (which, you recall, regulates emotion). Interesting, isn't it? No one is sure exactly why the depletion occurs, although it probably has something to do with norepinephrine being consumed faster than usual (rather than its being made more slowly than usual). Similarly, it is not understood why the depletion is localized to that area of the brain. Nevertheless, there appears to be an important link between stress and the anhedonia and/or psychomotor retardation features of depression. Along comes something stressful, down go norepinephrine levels, and we feel depressed and "blue." But we recover, or at least most of us do. How does recovery fit in? The final vital fact: stress not only depletes the brain of norepinephrine but simultaneously initiates the gradual synthesis of more norepinephrine. At the same time that norepinephrine content is plummeting, shortly after the onset of stress, the brain is making more of the key enzyme (called tyrosine hydroxylase) that synthesizes norepinephrine. Glucocorticoids probably have something to do with the induction of new tyrosine hydroxylase, but *how* is not completely clear. The main point is that, in most of us, stress may cause depletion of norepinephrine and thus some of the symptoms of depression—we feel "blue"— but at the same time, we are already building in the mechanisms of recovery, and we only feel depressed transiently.

What if there is a defect in people at risk for depression such that, following stress, they do not increase their levels of tyrosine hydroxylase? If true, this would begin to explain many of the features of depression. It would explain why this could be a disorder of *vulnerability*: in the absence of major stressors, a person with this biochemical abnormality would function normally. When something stressful did come along—the sort of thing that might be extremely difficult for any of us, but not psychiatrically crippling—the person with this biochemical vulnerability would be depleted of norepinephrine; for lack of protective tyrosine hydroxylase compensation, however, the deficit would continue to get worse, and the person would sink deeper into depression. In effect, this would be a neurochemical equivalent of cognitive overgeneralization—when something bad happens to most of us, we conclude that that was a bad thing about which we feel helpless and sad and anhedonic, but it's not the end of the world. And we heal. For the depressive, something awful happens and the neurochemical and perceptual and emotional consequences keep spreading; soon everything appears hopeless, out of control, and pleasureless, and there seems no point to getting out of bed.*

This is a hypothetical model, although evidence is accumulating in support of it. It would offer some insight into individual

---

*Many readers are likely to be familiar with the "tyrosine" element in the term "tyrosine hydroxylase." Tyrosine is an amino acid, a relatively simple chemical compound that is found plentifully in the diet and, in addition, can easily be synthesized by chemists and sold as tablets. Tyrosine hydroxylase, on the other hand, is an immensely complicated enzyme that begins the process of turning tyrosine into norepinephrine. At present, there is no way to take tyrosine hydroxylase as a dietary supplement.

differences in the patterns of disease — why some people seem to require little external stress to throw them into a depression. They may start off with relatively low levels of norepinephrine in the relevant parts of the brain, their norepinephrine levels may be driven down very readily by stress, they may be sluggish in their compensatory increase in tyrosine hydroxylase during stress. Laboratory mice vary considerably in how readily gluco-corticoids turn on their tyrosine hydroxylase activity.

This is admittedly a very simplistic model at this stage, but seems to have possibilities. In any case, it emphasizes how often a biochemical disorder can be about *propensities*, rather than about inevitabilities; how stress can be a critical trigger of de-pressions; and how depression can be both biological and envi-ronmental, in the elementary senses of each of those words. It also contains the seeds of hope. If the psychobiology of depres-sion is a lesson in the deleterious effects of extreme psychologi-cal stress, it is also a blueprint of where we can be most helped and protected from our psychological vulnerabilities by manip-ulating or compensating for those stressors.

AGING AND DEATH

Predictably, it comes at the most unpredictable times. I'll be lecturing, bored, telling the same story about neurons I did last year, daydreaming, looking at the ocean of irritatingly young undergraduates, and then it hits, producing almost a sense of wonderment. "How can you just sit there; am I the only one who realizes that all of you are going to die someday?" Or it can have a more personal tinge: I'll be at a scientific conference, this time barely understanding someone else's lecture, and amid the roomful of savants, the wave of bitterness will sweep over me. "All of you highfalutin' medical experts, and not one of you can make me live forever."

It first really dawns on us emotionally sometime around puberty. Woody Allen, once our untarnished high priest of death and love, captures its roundabout assault perfectly in *Annie Hall*. The protagonist is shown, in flashback, as a young adolescent. He is sufficiently depressed for the worried mother to drag him to the family doctor—"Listen to what he keeps saying, what's wrong with him, does he have the flu?" The

Allenesque adolescent, glazed with despair and panic, announces in a monotone: "The universe is expanding." It's all there — the universe is expanding, look how big infinity is and how finite we are — and he has been initiated into the great secret of our species: we will die and we know it. With that rite of passage, he has found the mother lode of psychic energy that fuels our most irrational and violent moments, our most selfish and our most altruistic ones, our neurotic dialectic of simultaneously mourning and denying, our diets and exercising, our myths of paradise and resurrection. It's as if we were trapped in a mine, shouting out for rescuers: save us, we're alive but we're getting old and we're all going to die.

Morris Zlapo, 1987: Gepetto's Dementia, *collage.*

Oh, it doesn't have to be that bad. Perhaps we will grow old with grace and wisdom. Perhaps we will be honored, perhaps surrounded by strong, happy children whose health and fecundity will feel like immortality to us. As I have noted, for 15 years I have spent part of each year doing stress research on wild baboons in East Africa. The people living there, like many people in the non-Westernized world, clearly think differently about these issues from the way we do. No one seems to find getting old depressing. How could they?—they wait their whole lives to become powerful elders. My nearest neighbors are Masai tribesmen, nomadic pastoralists. I often patch up their various minor injuries and ills. One day, one of the extremely old men of the village (perhaps sixty years old) tottered into our camp. Ancient, wrinkled beyond measure, tips missing from a few fingers, frayed earlobes, long-forgotten battle scars. He spoke only Masai and not Swahili, the lingua franca of East Africa, so he was accompanied by his more worldly, middle-aged neighbor, who translated for him. He had an infected sore on his leg, which I washed and treated with antibiotic ointment. He also had trouble seeing—cataracts was my barely educated guess—and I explained that they were beyond my meager curative powers. He seemed resigned, but not particularly disappointed, and as he sat there cross-legged, naked except for the blanket wrapped around him, basking in the sun, the woman stood behind him and stroked his head. In a voice as if describing last year's weather she said, "Oh, when he was younger, he was beautiful and strong. Soon he will die." That night in my tent, sleepless and jealous of the Masai, I thought "I'll take your malaria and parasites, I'll take your appalling infant mortality rates, I'll take the chances of being attacked by buffalo and lions. Just let me be as unafraid as you are."

Maybe we will luck out and wind up as respected village elders. Gerontologists studying the aging process find increasing evidence that most of us will age with a fair degree of grace and success; chapter 13 tells some of this pleasing story. Nevertheless, there are still so many other outcomes to fear: Wracking pain. Dementia so severe we can't recognize our children. Cat food. Forced retirement. Colostomy bags. Muscles that no

An elderly hunter-gatherer shaman in the Kalahari desert.

longer listen to our commands, organs that betray us, children who ignore us. Mostly that aching sense that just when we finally grow up and learn to like ourselves and to love and play, the shadows lengthen. There is so little time.

Not only are we in the Westernized world relatively alone in our fear of aging, but we are relatively alone in undergoing advanced stages of the process. Within the time scale of evolution, widespread aging within a species is a fairly recent invention. It is not a luxury readily available to most other animals on the planet, nor was it to most of our ancestors. Likewise the science of aging, gerontology, is a fairly new discipline. And

Anthony

almost from its beginning, theories about the nature of aging have been intertwined with ideas about stress. In general, these have taken two forms. The first is that advanced age is a time when organisms no longer cope well with stress. The second is that stress, especially prolonged and extreme forms of stress, can accelerate aging. This chapter explores the evidence supporting each of these ideas.

HOW DO AGED ORGANISMS DEAL WITH STRESS?

Not very well, it turns out. In many ways, aging can be defined as the progressive loss of the ability to deal with stress, and that certainly fits our perception of aged individuals as fragile and vulnerable. This can be stated more rigorously by saying that many aspects of the bodies and minds of old organisms work fine, just as they do in young ones—so long as they aren't pushed. Throw in an exercise challenge, an injury or illness, time pressure, novelty—any of a variety of physical, cognitive, or psychological stressors—and aged organisms are more likely to fall apart. The illustration on page 232 shows this in a schematic way. In the absence of stress (of whatever sort), young and old individuals perform roughly the same way. Under stress, performance declines in both age groups—but faster in the old individuals.

This occurs frequently. As one classic example, normal body temperature—98.6 degrees—does not change with age. Nevertheless, it takes the bodies of the elderly longer to restore a normal temperature after being warmed or chilled; or, to use the terminology of this book, it takes them longer to reestablish homeostasis after temperature stressors. Heart performance follows a similar pattern. Once you eliminate the elderly people in your study who have heart disease and look only at healthy individuals of different ages (so as to study aging, instead of inadvertently studying disease), many aspects of cardiac function remain the same despite age—heart rate, cardiac output,

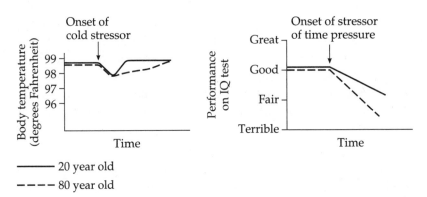

Two ways in which the stress-response may be impaired in an older individual. (Left) Young and old individuals may have the same function under nonstressed conditions (in this case, the same body temperature). However, in the face of a stressor that knocks that measure out of homeostatic balance (chilling the person one degree), it takes the older person longer to reestablish homeostasis. (Right) Young and old individuals may have the same function under nonstressed conditions (performance on an IQ test). However, as the stressor of time pressure is added to the test, performance declines in both individuals—but to a greater extent in the older person.

stroke volume, "stiffness" of cardiac muscle, end diastolic volume, and ejection fraction.* Stress the cardiovascular system with exercise, however, and old hearts do not respond the same as young ones. The maximal work capacity and the maximal heart rate that can be achieved are nowhere near as great as in a young person. Ejection volume decreases more dramatically than in the young, while cardiac muscle stiffness increases more dramatically. All of this is a fancy way of saying that even if some eighty-year-old still has the blood pressure and heart rate of a teenager, it still may not be such a hot idea for her to run a marathon.

---

*Heart rate is how often the heart beats per unit time (typically a minute). Cardiac output is the amount of blood pumped out in that period. Stroke volume is the amount pumped per heartbeat. Stiffness of cardiac muscle is an engineering term for expressing how efficiently the heart muscle meets changing blood pressure needs. End diastolic volume is the amount of blood in the heart just before it contracts, and ejection fraction is how much of that blood is pumped out with the next contraction.

Everything can be fine in the absence of a stressor, but the system's still vulnerable. This idea applies in other arenas of gerontology as well. For example, if the brain is damaged and neurons are killed, remaining neurons can sometimes grow new branches to try to compensate for the injury. The phenomenon occurs in old brains but, for the same degree of injury, more slowly than in young brains. Similarly, old and young rat brains contain roughly the same amount of energy (stored in molecules/chemicals called ATP), but when you stress the system by cutting off the flow of oxygen and nutrients, energy levels decline faster in the old brains.

The idea also applies to measures of cognition. What happens to IQ test scores as people get older? (You'll notice that I didn't say "intelligence," just "performance on IQ tests." Whether the latter tells us much about the former is a controversy I don't want to come within a hundred miles of.) The dogma in the field was once that IQ declined with age, then that it did not decline. It depends on how you test it. If you test young and old people and give them lots of time to complete the test, there is little difference. As you stress the system—in this case, by making the subjects race against a time limit—scores fall for all ages, but much further among older people.

So in many ways the elderly may function just as the young do, so long as they are not stressed. But throw in a stressor, and some dramatic vulnerabilities become evident. A lot of this relative dysfunction can be explained by a host of problems with the individual hormonal systems involved in the stress-response. In some respects, there is not *enough* of a stress-response. For example, during exercise old people secrete plenty of epinephrine and norepinephrine (a lot more than young people, in fact). This would predict that their cardiovascular systems should kick into high gear during the exercise. Yet, as just mentioned, maximal cardiac output during exercise declines with age. Why? Because the heart and various blood vessels for some reason do not respond as vigorously to the epinephrine and norepinephrine.

An even bigger problem is that aged organisms often have *too much* of a stress-response. For example, older individuals are not so good at turning off epinephrine and norepinephrine secretion after a stressor has finished; it takes longer for their levels of these substances to return to baseline. The same thing is seen with glucocorticoid secretion. Stress young and old rats by holding them still, and they have roughly the same sized burst of glucocorticoid secretion. But after the immobilization, glucocorticoid levels return to normal in young rats at least twice as fast as in old rats.

By now it should be clear that secreting hormones like epinephrine and glucocorticoids when there is no longer a stressor is a bad idea — once the emergency is over, your body should turn off the various alarms as rapidly as possible. Do old rats pay a price for not being able to promptly turn off their stress-responses after the end of stress? A colleague — Thomas Donnelly — and I tested this idea a few years ago. As discussed in the immunity chapter, if a tumor of a certain type is induced to grow in a rat, it will grow faster if that rat is repeatedly stressed, and this in part is because of the glucocorticoids secreted during stress. We first observed that, for the same pattern of stressors, these tumors grew faster in old rats than in young ones. Was this due to the extra glucocorticoids that old rats secrete because they are sluggish in turning off the stress-response? To test this, we infused some young rats with extra glucocorticoids at the end of each stressful event, in a way that mimicked the "shut-off" problem of old rats — and the young ones grew tumors faster as well.

Aged organisms not only have trouble turning off the stress-response after the end of stress, they also secrete more stress-related hormones even in their normal, nonstressed state. As an example of this, resting epinephrine and norepinephrine levels are typically elevated in old rats and aged humans. The same thing is seen with glucocorticoids: resting levels rise with age in the rat and human. The consensus in the field used to be that this did not happen in humans — numerous studies had found the same resting levels of glucocorticoids in old humans as in young. However, these studies were based on a dated concept of what is "old" in a human; they looked at people in their 60s and early 70s. Modern gerontologists do not consider someone aged until the late 70s or 80s, and the more recent studies show a big jump in resting glucocorticoid levels in that age group. A colleague — Jeanne Altmann — and I recently made a similar observation of wild baboons — the really old ones had elevated glucocorticoid levels, showing a jump of about the same magnitude with age as humans. (Studying aging in a wild population of a closely related species like the baboon is particularly useful because it eliminates many of the confounds in studying humans. Baboons of every age eat roughly the same thing and are still physically active; they're all somewhat related, so genetic differences aren't much of a factor; they don't drink coffee or smoke; and the old ones aren't taking half a dozen different medicines. Furthermore, you don't have to worry much that you are accidentally studying disease instead of aging — an old baboon living in the wild is a supremely healthy beast, because any who wasn't got eaten long ago.)

Old individuals of all sorts tend to have the stress-response turned on even when nothing stressful is happening. Do old organisms pay a price for this "normal" hormonal hyperactivity? It seems so. For example, the elevated resting epinephrine and norepinephrine levels probably have a lot to do with the elevated blood pressure often seen during aging. Studies also indicate that the elevated resting glucocorticoid levels in old rats are responsible for the increasing difficulty that neurons have sprouting new branches after an injury.

In previous chapters, we've seen that, ideally, the hormones of the stress-response should be nice and quiet when nothing bad is happening, secreted in tiny amounts. When a stressful emergency hits, your body needs a huge and fast stress-response. At the end of the stressor, everything should shut off immediately. And these traits are precisely what old individuals typically do not have.

CAN STRESS MAKE YOU AGE FASTER?

Intuitively, the idea that stress accelerates the aging process makes sense. We recognize that there is a connection between how we live and how we die. Around the turn of the century, a madly inspired German physiologist, Max Rubner, tried to define this connection scientifically. He looked at all sorts of different domestic species and calculated things like lifetime number of heartbeats and lifetime metabolic rate (not the sort of study that many scientists have tried to replicate). He concluded that there is only so long a body can go on—only so many breaths, so many heartbeats, so much metabolism that each pound of flesh can carry out before the mechanisms of life wear out. A rat, with approximately 400 heartbeats a minute, uses up its heartbeat allotment faster (after approximately two years) than an elephant (with approximately 35 beats per minute and a 60-year lifespan). Such calculations lay behind ideas about why some species lived far longer than others. Soon the same sort of thinking was applied to how long different individuals *within* a species live—if you squander a lot of your heartbeats and heavy breathing being nervous about blind dates when you're sixteen, there's that much less metabolic reserve available to you at seventy.

In general, Rubner's ideas about lifespans among different species have not held up well in their strictest versions, while the "rate of living" hypotheses about individuals within a species that his ideas inspired have held up even worse. Nevertheless, they led many people in the field to suggest that a lot of environmental perturbations can wear out the system prematurely. Such "wear and tear" thinking fit in naturally with the era of stressology that Selye introduced, and in his later years Selye theorized that a lifetime of stress depletes an individual of "adaptational" energies, leading to accelerated senescence.

Fascinating, especially the notion of adaptational energies, —but no one is really sure what that term means. We can, however, put the issue in more concrete terms: What does being exposed to a lot of glucocorticoids over the lifespan do to the aging process? We have a list hammered into our heads by now of problems that glucocorticoid excess brings about—fatigue, thinning muscles, adult-onset diabetes, hypertension, osteoporosis, reproductive decline, immune suppression. All of these conditions become more common among the elderly. Can glucocorticoids determine how fast aging occurs? It turns out that, in more than a dozen species, glucocorticoid excess is *the* cause of death during aging.

WHY YOU SELDOM SEE REALLY OLD SALMON

Pictures of heroic wild animals, à la Marlin Perkins: Penguins who stand all winter amid the Antarctic cold, keeping their eggs warm at their feet. Leopards dragging massive kills up trees with their teeth, in order to eat them free of harassment by lions. Dessicated camels marching scores of miles. And most of all, salmon leaping over dams and waterfalls to return to the freshwater stream of their birth. Where they spawn a zillion eggs. After which they all die over the next few weeks.

Why do salmon die so soon after spawning? No one is quite sure, but evolutionary biologists are rife with theories about why this and the rare other cases of "programmed die-offs" in the animal kingdom may make some evolutionary sense. What

A male sockeye salmon, after the onset of programmed aging.

is known, however, is the proximal mechanism underlying the sudden die-off. (Not "how come they die, in terms of evolutionary patterns over the millennia," but how come they *die*— which parts of the body's functioning suddenly go crazy?) It is glucocorticoid secretion.

If you catch salmon right after they spawn, just when they are looking a little green around the gills, you find they have huge adrenal glands, peptic ulcers, and kidney lesions; their immune systems have collapsed, and they are teeming with parasites and infections. Aha, kind of sounds like Selye's rats way back when. Moreover, the salmon have stupendously high glucocorticoid concentrations in their bloodstreams. When salmon spawn, regulation of their glucocorticoid secretion breaks down. Basically, the brain loses its ability to measure accurately the quantities of circulating hormones and keeps sending a signal to the adrenals to secrete more of them. Lots of glucocorticoids can certainly bring about all those diseases with which the salmon are festering. Is the glucocorticoid excess really responsible for their death? Yup. Take a salmon right after spawning, remove its adrenals, and it will live for a year afterward.

The bizarre thing is that this sequence of events not only occurs in five species of salmon, but also among a dozen species of Australian marsupial mice. All the male mice of these species die shortly after seasonal mating; cut out their adrenal glands, however, and they keep living as well. Pacific salmon and marsupial mice are not close relatives. At least twice in history, completely independently, two very different sets of species have come up with the identical trick: if you want to degenerate very fast, secrete a ton of glucocorticoids.

CHRONIC STRESS AND THE AGING PROCESS IN THE MAINSTREAM

That is all fine for the salmon looking for the fountain of youth, but we and most other mammals age gradually over time, not in catastrophic die-offs over the course of days. Does stress influence the rate of gradual mammalian aging? This turns out to be the case, in at least one fairly frightening way.

We return to the tendency of very old rats, humans, and primates to have elevated resting levels of glucocorticoids in the bloodstream. Some aspect of the regulation of normal glucocorticoid secretion is disrupted during aging. To get a sense of why this happens, we must become extremely technical and delve into the essential topic of why toilet bowls do not overflow when they are refilling. There is a source of water—a pipe that typically sticks straight up. There is a way for the system to know how much the tank has filled—the flotation device that bobs up higher as the water rises. And there is a connection between how much water there is in the tank and whether more water is released: the flotation device is attached to a valve on the top of the water pipe, and as the device bobs higher, it closes the valve. Engineers who study this sort of thing term that process "negative feedback inhibition" or "end-product inhibition": increasing amounts of water accumulating in the tank decrease the likelihood of further release of water.

Most hormonal systems, including the glucocorticoids, work by this feedback-inhibition process. The brain secretes CRF, which triggers pituitary release of ACTH, and finally, out come glucocorticoids from the adrenal. The brain needs to know whether to keep secreting more CRF. It does this by sensing the levels of glucocorticoids in the circulation (sampling the hormone from the bloodstream coursing through the brain) to see if levels are at, below, or above a "setpoint." If levels are low, the brain keeps secreting CRF—just as when water levels in the toilet tank are still low. Once glucocorticoid levels reach or exceed that setpoint, there is a negative feedback signal and the brain stops secreting CRF. As a fascinating complication, the setpoint can shift. In the absence of stress, the brain wants different levels of glucocorticoids in the bloodstream from those required when something stressful is happening. (This implies that the quantity of glucocorticoids in the bloodstream necessary to turn off CRF secretion by the brain should vary with different situations.)

This is how the system works normally, as can be shown experimentally by injecting a person with a massive dose of a synthetic glucocorticoid ("dexamethasone"). The brain senses the sudden increase and says, in effect, "My god, I don't know what is going on with those idiots in the adrenal, but they just secreted *way* too many glucocorticoids." The dexamethasone exerts a negative feedback signal, and soon the person has stopped secreting CRF, ACTH, and her own glucocorticoids. This person would be characterized as "dexamethasone responsive." If negative feedback regulation is not working very well, however, the person is "dexamethasone resistant"—she keeps secreting her hormones, despite the whopping glucocorticoid signal in the bloodstream. And that is precisely what happens in old people, primates, and rats. Glucocorticoid feedback regulation no longer works very well.

This may explain why very old organisms secrete excessive glucocorticoids (in the absence of stress and/or during the recovery period after the end of a stressor). Why the failure of feedback regulation? There is a fair amount of evidence that it is due to the degeneration during aging of one part of the brain. The entire brain does not serve as a "glucocorticoid sensor"; instead, that role is served by only a few areas with very high levels of receptors for glucocorticoids and the means to tell the hypothalamus whether or not to secrete CRF. One of those brain regions, the hippocampus, appears to undergo considerable degeneration with age—about 20 percent of the neurons die.* And when the hippocampus is damaged, some of the deleterious consequences include a tendency to secrete an excessive amount of glucocorticoids—aged persons may have elevated resting levels of the hormone, trouble turning off secretion after the end of stress, or may be dexamethasone resist-

*One of the great myths of science folklore is that, from some tender age, twenty-five or so, we all begin to lose massive amounts of neurons. This turns out to be a mistake occasioned by earlier researchers looking at the brains of people with dementia— probably Alzheimer's—and assuming that this represented "normal" aging, instead of a disease associated with aging. But although the extent of neuron loss as we age is not dramatic, the hippocampus tends to be one of the areas most consistently damaged. The other is a region called the "nigrostriatal system": neuron loss there has something to do with the tremors that many old people get. It is also the region dramatically damaged during Parkinson's disease.

ant. It is as if one of the brakes on the system has been damaged, and hormone secretion rushes forward now a little out of control.

The elevated glucocorticoid levels of old age, therefore, arise because of a problem with feedback regulation that, in turn, is related to neuron loss in the hippocampus. Why does the aging hippocampus lose so many neurons? The answer is a bombshell—the neurons probably die because of their lifetime of exposure to glucocorticoids.

The first evidence that glucocorticoids could damage the brain came in the late 1960s. Two researchers showed that if guinea pigs are exposed to pharmacological levels of glucocorticoids (that is, higher levels than the body ever normally generates on its own), the brain is damaged. Oddly, damage was mainly limited to the hippocampus. No one understood that at the time, but a few years later a neurochemist named Bruce McEwen first mapped steroid hormone receptors in the brain. It turned out that the hippocampus had huge numbers of receptors for glucocorticoids, making hippocampal neurons exquisitely sensitive to the hormones. Whatever glucocorticoids do to the brain, they do it first to the hippocampus.

Beginning in the early 1980s, various researchers including myself showed that this "glucocorticoid neurotoxicity" was not just a pharmacological effect, but was relevant to normal brain aging in the rat. Collectively, the studies that showed lots of glucocorticoid exposure (in the range seen during stress) or lots of stress itself would accelerate the degeneration of the aging hippocampus. Conversely, to diminish glucocorticoid levels (by removing the adrenals of the rat and maintaining low circulating levels of the hormone with injections of synthetic glucocorticoids) was to delay hippocampal aging. While the hippocampus plays a part in regulating glucocorticoid secretion, its most famous role has to do with learning and memory—the hippocampus is essential for certain types of learning. These studies showed that the extent of glucocorticoid exposure over the rat's lifetime not only determined how much hippocampal degeneration there would be in old age, but how much memory loss as well.

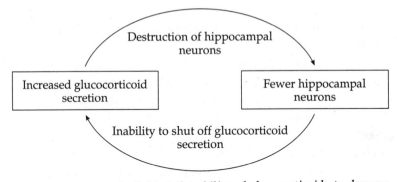

A degenerative cascade linking the ability of glucocorticoids to damage the hippocampus, and damage to the hippocampus resulting in enhanced secretion of glucocorticoids.

The reader will note something truly insidious embedded in these findings. Glucocorticoids appear capable of damaging the rat's hippocampus. When the hippocampus is damaged, the rat secretes more glucocorticoids. Which should damage the hippocampus further. Which should cause even more glucocorticoid secretion . . . Each makes the other worse, causing a degenerative cascade that appears to occur in many aging rats.

So glucocorticoids appear to be a major determinant of hippocampal aging. The next obvious question: Where do glucocorticoids get off killing brain cells? Sure, stress hormones can make you sick in lots of ways, but isn't neurotoxicity going a little beyond the bounds of good taste?

This is what my laboratory studies, and we are making some progress understanding what exactly glucocorticoids do to hippocampal neurons. It appears that the hormones don't kill the neurons directly; but they do make them more vulnerable. If nothing else happens at this point, the neurons recover just fine. But while the neuron is vulnerable, if some other challenge comes along, it is more likely than usual to meet its death. This suggests that all sorts of neurological insults that damage the hippocampus will become more damaging in the presence of glucocorticoids. And this is precisely what we and others have observed.

The hippocampus is either the principal or among the principal brain regions damaged by hypoglycemic coma, by chronic epilepsy, and by lack of blood flow due to cardiac arrest.* And in rat models of these neurological diseases, we and others have found that glucocorticoids make the damage worse. Give a rat more glucocorticoids after a seizure and it winds up with more hippocampal damage. Remove its adrenals and there's less damage. You can even grow hippocampal neurons in a dish, subject them to similar insults (take the sugar out of their petri-dish soup to mimic hypoglycemia, for example; put the dish in a chamber without oxygen to mimic the hypoxia that follows cardiac arrest, and so on) and the same thing occurs — the more glucocorticoids, the more dead neurons. (Remember, these are conditions in which the glucocorticoids alone are not killing the cells. The stress hormones endanger, rather than kill outright.)

How do glucocorticoids make hippocampal neurons more vulnerable to such disasters? It has something to do with energy. All these neurological diseases are energy crises for a neuron: cut off the glucose to a neuron (hypoglycemia), the glucose and oxygen (hypoxia-ischemia), or make a neuron work like mad (a seizure) and energy stores drop precipitously. Glucocorticoids seem to further disrupt the energy stores during these disasters. Think back to the metabolism chapter and the news that gluco-corticoids inhibit the transport of glucose into fat cells and non-exercising muscle cells. That's a strategy to divert glucose to the exercising muscles, but it turns out that glucocorticoids also inhibit glucose transport into hippocampal neurons. Nothing dramatic, not of a magnitude that would kill a neuron outright,

---

*Hippocampal damage seems to occur only in severe cases of chronic epilepsy. Brain damage due to cardiac arrest is an example of "hypoxia-ischemia," where the brain gets insufficient oxygen and glucose. When someone's heart has stopped, you face the classical clinical disaster of having only a few minutes to get the heart going again "before there is brain damage"; it is the hippocampus where such damage occurs first. Hypoxia-ischemia can also occur when someone has a "stroke" — when blood flow through a particular blood vessel to the brain ceases (because of blockage or a spasm of the vessel), or when a hemorrhage occurs and a vessel bleeds into the brain. In yet another set of circumstances, a blood vessel bursts elsewhere in the body or there is other internal bleeding, resulting in insufficient blood pressure to keep up circulation to the brain. In all these cases, there is a common theme: the brain is getting too little of the glucose and oxygen that it needs. Thus, I am going to make a technically incorrect simplification and use the familiar term "stroke" to refer to all of these instances.

but probably enough to make the energy crisis of a stroke or a seizure even more severe. And once that neurological disaster happens, the various neurochemical steps that would normally go awry in the endangered neuron are now going to alter even more dramatically.

It is not yet clear whether the glucocorticoid effects on the aging hippocampus are the same as on the hippocampus that has just undergone a neurological disaster. For example, after a massive hypoglycemic coma, a rat may lose one thousand hippocampal neurons; let us assume that the rat is exposed to high glucocorticoid levels at the time and, instead, loses fifteen hundred neurons — this is the "endangerment" that I have been discussing. It is not clear if the loss of neurons as the hippocampus ages over years works the same way. Perhaps each time a rat is fed a little late in the day and gets a bit hypoglycemic, it loses two hippocampal neurons; and if there are lots of glucocorticoids around at the time, it loses three. This would constitute the same pattern of glucocorticoids not killing, but making other threats worse, simply by acting in conjunction with tiny little insults spread over years. Alternatively, over the course of an organism's lifetime, glucocorticoids might really kill the neurons all on their own. No one knows at this point.

Clearly, however, glucocorticoids can exacerbate neurological damage to the hippocampus, in addition to playing a major role in determining the rate of hippocampal aging. This suggests some possible remedial interventions. If a rat has just had a stroke, these studies suggest that giving it glucocorticoids will make the hippocampal damage worse. Yet, glucocorticoids are often given to humans after strokes or head trauma, typically, to reduce "edema," or brain swelling that can occur at those times. (Glucocorticoids also appear to help decrease injury to the spinal cord, but for reasons very different from their actions discussed in this book.) Their usefulness in those circumstances has been controversial for decades, and various clinicians have urged that "nonsteroidal" substitutes be used instead. These new findings lend support to those voices.

But an additional intervention could be even more helpful. If the rat that has just had some neurological crisis is not given glucocorticoids by its neurologist, it will still secrete plenty on its own — rats (and humans) who have just had strokes or seizures have massive stress-responses.* Bursts of glucocorticoids at those times are enough to make the hippocampal damage worse. How do we know? Because if a rat's adrenals are removed right after its seizure or stroke, the hippocampal damage is decreased. This implies that what we think of as "normal" hippocampal damage after one of these disasters is, in fact, normal damage made worse by having a massive stress-response at the same time. Now, you can't adrenalectomize an animal just because it has had a seizure, since that animal is going to need those glands some other time. But there are drugs available that block glucocorticoid secretion for a few hours; give them to rats after the stroke or seizure, and there is less hippocampal damage.

This is encouraging news for those concerned with lessening the impact of neurological disease in rats. Does any of this apply to us? Millions of people in the United States and elsewhere take synthetic glucocorticoids each year, hundreds of thousands of these in very large quantities.† Will the hippocampi of these people age faster? Will they develop more severe memory problems in old age? Hundreds of thousands of people have strokes each year, millions have seizures of some sort — could their massive glucocorticoid stress-responses endanger their brains at those critical times? To ask the more frightening question: Could Alzheimer's disease, which primarily attacks

---

*Massive amounts of norepinephrine, moreover, are secreted in response to a spinal cord injury — and through a number of its actions, norepinephrine makes the damage worse. How did such maladaptive responses evolve? The most likely explanation is that the body simply has not evolved the tendency *not* to secrete glucocorticoid and norepinephrine during a neurological crisis. Until the last half-century or so, no mammal had much likelihood of surviving a stroke or a spinal injury, so there was no evolutionary pressure to make the body's response to massive neurological injury more logical.

†Benign low doses are used most often when ointment containing hydrocortisone (again, another term for the glucocorticoid secreted by primates and humans) is applied topically to control poison ivy or poison oak reactions (taking advantage of its anti-inflammatory effects). High doses are usually taken by people with arthritis or asthma (the glucocorticoids suppress the out-of-control inflammatory response), autoimmune diseases (where the steroids suppress the out-of-control immune system), or after an organ transplant (to keep the immune system from rejecting the foreign tissue).

the hippocampus and cortex, be made worse by stress or glucocorticoids?

At this point, there are only vague hints that glucocorticoids might be bad news for the human hippocampus. Recent work has shown that both stress and glucocorticoids will damage the primate hippocampi, just as in the rat, and the primate and human hippocampus are quite similar. As further evidence, people who take massive doses of glucocorticoids tend to develop some memory problems. It is not clear, however, whether these memory problems are permanent, and if they have more to do with taking the steroids or trying to get off them. Finally, before there was a treatment for it, people who had Cushing's disease (in which a tumor causes massive glucocorticoid secretion) were found to have memory problems while they were alive and seen at postmortem to have brain damage—but the studies that yielded these results were not particularly carefully done, because no one was attuned to issues of the brain in Cushing's patients at the time.

It is thus not yet clear whether the "glucocorticoid neurotoxicity" story applies to how our brains age, let alone to how they weather neurological diseases. Unfortunately, the answer is not likely to be available for years; the subject is very difficult to study in humans. Nevertheless, from what we know about this process in the rat and monkey, glucocorticoid toxicity stands as a striking example of ways in which stress can accelerate aging. And should it turn out to apply to us as well, it will be an aspect of our aging that will harbor a special threat. If we are crippled by an accident, if we lose our sight or hearing, if we are so weakened by heart disease as to be bed-bound, we cease having so many of the things that make our lives worth living. But when it is our brains that are damaged, when it is our ability to recall old memories or to form new ones that is destroyed, we cease to exist as sentient, unique individuals—the version of aging that haunts us most.

George Segal, 1969: Man in a Chair, *wood and plaster.*

13

MANAGING STRESS

By now, if you are not depressed by all of the bad news in the preceding chapter, you probably have only been skimming. Stress can wreak havoc with your metabolism, raise your blood pressure, burst your white blood cells, make you flatulent, ruin your sex life, and if that's not enough, possibly damage your brain.* Why don't we toss in the towel right now?

There is hope. Although it may sneak onto the scene in a quiet, subtle way, once you realize that the hope is there, it may change the way you think about stress. This frequently hits me at gerontology meetings. I'm sitting there, listening to the umpteenth lecture with the same general tone—the kidney expert speaking about how the kidney disintegrates with age, the immunology expert on how immunity declines, and so on. There is always a bar graph set to 100 percent for young subjects, with a

---

*An additional pathology, for those who are really trivia fans when it comes to stress-related disease: "alopecia areata." This is the technical term for that extraordinary state of getting so stressed, and terrified by something that your hair turns white or gray overnight. It really does occur.

Henri Matisse, 1910: The Dance, *oil on canvas.*

bar showing that the elderly have only 75 percent of the kidney filtration rate of young subjects, 75 percent of the limb strength, and so on.

Research typically involves the study of populations, rather than single individuals one at a time. The characteristics of various individuals never have exactly the same values — instead, the bars in a graph represent the average for each age (see the figure below). Suppose one group of three subjects has scores of 19, 20, and 21, for an average of 20. Another group may have scores of 10, 20, and 30. They also have an average score of 20, but the variance of those scores would be much larger. By the convention of science, the bars also contain a measure of how much variation there is within each age group: the size of the "T" above the bar indicates what percentage of the subjects in the group had scores within X number of steps of the average.

One thing that is utterly reliable is that the extent of variance increases a lot with age — the conditions of the elderly are always much more variable than those of the young subjects. What a drag, you say as a researcher, because with that variance

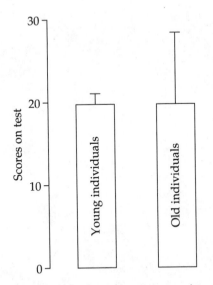

Schematic presentation of the fact that a group of young and old individuals may receive the same average score on a given test, yet the variability in the scores is typically greater among the older population.

your statistics are not as neat and you have to include more subjects in your aged population to get a reliable average. But really *think* about that fact for a minute. Look at the size of the bars for the young and old subjects, look at the size of the T-shaped variance symbols, do some quick calculations, and suddenly the extraordinary realization hits you — amid the population of, say, fifty subjects, for six of them things are *improving* with age. Their kidney filtration rates have gotten better, their blood pressures have decreased, they do better on memory tests. You're on the edge of your seat. Who *are* those six? What are they doing right? And with all scientific detachment abandoned, how can I do that, too?

This pattern used to be a statistical irritant to gerontologists. Now it's the trendiest subject in the field. "Successful aging." Not everyone falls apart miserably with age, not every organ system poops out, not everything is bad news.

The same pattern occurs in many other realms in which life tests us. Ten men are released from years spent as political hostages. Nine come out troubled, estranged from friends and family, with nightmares, difficulties readapting to everyday life. One or two succumb to a crippling post-traumatic stress disorder and never function well again. Yet invariably there is one guy who comes out saying, "Yeah, the beatings were awful, the times they put a gun to my head and cocked the trigger were the worst in my life, of course I would never want to do it again, but it wasn't until I was in captivity that I realized what is really important, that I decided to devote the rest of my life to X. I'm almost grateful." How did he do it? Physiological studies of people carrying out dangerous, stressful tasks — parachuting, learning to land on an aircraft carrier in choppy seas, carrying out underwater demolition — show the same pattern: some people have massive stress-responses and others are physiologically unflustered.

A similar phenomenon appears in the most mundane aspects of our everyday stressors. The supermarket line that you pick, naturally, turns out to move the slowest. You're simmering, your sense of irritation made worse by the fact that the person just behind you looks perfectly happy standing there, daydreaming.

Despite the endless ways in which stress can disrupt our well-being, we do not all collapse into puddles of stress-related disease and psychiatric dysfunction. Of course, we are not all exposed to identical external stressors; but given the same stressors, even the same major stressors, we vary tremendously in how our bodies and psyches cope. This final chapter asks the questions born of hope. Who makes up that subset who can cope? How do they do it? And how can we?

INDIVIDUAL DIFFERENCES IN THE STRESS-RESPONSE: SOME PLEASING EXAMPLES

Successful Aging Probably the best place to start is with successful aging, given all the bad news in the preceding chapter. One particularly grim set of findings had to do with glucocorticoids. Old rats, recall, secrete too much of these hormones

—elevated levels during basal, nonstressful situations, and difficulty shutting off secretion at the end of stress. I discussed the evidence that this could arise from damage to the hippocampus, the part of the brain that (in addition to playing a role in learning and memory) helps inhibit glucocorticoid secretion. Then, to complete the distressing story, it was revealed that glucocorticoids could hasten the death of hippocampal neurons. Furthermore, the tendency of glucocorticoids to damage the hippocampus worsens the oversecretion of glucocorticoids, which in turn leads to more hippocampal damage, more glucocorticoids, spiraling downward.

I proposed that "feedforward cascade" model half a dozen years ago. It seemed to describe a basic and inevitable feature of aging in the rat, one that seemed important (at least from my provincial perspective, having just spent 80 hours a week studying it in graduate school). I was pretty proud of myself. Then a few years ago an old friend, Michael Meaney of McGill University, did an experiment that deflated my grandiosity.

Meaney and colleagues studied that feedforward cascade in old rats. But they did something clever first. Before starting the studies, they tested the memory capacity of the rats. As is usual, on the average these old rats had memory problems, relative to young controls. But as usual there was a subset of old rats who were doing just fine, with no memory impairment whatsoever. Meaney and crew split the group of old rats into the impaired and the unimpaired. The latter turned out to show no evidence at all of that degenerative feedforward cascade. They had normal glucocorticoid levels basally and after stress. Their hippocampi had not lost neurons or lost receptors for glucocorticoids. All those awful degenerative features turned out not to be an inevitable part of the aging process. All those rats had to do was age successfully.

What was this subset of rats doing right? Oddly, it might have had something to do with their childhoods. If a rat is handled during the first few weeks of its life, it secretes less glucocorticoids as an adult. This generated a syllogism: If neonatal handling decreases the amount of glucocorticoids secreted as an adult, and such secretion in an adult influences the rate of hippocampal degeneration in old age, then handling a rat in the first few weeks of its life should alter the way it ages years later. Meaney's lab and I teamed up to test this and found exactly that. Do nothing more dramatic than pick a rat up and handle it fifteen minutes a day for the first few weeks of its life, put it back in its cage with the unhandled controls, come back two years later . . . and the handled rat is spared the entire feed-forward cascade of hippocampal damage, memory loss, and elevated glucocorticoid levels.

Maybe neonatal handling explains why a subset of old rats winds up aging successfully in this regard. Perhaps those are the ones whose mothers carried them around the cage before reading them Dr. Seuss, way back when. The chapter on growth reviewed various studies showing that the extent and quality of contact shortly after birth influence growth dramatically— why shouldn't other endocrine systems be similarly affected? It would seem particularly pleasing if this grim cascade of stress-related degeneration in old age could be derailed by something this subtle years earlier. No doubt there are other genetic and experiential factors that bias a rat toward successful or unsuccessful aging, a subject that Meaney still pursues. Of greatest importance, however, is the simple fact that this degeneration is not inevitable.

If the fates of inbred laboratory rats are this variable, how humans fare is likely to be even more diverse. Research on "successful aging" in humans is in its infancy. Some mammoth studies are beginning in which the characteristics of large numbers of middle-aged people will be monitored closely for the rest of their lives—diet, activity, cardiac function, personality profiles, cognitive skills, hormonal secretion, and so on. Ultimately, some of them will prove to be decrepit at age 70, others running marathons at 90. And then the hardy and patient researchers will be able to return to the decades of data and determine what, at the outset, distinguished the people who were destined to be successful agers. With any luck, they will have behavioral and physiological lessons to teach the rest of us.

Coping with Catastrophic Illness In the early 1960s, when scientists were just beginning to investigate whether psychological stress triggers the same hormonal changes that physical

Joseph Greenstein, "The Mighty Atom," in old age. An idol of my youth, Greenstein was still performing his feats of strength in Madison Square Garden as an octogenarian. He attributed it to clean, vegetarian living.

stressors do, a group of psychiatrists conducted what has become a classic study. It concerned the parents of children dying of cancer and the high glucocorticoid levels that those parents secreted. Predictably, there was great variance in this measure —some of the parents were secreting immense quantities of glucocorticoids; others were in the normal range. The investigators, in psychiatric interviews to explore in depth which parents were holding up best to this horrible stressor, identified a number of coping styles associated with a reduced glucocorticoid stress-response.

One important variable was whether the parent had a structure of religious rationalization to explain the illness. At one extreme was the parent who, while obviously profoundly distressed by her child's cancer, was deeply religious and perceived the cancer to be God's test of her family. She even reported an increase in her self-esteem—in effect, "God does not choose just anyone for a task like this; He chose us because He knew we were special, and could handle this." At the other extreme was the parent who said, in effect, "Don't tell me that God works in mysterious ways. In fact, I don't want to hear about God this decade at all." The researchers found that if you can look at your child dying of cancer and decide that God is choosing you for an extra-special assignment, you are likely to have less of a stress-response.

A second variable was the ability of parents to displace a major worry onto something less threatening. A father has been standing vigil by his sick child for weeks. It's clear to everyone that he needs to get away for a few days, to gain some distance, as he is near a breaking point. Plans are made for him to leave for a few days, but at the last moment he cancels the vacation, too anxious to go away. Why? At one extreme is the parent who says, "I've seen how rapidly medical crises can develop at this stage. What if he suddenly gets very sick and dies while I am away?" At the other extreme is the parent who is able to attribute the anxiety to something more manageable — "It would be good to get away now, but I worry that she will be lonely while I'm gone." The researchers found that the latter style was associated with lower glucocorticoid levels.

A third variable had to do with denial. When a child went into remission, which frequently happened, did the parents look at her and say to the doctor, "It's over with, there's nothing to worry about, we don't even want to hear the word remission, she is going to be fine"? Or did they peer anxiously at the child, wondering if every cough, every pain, every instant of fatigue was a sign that the disease had returned? During periods of remission, parents who denied that relapse and death were likely and instead focused on the seemingly healthy moment had lower glucocorticoid levels.

In the chapter on psychological stress, I noted that two organisms could have very different stress-responses in the face of the very same stressor, depending on whether they thought the stressor signaled that life was getting better or worse. Eventually, all of the children in the cancer study came out of remission and died. When that occurred, how did the parents fare? There were those who all along had accepted the possibility, even probability, of a relapse, and there were those who staunchly denied the possibility. As noted, during the period of remission the latter parents tended to be the low glucocorticoid secretors. But when their illusions were shattered and the disease returned, they had the largest increases in glucocorticoid concentrations. This grim and poignant finding foreshadows the main point of the latter half of this chapter. In applying notions about control, predictability, denial, and displacement to stress management, one must do so with great caution. These are powerful and double-edged swords.

Differences in Vulnerability to Learned Helplessness   In chapter 11, I described the learned helplessness model and its relevance to depression. I emphasized there how generalized the model appears to be: animals of many different species show some version of giving up on life in the face of something aversive and out of their control. Yet when you look at research papers based on the learned helplessness model, they are like those of any other stress-related field—dozens of bar graphs with T-shaped variance bars indicating large differences in response. For example, of the laboratory dogs put through one learned helplessness paradigm, about one third wind up being resistant to the phenomenon. This is the same idea as the one out of ten hostages who comes out of captivity a mentally healthier person than when he went in. Some folks and some animals are much more resistant to learned helplessness than average. Who are the lucky ones?

In that same chapter, we saw that an important factor in a person's resiliency was whether he had developed an "internalized" locus of control—the perception that he is the master of his destiny—or an "externalized" locus—in which he tends to perceive himself as having little control over the events of everyday life. Those who were internalizing in nature were far more resistant to learned helplessness. In effect, if you generally feel as if you have your hands on the wheel, you view an individual case of uncontrollable bad news to be only that—a single case, and not the whole world.

Why are some dogs naturally resistant to learned helplessness? An important clue: dogs born and raised in laboratories, bred only for research purposes, are more likely to succumb to learned helplessness than those who have come to the lab by way of the pound. Martin Seligman, one of the originators of helplessness research, offers this explanation: if a dog has been out in the real world, experiencing life and fending for itself (as the dogs who wind up in a pound are likely to have done), it has learned about how many controllable things there are in life. When the experience with an uncontrollable stressor occurs, the dog, in effect, is more likely to conclude that "this is awful, but it isn't the entire world." It resists globalizing the stressor into learned helplessness.

Stress and the Successful Baboon   If you are interested in understanding the stressors in our everyday lives and how to cope with them, study a troop of baboons in the Serengeti—big, smart, long-lived, highly social animals who live in groups of from 50 to 150. The Serengeti is a great place for them to live, offering minimal problems with predators, low infant mortality rates, easy access to food. Baboons there work perhaps four hours a day, foraging through the fields and trees for fruits, tubers, and edible grasses. This has a critical implication that makes them the perfect study subjects for what I've been interested in over the past fifteen summers I've snuck away from my laboratory to go there—the characteristics of the baboons who deal best with stress. If baboons are only spending four hours a day filling their stomachs, that leaves them with eight hours a day to be vile to each other. Social competition, coalitions forming to gang up on other animals, big males in bad moods beating up on someone smaller, snide gestures behind someone's back —just like us.

I am not being facetious. Think about some of the themes of the first chapter—how few of us are getting our ulcers because we have to walk ten miles a day looking for grubs to eat, how few of us become hypertensive because we are about to punch it out with someone over the last gulp from the water hole. We are ecologically buffered and privileged enough to get stressed mainly over social and psychological matters. Because the ecosystem of the Serengeti is so ideal for savanna baboons, they have the same luxury to make each other sick with social

Grooming, a wonderful means of social cohesion and stress reduction, in a society where everyone's back is not scratched equally.

and psychological stressors. Of course it is a world filled with affiliation, friendships, relatives who support each other; but it is a viciously competitive society as well. If a baboon in the Serengeti is miserable, it is almost always because another baboon has worked hard and long to bring about that state.

A tremendous percentage of that misery revolves around social rank. No matter how ideal an ecosystem is, resources are still finite, and in many species, including baboons, these are divided unevenly along lines of social rank. A dominance hierarchy exists with markedly different degrees of access to all sorts of resources: food, a safe place when predators are near, a shady spot during the day's heat, someone to groom them or mate with them. What goes into attaining a high rank and then maintaining it? Among female baboons, rank is inherited; you get a rank one below that of your mother or, if one exists, your older sister. Among males, rank changes over time. The high-ranking male is typically of prime age, in good health, with an impressive array of muscles and a terrifying set of canines. But dominance among the males is not merely a matter of being

A middle-ranking male baboon, who has spent all morning predating an impala, has the kill stolen from him by a high-ranking male.

good at fighting. These are far more sophisticated animals than that, and much of what they do falls into the realm of what must be described as psychologically stressing each other— intimidating someone with just the start of a threatening gesture until he gives up; forming a cooperative partnership with another male, so that anyone who challenges you suddenly finds himself dealing with two adversaries; harassing another male's sexual relationships with a female—no overt fighting or threatening, just relentlessly shadowing the guy until you so wear him down that he gives up the consortship. It's a socially complex world, in which the successful male is aided by familiarity with the writings of Machiavelli as much as by working out in the gym.

Given the drama and conspicuousness of dominance rank as an organizing principle of the troop, I began my work asking whether the stress-responses of males differed according to their rank. I watched them, collected detailed behavioral data, and then would anesthetize the animals under controlled conditions, using a blowgun.* Once they were unconscious, I could measure their glucocorticoid levels, their ability to make antibodies, their cholesterol profiles, and so on, under basal and stressed conditions.

As I had hoped to see, essentially every hormonal and physiological system relevant to stress that I studied varied as a

---

*The controls are daunting. You have to find an anesthetic that does not distort the levels of hormones that you are measuring. You have to dart every animal at the same time of day to control for daily fluctuations in hormone levels. If you want to get a first blood sample in which hormone levels reflect basal, nonstressed conditions, you can't dart someone who is sick or injured or who has had a fight or intercourse that day. For some of the cholesterol studies, I could not dart anyone who had eaten in the preceding twelve hours. If you are trying to measure resting hormone levels, you can't spend all morning making the same animal nervous as you repeatedly try to dart him; instead you get one shot, and you can't let him see it coming. Finally, once you dart him, you have to obtain the first blood sample rapidly, before hormone levels change in response to the dart. Quite a thing to do with your college education.

Why are these studies exclusively about males? Because of the difficulties inherent in trying to dart and anesthetize females. At any given time in this baboon population, approximately 80 percent of the adult females are either pregnant or nursing their young. You don't want to dart someone who is pregnant, as there is a good chance that the anesthesia will endanger the pregnancy. And you don't want to dart someone who has a young child holding onto her in a panic as she goes down, or spends a day badly endangered for lack of milk while mom is anesthetized.

function of rank. And consistently, when the dominance hierarchy was stable and everyone knew his place, subordinate males had the profiles that were more likely to set them up for stress-related disease. Their stress-responses were always turned on a little bit under basal conditions; for example, they had higher resting levels of glucocorticoids than dominant males did, fewer circulating lymphocytes, less "good" HDL cholesterol (the cholesterol that is being removed from the body, rather than potentially being deposited in blood vessels). And when a stressor occurred, their stress-responses weren't as efficient. Glucocorticoid levels and blood pressure rose more slowly than in the dominant animals, testosterone levels plummeted faster. Did rank cause the distinctive physiological profiles of these males, or did their physiological profiles determine their rank? With captive animals, you can study individuals before and after group formation and thus see whether the distinctive rank or the distinctive physiology emerged first. Consistently, those studies showed that the establishment of a rank caused the distinctive physiological profile to emerge, not the other way around.

This was all very gratifying, and I thought I was on to something important about the links between rank and stress-related physiology. Then, a dozen years into the project, it began to dawn on me that I was not looking at some of the most interesting variables in the lives of these animals.

If you look at a troop of baboons for a week, you will sense that these are strongly individualistic animals, with very distinct personalities. What do I mean by a baboon personality? Two males of similar ranks may differ dramatically as to how readily they form partnerships with other males, how much they like to groom females, whether they play with kids, whether they sulk after losing a fight or go beat up on someone smaller. A student of mine, Justina Ray, and I analyzed years of behavioral data to try to formalize different elements of style and personality among these animals. We found that many of the physiologic features that we thought were associated with rank were instead associated with personality styles. It turned out that not all dominant males had the great trait of low resting glucocorticoid levels; instead, it was only the large subset with certain types of personalities, and high-ranking males without those personality traits had glucocorticoid levels just as high as the lowest ranking males in the troop.

Thus, the sixty-four-dollar question: What personality traits and styles of behavior work best for a baboon? Who had the lowest glucocorticoid levels, for example? If you took some of the best books on human stress management techniques and could somehow translate them into baboon, they would suggest the precise patterns observed in these "successful" males.

Among the dominant males, we observed a cluster of behavioral traits associated with low resting glucocorticoid levels independent of rank. Some of these traits were related to how males competed with each other. The first trait was whether a male could tell the difference between a threatening and a neutral interaction with a rival. How does one spot this in a baboon? Look at a particular male. Along comes his worst rival, sits down next to him, and makes a threatening gesture. What does our male subject do next? Alternative scenario: our guy is sitting there, his worst rival comes along and . . . wanders off to the next field to fall asleep. What does our guy do in this situation?

Some males can tell the difference between these situations. Threatened from a foot away, they get agitated, vigilant, prepared; when their rival is taking a nap, they keep doing whatever they were doing. They can tell that one situation is bad news, the other is meaningless. But some males get agitated when their rival is taking a nap across the field—the sort of situation that happens five times a day. If a male baboon can't tell the difference between the two situations, on the average his resting glucocorticoid levels are twice as high as those of the guy who can tell the difference—after correcting for rank as a variable. If a rival napping across the field throws a male into turmoil, he is going to be in a constant state of stress. No wonder his glucocorticoid levels are elevated.

Next variable. If the situation really is threatening (the rival is a foot away and making menacing moves), does our male sit there passively and wait for the fight, or does he take control of the situation and strike first? Males who sit there passively, abdicating control, have much higher glucocorticoid levels than the take-charge types, after rank is eliminated as a factor in the analysis.

A third variable: after a fight, can the baboon tell whether he won or lost? Some guys are great at it; they win a fight, and they groom their best friend. They lose a fight, and they beat up someone smaller. Other baboons react the same way regardless of outcome; they can't tell if life is improving or worsening. The baboon who can't tell the difference between winning and losing a fight has much higher glucocorticoid levels, on the average, than the guys who can, independent of rank.

Final variable. If a male has lost a fight, what does he do next? Does he sulk by himself, groom someone, or beat someone up? Discouragingly, it turns out that the males who are most likely to go beat on someone—"displaced aggression" is the term—have lower glucocorticoid levels, again after rank is eliminated as a variable.

Thus, independent of rank, lower basal glucocorticoid levels are found in males who are best at telling the difference between threatening and neutral interactions, who take the initiative if the situation clearly is threatening, who are best at telling whether they won or lost, and in the latter case, most likely to make someone else pay for it. This echoes some of the themes from the chapter on psychological stress. The males who were coping best (at least by this endocrine measure) had high degrees of social control (initiating the fights), predictability (they can accurately assess whether a situation is threatening, whether an outcome is good news), and outlets for frustration (a tendency to give rather than get ulcers).

Our subsequent studies have shown another set of traits that also predicts low basal glucocorticoid levels. These traits have nothing to do with how males compete with each other. Instead, they are related to patterns of social affiliation. Males who spent the most time grooming females not in heat (not of immediate sexual interest), who are groomed by them the most frequently, who spend the most time playing with the young— these are the low glucocorticoid guys. Put most basically (and not at all anthropomorphically), these are male baboons who are most capable of developing friendships. This finding is re-markably similar to those discussed in previous chapters regard-ing the protective effects of social affiliation against stress-re-lated disease in humans.

Another student of mine, Charles Virgin, and I are now analyzing personality styles among the subordinate animals. If you have to be low-ranking, are there certain behavioral styles that are associated with a more adaptive physiological profile? While our results are still preliminary, we are seeing evidence that, again, the subset of males who are most socially affiliated have the lowest glucocorticoid levels.

What is the background of these few males on the Seren-geti who appear least susceptible to stress? At the moment, we haven't a clue. Male baboons change troops at puberty, often moving dozens of miles before finding an adult troop to join. It is virtually impossible to track the same individuals from birth to adulthood, so I have no idea what their childhoods were like, if their mothers were permissive or stern, whether they were forced to take piano lessons, and so on. Given the unique fea-tures of this population, I will never get these answers. Steven Suomi, however, of the National Institute of Mental Health, has studied these issues in captive primates. Predictably, he finds that both genetics and mothering style contribute to the behav-ioral "personality" a primate will grow up to have. In general, it is the children of mothers who are less anxious and more per-missive who grow up to be more confident and exploratory.

There is an association between a baboon's social rank and how his body responds to stress. In effect, rank is one way of describing how the real world treats you. By contrast, individual differences in personality are a way of describing how the ani-mal *perceives, responds to*, and *copes* with that real world, and these personality variables are turning out to be at least as important as the external reality of rank in predicting differences in stress-related physiology. Baboons appear to differ dramati-cally in whether they see the world full of water holes half full or half empty, and their physiology appears to reflect this as well. An obvious but encouraging point: if some baboons have the psychological means to take life's ups and downs in stride, the same is certainly a plausible goal for humans.

COPING WITH STRESS: SOME SUCCESS STORIES

Parents somehow shouldering the burden of their child's fatal illness, a low-ranking baboon who has a network of friends, a dog resisting learned helplessness — these are striking examples of individuals who, faced with a less than ideal situation, nevertheless excel at coping. That's great, but what if you don't already happen to be that sort of individual? When it comes to rats, if you are not among those aging successfully and preserving their hippocampi, you are probably out of luck. The first few weeks of these rats' lives appear to have been critical in determining their aging, and none of us, rat or human, can go back and change our infancies (let alone change our genes, which sometimes play a not insignificant role in how much of a hormone you make and secrete, how long it persists in the bloodstream, how many receptors there are for it on target tissues, and so on). The other cases of successfully coping with stress may not be any more encouraging to the rest of us. What if we happen not to be the sort of baboon who looks at the bright side, the person who holds on to hope when others become hopeless, the parent of the child with cancer who somehow psychologically manages the unmanageable? These are all stories of individuals who have supreme gifts of coping. For us ungifted ones, are there ways to change the world around us and to alter our perceptions of it so that psychological stress becomes at least a bit less stressful?

A first thing to emphasize is that we can change the way we cope, both physiologically and psychologically. As the most obvious example, physical conditioning brought about by regular exercise will lower blood pressure and resting heart rate and increase lung capacity, just to mention a few of its effects. Among Type A people, psychotherapy has been shown to change not only behaviors but also cholesterol profiles, risk of heart attack, and risk of dying, independent of changes in diet or other physiological regulators of cholesterol. Some preliminary studies have also shown that various relaxation techniques or techniques that "alter consciousness" may have beneficial physiological effects. For example, trained practitioners of transcendental meditation are reported to be able to reduce glucocorticoid levels and various indices of their bodies' metabolism, at least while they are actually meditating. As another example, the pain and stressfulness of delivery can be modulated by relaxation techniques such as Lamaze. Sheer repetition of certain activities can change the connection between your behavior and activation of your stress-response. In one classic study, Norwegian soldiers learning to parachute were studied over the course of months of training. At the time of their first jump, they were all terrified; they felt like vats of Jell-O, and their bodies reflected it. Glucocorticoids and epinephrine levels were elevated, testosterone levels were suppressed — all for hours before and after the jump. As they repeated the experience, mastered it, and, most of all, learned not to be terrified, their hormone secretion patterns changed. By the end of training they were no longer turning on their stress-response hours before and after the jump, only at the actual time. They were able to confine their stress-response to an appropriate moment, when there was a physical stressor; the entire psychological component of the stress-response had been habituated away.

All of these examples show that the workings of the stress-response can change over time. We grow, learn, adapt, get bored, develop an interest, mature, harden, forget. We are malleable beasts. What are the buttons we can use to manipulate the system in a way that will benefit us?

The issues raised in the chapter on the psychology of stress are obviously critical: control, predictability, social support, outlets for frustration. Seligman and colleagues, for example, have reported some success in the laboratory in buffering people from learned helplessness when confronted with an unsolvable task — if subjects are first given "empowering" exercises (various tasks that they readily can master and control). But this is a fairly artificial setting. Some classic studies have manipulated similar psychological variables in the real world — some of the grimmest parts of the real world. The results have been startling.

SELF-MEDICATION AND CHRONIC PAIN SYNDROMES

Whenever something painful happens to me, amid all the distress I am surprised at being reminded of how painful pain is. That thought is always followed by another, "What if I hurt like this all the time?" Chronic pain syndromes are extraordinarily debilitating. Diabetic neuropathies, crushed spinal nerve roots, severe burns, recovery after surgery can all be immensely painful. This poses a medical problem, insofar as it is often difficult to give enough drugs to control the pain without causing addiction or putting the person in danger of an overdose. As any nurse will attest, this also poses a management problem, as the chronic pain patient spends half the day hitting the call button, wanting to know when his next painkiller is coming, and the nurse has to spend half the day explaining that it is not yet time. A memory that will always make me shudder: a few years back, my father was hospitalized. In the room next door was an elderly man who, seemingly around the clock, every thirty seconds, would plaintively shout in a heavy Yiddish accent, "Nurse. Nurse! It hurts. It hurts! Nurse!" The first day it was horrifying. The second day it was irritating. By the third day, it had all the impact of the rhythmic chirping of crickets.

A while back some researchers got an utterly mad idea, the thought of frothing lunatics. Why not give the painkillers to the patients and let them decide when they need medication? You can just imagine the apoplexy that mainstream medicine would have over that one—patients will overdose, become addicts, you can't let patients do that. It was tried with cancer patients and postsurgical patients, and it turned out that the patients did just fine when they self-medicated. In fact, the total amount of painkillers consumed decreased.

Why should consumption go down? Because when you are lying there in bed, in pain, uncertain of the time, uncertain if the nurse has heard your call or will have time to respond, uncertain of everything, you are asking for painkillers not only to stop the pain but also to stop the uncertainty. Reinstitute control, give the patient the knowledge that the medication is there for the instant that the pain becomes too severe, and the pain often becomes far more manageable.

INCREASING CONTROL IN NURSING HOMES

I can imagine few settings that better reveal the nature of psychological stress than a nursing home. Under the best of circumstances, the elderly tend to have a less active, less assertive coping style than young people. When confronted by stressors, the latter are more likely to try to confront and solve the problem, while the former are more likely to distance themselves from the stressor or adjust their attitude towards it. The nursing home setting worsens these tendencies toward withdrawal and passivity: It's a world in which you are often isolated from the social support network of a lifetime and in which you have little control over your daily activities, your finances, often your own body. A world of few outlets for frustration, in which you are often treated like a child—"infantilized." What you can most easily predict: life will get worse.

A number of psychologists have ventured into this world to try to apply some of the ideas about control and self-efficacy outlined in chapter 10. In one study, for example, residents of a nursing home were given more responsibility for everyday decision making. They were made responsible for choosing their meals for the next day, signing up in advance for social activities, picking out and caring for a plant for their room, instead of having one placed there and cared for by the nurses ("Oh, here, I'll water that, dear, why don't you just get back into bed"). People became more active—initiating more social interactions—and described themselves in questionnaires as happier. Their health improved, as rated by doctors unaware of whether they were in the increased-responsibility group or the control group. Most remarkable of all, the death rate in the former group was half that of the latter.

In other studies, different variables of control were manipulated. Almost unanimously, these studies show that a moderate increase in control produces all of the salutary effects just described; in a few studies, physiological measures were even taken, showing changes like reductions in glucocorticoid levels or improved immune function. The forms that increased control could take were many. In one study, the baseline group was left alone, while the experimental group was organized into a residents' council that made decisions about life in the nursing home. In the latter group, health improved and individuals showed more voluntary participation in social activities. In another study, residents in a nursing home were being involuntarily moved to a different residence because of the financial collapse of the first institution. The baseline group was moved in the normal manner, while the experimental group was given extensive lectures on the new home and given control of a wide variety of issues connected with the move (the day of the move, the decor of the room they would live in, and so on). When the move occurred, there were far fewer medical complications for the latter group. The infantilizing effects of loss of control were shown explicitly in another study in which residents were given a variety of tasks to do. When the staff present *encouraged* them, performance improved; when the staff present *helped* them, performance declined.

Another study of increased self-control among nursing home populations yielded the (by now) expected results plus an unexpected one, one that was an even more poignant affirmation of some of the principles outlined here. This study concerned visits by college students to people in nursing homes. One nursing-home group, the baseline group, received no student visitors. In a second group, students would arrive at unpredictable times to chat. There were various improvements in functioning and health in this group, testifying to the positive effects of increased social contact. In the third and fourth groups, control and predictability were introduced — in the third group, the residents could decide when the visit occurred, whereas in the fourth they could not control it, but at least were told when the visit would take place. Functioning and health improved even more in both of those groups, compared to the second. Control and predictability help.

It was then that the investigators got their extra, unexpected finding. End of the study, celebration, everyone delighted with the clear-cut and positive results, papers to be published, lectures to the given. Students visit the people in the nursing home for a last time, offer an awkward, "It's been wonderful getting to know you, I'll be dropping by, er, sometime soon, best of luck . . . " What happens then? Do the people whose functioning, happiness, and health improved now decline back to preexperiment levels? No. They drop even further, winding up worse off than before the study.

This makes perfect sense. Think of how it is to get 25 shocks an hour when yesterday you got 10, compared to 25 shocks an hour when yesterday you got 50. Think of what it feels like to have your child come out of remission after you had spent the last year denying the possibility that it could ever happen. In both cases, a perception of things worsening. It is one thing to be in a nursing home, lonely, isolated, visited once a month by your bored children. It is even worse to be in that situation and having a chance to spend time with bright, eager young people who seemed interested in you, to now find they aren't coming anymore. All but the most heroically strong among us would slip another step in the face of this loss. It is true that hope, no matter how irrational, can sustain us in the darkest of times. But nothing can break us more effectively than hope given and then taken away capriciously.

STRESS MANAGEMENT: READING THE LABEL CAREFULLY

These studies generate some simple answers to coping with stress that are far from simple to implement in everyday life. They emphasize the importance of manipulating feelings of control, predictability, outlets for frustration, social connectiveness, the perception of whether things are worsening or improving. In effect, the nursing home and pain studies are encouraging dispatches from the front lines in this war of coping. Their simple, empowering, liberating message: if manipulating such psychological variables can work in these trying circumstances, it certainly should for the more trivial psychological stressors that fill our daily lives.

This is the message that fills stress management seminars, therapy sessions, and the many books on the topic. Uniformly, they emphasize finding means to gain at least some degree of control in difficult situations, viewing bad situations as discrete events rather than permanent or pervasive ones, finding appropriate outlets for frustration and means of social support and solace in difficult times. But the really good ones also teach that the story is not that simple. It is critical that one not walk away with the conclusion that in order to manage and minimize psychological stressors, the solution is always more control, more predictability, more outlets, more social affiliation.

Social affiliation is not always the solution to psychological turmoil. We can easily think of people who would be the last ones on earth we would want to be stuck with when we are troubled. We can easily think of troubled circumstances where being with *anyone* would make us feel worse. Physiological studies have demonstrated this as well. Take a rodent or a primate that has been housed alone and put it into a social group. The typical result is a massive stress-response. In the case of monkeys, this can go on for weeks or months while they tensely go about figuring out who dominates whom in the group's social hierarchy.* In another demonstration of this principle, infant monkeys were separated from their mothers. Predictably, they had pretty sizable stress-responses, with elevations in glucocorticoid levels. The elevation could be prevented if the infant was placed in a social group of monkeys—but only if the infant already knew those animals. There is little to be derived in the way of comfort from strangers.

Even once animals are no longer strangers, on the average half of those in any social group will be socially dominant to any given individual, and having more dominant animals around is not necessarily a comfort during trouble. Even intimate social affiliation is not always helpful. We saw in the psychoimmunity chapter that being married is associated with all sorts of better health outcomes. There is an obvious but important exception to this general rule, however: being in a *bad* marriage is associated with immune suppression.

Increased degrees of predictability and information about the future are not always good news, either. As noted in chapter 10, it does little good to get predictive information about very common events (because they are basically inevitable) or very rare ones (because you weren't anxious about them anyway). It does little good to get predictive information a few seconds before something bad happens (because there isn't time to derive the psychological advantages of being able to relax a bit) or way in advance of the event (because who's worrying anyway?).

In some cases, predictive information can even make things worse—for example, when the information tells you little. Suppose you are incredibly nervous about an important examina-

---

*A few years ago, the U.S. government proposed new guidelines to improve the psychological well-being of primates used for research; one well-intentioned but uninformed feature was that monkeys housed individually during a study should, at least once a week, spend time in a group of other monkeys. That precise social situation had been studied for years as a model of chronic social stress, and it was clear that the regulations would do anything but increase the psychological well-being of these animals. Fortunately, the proposed rules were changed after some expert testimony.

tion you are about to take, and a friend furtively gives you a piece of news: "I just heard that they are really going to be hard on you, absolutely rake you over the coals." How? "I don't know, I couldn't find out that part." I would wager that most of us would be more anxious with that extra information, not less.

An overabundance of information can be stressful as well. One of the places I dreaded most in graduate school was the "new journal desk" in the library, where all the science journals received the previous week were displayed, thousands of pages of them. Everyone would circle around it, teetering on the edge of anxiety attacks. All that available information seemed to taunt us with how out of control we felt—stupid, left behind, out of touch, and overwhelmed.

Manipulating a sense of control is probably the most double-edged variable in psychological stress. Too much of a sense of control can be crippling, whether the sense is accurate or not. I offer two disparate examples.

When he was a medical student, a friend embarked on his surgery rotation. That first day, nervous, with no idea what to expect, he went to his assigned operating room and stood at the back of a crowd of doctors and nurses doing a kidney transplant. Hours into it, the chief surgeon suddenly turned to him: "Ah, you're the new medical student, good, come here, grab this retractor, hold it right here, steady, good boy." Surgery continued; my friend was ignored as he precariously maintained the uncomfortable position the surgeon had put him in, leaning forward at an angle, one arm thrust amid the crowd, holding the instrument, unable to see what was going on. Hours passed. He grew woozy, faint from the tension of holding still. He found himself teetering, eyes beginning to close—when the surgeon loomed before him. "Don't move a *muscle*, because you're going to screw up everything!" Galvanized, panicked, half-ill, he barely held on . . . only to discover that the "you're going to screw up everything" scenario was a stupid hazing trick done to every new med student. He had been holding an instrument over some irrelevant part of the body the entire time, tricked into feeling utterly responsible for the survival of the patient, when in fact, his actions had no consequence at all. (He chose another medical specialty.)

The second example concerns one of the heaviest burdens of psychological stress imaginable. It involved a lone man given an extraordinary sense of control over a situation that simply could not be ameliorated by any action. In 1947, Lord Mountbatten surprised the world by announcing that Britain was pulling out of the British Raj within months, that the Indian subcontinent would get its independence far sooner than had been expected. What should be done about the Hindu and Muslim populations — different cultures, seething with tensions for centuries? The awful decision was made to divide the subcontinent into two countries, Hindu India and Muslim Pakistan.

Where would the boundary be drawn? Endless unworkable solutions were raised and scuttled until everyone agreed to choose an outside arbitrator. The call went to Sir Cyril Radcliffe, an English barrister known for his brilliance, fairness, and most of all, his utter disinterest in and ignorance about the Indian subcontinent. With all the force of imperial noblesse oblige used to twist his arm, he was whisked off to India and given seven weeks to decide the fate of 88 million people and 15,000 square miles of land, working with unreliable maps and unreliable advisors, every Indian he encountered frantic to cajole, bully, threaten, and beg Radcliffe into drawing the border at a particular point.

For weeks Radcliffe worked, trying to determine when to make a decision based on ethnicity, when on topography, when on economics. Should he separate an agricultural region from the irrigation system that watered it, or leave a Muslim village stranded in Hindu India? Separate a factory and the port used to ship its products from the roads by which raw materials were delivered, or sentence a Hindu holy city to control by Muslim Pakistan? Under stupefying time pressure he demarcated thirty miles of border a day, locked away in a cottage under increasing threats of violence, certain that no matter what he did it would be a disaster in a land too heterogeneous to ever be divided peacefully and too hostile and fragmented to ever be left peacefully as one. His task finished, he left, the most hated man in the subcontinent, under military protection.

In the coming months, the line Radcliffe drew circumscribed one of the greatest tragedies of history, as 10 million people were forced to flee their ancestral lands for their new national homes. Somewhere between 200,000 and 500,000 people were slaughtered amid ethnic and religious fighting. In our more grandiose moments, some of us might relish the opportunity to affect the lives of 88 million people — but never, absolutely never, when the sense of control is illusory and any action you take leads inevitably to disaster. It is anything but psychologically comforting to believe that you can control the uncontrollable.

Yet, remarkably, the story of Cyril Radcliffe not only teaches us about the dangers of having an illusory sense of control but also about the enormous range of individual responses to stress. Apparently Mountbatten had found the one human capable of performing the impossible task who could cope with its stressfulness, utterly unaffected by the human drama. (Or perhaps, British gentleman that he was, Radcliffe thought that any emotions he might feel were none of the world's damn business.) A book of Radcliffe's legal and political essays includes the transcript of a broadcast he gave on the BBC in October 1947, a few months after his return and the granting of independence. It was a month in which the British news was dominated daily by sickening reports of massacre after massacre, Muslims and Hindus and Sikhs butchering each other, mass rapes, villages of people burned to death in their homes, ritual mutilation of victims, all amid columns of dying refugees crawling toward their new countries. And what did Radcliffe speak about? The excellent values and standards of the British civil servants who had served in India over the centuries; he lamented how little art and literature there was to commemorate them. To quote W. H. Auden's poem, "Partition":

In seven weeks it was done, the frontiers decided,
A continent for better or worse divided.
The next day he sailed for England, where he quickly forgot
The case, as a good lawyer must. Return he would not,
Afraid, as he told his Club, that he might get shot.

Finally, recall the discussion in chapter 9 on the links between psychological factors and cancer. There is indeed a link between the two — certain types of emotional stress appear to be associated with an increased risk of cancer in humans and accelerated tumor growth in experimental animals — but the association is a fairly weak one. It is clearly a travesty to lead cancer patients or their families to believe, misinterpreting the power of these studies, that there is more possibility for control over the causes and courses of cancers than actually exists. Doing so is simply teaching the victims of cancer and their families that the disease is their own fault, which is neither true nor conducive to reducing stress in an already stressful situation.

Control is not always a good thing psychologically, and a principle of good stress management cannot be simply to increase the perceived amount of control in one's life. It depends on what that perception implies, as we saw in chapter 10. Is it stress-reducing to feel a sense of control when something bad happens? If you think, "Whew, that was bad, but imagine how much worse it would have been if I hadn't been in charge," a sense of control is clearly working to buffer you from feeling more stressed. However if you think, "What a disaster and it's all my fault. I should have prevented it," a sense of control is working to your detriment. This dichotomy can be roughly translated into the following rule for when something stressful occurs: The more disastrous a stressor is, the worse it is to believe you had some control over the outcome, because you are inevitably led to think about how much better things would have turned out, if only you had done something more. A sense of control works best for milder stressors. (Remember, this advice concerns the sense of control you *perceive* yourself having, as opposed to how much control you actually have.)

SOME CONCLUSIONS AND TENTATIVE PRESCRIPTIONS

All of these cautionary tales run through the work of the scientists and clinicians giving the best advice in stress management. Judith Rodin, for example, a Yale psychologist who is one of the leaders in the field of encouraging greater control among people in nursing homes, emphasizes this in her writing — do not inadvertently overload the elderly with a sense of responsibility for things that they cannot plausibly control; pick the battles carefully. A similar theme is found in the writings of Ellen Langer, a Harvard psychologist who has been a frequent collaborator of Rodin's.

Redford Williams, the Duke University physician perhaps most responsible for focusing attention on the hostility component of Type A personalities, writes extensively about the particular dangers of "unrealistic anger." He warns against trying to assert control over something that does not need correcting or that cannot be corrected — an approach at which Type A's tend to excel.

Similar ideas are emphasized by David Spiegel, the Stanford psychiatrist who surprised both the medical community and himself with his observations that a supportive therapy setting caused a significant extension of survival time in breast cancer patients. "We encourage our patients to hope for the best, but prepare for the worst," he writes, citing research to show that increasing a patient's sense of control over the *future* course of the disease is associated with an increase in spirit, whereas increasing a patient's belief in her control over what *caused* the disease produces the opposite. Once again, if the outcome of something is awful, it does not do great things for morale to be led to believe that you had the power to have prevented it.

Richard Lazarus, the University of California (Berkeley) psychologist who is a leading theorist on stress and coping, has written extensively about the occasional advantages of denial and lack of information. In the immediate aftermath of some medical disaster, for example, when a person is too weak to act constructively in a problem-solving way, the last things he needs is detailed information about how bad reality is or advice to start working on a sense of control. It is only later that these strategies are likely to be helpful, rather than hurtful.

This idea is also encompassed in a personality test found in a recent book by Martin Seligman, the University of Pennsylvania psychologist who pioneered thinking about learned help-lessness. He is now concentrating on the subset of individuals who are resistant to the phenomenon, asking what they are doing right and how we can make use of these attitudes our-selves. To use the title of his new book, he is now studying "learned optimism." The personality test measures people's at-tributional style: when something happens, to what do they attribute its cause? How *externalized* are they: do they attribute outcomes to their own actions, to those of others, or to chance? How *pervasive* do they view events as being: is this occurrence an isolated event, or is this how everything works? How *perma-nent* do they view events as being: is this a one-time occurrence, or are things always going to be this way? Critically, the extent to which people are pervasive, permanent, or externalizing in their beliefs does not by itself predict how they fare in the face of life's challenges. Seligman argues that it depends on whether the news is good or bad. If the news is good, the healthiest people think, "This is always how it is in all sorts of situations, and it came about as a result of my efforts." When the news is bad, those same healthy people use an opposite attributional strategy: "That was awful, but it was due to this one flukey event, out of my control and unlikely to happen again or to apply to other parts of my life." Good news viewed as generated by your own actions; bad news viewed as an isolated exception.

What general strategies can help us the most in the face of psychological stressors? Obviously, the first step is to accurately recognize signs of the stress-response and to identify the situa-tions most responsible for it. Once you have done that, there are some ways to proceed:

- One successful strategy is to find an outlet for life's frustrations that can be used regularly. Make it a benign one for those around you—one should not give ulcers in order to avoid getting them—and choose one that you find personally com-patible. Prayer, meditation, ballroom dancing, psychoanalysis, Bach, competitive sports—each may help some people but not others. Read the fine print and the ingredient list on each new form of supposed antistress salvation, be skeptical of hype,

"Is there anyone here who specializes in stress management?"

listen to your own responses with each new exploration and trust them.

- In the face of terrible news beyond control, beyond prevention, beyond healing, those who are able to find the means to deny tend to cope best. Such denial is not only permissible, it may be the only means of sanity. But in the face of lesser problems, one should hope, but protectively and rationally. Find ways to view even the most stressful of situations as holding the promise of improvement but do not deny the possibility that things will not improve. Balance these two opposing trends carefully. Hope for the best and let that dominate most of your emotions, but at the same time let one small piece of you prepare for the worst.

- Those who cope with stress successfully tend to seek control in the face of stressors but do not try to control in the present things that have already come to pass. They do not try to control future events that are uncontrollable and do not try to fix things that are not broken or that are broken beyond repair. When faced with the large wall of a stressor, one should not assume there will be a breakthrough, one single, controlling solution that will make the wall disappear. Assume instead that the wall can be scaled by a series of footholds of control, each one small but still capable of giving support.

- It is generally helpful to seek predictable, accurate information. However, such information is not useful if it comes too soon or too late, if it is unnecessary information, if there is so much information that it is stressful in and of itself, or if the information is about news far worse than one wants to know.

- It is important to find sources of social affiliation and support. Even in this most obsessively individualistic of societies, most of us yearn to feel part of something larger than ourselves. But one should not mistake true affiliation and support for mere socializing. A person can feel vastly lonely in a crowd or when faced with a supposed intimate who has proved to be a stranger. Be patient; most of us spend a lifetime learning how to be truly good friends and spouses.

Two far more beautiful ways of expressing these ideas about flexibility, resiliency, picking your battles and your weapons carefully include something I once heard at a Quaker meeting:

In the face of strong winds, let me be a blade of grass.
In the face of strong walls, let me be a gale of wind.

And the prayer of the theologian Reinhold Niebuhr, adopted by Alcoholics Anonymous:

God grant me the serenity to accept the things I cannot change, courage to change the things I can, and wisdom to know the difference.

Stress is not everywhere. Every twinge of dysfunction in our bodies is not a manifestation of stress-related disease. It is true that the real world is full of bad things that we can finesse away by altering our outlook and psychological makeup, but it is also full of awful things that cannot be eliminated by a change in attitude, no matter how heroically, fervently, complexly, ritualistically we may wish. Once we are actually sick with the illnesses, the fantasy of which keeps us anxiously awake at two

Constantin Brancusi, 1912: The Kiss, *limestone.*

in the morning, the things that will save us have little to do with the content of this book. Once we have that cardiac arrest, once a tumor has metastasized, once our brain has been badly deprived of oxygen, little about our psychological outlook is likely to help. We have entered the realm where someone else—a highly trained physician—must use the most high-tech of appropriate medical interventions.

These caveats must be emphasized repeatedly in teaching what cures to seek and what attributions to make when confronted with many diseases. But amid this caution, there remains a whole realm of health and disease that is sensitive to the quality of our minds—our thoughts and emotions and behaviors. And sometimes whether we become sick with the diseases that frighten us at two in the morning will reflect this realm of the mind. It is here that we must turn from the physicians and their ability to clean up the mess afterward, and recognize our own capacity to *prevent* some of these problems beforehand in the small steps with which we live our everyday lives.

Perhaps I'm beginning to sound like your grandmother, advising you to be happy and not to worry so much. This advice may sound platitudinous, trivial, or both. But change the way even a rat perceives its world and you dramatically alter the likelihood of it getting a disease. These ideas are no mere truisms. They are powerful, potentially liberating forces to be harnessed. As a physiologist who has studied stress for many years, I clearly see that the physiology of the system is often no more decisive than the psychology. We return to the catalogue at the beginning of the first chapter, the things we all find stressful—traffic jams, money worries, overwork, the anxieties of relationships. Few of them are "real" in the sense that that zebra or that lion would understand. In our privileged lives, we are uniquely smart enough to have invented these stressors and uniquely foolish enough to have let them, too often, dominate our lives. Surely we have the potential wisdom to banish their stressful hold.

NOTES

The following annotated references are quite specific; I have gone into this much detail both to show why I have made some of the statements I have and as a guide for the hordes of you out there who are going to want to read those original Russian references on metabolic rates in chess players. In many of these cases, there are a vast number of references supporting some statement in the book. In those instances, I cite only a few, typically the original demonstration, any that are particularly good, classic or accessible, and one that is as recent as possible.

CHAPTER 1: WHY DON'T ZEBRAS GET ULCERS?

For years, in lectures, I've rhetorically compared disease patterns in humans with those of zebras, and when sitting down to write this book, it suddenly scared the willies out of me that I wasn't sure about the business with zebras and ulcers. And then where would we be? What good is a book entitled something like *Why Do Zebras Get Ulcers Less Frequently Than We Do and for Some Fairly Different Reasons, Although It's Complicated?* However, according to *Zoo and Wild Animal Medicine* (M. Fowler; Philadelphia: Saunders, 1986, 2nd ed.), and phone calls to the zebra vets at the Brookfield, Bronx, National, Philadelphia, and San Diego zoos, ulcers are extremely uncommon in zebras. They occur in animals undergoing severe and unnatural stress (e.g., when they are first transported into a zoo), but that is about the only circumstance. Stated in the framework of this book, when left to their own devices (either in the wild or in reasonably large enclosures in a zoo), zebras don't develop ulcers.

Many of the ideas in this chapter have a long history in stress physiology. The main point was stated well by Walter Cannon over half a century ago: "A highly important change has occurred in the incidence of disease in our country. . . . serious infections, formerly extensive and disastrous, have markedly decreased or almost disappeared, . . . meanwhile conditions involving strain in the nervous system have been greatly augmented" ("The role of emotion in disease," *Annals of Internal Medicine,* vol. 9, no. II, May 1936).

PAGE 2: Viewed through the eclipse of World War II, we seem to remember World War I with odd fondness — Irving Berlin tunes, colorful uniforms, rickety motorcars, and heads of states with silly titles and big mustaches. Eight and a half million people were killed in the pointless bloodbath we know as World War I (D. Fromkin. 1989. *A Peace to End All Peace.* New York: Avon Books, 379). The flu that swept the planet at the same time, by contrast, killed twenty million (W. McNeill. *Plagues and Peoples.* New York: Doubleday Books, 255). "The sum of American sailors and soldiers who died of flu and pneumonia in 1918 is over 43,000, about 80 percent of American battle deaths in the war" (A. Crosby. 1918, 1976. *Epidemic and Peace.* London: Greenwood Press, 36).

PAGE 6: The definitive study on chess players was carried out by the physiologist Leroy DuBeck and his graduate student, Charlotte Leedy. They wired up chess players in order to measure their breathing rates, blood pressure, muscle contractions, and so on, and monitored the players before, during, and after major tournaments. They found tripling of breathing rates, muscle contractions, systolic blood pressures that soared to over 200 — exactly the sort of thing seen in athletes during physical competition. See the original report, Leedy's thesis "The effects of tournament chess playing on selected physiological responses in players of varying aspirations and abilities" (Temple University, 1975) or their brief report (Leedy, C., and DuBeck, L. 1971. "Physiological changes during tournament chess." *Chess Life and Review,* 708). In a telephone conversation, DuBeck also tells the story of the international match in the early 1970s between grand masters Bent Larson and Bobby Fischer, in which the former had to be given antihypertensive medication in the middle of his losing match; his blood pressure remained elevated for days afterward. The Kasparov/Karpov report is from *The New York Times,* 20 December 1990. And for that special chess fan out there who just can't get enough of this subject, may I suggest as the perfect gift a copy of Glezerov, V., and Sobol, E. 1987. "Hygenic evaluation of the changes in work capacity of young chess players during training." *Gigiena i Sanitariia* 24, in the original Russian.

PAGE 8: Selye published numerous autobiographical articles and books, many of which contain the story of the ovarian extract and his discovery of the nonspecific stress-response; a good example is *The Stress of My Life* (New York: Van Nostrand, 1979). The book also contains Selye's claim that he was the first to use the word "stress" in a biomedical, rather than engineering, sense. Actually, Walter Cannon beat him to it by decades (1914. "The interrelations of emotions as suggested by recent physiological researches." *American Journal of Psychology* 25, 256). This point was brought up in a colorful debate between Selye and John Mason, a psychiatrist whose pioneering work on the psychological stress-response is discussed later (Mason, J., 1975. "A historical view of the stress field." *Journal of Human Stress* 1, 6; part II: 1, 22. Selye, H., 1975. "Confusion and controversy in the stress field." *Journal of Human Stress* 1, 37).

PAGE 16: Descriptions of Addison's disease can be found in all endocrinology textbooks, as it is one of the best-studied endocrine disorders. Shy-Drager is rarer and more recent, first described in 1960. For a description right from the horses' mouths, see Shy, G., and Drager, G., 1960. "A neurological syndrome associated with ortho-static hypotension." *A.M.A. Archives of Neurology* 2, 41/511. Also see Low, P., *Seminars in Neurology*, vol. 7, no. 1 (March 1987), 53; and Bannister, R. and Mathios, C. 1992. *Autonomic Failure* (New York: Oxford University Press).

For a good history of stress physiology, see Weiner, H. 1992. *Perturbing the Organism: The Biology of Stressful Experience* (Chicago: University of Chicago Press).

CHAPTER 2: GLANDS, GOOSEFLESH, AND HORMONES

PAGE 20: The D. H. Lawrence quotation is, of course, from *Lady Chatterley's Lover* (Cutchogue, N.Y.: Buccaneer Books, Inc., 1983). The idea for this example comes from a colleague, the British immunologist Nick Hall. He regularly lectures to halls of distracted scientists clicking away with their three-color pens, starts off with some really steamy passage of Lawrence recited in his impressive English accent, and rivets their attention.

P A G E 2 6 : The testicular injection mania began in 1889, with a paper published by the formidable Charles-Edouard Brown-Sequard, entitled "On the physiological and therapeutic role of a juice extracted from the testicles of animals according to a number of facts observed in man" (*Archives de physiologie normale et pathologique* [5e series], 1889, 1, 739).

A lot of the facts Brown-Sequard collected had been observed in one man, himself. Brown-Sequard was arguably the most august physiologist in the world at the time, age seventy-two and with somewhat declining energies. He had theorized that some features of senescence of humans were due to declining gonadal function (the more global statements about such decline as *the* cause of aging came from later followers). He felt that the testes contained some sort of active secreted substance, and he started injecting himself subcutaneously with extracts of testes from dogs and guinea pigs. He was absolutely right that the testes secreted a substance — testosterone (which had not yet been discovered; the term "hormone" did not even exist then) — but his experiment couldn't possibly work, since he made his extracts in water; testosterone, because of its chemical nature, does not dissolve in water.

Despite that, he reported wondrous results (increased physical vitality, increased length of his jet of urine — the latter no doubt being the sort of thing we all hope to retain into our golden years). All placebo. The reproductive physiologist Roger Gosden of the University of Edinburgh, who is writing a book on the subject, suspects that Brown-Sequard was probably depressed at the time of his experiments and thus was particularly vulnerable to such a placebo effect (personal communication). Nevertheless, doctors were thrilled at the report, and within two years, organotherapy, as it was called, was being used worldwide. Brown-Sequard took particular umbrage at the charlatans making quick money using his (altogether incorrect and ineffectual) discovery, particularly the American hucksters soon selling "Dr. Brown-Sequard's Elixir of Life." He also expanded his theory a bit, noting that loss of semen resulted in loss of strength (twenty years earlier he had speculated on the rejuvenative effects of intravenous injections of sperm into men, an idea fortunately not tried), citing the well-known physical and mental weaknesses of men who masturbated frequently or who had frequent intercourse. (For the original citations and a thorough review of the subject, see M. Borell. 1976. "Brown-Sequard's organotherapy and its appearance in America at the end of the nineteenth century." *Bulletin of the History of Medicine* 50, 309.)

PAGE 28: The history of hypothalamic hormones (Harris's theory that the brain was an endocrine organ, and the work of Guillemin and Schally) has been well documented, especially in the aftermath of the award of the Nobel Prize to the latter pair. This is because of the ferocity and colorfulness of the Guillemin/Schally race, and because the huge, "corporate" lab that each evolved in the process seemed the wave of the scientific future at the time. For a particularly readable account, see *The Nobel Duel: Two Scientists' 21-Year Race to Win the World's Most Coveted Research Prize* (N. Wade; Garden City, N.Y.: Anchor Press, 1981). The quotation from Schally about the competition with Guillemin is in Wade's book, page 7. For a dauntingly academic account of the sociology of Guilleman's lab (although it is not identified as Guilleman's by name), see Latour, B. and Woolgar, S. 1979. *Laboratory Life: The Social Construction of Scientific Facts* (Beverly Hills, Calif.: Sage Publications).

   New releasing and inhibiting factors continue to be isolated, still often in sprints to the finish line by groups in frenzied competition with each other. An exception to this pattern came in 1981 with the isolation of what was perhaps the most sought-after of the brain hormones. This hormone, which will be discussed throughout the book, is the main way in which the brain controls a principal branch of the stress-response. CRF, as it is called, was the first brain hormone whose existence was inferred (in 1955) but one of the last ones isolated, because it turned out to be among the most chemically complex. In a wrinkle on the old Guillemin/Schally dichotomy, its isolation was carried out by a team headed by Wylie Vale, once Guillemin's right-hand man. Vale and his band of renegades, in a lab of their own, had the audacity to look for CRF in places none of the other researchers had tried in the 25 years of investigation, considering very unlikely chemical structures for CRF. One turned out to be the right one, and they beat the competition by miles. See Vale, W., Speiss, J., Rivier, C., and Rivier, J. 1983. "Characterization of a 41-residue ovine hypothalamic peptide that stimulates the secretions of corticotropin and beta-endorphin." *Science* 213, 1394.

PAGE 36: Hormonal "signatures" of different stressors: Henry, J. P. 1977. *Stress, Health, and the Social Environment* (New York: Springer-Verlag); Frankenhaeuser, M. 1983. "The sympathetic-adrenal and pituitary-adrenal response to challenge." In Dembroski, T., Schmidt, T., and Blumchen, G. (eds.). *Biobehavioral Basis of Coronary Heart Disease* (Basel: Karger), 91. For a nice discussion of signatures involving epinephrine versus norepinephrine, see chapter 8 of Weiner, H. 1992. *Perturbing the Organism: The Biology of Stressful Experience* (Chicago: University of Chicago Press).

CHAPTER 3: STROKE, HEART ATTACKS, AND VOODOO DEATH

PAGE 37: Good general overviews of what the cardiovascular system does during stress can be found in most physiology textbooks, although the information is rarely explicitly organized under the topic of "stress." Instead, it can usually be found in a chapter on the heart itself, or on the physiologic response to exercise.

PAGE 39: The 1833 study showing that emotional stress would shut down blood flow to the guts of the Canadian with the gunshot wound: Beaumont, W. 1833. *Experiments and Observations on the Gastric Juice and the Physiology of Digestion* (Plattsburgh, N.Y.).

For a discussion of the role of kidneys in increasing blood pressure during stress, see Guyton, A. 1991. "Blood pressure control—special role of the kidneys and body fluids." *Science* 252, 1813.

PAGE 40: The bladder conundrum. One of my intrepid research assistants, Michelle Pearl, called up some of America's leading urologists to ask them why bladders evolved. One comparative urologist (as well as Jay Kaplan, whose research is discussed in this chapter) took the findings about territorial rodents having bladders to make scent trails and inverted the argument—maybe we have bladders so that we can avoid continual dribble of urine that would leave a scent trail so some predator could track us. The same urologist noted, however, that a weakness with his idea is that fish also have bladders, and they presumably don't have to worry about leaving scent trails. A number of urologists suggested that maybe the bladder acts as a buffer between the kidney and the outside world, to reduce the chance of kidney infections. However, it seems odd to develop an organ exclusively for the purpose of protecting another organ from infection. Pearl suggested that it may have evolved for male reproduction — the acidity of urine isn't very healthy for sperm (in ancient times, women would use half a lemon as a diaphragm), so perhaps it made sense to evolve a storage site for the urine. A remarkable percentage of the urologists questioned said something like, "Well, it would be an extreme social liability to not have a bladder" before realizing that they had just suggested that vertebrates evolved bladders tens of millions of years ago so that we humans wouldn't inadvertently pee on our party clothes. Mostly, however, the urologists said things like, "To be honest, I've never thought about this before," "I don't know and I talked to everyone here and they don't know anything either," and "Beats me."

The strangest thing about it all is that many animals may not actually take advantage of their bladder's storage capacity. In my vast experience watching baboons go about their urinary business, it is apparent that they very rarely hold it in when they have to go.

Clearly, there's a lot of work to be done in this area.

PAGE 41: The difference in cardiovascular responses to overt physical stressors and to quiet vigilance: Fisher, L. 1991. "Stress and cardiovascular physiology in animals." In Brown, M., Koob, G., and Rivier, C. 1991. *Stress: Neurobiology and Neuroendocrinology* (New York: Marcel Dekker, Inc.). 2 hours, 10 minutes; black and white. With Claude Rains, Lily Pons, and the young Robert Mitchum as the descending aorta.

PAGE 42: Detailed discussions about how damage to the vascular lining, various hormones, and high levels of fat in the bloodstream interact to cause atherosclerosis: DeSilva, R. 1986. "Psychological stress and sudden cardiac death." In Schmidt, T., Dembroski, T., and Blumchen, G. *Biological and Psychological Factors in Cardiovascular Disease* (Berlin: Springer-Verlag). Also Rozanski, A., Krantz, D., Klein, J., and Gottdiener, J. 1991. "Mental stress and the induction of myocardial ischemia." In Brown, et al. 1991. *Stress: Neurobiology and Neuroendocrinology* (New York: Marcel Dekker, Inc.). Also see Fuster, V., Badimon, L., Badimon, J., and Chesebro, J. 1992. "The pathogenesis of coronary artery disease and the acute coronary syndromes." *New England Journal of Medicine* 326, 242. The work regarding social stress and the heart disease in rodents can be found in Henry, J. P., 1977. *Stress, Health, and the Social Environment* (New York: Springer-Verlag).

The work regarding social stress and plaque formation in primates is reviewed in Kaplan, J. "Social behavior and gender in biomedical investigations using monkeys: Studies in atherogenesis." *Laboratory Animal Science*, in press. The work regarding interactions of the hormones of the metabolic stress-response in causing atherosclerosis can be found in Brindley, D. and Rolland, Y. 1989. "Possible connections between stress, diabetes, obesity, hypertension and altered lipoprotein metabolism that may result in atherosclerosis." *Clinical Science* 77, 453.

PAGE 46: Myocardial ischemia, damaged heart muscle, and its subsequent vulnerability to stress: *Stress: Neurobiology and Neuroendocrinology* (Brown, M. et al.; New York: Marcel Dekker, 1991) contains a number of chapters with useful information. These include chapters 20 (Verrier, R. "Stress, sleep and vulnerability to ventricular fibrillation"), 21 (Fisher, L. "Stress and cardiovascular physiology in animals"), 22 (Brodsky, M. and Allen, B. "Effects of psychological stress on cardiac rate and rhythm"), and 23 (Rozanski, A., Krantz, D., Klein, J., and Gottdiener, J. "Mental stress and the induction of myocardial ischemia"). Chapters 20 and 23 contain good reviews of ambulatory electrocardiography; the former chapter details Verrier's own studies showing that psychological stress in humans and dogs can cause acute ischemia in damaged heart tissue. (Also see Rozanski, A., and Berman, D. 1987. "Silent myocardial ischaemia. I. Pathophysiology, frequency of occurrence and approaches toward detection." *American Heart Journal* 114, 615.) For a review of the paradoxical vasoconstriction, rather than vasodilation, during stress in damaged coronary arteries, see Fuster, V., Badimon, L., Badimon, J., and Chesebro, J. 1992. "The pathogenesis of coronary artery disease and the acute coronary syndromes, Part II." *New England Journal of Medicine* 326, 310. For more examples of ischemia in heart patients being brought on by subtle psychological stressors (in this case, public speaking), see Taggert, P., Carruthers, M., and Somerville, W. 1973. "Electrocardiogram, plasma catecholamines, and their modification by oxyprenolol when speaking before an audience." *The Lancet* 2, 341. In another demonstration, patients were shown to have as much myocardial ischemia when describing a personal problem to a stranger as they did during exercise: Rozanski, A. 1988. "Mental stress and the induction of silent myocardial ischemia in patients with coronary artery disease." *New England Journal of Medicine* 318, 1005.

PAGE 48: Instances of sudden cardiac death during stress in humans: Engel, G. 1971. "Sudden and rapid death during psychological stress: Folklore or folk wisdom?" *Annals of Internal Medicine* 74, 771. According to the Israeli Consulate in San Francisco, the final result of the SCUD attacks during the Gulf War was one Israeli dead as a direct result of a missile attack, and three dead of heart attacks. A recent report shows a tripling in the incidence of myocardial infarctions of the Tel Aviv population during the first three days of the SCUD attacks, as compared to the same three days of January the year before: Meisel, S., Kutz, I., Dayan, K., Pauzner, H., Chetboun, I., Arbel, Y., and David, D. 1991. "Effect of Iraqi missile war on incidence of acute myocardial infarction and sudden death in Israeli civilians." *The Lancet* 338, 660. The mechanisms underlying sudden cardiac death: DeSilva, R. 1986. "Psychological stress and sudden cardiac death." In Schmidt, T., Dembroski, T., and Blumchen, G. *Biological and Psychological Factors in Cardiovascular Disease* (Berlin: Springer-Verlag).

PAGE 51: The Irven DeVore quotation is reproduced as a personal communication.

Psychophysiological death: Davis, W., and DeSilva, R. "Psychophysiological death: A cross-cultural and medical appraisal of voodoo death." *Anthropologia*, in press. Walter Cannon contacted a variety of missionaries, anthropologists, and medical people working in the third world, collecting their descriptions of voodoo death in order to decide that it sounded like too much sympathetic nervous system to him (1942. "'Voodoo' death." *American Anthropologist* 44, 169). Curt Richter, by contrast, didn't gather any firsthand accounts of his own. Instead, he noted the similarity between the accounts in Cannon's paper and cases of parasympathetic-induced death in rats undergoing severe stressors in his own laboratory (he noted that the phenomenon occurred much more readily in wild rats captured and brought to his lab than in the lab-bred strains, and made comparisons between "uncivilized primitive humans" and undomesticated wild rats) (1957. "On the phenomenon of sudden death in animals and man." *Psychosomatic Medicine* 19, 191).

As he described in *The Serpent and the Rainbow* (New York: Warner Books, 1985), Wade Davis believed he had isolated the critical substance—a poison called tetrodotoxin isolated from puffer fish—that the Haitian witch doctors use to put someone in a zombified state. This is the same poison found in the fugu fish, used in Japanese cooking. (When the fugu chef leaves a smidgen of the tetrodotoxin gland in the fish, the well-paying customer gets a mild buzz. When the chef leaves too much in, the well-paying customer gets put into a coma. Fugu chefs, by the way, are carefully licensed.) Davis made a fascinating argument that zombification in Haiti reflected the intersection of the biology of tetrodotoxin action and the anthropology of traditional Haitian religion: when a Japanese businessman gets major tetrodotoxin poisoning and recovers, he sues the chef and switches restaurants. When a Haitian villager gets the same tetrodotoxin poisoning and recovers, he realizes that his village had hired a shaman to poison him because he has done something terrible — he awakes as an ostracized zombie with no will, and then is often used for slave labor (although in some cases, the zombified person's passive state is promoted by continually drugging him). It's a charming story, although the isolation of tetrodotoxin remains controversial. Davis and tetrodotoxin zombification became so trendy in the 1980s that in Garry Trudeau's *Doonesbury*, Uncle Duke was zombified at one point, and "Miami Vice" used the zombie motif in an episode about drug runners from Haiti.

PAGE 54: The Sisyphus pattern of personality was first identified in Bruhn, J., Paredes, A., Adsett, C., and Wolf, S. 1974. "Psychological predictors of sudden death in myocardial infarction." *Journal of Psychosomatic Research* 18, 187.

Type A: The definitive prospective study showing a link between Type A personality and coronary heart disease is Rosenman, R., Brand, R., Jenkins, C., Friedman, M., Straus, R., and Wurm, M. 1975. "Coronary heart disease in the Western Collaborative Group Study: Final follow-up experience of $8\frac{1}{2}$ years." *Journal of the American Medical Association* 233, 872. See also Friedman, M., and Rosenman, R. 1974. *Type A Behavior and Your Heart* (New York: Knopf). The blue-ribbon panel that endorsed the Type A concept published its report as: Cooper, T., Detre, T., and Weiss, S. 1981. "Coronary prone behavior and coronary heart disease; A critical review." *Circulation* 63, 1199.

PAGE 55: Problems with replicating the original Type A finding: The most influential study was Shekelle, R., Billings, J., and Borhani, N. 1985. "The MRFIT behavior pattern study. II. Type A behavior and incidence of coronary heart disease." *American Journal of Epidemiology* 122, 599. Others are discussed in Barefoot, J., Peterson, B., Harrell, F., et al. 1989. Type A behavior and survival: A follow-up study of 1,467 patients with coronary artery disease." *American Journal of Cardiology* 64, 427.

The demonstration that Type A behavior is associated with better survivorship: the Barefoot study just cited, plus Ragland, D. and Brand, R. 1988. "Type A behavior and mortality from coronary heart disease." *New England Journal of Medicine* 313, 65. That finding is a good lesson in how incredibly subtle some confounds can be in epidemiology research. Why should being Type A be associated with better survivorship, once you are diagnosed with coronary heart disease? Some possibilities: Type A people, because of their driven and disciplined nature, are more likely to comply with the medicine/dieting/exercise schedules given them by their doctors. Or certain people may immediately be recognized as being Type A by their doctors, who then think "Aha, here's this Type A patient with coronary heart disease. I know all about Friedman and Rosenman's studies; I'd better take extra good care of this person." Or Type A people may be more disciplined about annual checkups with doctors, and thus be diagnosed with coronary heart disease earlier than average, when it is still pretty mild—leading to seemingly better survivorship. This last factor has probably been ruled out, but no one is sure about the other possible confounds yet, as the studies showing better Type A survivorship are quite recent. Some of the possible sources of confounds in these finding are discussed in Matthews, K. and Haynes, S. 1986. "Type A behavior pattern and coronary disease risk." *American Journal of Epidemiology* 123, 923.

The importance of hostility as a predictor of heart disease: The demonstration of this by reanalysis of the original Friedman and Rosenman data: Hecker, M., Chesney, M. N., Black, G., and Frautsch, N. 1988. "Coronary-prone behaviors in the Western Collaborative Group Study." *Psychosomatic Medicine* 50, 153. Hostility in medical students: Barefoot, J., Dahlstrom, W., and Williams, R. 1983. "Hostility, CHD incidence, and total mortality: A 25-year follow-up study of 255 physicians." *Psychosomatic Medicine* 45, 59. In lawyers: Barefoot, J., Dodge, K., Peterson, B., Dahlstrom, W., and Williams, R. 1989. "The Cook-Medley Hostility scale: item content and ability to predict survival." *Psychosomatic Medicine* 51, 46. In Finnish twins: Koskenvuo, M., Kaprio, J., Rose, R., Kesaniemi, A., Sarna, S., Heikkila, K., and Langinvainio, H. 1988. "Hostility as a risk factor for mortality and ischemic heart disease in men." *Psychosomatic Medicine* 50, 330. In Western Electric employees: Shekelle, R., Gale, M., Ostfeld, A., and

Paul, O. 1983. "Hostility, risk of coronary disease, and mortality." *Psychosomatic Medicine* 45, 219. For general reviews, see Williams, R. 1991. "A relook at personality types and coronary heart disease." *Progress in Cardiology* 4 (October) and Matthews, K., and Haynes, S. 1986. "Type A behavior pattern and coronary disease risk." *American Journal of Epidemiology* 123, 923. For a more accessible entrée to this literature, see Williams, R. 1989. *The Trusting Heart: Great News About Type A Behavior* (New York: Random House). For some criticisms of the linking of hostility to heart disease, see Thoresen, C., and Powell, L. 1992. "Type A behavior pattern: New perspectives on theory, assessment and intervention." *Journal of Consulting and Clinical Psychology*, in press.

PAGE 56: Hormonal and cardiovascular function in hostile versus nonhostile people. Demonstration that hostile and nonhostile people do not differ in hormone and blood pressure measures during rest or during nonsocial stressors: Sallis, J., Johnson, C., Treverow, T., Kaplan, R., and Hovell, M. 1987. "The relationship between cynical hostility and blood pressure reactivity." *Journal of Psychosomatic Research* 31, 111. See also Smith, M. and Houston, B. 1987. "Hostility, anger expression, cardiovascular responsivity, and social support." *Biological Psychology* 24, 39. Also Krantz, D., and Manuck, S. 1984. "Acute psychophysiologic reactivity and risk of cardiovascular disease: A review and methodological critique." *Psychological Bulletin* 96, 435.

Demonstration of larger responses in hostile people to social provocations: Being interrupted during a task: Suarez, E. and Williams, R. 1989. "Situational determinants of cardiovascular and emotional reactivity in high and low hostile men." *Psychosomatic Medicine* 51, 404. During a rigged game against a disparaging opponent: Glass, D., Krakoff, L., and Contrada, R. 1980. "Effect of harassment and competition upon cardiovascular and catecholamine responses in Type A and Type B individuals." *Psychophysiology* 17, 453. During a role-play of social conflict: Hardy, J. and Smith, T. 1988. "Cynical hostility and vulnerability to disease: Social support, life stress, and physiological response to conflict." *Health Psychology* 7, 477. Unsolvable tasks with bad instructions: Weidner, G., Friend, R., Ficarrotto, T., and Mendell, N. 1989. "Hostility and cardiovascular reactivity to stress in women and men." *Psychosomatic Medicine* 51, 36. Note that many of these studies were done when everyone was still dichotomizing between Type A and Type B people, rather than hostile and nonhostile.

P A G E 5 7 : If you can change Type A tendencies, you decrease risk of coronary heart disease: Friedman, M., Thoresen, C., and Gill, J. 1986. "Alteration of Type A behavior and its effect on cardiac recurrences in post-myocardial infarction patients: Summary results of the Recurrent Coronary Prevention Project." *American Heart Journal* 112, 653.

Finally, for an analysis of the medical histories and the significantly shortened life spans of the American Presidents, in which the author concludes that they have died disproportionately from stress-related cardiovascular disease: Gilbert, R. 1993. "Travails of the chief." *The Sciences* (January/February) 8.

CHAPTER 4: STRESS, METABOLISM, AND LIQUIDATING YOUR ASSETS

P A G E 5 9 : Energy storage and mobilization: The basics of this vastly complicated subject, involving storage tissues throughout the body, a variety of different hormonal messengers, and the liver serving as Grand Central Station for various nutrients coming and going, is covered in any physiology textbook. A fairly lucid presentation of the subject on an introductory college level can be found in chapter 17, "Regulation of organic metabolism, growth, and energy balance," in Vander, A., Sherman, J., and Luciano, D. 1990. *Human Physiology: The Mechanisms of Body Function*, 5th ed. (New York: McGraw-Hill). It discusses the mechanisms by which insulin promotes energy storage during surplus, how insulin secretion is turned off and the various "counterregulatory" hormones (glucocorticoids, epinephrine, norepinephrine, glucagon) are turned on during stress, and how they help mobilize energy. Also see Havel, P., and Taborsky, G. 1989. "The contribution of the autonomic nervous system to changes of glucagon and insulin secretion during hypoglycemic stress." *Endocrine Reviews* 10, 332.

P A G E 6 4 : The inefficiency of the repeated activation of the metabolic stress-response: This is horrendously complicated. The introductory reference given above will teach the general principle that it is inefficient to repeatedly store away energy and then reverse the process by mobilizing it. However, in order to gain a detailed, quantitative understanding of it, one must become something of an accountant — learning what the currency of energy is in the body and how much it costs to make all those deposits and withdrawals in the body's metabolic banks. For this, one must consult biochemistry texts (typically, of the early graduate school level of difficulty); among the best is Stryer, L. 1988. *Biochemistry*, 3rd ed. (New York: W. H. Freeman).

P A G E 6 5 : Chronic glucocorticoid exposure causes muscle wastage: for a classic demonstration of this, see Kaplan, S. and Nagareda Shimizu, C. 1963. "Effects of cortisol on amino acid in skeletal muscle and plasma." *Endocrinology* 72, 267. (Cortisol is the glucocorticoid found in humans and primates.)

Adult-onset diabetes: The disease — how it differs from juvenile diabetes, its possible origins, how it makes you sick — dominates chapters of every endocrinology, pathophysiology, and gerontology textbook. For a classic demonstration that type 2 (adult-onset) diabetes involves impaired sensitivity to insulin, rather than impaired secretion of insulin, see: Reaven, G., Bernstein, R., Davis, B., and Olefsky, J. 1976. "Nonketotic diabetes mellitus: Insulin deficiency or insulin resistance?" *American Journal of Medicine* 60, 80. For demonstrations that the insulin resistance arises from a loss of insulin receptors see: Gavin, J., Roth, J., Neville, D., DeMeyts, P., and Buell, D. 1974. "Insulin-dependent regulation of insulin receptor concentrations: A direct demonstration in cell culture." *Proceedings National Academy of Sciences USA* 71, 84; Olefsky, J. 1976. "The insulin receptor: Its role in insulin resistance of obesity and diabetes." *Diabetes* 25, 1154. For a discussion of how the insulin resistance also arises from the remaining insulin receptors not working properly (what is called a "postreceptor" defect), see Flier, J. 1983. "Insulin receptors and insulin resistance." *Annual Review of Medicine* 34, 145. For an emphasis on the fatty acid problems in diabetes, rather than the usual emphasis on the glucose problems, see McGarry, J. 1992. "What if Minkowski had been ageusic? An alternative angle on diabetes." *Science* 258, 766. Finally, despite the primary defect of target tissue resistance to insulin's actions, a subset of patients also has a defect in the secretion of insulin. The mechanisms underlying this are reviewed by Unger, R. 1991. "Role of impaired glucose transport by β cells in the pathogenesis of diabetes." *Journal of NIH Research* 3, 77.

In Western societies, rates of glucose intolerance and insulin resistance rise with age: Andres, R. 1971. "Aging and diabetes." *Medical Clinics of North America* 55, 835; Davidson, M. 1979. "The effect of aging on carbohydrate metabolism: A review of the English literature and a practical approach to the diagnosis of diabetes mellitus in the elderly." *Metabolism* 28, 687. For a discussion of the increasing rate of overt type 2 diabetes with age in Western societies, see Harris, M. 1982. "The prevalence of diabetes, undiagnosed diabetes and impaired glucose tolerance in the United States." In Melish, H., Hanna, J., and Baba, S. (eds.), *Genetic Environmental Interaction in Diabetes Mellitus* (Amsterdam: Excerpta Medica), 70.

Despite this trend, type 2 diabetes seems not to be an obligatory part of aging: aging rats and aging humans in our own society do not become more glucose intolerant with age, as long as they are active and lean: Reaven, G. and Reaven, E. 1985. "Age, glucose intolerance and non-insulin-dependent diabetes mellitus." *Journal of the American Geriatrics Society* 33, 286. Also see Goldberg, A. and Coon, P. 1987. "Non-insulin-dependent diabetes mellitus in the elderly: Influence of obesity and physical inactivity." *Endocrinology and Metabolism Clinics* 16, 843.

For a demonstration of extremely low rates of type 2 diabetes in non-Westernized populations (for example, the Inuit and other Native Americans, New Guinea islanders, inhabitants of rural India, and North African nomads), see table 5 in Eaton, S., Konner, M., and Shostak, M. 1988. "Stone agers in the fast lane: Chronic degenerative diseases in evolutionary perspective." *American Journal of Medicine* 84, 739.

The low rates of type 2 diabetes in non-Westernized populations pose a fascinating mystery. If these people begin eating Westernized diets, they get astonishingly high rates of type 2 diabetes. Part of this has an obvious explanation; once these various groups gain entrée into our world of packaged food and processed sugars, they tend to eat themselves into obesity (and, thus, high rates of type 2 diabetes). However, the mystery is that given the *same* diet and degree of obesity, most people of the third world are at far greater risk for type 2 diabetes than people in Western societies. Diabetes rates have soared among Mexicans and Japanese after they emigrated to the United States, among Asian Indians moving to Britain and Yemenite Jews moving to Israel. In the most striking cases, the residents of the Pacific island of Nauru have a 33 percent rate of diabetes (ten times the rate in the United States), while more than 70 percent of the Pima people of Arizona over age 55 have diabetes.

Why should those in the developing world be at such risk for diabetes once they start consuming a Western diet, despite having such low rates of the disease on their own traditional diet (remember, this risk is for individuals not yet obese)? One fascinating theory is that the gene for a propensity to diabetes is adaptive in non-Westernized settings. Normally, we in the West are a bit inefficient in how we handle sugar in our diet: we don't absorb all of it from the circulation, and a certain amount gets lost in the urine. The notion is that people of the third world are more efficient at utilizing sugar; the second they get any in their circulation, they have a burst of insulin secretion and every bit of the sugar gets stored, instead of urinated away. This makes sense, given tough environments with intermittent food sources, where every little bit must be exploited. And it is easy to imagine this as a genetic trait—for example, genes altering the sensitivity with which the pancreas senses circulating glucose concentrations and releases insulin. These putative genes have even been termed "thrifty genes."

With traditional third world diets, this trigger-happy insulin secretion keeps the body from wasting any sugar. Once people begin eating a Westernized, high-sugar diet, this tendency leads to constant bursts of insulin secretion, which is more likely to cause storage tissues to become insulin resistant, leading to type 2 diabetes. People in Western countries, in contrast, are theorized to have more sluggish insulin responses to sugar; the net result is less efficient storing of sugar from the circulation, but lower risk of diabetes. And why are people in Westernized societies theorized to be genetically less efficient in handling blood sugar? Because a few centuries back, as we first began eating typical Westernized diets, those people with the greatest tendency toward insulin secretion failed to survive and pass on their genes. This predicts that populations like the Nauru islanders and Pima are undergoing the same process now; in a few centuries, most of their descendants will be the offspring of the rare individuals now with the lower diabetes risk. In support of this prediction, the rate of diabetes has already peaked among the Nauru islanders. But at present the existence of thrifty genes, and their differential presence in different human populations, is purely speculative. For a nontechnical discussion of these ideas, see Diamond, J. 1992. "Sweet death." *Natural History* (February), 2. For technical discussions from the originator of the idea, see Neel, J. 1962. "Diabetes mellitus: a 'thrifty' genotype rendered detrimental by 'progress'?" *American Journal of Human Genetics* 14, 353; Neel, J. 1982. "The thrifty genotype revisited." In Kobberling, J., and Tattersall, R. (eds.), *The Genetics of Diabetes Mellitus* (London: Academic Press, Proceedings of the Serono Symposia, vol. 47), 283. For some technical discussions of the change in the incidence of diabetes with Westernization, see Bennett, P., LeCompte, P., Miller, M., and Rushforth, N. 1976. "Epidemiological studies of diabetes in the Pima Indians." *Recent Progress in Hormone Research* 32, 333; O'Dea, K., Spargo, R., and Nestle, P. 1982. "Impact of Westernization on carbohydrate and lipid metabolism in Australian Aborigines." *Diabetologia* 22, 148; Cohen, A., Chen, B., Eisenberg, S., Fidel, J., and Furst, A. 1979. "Diabetes, blood lipids, lipoproteins and change of environment. Restudy of the 'new immigrant Yemenites' in Israel." *Metabolism* 28, 716. For information on the rate of diabetes having peaked among the Nauru islanders, see Diamond, J. 1992. "Diabetes running wild." *Nature* 357, 362. For a broader discussion of the genetics of the disorder, see Unger, R. and Foster, D. 1985. "Diabetes mellitus." In Wilson, J. and Foster, D. *Williams Textbook of Endocrinology*, 7th ed. (Philadelphia: W. B. Saunders Co.).

PAGE 66: One of the puzzles of how diabetes affects your health has been solved in recent years. It is relatively easy to understand how extra glucose in the bloodstream can clog blood vessels and cause damage. One of the mysteries, however, is why high levels of circulating glucose damage the eye (diabetes is the leading cause of blindness in this country). It turns out that glucose can stick to all sorts of proteins, causing them to form aggregates; indeed, because of its structure, glucose can stick onto proteins without the aid of enzymes to mediate the process. The term "nonenzymatic modification" has been given to this recently discovered phenomenon. Once glucose fuses these proteins, they have to be broken apart and replaced. However, in some tissues—such as the lens of the eye—proteins are not recycled very frequently, and those cells are stuck with the fused mess. For a discussion of the nonenzymatic chemistry of sugars focusing on its implications for aging and adult-onset diabetes, by the main workers in that area, see Lee, A. and Cerami, A. 1990. "Modifications of proteins and nucleic acids by reducing sugars: Possible role in aging." In Schneider, E. and Rowe, J. *Handbook of the Biology of Aging*, 3rd ed. (New York: Academic Press).

Glucocorticoids promote insulin resistance: Rizza, R., Mandarino, L., and Gerich, J. 1982. "Cortisol-induced insulin resistance in man: Impaired suppression of glucose production and stimulation of glucose utilization due to a postreceptor defect of insulin action." *Journal of Clinical Endocrinology and Metabolism* 54, 131. Glucocorticoids and stress can exacerbate the symptoms of type 2 diabetes: Surwit, R., Ross, S., and Feingloss, M. 1991. "Stress, behavior, and glucose control in diabetes mellitus." In McCabe, P., Schneidermann, N., Field, T., and Skyler, J. (eds.), *Stress, Coping and Disease* (Hillsdale, N.J.: L. Erl-baum Assoc.), 97.

PAGE 68: Statistics regarding the incidence and impact of diabetes: Rifkin, H., and Porte, D. 1990. *Diabetes Mellitus. Theory and Practice*, 4th ed. (New York: Elsevier).

CHAPTER 5: ULCERS, COLITIS, AND THE RUNS

PAGE 69: Stressors tend to inhibit gastrointestinal function: Desiderato, O., MacKinnon, J., and Hissom, R. 1974. "Development of gastric ulcers following stress termination." *Journal of Comparative and Physiological Psychology* 87, 208; Hess, W. 1957. *Diencephalon; Autonomic and Extrapyramidal Functions* (New York: Grune and Stratton); Kiely, W. 1977. "From the symbolic stimulus to the pathophysiological response." In Lipowski, Z., Lipsitt, D., and Whybrow, P. (eds.), *Current Trends and Clinical Applications* (New York: Oxford University Press); Murison, R. and Bakke, H. 1990. "The role of corticotropin-releasing factor in rat gastric ulcerogenesis." In Hernandez, D. and Glavin, G. (eds.), *Neurobiology of Stress Ulcers* (Annals of the New York Academy of Sciences, Vol. 597), 71; Tache, Y. 1991. "Effect of stress on gastric ulcer formation." In Brown, M., Koob, G., and Rivier, C. (eds.), *Stress: Neurobiology and Neuroendocrinology* (New York: Marcel Dekker), 549.

PAGE 70: Mediators of the stress-response, such as CRF, also inhibit gastrointestinal function: reviewed in Murison, R. and Bakke, H. 1990. "The role of corticotropin-releasing factor in rat gastric ulcerogenesis," cited immediately above.

PAGE 72: Selye was the first to note that stress could cause peptic ulcers (1936. "A syndrome produced by diverse nocuous agents." *Nature* 138, 32). The first researchers to systematically explore the role of psychological stress in causing ulcers were Brady, J., Porter, D., Conrad, D., and Mason, J. 1958. "Avoidance behavior and the development of gastroduodenal ulcers." *Journal of Experimental Analysis of Behavior* I, 69; Weiss, J. 1968. "Effects of coping responses on stress." *Journal of Comparative and Physiological Psychology* 65, 251. What it is about psychological stress that is ulcerogenic is explored in detail in chapter 10.

The evidence that major and short-term traumas in humans can cause rapidly emerging stress ulcers can be found in Skillman, J., Bushnell, L., Goldman, H., and Silen, W. 1969. "Respiratory failure, hypotension, sepsis, and jaundice. A clinical syndrome associated with lethal hemorrhage from acute stress ulceration of the stomach." *American Journal of Surgery* 117, 523; Lucas, C., Sugawa, C., Riddle, J., Rector, F., Rosenberg, B., and Walt, A. 1971. "Natural history and surgical dilemma of 'stress' gastric bleeding." *Archives of Surgery* 102, 266; Butterfield, W. 1975. "Experimental stress ulcers: A review." *Surgical Annual* 7, 261. For evidence that more subtle psychological stress can cause gradually emerging peptic ulcers in humans see Feldman, M., Walker, P., Green, J., and Weingarden, K. 1986. "Life events, stress and psychosocial factors in men with peptic ulcer disease: A multidimensional case-controlled study." *Gastroenterology* 91, 1370. Also see Weiner, H. 1992. *Perturbing the Organism: The Biology of Stressful Experience* (Chicago: University of Chicago Press).

PAGE 73: Ulcers are predominantly formed during the poststress recovery period, rather than during the stressor itself: Overmier, J., Murison, R., and Ursin, H. 1986. "The ulcerogenic effect of a rest period after exposure to water-restraint stress." *Behavioral and Neural Biology* 46, 372; Vincent, G. and Pare, W. 1982. "Post stress development and healing of supine-restraint induced stomach lesions in the rat." *Physiology and Behavior* 29, 721; Desiderato, O., MacKinnon, J., and Hissom, H. 1974. "Development of gastric ulcers in rats following stress termination." *Journal of Comparative and Physiological Psychology* 87, 208; Glavin, G. 1980. "Restraint ulcer: History, current research and future implications." *Brain Research Bulletin* 5, supplement 1, 51. For the evidence for how this is due to rebound of the parasympathetic nervous system, see the Glavin paper just cited; also see Klein, H., Gheorghiu, T., and Hubner, G. 1975. "Morphological and functional gastric changes in stress ulcer." In Gheorghiu, T. (ed.), *Experimental Ulcer: Models, Methods and Clinical Validity* (Baden-Baden: Witzstrock).

Back to hydrochloric acid digesting the stomach in which it is secreted: if the mucous layer prevents the acid from penetrating it, how can acid, first secreted by the stomach wall, ever get through the mucous layer to digest food? This conundrum is answered by Bhaskar, K., Garik, P., Turner, B., Bradley, J., Bansil, R., Stanley, H., and Lamont, J. 1992. "Viscous fingering of hydrochloric acid through gastric mucin." *Nature* 360, 458.

PAGE 74: Bicarbonate secretion decreases in ulcer patients: Isenberg, J., Selling, J., Hogan, D., and Koss, M. 1987. "Impaired proximal duodenal mucosal bicarbonate secretion in duodenal ulcer patients." *New England Journal of Medicine* 316, 374. Bicarbonate secretion decreases with sustained stress in an animal ulcer model: Takeuchi, K., Furukawa, O., and Okabe, S. 1986. "Induction of duodenal ulcers in rats under water-immersion stress conditions. Influence on gastric acid and duodenal alkaline secretion." *Gastroenterology* 91, 554. Mucus secretion decreases with stress and with glucocorticoid administration: Schuster, M. 1989. "Irritable bowel syndrome." In Sleisenger, M. and Fordtron, J. *Gastrointestinal Disease: Pathophysiology, Diagnosis, Management*, 4th ed. (Philadelphia: Saunders), 1402.

In approximately half the cases, during this rebound period the amount of gastric acid secreted is normal, implying that the problem is that the stomach wall is relatively more vulnerable, since the acidic attack is not stronger than usual: Dayal, Y. and DeLellis, R. 1989. "The gastrointestinal tract. In Robbins, S., Cotran, R., and Kumar, V. *Pathologic Basis of Disease*, 4th ed. (Philadelphia: Saunders), 827; also Weiner, H. 1991. "From simplicity to complexity (1950–1990): The case of peptic ulceration—I. Human studies." *Psychosomatic Medicine* 53, 467; and Weiner, H. 1991. "From simplicity to complexity (1950–1990): The case of peptic ulceration—II. Animal studies." *Psychosomatic Medicine* 53, 491; Grossman, M. 1978. "Abnormalities of acid secretion in patients with duodenal ulcer." *Gastroenterology* 75, 524; also Brodie, D., Marshall, R., and Moreno, O. 1962. "The effect of restraint on gastric acidity in the rat." *American Journal of Physiology* 202, 812.

As noted, an interesting implication of the rebound phenomenon is that in a person at risk for a stress ulcer, continuous stress may protect against the formation of an ulcer (although, as noted, this is not a good prescriptive idea for many other reasons). As a building block of that idea, sustained administration of CRF will protect against ulcer formation: Murison, R. and Bakke, H. 1990. "The role of corticotropin-releasing factor in rat gastric ulcerogenesis." In Hernandez, D. and Glavin, G. (eds.), *Neurobiology of Stress Ulcers* (Annals of the New York Academy of Sciences, Vol. 597), 71.

In some cases, there is hypersecretion of gastric acid, and this is thought to be due to impaired shut-off acid secretion. Walsh, J., Richardson, C., and Fordtran, J. 1975. "pH dependence of acid secretion and gastrin release in normal and ulcer subjects." *Journal of Clinical Investigation* 79, 582; Wormsley, K. 1974. "The pathophysiology of duodenal ulceration." *Gut* 15, 59; Lam, S., Isenberg, J., Grossman, M., Lane, W., and Walsh, J. 1980. "Gastric acid secretion is abnormally sensitive to endogenous gastrin released after peptone test meals in duodenal ulcer patients." *Journal of Clinical Investigation* 65, 555.

Ulcers form as a result of decreased blood flow to the stomach, causing ischemic lesions, due to both acid accumulation and to formation of oxygen radicals. These ideas are reviewed in Tsuda, A. and Tanaka, M. 1990. "Neurochemical characteristics of rats exposed to activity stress." In Hernandez, D. and Glavin, G. (eds.), *Neurobiology of Stress Ulcers* (Annals of the New York Academy of Sciences, Vol. 597), 146; also Yabana, T. and Yachi, A. 1988. "Stress-induced vascular damage and ulcer." *Digestive Disease Science* 33, 751; also Menguy, R. 1980. "The prophylaxis of stress ulceration." *New England Journal of Medicine* 302, 461; also Robert, A. and Kauffman, G. 1989. "Stress ulcers, erosions and gastric motility injury." In Sleisenger, M. and Fordtron, J. *Gastrointestinal Disease: Pathophysiology, Diagnosis, Management*, 4th ed. (Philadelphia: Saunders), 1402. Original data regarding how hemorrhage stress can cause oxidative damage: Itoh, M. and Guth, P. 1985. "Role of oxygen-derived free radicals in hemorrhagic shock-induced gastric lesions in the rat." *Gastroenterology* 88, 1162.

PAGE 75: The bacterial story: *Helicobacter pylori* is associated with the occurrence of ulcers: Blaser, M. 1987. "Gastric *Campylobacter*-like organisms, gastritis, and peptic ulcer disease." *Gastroenterology* 93, 371; Dooley, C. and Cohen, H. 1988. "The clinical significance of *Campylobacter pylori*." *Annals of Internal Medicine* 108, 70.

Although glucocorticoids may cause ulcer formation by suppressing the immune system during stress via this route, it is not clear how important this is for mild stressors. During mild or infrequent stressors, the levels of glucocorticoids secreted do not predict whether ulcers form or not: Murison, R. and Overmeir, J. 1988. "Adrenocortical activity and disease, with reference to gastric pathology in animals." In Hellhammer, D., Florin, I., and Weiner, H. (eds.), *Neurobiological Approaches to Human Disease* (Toronto: Hans Huber), 335. Moreover, removal of glucocorticoids by adrenalectomizing a rat actually protects against ulcers: Brodie, D. 1968. "Experimental peptic ulcer." *Gastroenterology* 55, 125.

All of this suggests that glucocorticoids are unlikely to be the cause of ulcers during stress. However, with more sustained or repeated stressors, the amount of glucocorticoids secreted does predict the severity of ulceration: Weiss, J. 1980. "Somatic effects of predict-able and unpredictable shock." *Psychosomatic Medicine* 32, 397; Weiss, J. 1981. "Effects of coping behavior in different warning signal condi-tions on stress pathology in rats." *Journal of Comparative and Physio-logical Psychology* 77, 1; Murphy, H., Wideman, C., and Brown, T. 1979. "Plasma corticosterone levels and ulcer formation in rats with hippocampal lesions." *Neuroendocrinology* 28, 123. In addition, supra-physiological levels of glucocorticoids (levels that are higher in the bloodstream than the body can normally generate, even during stress, but are induced by taking glucocorticoid medication) can cause ulcers: Robert, A. and Nezmis, J. 1964. "Histopathology of steroid-induced ulcers: An experimental study in the rat." *Archives of Pathology* 77, 407.

The role of prostaglandins in ulcerogenesis: The protective ef-fects of prostaglandins are discussed in Kauffman, G., Zhang, L., Xing, L., Seaton, J., Colony, P., and Demers, L. 1990. "Central neurotensin protects the mucosa by a prostaglandin-mediated mechanism and inhibits gastric acid secretion in the rat." In Hernandez, D. and Gla-vin, G. (eds.), *Neurobiology of Stress Ulcers* (Annals of the New York Academy of Sciences, Vol. 597), 175. See also Schepp, W. Steffen, B., Ruoff, H., Schusdziarra, V., and Classen, M. 1988. "Modulation of rat gastric mucosal prostaglandin E2 release by dietary linoleic acid: Ef-fects on gastric acid secretion and stress-induced mucosal damage." *Gastroeneterology* 95, 18.

Aspirin is ulcerogenic by blocking prostaglandin synthesis: Her-nandez, D., Burke, J., Orlando, C., and Prang, A. 1986. "Differential effects of intracisternal neurotensin and bombesin on stress and eth-anol-induced gastric ulcers." *Pharmacological Research Communica-tions* 187, 617; Adcock, J., Hernandez, D., Nemeroff, C., and Prang, A. 1983. "Effect of prostaglandin synthesis inhibitors on neurotensin and sodium salicylate-induced gastric cytoprotection in rats." *Life Science* 32, 2905. Glucocorticoids block prostaglandin synthesis: Flowers, R. and Blackwell, G. 1979. "Anti-inflammatory steroids induce biosyn-thesis of a phospholipase A2 inhibitor which prevents prostaglandin generation." *Nature* 278, 456.

PAGE 76: The role of stomach contractions in causing ulcers is discussed at length in Weiner, H. 1991. "From simplicity to complexity (1950–1990): The case of peptic ulceration—II. Animal studies." *Psy-chosomatic Medicine* 53, 491.

PAGE 77: Stress decreases contractions in the small intestines: Thompson, D., Richelson, E., and Malagelada, J. 1982. "Perturbation of gastric emptying and duodenal motility through the central nervous system." *Gastroenterology* 83, 1200; Thompson, D., Richelson, E., and Malagelada, J. 1983. "Perturbation of upper gastrointestinal function by cold stress." *Gut* 24, 277; O'Brien, J., Thompson, D., Holly, J., Burnham, W., and Walker, E. 1985. "Stress disturbs human gastrointestinal transit via a beta-1 adrenoreceptor mediated pathway." *Gastroenterology* 88, 1520.

Stress increases contractions in the large intestines: Almy, T. 1951. "Experimental studies on irritable colon." *American Journal of Medicine* 10, 60; Almy, T. and Tulin, M. 1947. "Alterations in colonic function in man under stress: Experimental production of changes simulating the 'irritable colon.'" *Gastroenterology* 8, 616; Narducci, F., Snape, W., Battle, W., London, R., and Cohen, S. 1985. "Increased colonic motility during exposure to a stressful situation." *Digestive Disease Science* 30, 40.

Chemical mediators of the sympathetic stress-response bring about the changes in contractions: Williams, C., Peterson, J., Villar, R., and Burks, T. 1987. "Corticotropin-releasing factor directly mediates colonic responses to stress." *American Journal of Physiology* 253, G582. Also Burks, T. 1990. "Central nervous system regulation of gastrointestinal motility." In Hernandez, D. and Glavin, G. (eds.), *Neurobiology of Stress Ulcers* (Annals of the New York Academy of Sciences 597), 36. Glucocorticoids are not mediators of the contractions: Williams, C., Villar, R., Peterson, J., and Burks, T. 1988. "Stress-induced changes in intestinal transit in the rat: A model for irritable bowel syndrome." *Gastroenterology* 94, 611.

PAGE 78: Colitis is usually stress-related: Kumar, D. and Wingate, D. 1988. "Irritable bowel syndrome." In Kumar, D. and Gustavsson, S. (eds.), *An illustrated Guide to Gastrointestinal Motility* (Chichester: John Wiley), 401. (Note: unique Christmas gift.) Also Mendeloff, A., Monk, M., Siegel, C., and Lilienfeld, A. 1970. "Illness, experience and life stress in patients with irritable colon syndrome and with ulcerative colitis. An epidemiological study of ulceration and regional enteritis in Baltimore, 1960–1964." *New England Journal of Medicine* 282, 14.

The symptoms of gut motility disorders: Burks, T. 1991. "Gastrointestinal motility disorders." In Brown, M., Koob, G., and Rivier, C. *Stress: Neurobiology and Neuroendocrinology* (New York: Marcel Dekker), 565.

PAGE 79: People with colitis have guts that are often hyperreactive: experimental stressors induce greater motility changes in them than in control subjects: reviewed in Burks, T. 1991. "Gastrointestinal motility disorders." In Brown, M., Koob, G., and Rivier, C. *Stress: Neurobiology and Neuroendocrinology* (New York: Marcel Dekker), 565. Original report: Wangle, A. and Deller, D. 1965. "Intestinal motility in man." *Gastroenterology* 48, 69.

PAGE 80: The effects of CRF in the brain, including the effect on appetite and feeding: Dunn, A. and Berridge, C. 1990. "Physiological and behavior responses to corticotropin-releasing factor administration: Is CRF a mediator of anxiety or stress response?" *Brain Research Reviews* 15, P71. The effects of glucocorticoids on appetite are discussed in McEwen, B., de Kloet, E., and Rostene, W. 1986. "Adrenal steroid receptors and actions in the nervous system." *Physiological Reviews* 66, 1121. I am not aware of any publication in which the opposing effects of CRF and glucocorticoids on appetite are analyzed in the manner done in this chapter. However, a similar flavor (viewing some glucocorticoid actions as mediating the "recovery" from the stress-response, rather than the "mediation" of the stress-response) can be found in a very influential paper: Munck, A., Guyre, P., and Holbrook, N. 1984. "Physiological functions of glucocorticoids during stress and their relation to pharmacological actions." *Endocrine Reviews* 5, 25.

CHAPTER 6: DWARFISM AND THE IMPORTANCE OF MOTHERS

PAGE 85: The mechanisms of growth and its regulation by various hormones can be found in any basic endocrine or physiology textbook. A relatively accessible version for nonspecialists can be found in chapter 17, "Regulation of organic metabolism, growth, and energy balance," in Vander, A., Sherman, J., and Luciano, D. 1990. *Human Physiology, The Mechanisms of Body Function*, 5th ed. (New York: McGraw-Hill).

PAGE 87: Short summaries of stress dwarfism and of failure to thrive can be found in most endocrine or pediatric textbooks. A relatively recent technical summary of the subject can be found in Green, W., Campbell, M., and David, R. 1984. "Psychosocial dwarfism: A critical review of the evidence." *J. Am. Acad. Child Psychiatry* 23, 1. A somewhat dated but very readable nontechnical account can be found in Gardner, L. 1972. "Deprivation dwarfism." *Scientific American* 227, 76. A specific discussion of the intellectual impairments found in such children can be found in Dowdney, L., Skuse, D., Heptinstall, E., Puckering, C., and Zur-Szpiro, S. 1987. "Growth retardation and developmental delay amongst inner-city children." *J. Child Psychology and Psychiatry* 28, 529.

PAGE 88: Fairly consistent versions of the King Frederick story are reported by a number of his biographers, including T. Kingston, *History of Frederick the Second, Emperor of the Romans* (Cambridge: Macmillan and Co., 1862), L. Allshorn, *Stupor Mundi: The Life and Times of Frederick II, Emperor of the Romans, King of Sicily and Jerusalem 1194–1250* (London: Martin Secker, 1912), and E. Kantorowicz, *Frederick the Second, 1194–1250* (London: Constable and Co., 1931). The quotation by Salimbene comes from A. Montagu, *Touching: The Human Significance of the Skin* (New York: Harper and Row, 1978). Another story about the intersection of the monarch's scientific curiosity and barbarity concerned his interest in rates of digestion. Frederick wondered whether digestion was faster when you rested after eating or if you exercised. He had two men fed identical and sumptuous dinners and sent one off to nap afterward, while the other went for a strenuous hunt. That phase of the experiment completed, he had both men returned to his court, disemboweled in front of him, and their innards examined. The sleeper had digested his food better.

PAGE 89: The tale of the two orphanages: Widdowson, E. 1951. "Mental contentment and physical growth." *The Lancet* (16 June), 1316. The information on the appalling survivorship in orphanages comes from Chapin, H. 1915. "A plea for accurate statistics in children's institutions." *Transactions of the American Pediatric Society* 27, 180. The quotation comes from Gardner, L. 1972. "Deprivation dwarfism." *Scientific American* 227, 76.

PAGE 91: The discussion of child-rearing practices at the time can be found in A. Montagu, *Touching: The Human Significance of the Skin*, cited above. The authoritative "expert" who advised against such unscientific practices as handling infants too much was Dr. Luther Holt, professor of pediatrics at Columbia University and the author of *The Care and Feeding of Children* (East Norwalk, Conn.: Appleton-Century), which went through 15 editions between 1894 and 1915.

J. M. Barrie and stress dwarfism: The discussion of Barrie that so caught my attention during my student days can be found in J. Martin and S. Reichlin, *Clinical Neuroendocrinology*, 1st ed. (Philadelphia: Davis Company, 1977). I am particularly grateful to Seymour Reichlin, one of the giants of endocrinology and my teacher at the time, for remembering this source.

In preparing this book, I decided to read up a bit more on Barrie. I was surprised to discover a vast number of Barrie biographies; this now fairly obscure man was once the most popular author and playwright in Britain. The details of his life are both fascinating and grotesque. He retained a lifelong obsession with his mother, forever attempting to win her love. In one remarkable passage that encapsulated both his Oedipal wooing of her and his pathological identification with her, he predicted that in his later years, "when age must dim my mind and the past comes sweeping back like the shades of night over the bare road of the present, it will not, I believe, be my youth I shall see but hers, not a boy clinging to his mother's skirt and crying, 'Wait till I'm a man, and you'll lie on feathers,' but a little girl in a magenta frock and a white pinafore." He also had a lifelong obsession with young boys, and his private writing includes passages of sadomasochism and pedophilia.

What is perhaps most fascinating is the transition of Barrie from a rather pathetic and sympathetic loner as a young man to a far-from-sympathetic manipulator in his later years, all because his writing success brought him the power and wealth to disrupt lives around him. As he grew older, alone and childless, he inveigled his way into the lives of a succession of young couples, appearing as a generous benefactor and gradually coming to dominate them more and more, especially the fates of the sons in these families. For the most interesting of the Barrie biographies (from which the above quotation was taken), I recommend A. Birkin, *J. M. Barrie and the Lost Boys* (London: Constable, 1979). Also see the elegaic piece by Alison Lurie, "The boy who couldn't grow up," *New York Review of Books* (6 February 1975), 11.

PAGE 92: In addition to the references given above on the clinical profiles of kids with various deprivation syndromes, the following could be checked for details of the endocrinology of the disruption of growth: chapter 8, "Regulation of growth hormone secretion and its disorders." In Martin, J. and Reichlin, S. 1987. *Clinical Neuroendocrinology*, 2nd ed. (Philadelphia: Davis Company); chapters 8 (Underwood, L. and Van Wyk, J. "Normal and aberrant growth") and 20 (Rose, R. "Psychoendocrinology") in Wilson, J. and Foster, D. 1985. *Williams Textbook of Endocrinology*, 7th ed. (Philadelphia: Saunders); Reichlin, S. 1988. "Prolactin and growth hormone secretion in stress." In Chrousos, G., Loriaux, D., and Gold, P. *Mechanisms of Physical and Emotional Stress* (New York: Plenum Press). These references also discuss the differences between growth hormone regulation in the adult versus the developing child, and in primates and humans versus rodents.

PAGE 93: For a review of the regulation of ODC levels by psychological factors, see Schanberg, S., Evoniuk, G., and Kuhn, C. 1984. "Tactile and nutritional aspects of maternal care: Specific regulators of neuroendocrine function and cellular development." *Proceedings of the Society for Experimental Biology and Medicine* 175, 135. Information on the requirement of active contact with the mother to normalize growth hormone levels in infant rats can be found in Kuhn, C., Paul, J., and Schanberg, S. 1990. "Endocrine responses to mother-infant separation in developing rats." *Developmental Psychobiology* 23, 395. For a discussion of the effects of maternal separation on glucocorticoid levels, see the Kuhn et al. paper just cited, plus the earlier work by Stanton, M., Guitierrez, Y., and Levine, S. 1988. "Maternal deprivation potentiates pituitary-adrenal stress responses in infant rats." *Behavioral Neuroscience* 102, 692. For the classic demonstration of the effects of neonatal handling in rats on growth rates see any of the following three reports by V. Denenberg and G. Karas: "Effects of differential handling upon weight gain and mortality in the rat and mouse." *Science*, 1959, 130, 629; "Interactive effects of age and duration of infantile experience on adult learning." *Psychological Reports*, 1960, 7, 313; "Interactive effects of infant and adult experience upon weight gain and mortality in the rat." *Journal of Comparative and Physiological Psychology*, 1961, 54, 658.

PAGE 94: The data from the study of the child with stress dwarfism whose nurse went on vacation comes from Saenger, P., Levine, L., Wiedemann, E., Schwartz, E., Korth-Schutz, S., Pareira, J., Heinig, B., and New, M. 1977. "Somatomedin and growth hormone in psychosocial dwarfism." *Padiatr. Padol. Suppl.* 5, 1.

PAGE 95: The importance of touch in rat development: Hofer, M. 1984. "Relationships as regulators." *Psychosomatic Medicine* 46, 183.

The work on touching of premature human infants is described in Field, T., Schanberg, S., Scarfidi, F., Bauer, C., Vega-Lahr, N., Garcia, R., Nystrom, J., and Kuhn, C. 1986. "Tactile/kinesthetic stimulation effects on preterm neonates." *Pediatrics* 77, 654. Also Scarfidi, F., Field, T., Schanberg, S., Bauer, C., Vega-Lahr, N., Garcia, R., Poirier, J., Nystrom, J., and Kuhn, C. 1986. "Effects of tactile-kinesthetic stimulation on the clinical course and sleep-wake behavior of pre-term infants." *Infant Behavior and Development* 9, 71. A similar experiment was carried out some years earlier in a much sketchier form with only five infants, as reported in Sokoloff, N., Yaffe, S., Weintraub, D., and Blase, G. 1969. "Effects of handling on the subsequent development of premature infants." *Developmental Psychology* 1, 765. That work, in turn, was inspired by the research of some pioneers in the field: the developmental biologist Rene Spitz and the famed pediatrician T. Berry Brazelton.

The estimate of one billion dollars in savings is based on the following (admittedly very crude) analysis. A federal report in 1987 ("Neonatal Intensive Care for Low Birthweight Infants: Costs and Effectiveness." *Health Technology Case Study 38,* Office of Technology Assessment, Washington, D.C.) reported 150,000–200,000 infants admitted annually to neonatal intensive care units, of whom approximately 20 percent were of very low weight (less than 3 pounds). The average length of stay for that most vulnerable group was approximately 48 days at a cost of $41,000; for the other 80 percent, average stay was approximately 28 days at a cost of $24,000. Total hospitalization bills thus come to something in excess of $5 billion, based on an average individual stay of approximately 32 days (weighting the two different groups). Thus an average reduction of one week's stay in the intensive care unit constitutes an approximate 20 percent reduction and (assuming, probably incorrectly, that the rate of expense incurred is constant over time) produces savings something in excess of a billion dollars. This does not even count savings on the considerable costs of outpatient care lasting months to years for preemies after discharge (discussed in Blackman, J. 1991. "Neonatal intensive care: Is it worth it?" *Pediatric Clinics of North America*, vol. 38, no. 6).

PAGE 97: Most basic physiology textbooks include descriptions of bone growth and resorption in the adult and its hormonal regulation. A particularly clear discussion can be found in Rhoades, R. and Pflanzer, R. 1989. *Human Physiology* (Philadelphia: Saunders College Publishing). Some good recent reviews of how glucocorticoids cause osteoporosis can be found in Reid, I. 1989. "Pathogenesis and treatment of steroid osteoporosis." *Clinical Endocrinology* 30, 83 (clinicians often use the term "steroid" or "corticosteroid" to refer to glucocorticoids); and Dempster, D. 1989. "Bone histomorphometry in glucocorticoid-induced osteoporosis." *Journal of Bone and Mineral Research* 4, 137. As an example of current, ongoing research in the area (in this case, on the specific question of how much the glucocorticoid effect on bone is due to inhibition of growth, versus stimulation of resorption) see Prummel, M., Wiersinga, W., Lips, P., Sanders, G., and Sauerwein, H. 1991. "The course of biochemical parameters of bone turnover during treatment with corticosteroids." *Journal of Clinical Endocrinology and Metabolism* 72, 382. The first report of bone fractures in patients with Cushing's syndrome came, of course, from Dr. Harvey Cushing himself: 1932. "The basophil adenomas of the pituitary body and their clinical manifestations as basophilism." *Bulletin of the Johns Hopkins Hospital* 1, 137. A classic report on how patients being treated with glucocorticoids to control a disease (in this case, asthma) will get osteoporosis can be found in Adinoff, A. and Hollister, J. 1983. "Steroid-induced fractures and bone loss in patients with asthma." *New England Journal of Medicine* 309, 265. For a demonstration that sustained social stress is associated with loss of bone mass in female primates, see Kaplan, J. and Manuck, S. 1989. "Behavioral and evolutionary considerations in predicting disease susceptibility in nonhuman primates." *American Journal of Physical Anthropology* 78, 250; and Shively, C., Jayo, M., Weaver, D., and Kaplan, J. 1991. "Reduced vertebral bone mineral density in socially subordinate female cynomolgus macaques." *American Journal of Primatology* 24, 135.

PAGE 99: Brief stressors can actually stimulate growth hormone secretion in humans: This can be found in most discussions of psychoendocrine regulation of growth hormone secretion. For example: chapter 8 ("Regulation of growth hormone secretion and its disorders") in Martin, J. and Reichlin, S. 1987. *Clinical Neuroendocrinology*, 2nd ed. (Philadelphia: Davis Company); chapters 8 (Underwood, L. and Van Wyk, J. "Normal and aberrant growth") and 20 (Rose, R. "Psychoendocrinology") in Wilson, J. and Foster, D. 1985. *Williams Textbook of Endocrinology*, 7th ed. (Philadelphia: Saunders); Reichlin, S. 1988. "Prolactin and growth hormone secretion in stress." In Chrousos, G., Loriaux, D., and Gold, P. *Mechanisms of Physical and Emotional Stress* (New York: Plenum Press).

PAGE 101: The cross-cultural studies of the stressfulness of developmental rituals: Landauer, T. and Whiting, J. 1964. "Infantile stimulation and adult stature of human males." *American Anthropologist* 66, 1007. A similar theme emerges from their later studies showing that the physical stressor of immunization (and the subsequent brief illness) of children under two years of age resulted in taller adults. The population was Americans who had been children in the 1930s, a time when immunization was far from universal: Whiting, J., Landauer, T., and Jones, T. 1968. "Infantile immunization and adult stature." *Child Development* 39, 59.

PAGE 105: The quotation by Harry Harlow comes from "The nature of love." 1958. *American Psychologist* 13, 673. More technical reports of his work can be found in Harlow, H. and Zimmerman, R. 1959. "Affectional responses in the infant monkey." *Science* 130, 421; Harlow, H., Harlow, M., Dodsworth, R., and Arling, G. 1966. "Maternal behavior of rhesus monkeys deprived of mothering and peer associations in infancy." *Proceedings of the American Philosophical Society* 110, 58.

CHAPTER 7: SEX AND REPRODUCTION

PAGE 107: Basic male reproductive endocrinology and the effects of the various hormonal changes described during stress on reproduction are covered in most basic textbooks. A good example is Rhoades, R., and Pflanzer, R. 1992. *Human Physiology*, 2nd ed. (Philadelphia: Saunders).

Some of the original papers showing how physical stressors (such as surgery, immobilization, drought for a wild primate population, foot shock, or forced swimming) will suppress hormones of the male reproductive system: Bardin, C. and Peterson, R. 1967. "Studies of androgen production by the rat: Testosterone and androstenedione content of blood." *Endocrinology* 80, 38; Free, M. and Tillson, S. 1973. "Secretion rate of testicular steroids in conscious and halothane-anesthetized rat." *Endocrinology* 93, 874; Matsumoto, K., Takeyasu, K., Mizutani, S., Hamanaka, Y., and Uozumi, T. 1970. "Plasma testosterone levels following surgical stress in male patients." *Acta Endocrinology* 65, 11; Sapolsky, R. 1986. "Endocrine and behavioral correlates of drought in the wild baboon." *American Journal of Primatology* II, 217.

Psychological stressors will also suppress these hormones. Examples follow. A drop in social rank for a male primate: Rose, R., Bernstein, I., and Gordon, T. 1975. "Consequences of social conflict on plasma testosterone levels in rhesus monkeys." *Psychosomatic Medicine* 37, 50; Mendoza, S., Coe, C., Lowe, E., and Levine, S. 1979. "The physiological response to group formation in adult male squirrel monkeys." *Psychoneuroendocrinology* 3, 221. A difficult learning task for a primate: Mason, J., Kenion, C., and Collins, D. 1968. "Urinary testosterone response to 72-hour avoidance sessions in the monkey." *Psychosomatic Medicine* 30, 721. A first parachute jump: Davidson, J., Smith, E., and Levine, S. 1978. "Testosterone." In Ursin, H., Baade, E., and Levine, S. (eds.), *Psychobiology of Stress* (New York: Academic Press), 57. Social instability for primates: Sapolsky, R. 1983. "Endocrine aspects of social instability in the olive baboon." *American Journal of Primatology* 5, 365.

PAGE 109: The suppressive effects of Officer Candidate School on testosterone levels: Kreuz, L., Rose, R., and Jennings, J. 1972. "Suppression of plasma testosterone levels and psychological stress." *Archives of General Psychiatry* 26, 479.

Opiate drugs and opioidlike hormones (for instance, beta-endorphin) block the release of LHRH: Delitala, G., Devilla, L., and Arata, L. 1981. "Opiate receptors and anterior pituitary hormone secretion in man. Effect of naloxone infusion." *Acta Endocrinology (Copenhagen)* 97, 150; Jacobs, M. and Lightman, S. 1980. "Studies in the opioid control of anterior pituitary hormones." *Journal of Physiology (London)* 300, 53; Rasmussen, D., Liu, J., Wolf, P., and Yen, S. 1983. "Endogenous opioid regulation of gonadotropin-releasing hormone release from the human fetal hypothalamus in vitro." *Journal of Clinical Endocrinology and Metabolism* 57, 881; Hulse, G. and Coleman, G. 1983. "The role of endogenous opioids in the blockade of reproductive function in the rat following exposure to acute stress." *Pharmacology, Biochemistry, and Behavior* 19, 795.

Exercise stimulates beta-endorphin release: Colt, E., Wardlaw, S., and Frantz, A. 1981. "The effect of running on plasma beta-endorphin." *Life Science* 28, 1637. For an interesting demonstration of the potential for this release to disrupt reproduction, see McArthur, J., Bellen, B., Beitins, T., Pagaon, M., Badger, T., and Klibanski, A. 1980. "Hypothalamic amenorrhea in runners of normal body composition." *Endocrine Research Communications* 7, 13. This study examined an amenorrheic runner with low LH levels; when she was given a drug (naloxone) that blocked beta-endorphin's actions, LH levels rose. Also see Samuels, M., Sanborn, C., Hofeldt, F., and Robbins, R. 1991. "The role of endogenous opiates in athletic amenorrhea." *Fertility and Sterility* 55, 507.

A moderate amount of exercise will stimulate testosterone levels: Elias, M. 1981. "Cortisol, testosterone and testosterone-binding globulin responses to competitive fighting in human males." *Aggressive Behavior* 7, 215. By contrast, sustained major exercise suppresses the system: Dessypris, A., Kuoppasalmi, K., and Adlercreutz, H. 1976. "Plasma cortisol, testosterone, androstenedione and leuteinizing hormone (LH) in a non-competitive marathon run." *Journal of Steroid Biochemistry* 7, 33; MacConnie, S., Barkan, A., Lampman, R., Schorok, M., and Beitins, I. 1986. "Decreased hypothalamic gonadotropin-releasing hormone secretion in male marathon runners." *New England Journal of Medicine* 315, 411; Grandi, M., and Celani, M. 1990. "Effects of football on the pituitary-testicular axis: Differences between professional and non-professional soccer players." *Experimental and Clinical Endocrinology* 96, 253.

PAGE 110: Similarly, major amounts of exercise suppress reproductive physiology in women. As one example, highly active ballet dancers have their onset of puberty delayed: Warren, M. 1980. "The effects of exercise on pubertal progression and reproductive function in girls." *Journal of Clinical Endocrinology and Metabolism* 51, 1150; Frisch, R., Wyshak, G., and Vincent, L. 1980. "Delayed menarche and amenorrhea in ballet dancers." *New England Journal of Medicine* 303, 17. Amenorrhea occurs among women who exercise heavily: Feicht, C., Johnson, T., Martin, B., Sparkes, K., and Wagner, W. 1978. "Secondary amenorrhea in athletes." *The Lancet* 2, 1145; Dale, E., Gerlach, D., and Wilhite, A. 1979. "Menstrual dysfunction in distance runners." *Obstetrics and Gynecology* 54, 47. In these cases, the degree of dysfunction is very tightly coupled to body weight or body fat content: Sanborn, C., Martin, B., and Wagner, W. 1982. "Is athletic amenorrhea specific to runners?" *American Journal of Obstetrics and Gynecology* 143, 859; Shangold, M. and Levine, H. 1982. "The effect of marathon training upon menstrual function." *American Journal of Obstetrics and Gynecology* 143, 862.

Some of the additional effects of overexercising. A moderate amount of exercise will increase bone density, particular in the bones most heavily utilized in the exercise: Nilsson, B. and Westlin, N. 1971. "Bone density in athletes." *Clinical Orthopedics* 77, 179; Lanyon, L.

1989. "Bone loading, exercise, and the control of bone mass; the physiological basis for the prevention of osteoporosis." *Bone* 6, 19. Nevertheless, extremes of exercise can reverse this trend, leading to bone thinning, increased risk of osteoporosis, scoliosis, and stress fractures: Myburgh, K., Hutchins, J., Fataar, A., Hough, S., and Koakes, T. 1990. "Low bone density is an etiologic factor for stress fractures in athletes." *Annals of Internal Medicine* 113, 754; Lindberg, J., Fears, W., Hunt, M., Powell, M., Boll, D., and Wade, C. 1984. "Exercise-induced amenorrhea and bone density." *Annals of Internal Medicine* 101, 647; Drinkwater, B., Nilson, K., and Chesnut, C. 1984. "Bone mineral content of amoenorrheic and eumenorrheic athletes." *New England Journal of Medicine* 311, 277; Marcus, R., Cann, C., Madvig, P., Minkoff, J., Goddard, M., Bayer, M., Martin, M., Gaudiani, L., Haskell, W., and Genant, H. 1985. "Menstrual function and bone mass in elite women distance runners: endocrine and metabolic factors." *Annals of Internal Medicine* 102, 158; Barrow, G. and Saha, S. 1988. "Menstrual irregularity and stress fractures in collegiate female distance runners." *American Journal of Sports Medicine* 16, 209. In prepubescent athletes, the risks also include scoliosis: Warren, M., Brooks-Gunn, J., Hamilton, J., Warren, L., and Hamilton, G. 1986. "Scoliosis and fractures in young ballet dancers: Relation to delayed menarche and secondary amenorrhea." *New England Journal of Medicine* 314, 1348.

These deleterious effects may be due, in part, to the elevated levels of glucocorticoids seen in serious athletes: Luger, A., Deuster, P., Kyle, S., Gallucci, W., Montgomery, L., Gold, P., Loriaux, L., and Chrousos, G. 1987. "Acute hypothalamic-pituitary-adrenal responses to the stress of treadmill exercise." *New England Journal of Medicine* 316, 1309; Willaneuva, A., Schlosser, C., Hopper, B., Liu, J., Hoffman, D., and Rebar, R. 1986. "Increased cortisol production in women runners." *Journal of Clinical Endocrinology and Metabolism* 63, 133; Loucks, A., Mortola, J., Girton, L., and Yen, S. 1989. "Alterations in the hypothalamic-pituitary-ovarian and the hypothalamic-pituitary-adrenal axes in athletic women." *Journal of Clinical Endocrinology and Metabolism* 68, 402. These cases documented pretty substantial increases in the levels of these hormones.

PAGE 111: Glucocorticoids work at the pituitary and the testes to block LH and testosterone release, respectively: Cummings, D., Quigley, M., and Yen, S. 1983. "Acute suppression of circulating testosterone levels by cortisol in men." *Journal of Clinical Endocrinology and Metabolism* 57, 671; Bambino, T. and Hseuh, A. 1981. "Direct inhibitory effect of glucocorticoids upon testicular luteinizing hormone receptors and steroidogenesis in vivo and in vitro." *Endocrinology* 108, 2142; Johnson, B., Welsh, T., and Juniewicz, P. 1982. "Suppression of luteinizing hormone and testosterone secretion in bulls following adrenocorticotropin hormone treatment." *Biology of Reproduction* 26, 305; Vierhapper, H., Waldhausl, W., and Nowotny, P. 1982. "Gonadotropin-secretion in adrenocortical insufficiency: Impact of glucocorticoid substitution." *Acta Endocrinology (Copenhagen)* 101, 580; Sapolsky, R. 1985. "Stress-induced suppression of testicular function in the wild baboon: Role of glucocorticoids." *Endocrinology* 116, 2273.

Prolactin inhibits multiple steps in the male reproductive system: Bartke, A., Smith, M., Michael, S., Peron, F., and Dalterio, S. 1977. "Effects of experimentally-induced chronic hyperprolactinemia on testosterone and gonadotropin levels in male rats and mice." *Endocrinology* 100, 182; Bartke, A., Goldman, B., Bex, F., and Dalterio, S. 1977. "Effects of prolactin on pituitary and testicular function in mice with hereditary prolactin deficiency." *Endocrinology* 101, 1760; McNeilly, A., Sharpe, R., and Fraser, H. 1983. "Increased sensitivity to the negative feedback effect of testosterone induced by hyperprolactinemia in the adult male rat." *Endocrinology* 112, 22.

A good introductory summary of the basic workings of erections and ejaculation can be found in Previte, J. 1983. *Human Physiology* (New York: McGraw-Hill). A more detailed version is found in Guyton, A. 1986. *Textbook of Medical Physiology*, 7th ed. (Philadelphia: Saunders), 959. The parasympathetic neurotransmitter acetylcholine promotes erections: Saenz de Tejada, I., Blanco, R., Goldstein, I., Azadzoi, K., De Las Morenas, A., and Krane, R. 1988. "Cholinergic neurotransmission in human corpus cavernosum. I. Responses of isolated tissue." *American Journal of Physiology* 254, H459. The sympathetic neurotransmitter noradrenaline (norepinephrine) inhibits erections: Saenz de Tejada, I., Kim, N., Lagan, I., Krane, R., and Goldstein, I. 1989. "Regulation of adrenergic activity in penile corpus cavernosum." *Journal of Urology* 142, 1117. Just to make life and sex more complicated, researchers are coming to recognize that there are mechanisms for inducing erections that do not involve the parasympathetic nervous system. These are poorly understood, but it appears that these nerve endings make the arteries into the penis dilate (and thus engorge the penis with blood) by way of nitric oxide, a newly identified gaseous neurotransmitter that is closely related to nitrous oxide (laughing gas): Ignarro, L. 1992. "Nitric oxide as the physiological mediator of penile erection." *Journal of NIH Research* 4, 59.

PAGE 1 1 2 : Incidences of psychogenic impotency: It remains controversial just how common this disorder is. Older studies reported
that 90 to 95 percent of all cases of impotency were psychogenic in
origin. For example, see Strauss, E. 1950. "Impotence from a psychiatric standpoint." *British Medical Journal* I, 697; or Kaplan, H. 1974. *The
New Sex Therapy: Active Treatment of Dysfunctions* (New York: Brun-
ner-Mazel). These numbers are almost certainly high, as they come
from a time when many subtle organic causes of impotency were not
yet understood. Some more recent studies report extremely low rates
(perhaps 10 to 15 percent) of psychogenic impotency. For example, see
Spark, R., White, R., and Connolly, P. 1980. "Impotence is not always
pyschogenic." *Journal of the American Medical Association* 243, 750. In
general, recent studies indicate rates ranging from 14 percent of cases
of impotency being psychogenic in nature, to one study showing that
55 percent were, with another 15 percent being of unknown origin.
These are summarized in Leiblum, S. and Rosen, R. 1989. *Principles
and Practices of Sex Therapy* (New York: Guilford Press).

PAGE 1 1 4 : For an introduction to revisionist ecology about this
species (their role as hunters, rather than just scavengers) see Kruuk,
H. 1972. *The Spotted Hyena: A Study of Predation and Social Behavior*
(Chicago: University of Chicago Press). For studies of their anatomy,
physiology, and behavior, see Frank, L. 1986. "Social organization of
the spotted hyena: II. Dominance and reproduction." *Animal Behavior*
35, 1510; Frank, L., Glickman, S., and Licht, P. 1991. "Fatal sibling
aggression, presocial development and androgens in neonatal spotted
hyenas." *Science* 252, 702; Glickman, S., Frank, L., Licht, P., Yalcin-
kaya, T., Siiteri, P., and Davidson, J. 1993. "Sexual differentiation of
the female spotted hyena: one of nature's experiments." *Annals of the
New York Academy of Sciences,* in press.

    The final reference discusses the possible evolution of the unique
hyena anatomy and social system. The most plausible scenario revolves around the fact that most large carnivores in Africa, such as
lions, have large litters; relatively few of the offspring survive. Most
starve to death, and this is because a lioness and her cubs are usually
excluded from feeding on a kill until the males are sated (despite the
fact that the females do the bulk of the hunting—there, one less
feature to admire lions for).

    By contrast, hyenas tend to have fewer progeny than these other
carnivores. Suddenly the pressure is on to get those few to survive.
Somewhere back when, a female hyena had a wondrous mutation—

her ovaries started secreting huge amounts of the male sex hormone androstenedione, in addition to the normal estrogen. As a result, when she was pregnant, her female fetuses were exposed to the hormone and, as a result, they grew up more muscular and aggressive than typical female mammals; and the tables got turned. Within a few generations, the starving, intimidated male hyenas go and kill something, and just as they are about to gorge, the females boot them off. The kids of high-ranking moms eat before any adult males do; they survive. Thus the tendency in females toward secreting large amounts of androstenedione is highly adaptive, likely to be passed on over the generations.

There is one problem with this, however. Your average female mammal, exposed to those sorts of male sex hormone levels at birth, wouldn't be having kids. The androstenedione would have "masculinized" her hypothalamus, which is to say that as an adult, her hypothalamus would secrete LHRH at a roughly constant rate (as males do) instead of in the cyclic pattern that females need to ovulate. In any other species, this "perinatal androgenization" (masculinization around the time of birth) would make it impossible to reproduce.

Therefore, female hyenas are speculated to have a second mutation, one that protects the reproductive part of the hypothalamus from the masculinizing effects of the hormones. (By contrast, the "aggressive" part of the brain—a phrase that is obviously simplistic—is plenty sensitive to the adrenostenedione: the female hyenas are terrifyingly aggressive.) At present, no one has a clue what that second mutation may be.

PAGE 118: The subject of the effects of starvation, fat depletion, and muscle-to-fat ratios on female reproduction is reviewed in Frisch, R. 1991. "Body weight, body fat and ovulation." *Trends in Endocrinology and Metabolism* 2, 191. This review also gives a good introduction to the reproductive abnormalities seen in anorexia nervosa. Anorexia and the related eating disorder bulimia are peculiar in that more is going on than just loss of weight. Specifically, reproductive suppression occurs even before there is substantial weight loss; in other words, the reproductive systems of anorexics and bulimics are more vulnerable to such suppression than those of healthy women and girls.

Opiates and opioids inhibit LHRH release in the female: Pfeiffer, A. and Herz, A. 1984. "Endocrine actions of opioids." *Hormone and Metabolic Research* 16, 386; Ching, M. 1983. "Morphine suppresses the proestrus surge of GnRH in pituitary portal plasmas of rats." *Endocri-*

nology 112, 2209. (GnRH, LHRH, and LHRF all refer to the same hypothalamic hormone, which causes release of LH and FSH from the pituitary.) For an interesting example of how this is relevant to female athletes, see McArthur, J., Bullen, B., Beitins, T., Pagaon, M., Badger, T., and Klibanski, A. 1980. "Hypothalamic amenorrhea in runners of normal body composition." *Endocrine Research Communications* 7, 13. This study examined an amenorrheic runner with low LH levels; when she was given a drug (naloxone) that blocked the action of beta-endorphin, LH levels rose. See immediately above in the male section for additional references regarding disrupted reproductive physiology in female athletes.

Glucocorticoids suppress the responsiveness of the pituitary to LHRH: Suter, D. and Schwartz, N. 1985. Effects of glucocorticoids on secretion of luteinizing hormone and follicle-stimulating hormone by female rat pituitary cells in vitro. *Endocrinology* 117, 849. References above show how glucocorticoid levels are elevated in heavily-exercising female athletes.

The follicular stage of the menstrual cycle is more vulnerable to disruption than the luteal phase: This is reported in many places. For an accessible version, see R. Hatcher, *Contraceptive Technology, 1984 – 85* (New York: Irvington Publishers, 1984). For a more detailed account, see L. Speroff, R. Glass, and N. Kase, *Clinical Gynecologic Endocrinology and Infertility* (Baltimore: Williams and Wilkins, 1989).

PAGE 119: The assertion that breastfeeding prevents more pregnancies than any other type of contraception comes from Carl Djerassi, the chemist who invented the pill and has spent much of the rest of his extraordinary career studying the social, economic, and political consequences of the revolution he caused, in *The Politics of Contraception* (San Francisco: W. H. Freeman, 1979).

Nursing, prolactin, and the Kalahari bushmen: Konner, M. and Worthman, C. 1980. "Nursing frequency, gonadal function, and birth spacing among !Kung hunter-gathers." *Science* 207, 788. The paper reviews what is known about how quickly prolactin rises in response to breastfeeding and how long it stays up following the end of an episode of nursing. The Kalahari !Kung have been the darlings of anthropologists for decades, and they are often considered to be the prototypical hunter-gatherer society. Their "affluent" preagricultural life has been described in Lee, R. 1979. *!Kung San: Men, Women and Work in a Foraging Society* (New York: Cambridge University Press); Lee, R. and DeVore, I. 1976. *Kalahari Hunter-Gatherers* (Cambridge,

Mass.: Harvard University Press); Jenkins, T. and Nurse, G. 1978. *Health and the Hunter-Gatherers* (Basel: Karger); Marshall, L. 1976. *The !Kung of Nyae Nyae* (Cambridge, Mass.: Harvard University Press); Shostak, M. 1981. *Nisa: The Life and Words of a !Kung Woman* (Cambridge, Mass.: Harvard University Press). Of late there has been some questioning of just how typical they are of hunter-gatherers: Lewin, R. 1988. "New views emerge on hunters and gatherers." *Science* 240, 1146. The link among Westernized women between a large number of menstrual cycles and a proclivity toward gynecological diseases is discussed by MacDonald, P., Dombroski, R., and Casey, M. 1991. "Recurrent secretion of progesterone in large amounts: An endocrine/ metabolic disorder unique to young women?" *Endocrine Reviews* 12, 372.

PAGE 122: The effects of stress on female libido are discussed in two chapters by Sue Carter, "Neuroendocrinology of sexual behavior in the female," and "Hormonal influences on human sexual behavior," both in Becker, J., Breedlove, S., and Crews, D. (eds.), *Behavioral Endocrinology* (Cambridge: MIT Press, 1992). Also see Rose, R. 1985. "Psychoendocrinology." In Wilson, J. and Foster, D. (eds.), *Williams Textbook of Endocrinology*, 7th ed. (Philadelphia: Saunders).

PAGE 124: Hippocrates' advice to pregnant women is noted in Huisjes, H. 1984. *Spontaneous Abortion* (Edinburgh: Churchill Livingstone), 108. Anne Boleyn's attribution is found in Ives, E. 1986. *Anne Boleyn* (Oxford: Basil Blackwell, Ltd.). George Eliot's *Middlemarch* (London: Zodiac Press, 1982 ed.), 557. Also see Hansteen, I. 1990. "Occupational and lifestyle factors and chromosomal aberrations of spontaneous abortions." In *Mutation and the Environment*, Part B (New York: Wiley-Liss, Inc.), 467. Much of this paper reviews the links between various occupational hazards and increased risk of miscarriage; however, it also presents epidemiologic data linking stressful lifestyles to increased rates of miscarriage.

PAGE 125: Abortions, miscarriages, and pregnancy terminations in animals: Competitive infanticide in animals is reviewed in Hausfater, G., and Hrdy, S. 1984. *Infanticide: Comparative and Evolutionary Perspectives* (Hawthorne, N.Y.: Aldine). Harassment and abortion: Berger, J. 1983. "Induced abortion and social factors in wild horses." *Nature* 303, 59; Pereira, M. 1983. "Abortion following the immigration of an adult male baboon (*Papio cynephalus*)." *American Journal of Primatology*, 4, 93; Alberts, S., Sapolsky, R., and Altmann, J. 1992. "Behavioral, endocrine, and immunological correlates of immigration by an aggressive male into a natural primate group." *Hormones and Behavior,* in press. Olfactory-induced abortions in rodents: Bruce, H. 1959. "An exteroceptive block to pregnancy in the mouse." *Nature* 184, 105.

PAGE 126: Miscarriages typically occur many days to weeks after the death of the fetus: chapter 24 ("Abortions") in Pritchard, J., Mac-Donald, P., and Gant, N. 1985. *Williams Obstetrics,* 17th ed. (East Norwalk, Conn.: Appleton-Century-Crofts).

For a good review of the possible mechanisms of stress-induced miscarriage, see Myers, R. 1979. "Maternal anxiety and fetal death." In Ziochella, L. and Pancheri, P. (eds.), *Psychoneuroendocrinology in Reproduction* (New York: Elsevier). The notion that decreased blood flow to the fetus can be the mechanism underlying miscarriage is found in Lapple, M. 1988. "Stress as an explanatory model for spontaneous abortions and recurrent spontaneous abortions." *Zentralblatt fur Gynakologie* 110, 325 (in German).

PAGE 127: For the most detailed review of the literature on psychogenic abortions, see Huisjes, H. 1984. *Spontaneous Abortion* (New York: Churchill Livingstone).

PAGE 129: The Kenyan birth rate: Hatcher, J., Kowal, N., Guest, S., Trussell, J., Stewart, M., Stewart, N., Bowen, T., and Cates, J. *Contraceptive Technology: International Edition* (Atlanta, Ga.: Printed Matter, Inc.), 21. Hutterite studies: Eaton, J. and Mayer, A. 1953. "The social biology of very high fertility among the Hutterites: The demography of a unique population." *Human Biology* 25, 206 (for an estimate of 9 children per family). See Frisch, R. 1978. "Population, food intake and fertility." *Science* 199, 22 (for an estimate of 10 to 12 kids per family).

PAGE 130: The Nazi studies of the women in the Theresienstadt death camp are discussed, without attribution, in Reichlin, S. 1974. "Neuroendocrinology." In Williams, R. (ed.), *Textbook of Endocrinology,* 6th ed. (Philadelphia: Saunders).

CHAPTER 8: IMMUNITY, STRESS, AND DISEASE

PAGE 132: For an introduction to psychoimmunology, or psychoneuroimmunology (the study of the links among the nervous, endocrine, and immune systems), there is the multisyllabic review by A. Dunn. 1989. "Psychoneuroimmunology for the psychoneuroendo-crinologist: A review of animal studies of nervous system-immune system interactions." *Psychoneuroendocrinology* 14, 251. The bible in the field is Ader, R., Felten, D., and Cohen, N. *Psychoneuroimmuno-logy,* 2nd ed. (San Diego: Academic Press).

P A G E   1 3 4 : Most college physiology textbooks will have introductions to the workings of the immune system. For those who want even more, a good introductory text for immunology is Benjamini, E., and Leskowitz, S. 1991. *Immunology: A Short Course,* 2nd ed. (New York: Wiley-Liss).

P A G E   1 3 9 : Effects of glucocorticoids on the immune system: The most up-to-date and masterly of reviews can be found in Munck, A., and Guyre, P. 1991. "Glucocorticoids and immune function." In Ader, R., Felten, D., and Cohen, N. *Psychoneuroimmunology,* 2nd ed. (San Diego: Academic Press). It should be noted that glucocorticoids don't always suppress the immune system. Nevertheless, as far as parts of the nervous and endocrine systems go, "glucocorticoids generally suppress immune function" is one of the more confident statements that can be made.

Glucocorticoids kill cells of the immune system in many species and do so by causing the DNA to be chopped into small pieces. This has been shown in many studies; some of the classic ones are Wyllie, A. 1980. "Glucocorticoid-induced thymocyte apoptosis is associated with endogenous endonuclease activation." *Nature* 284, 555. Cohen, J. and Duke, R. 1984. "Glucocorticoid activation of a calcium-dependent endonuclease in thymocyte nuclei leads to cell death." *Journal of Immunology* 132, 38. Compton, M., and Cidlowski, J. 1986. "Rapid in vivo effects of glucocorticoids on the integrity of rat lymphocyte genomic DNA." *Endocrinology* 118, 38. As noted throughout the chapter, a frequent question runs along the line of "Okay, so if you inject an animal with a ton of glucocorticoids and you mess up its immune system in some way (in this case, by killing lymphocytes), is that a 'physiological' effect—will the smaller amounts of glucocorticoids secreted during stress (or stress itself) do the same thing?" The last paper also presents a small amount of data suggesting that stress will damage lymphocytes in the same way: Compton, M., Haskill, J., and Cidlowski, J. 1988. "Analysis of glucocorticoid actions on rat thymocyte DNA by fluorescence-activated flow cytometry." *Endocrinology* 122, 2158.

Effects of beta-endorphins and of the sympathetic nervous system on the immune system. For reviews of the confusions in the literature, see Shavit, Y. 1991. "Stress-induced immune modulation in animals: Opiates and endogenous opioid peptides" (beta-endorphin, it should be remembered, is an endogenous opioid); see also Madden, K. and Livnat, S. 1991. "Catecholamine action and immunologic reactivity." (Catecholamines are the chemical messengers released by the sympathetic nervous system.) Both are chapters in Ader, R., Felten, D., and Cohen, N. *Psychoneuroimmunology*, 2nd ed. (San Diego: Academic Press).

PAGE 140: Why does it make sense to suppress immunity at all during stress? For thoughtful discussions of this idea, see Besedovsky, H., and del Rey, A. 1991. "Physiological implications of the immune-neuro-endocrine network"; and Munck, A., and Guyre, P. 1991. "Glucocorticoids and immune function." Both in Ader, R., Felten, D., and Cohen, N. *Psychoneuroimmunology*, 2nd ed. (San Diego: Academic Press). Also see Munck, A., Guyre, P., and Holbrook, N. 1984. "Physiological actions of glucocorticoids in stress and their relation to pharmacological actions." *Endocrine Reviews* 5, 25. The latter is the very influential paper that introduced the idea that glucocorticoids are immunosuppressive as a means of recovering from the stress-response, rather than as a means of mediating the stress-response.

PAGE 143: The effects of illness on the behavior of animals: Hart, B. 1988. "Biological bases of the behavior of sick animals." *Neuroscience and Biobehavioral Reviews* 12, 123.

PAGE 145: The idea that not all of the traits of an organism are necessarily sculpted by evolution to be adaptive runs through much of Stephen Jay Gould's writing. It is most succinctly presented in "The spandrels of San Marco and the Panglossian paradigm: A critique of the adaptationist programme." Written with the geneticist Richard Lewontin, 1979. *Proceedings of the Royal Society of London* B 205, 581.

PAGE 145: Interleukin-1 causes the release of CRF from the hypothalamus: Sapolsky, R., Rivier, C., Yamamoto, G., Plotsky, P., and Vale, W. 1987. "Interleukin-1 stimulates the secretion of hypothalamic corticotropin-releasing factor." *Science* 238, 522; Berkenbosch, F., van Oers, J., del Rey, A., Tilders, F., and Besedovsky, H. 1987. "Corticotropin-releasing factor-producing neurons in the rat activated by interleukin-1." *Science* 238, 524. Just to make things worse, the same issue contained a report that IL-1 works at the level of the pituitary, rather than the hypothalamus in the brain, to stimulate the stress-response: Bernton, E., Beach, J., Holaday, J., Smallridge, R., and Fein, H. 1987. "Release of multiple hormones by a direct action of interleukin-1 on pituitary cells." *Science* 238, 519. I think a vague consensus is emerging in the field that the effect on the hypothalamus occurs reproducibly in an animal, whereas the pituitary effect depends on the use of pituitary cells in a petri dish (rather than in the living animal) and on the conditions under which the cells are grown in the dish.

P A G E   1 4 7 : Bereavement decreases immune function and increases the risk for mortality: Kiecolt-Glaser, J., and Glaser, R. 1991. "Stress and immune function in humans." In Ader, R., Felten, D., and Cohen, N. (eds.). *Psychoneuroimmunology*, 2nd ed. (San Diego: Academic Press); Levav, I., Friedlander, Y., Kark, J., and Peritz, E. 1988. "An epidemiological study of mortality among bereaved parents." *New England Journal of Medicine* 319, 457. One facet of this paper's conclusions was widely publicized. The researchers studied the parents of soldiers killed in the Yom Kippur War in Israel. After doing all the appropriate controls, the researchers found that these parents were at no increased risk for death during this bereavement period. This fact was widely cited as evidence against psychoimmunologic mechanisms in humans. Generally ignored, however, was the finding that mortality was significantly increased among the parents who were widows, widowers, or divorced. In other words, bereavement was associated with enhanced mortality among those with little social support.

A major depression is associated with an increased risk of mortality from cancer even decades later: Shekelle, R., Raynor, W., Ostfeld, A., Garron, D., Bieliauskas, L., Liu, S., Maliza, C., and Paul, O. 1981. "Psychological depression and 17-year risk of death from cancer." *Psychosomatic Medicine* 43, 117.

Factors like divorce, marital discord, and caregiving to an Alzheimer's patient are associated with suppressed aspects of immune function. Reviewed in Kiecolt-Glaser, J., and Glaser, R. 1991. "Stress and immune function in humans." In Ader, R., Felten, D., and Cohen, N. (eds.). *Psychoneuroimmunology*, 2nd ed. (San Diego: Academic Press).

One example of a body of studies showing stress-induced changes in immune function in college students taking examinations: Kiecolt-Glaser, J., Glaser, R., Strain, E., Stout, J., Tarr, K., Holliday, J., and Speicher, C. 1986. "Modulation of cellular immunity in medical students." *Journal of Behavioral Medicine* 9, 5.

Links between stress and the onsets of post-polio syndrome, multiple sclerosis and juvenile diabetes: Bruno, R., Frick, N., and Cohen, J. 1991. "Polioencephalitis, stress, and the etiology of post-polio sequelae." *Orthopedics* 14, 1269; Leclere, J. and Weryha, G. 1989. "Stress and auto-immune endocrine diseases." *Hormone Research* 31, 90; Weiner, H. 1991. "Social and psychobiological factors in autoimmune diseases." In Ader, R., Felten, D., and Cohen, N. *Psychoneuroimmunology*, 2nd ed. (San Diego: Academic Press).

Stress and the common cold: Cohen, S., Tyrrell, D., and Smith, A. 1991. "Psychological stress and susceptibility to the common cold." *New England Journal of Medicine* 325, 606. This paper came out of the famed Common Cold Unit of the Medical Research Council in Salisbury, England, which recruited volunteers for their frequent two-week experiments about various aspects of coming down with and recovering from the common cold. Apparently quite an experience: all expenses covered plus a small salary, many recreational activities in the peaceful Salisbury countryside, daily blowing of noses into collection tubs for the staff, questionnaires to fill out, and being spritzed up the nose with either placebo or a cold-causing virus. One in three chance, on the average, of getting a cold while there. People would compete for slots as volunteers; couples have met there, married, returned for honeymoons; folks with connections would maneuver for return visits, making it an annual paid vacation. (All was not idyllic sniffling heaven at the Cold Unit, however. An occasional group would be involved in studies showing that, for example, being chilled and damp does not cause colds, and would have to stand around for hours in wet socks.) Unfortunately, because of budget limitations, the unit has been closed. For a particularly amusing account of the place, see Roach, M. 1990. "How I blew my summer vacation." In *Health* (January/February), 73.

Stress increases the rate of spontaneous tumors in mice: Henry, J., Stephens, V., and Watson, F. 1975. "Forced breeding, social disorder, and mammary tumor formation in CBA/USC mouse colonies: A pilot study." *Psychosomatic Medicine* 37, 277. Stress accelerates tumor growth in rats: Sklar, L. and Anisman, H. 1979. "Stress and coping factors influence tumor growth." *Science* 205, 513. Riley, V.

1981. "Psychoneuroendocrine influences on immunocompetence and neoplasia." *Science* 212, 1100. Visintainer, M., Volpicelli, J., and Seligman, M. 1982. "Tumor rejection in rats after inescapable or escapable shock." *Science* 216, 437. Sapolsky, R. and Donnelly, T. 1985. "Vulnerability to stress-induced tumor growth increases with age in rats: Role of glucocorticoids." *Endocrinology* 117, 662.

Social relationships are associated with decreased mortality rates: House, J., Landis, K., and Umberson, D. 1988. "Social relationships and health." *Science* 241, 540.

PAGE 149: Patients with Cushing's syndrome are immunosuppressed because of their very high glucocorticoid levels: Krieger, D. 1982. "Cushing's syndrome." *Monographs in Endocrinology*, Vol. 22 (Berlin: Springer-Verlag). Small amounts of glucocorticoids can actually stimulate aspects of the immune system: Munck, A. and Guyre, P. 1991. "Glucocorticoids and immune function." In Ader, R., Felten, D., and Cohen, N. *Psychoneuroimmunology*, 2nd ed. (San Diego: Academic Press).

PAGE 151: Some subtle confounds in lifestyle/disease relationships: Some particularly thoughtful discussions can be found in House, J., Landis, K., and Umberson, D. 1988. "Social relationships and health." *Science* 241, 540; Levav, I., Friedlander, Y., Kark, J., and Peritz, E. 1988. "An epidemiological study of mortality among bereaved parents." *New England Journal of Medicine* 319, 457; and throughout Ader, R., Felten, D., and Cohen, N. *Psychoneuroimmunology*, 2nd ed. (San Diego: Academic Press).

Excellent studies showing that social relationships decrease the risk for mortality: House, J., Landis, K., and Umberson, D. 1988. "Social relationships and health." *Science* 241, 540. Berkman, L. 1983. *Health and Ways of Living: Findings from the Alameda County Study* (New York: Oxford University Press). Lonelier individuals had less Natural Killer cell activity: Kiecolt-Glaser, J., Garner, W., Speicher, C., Penn, G., and Glaser, R. 1984. "Psychosocial modifiers of immunocompetence in medical students." *Psychosomatic Medicine* 46, 7. Monkeys separated from their mothers become immunosuppressed, but are somewhat protected by being put in a social group: Coe, C., Lubach, G., and Ershler, W. 1989. "Immunological consequences of maternal separation in infant primates." In Lewis, M. and Worobey, J. (eds.). *Infant Stress and Coping* (San Francisco: Jossey-Bass), 65.

PAGE 152: Parents of children killed by war or accident were at greater risk for death during the bereavement period if they lacked social support: Levav, I., Friedlander, Y., Kark, J., and Peritz, E. 1988. "An epidemiological study of mortality among bereaved parents." *New England Journal of Medicine* 319, 457.

Depression and increased cancer risk: Shekelle, R., Raynor, W., Ostfeld, A., Garron, D., Bieliauskas, L., Liu, S., Maliza, C., and Paul, O. 1981. "Psychological depression and 17-year risk of death from cancer." *Psychosomatic Medicine* 43, 117; Persky, V., Kempthorne-Rawson, J., and Shekelle, R. 1987. "Personality and risk of cancer: 20-year follow-up of the Western Electric Study." *Psychosomatic Medicine* 49, 435.

Being in a support group extends cancer survivorship: Spiegel, D., Bloom, J., and Kraemer, H. 1989. "Effect of psychosocial treatment on survival of patients with metastatic breast cancer." *The Lancet* 2, 888. See also Spiegel, D. 1991. "A psychosocial intervention and survival time of patients with metastatic breast cancer." *Advances* 7, 10.

PAGE 153: Reports that stress can exacerbate some autoimmune diseases: Leclere, J., and Weryha, G. 1989. "Stress and auto-immune endocrine diseases." *Hormone Research* 31, 90. Weiner, H. 1991. "Social and psychobiological factors in autoimmune diseases." In Ader, R., Felten, D., and Cohen, N. *Psychoneuroimmunology*, 2nd ed. (San Diego: Academic Press).

PAGE 154: Tumor growth rates in rodents can be accelerated by housing them in stressful conditions, giving them rotational stress, and/or glucocorticoids: Riley, V. 1981. "Psychoneuroendocrine influences on immunocompetence and neoplasia." *Science* 212, 1100. Tumor growth can also be accelerated by inescapable shock: Visintainer, M., Volpicelli, J., and Seligman, M. 1982. "Tumor rejection in rats after inescapable or escapable shock." *Science* 216, 437.

Stress and glucocorticoid effects on natural killer cell activity: Munck, A. and Guyre, P. 1991. "Glucocorticoids and immune function." In Ader, R., Felten, D., and Cohen, N. *Psychoneuroimmunology*, 2nd ed. (San Diego: Academic Press); effects on angiogenesis: Folkman, J., Langer, R., Linhardt, R., Haudenschild, C., and Taylor, S. 1983. "Angiogenesis inhibition and tumor regression caused by heparin or a heparin fragment in the presence of cortisone." *Science* 221, 719. Effects of glucocorticoids on tumor metabolism: Romero, L., Raley-Susman, K., Redish, K., Brooke, S., Horner, H., and Sapolsky, R. 1992. "A possible mechanism by which stress accelerates growth of virally-derived tumors. *Proceedings of the National Academy of Sciences, USA,* 89, 11084.

The links between stress and cancer mostly involve induced tumors, acceleration of tumor growth rather than initial establishment of tumors, and virally derived tumors: Fitzmaurice, M. 1988. "Physiological relationships among stress, viruses, and cancer in experimental animals." *International Journal of Neuroscience* 39, 307; Justice, A. 1985. "Review of the effects of stress on cancer in laboratory animals: Importance of time of stress application and type of tumor." *Psychological Bulletin* 98, 108.

PAGE 155: Some very similar sentiments to those in Bernie Siegel's magnum opus, *Love, Medicine and Miracles,* 1986, can be found in other books, including one by a Siegel's mentors: Simonton, O., Matthews-Simonton, S., and Creighton, J. 1978. *Getting Well Again* (Los Angeles: Tarcher, Inc.). The lack of an effect of Siegel's program on survivorship can be found in Morgenstern, H., Gellert, G., Walter, S., Ostfeld, A., and Siegel, B. 1984. "The impact of a psychosocial support program on survival with breast cancer: The importance of selection bias in program evaluation." *Journal of Chronic Disease* 37, 273. The program's lack of efficacy is pointed out in a 1992 debate between Siegel and David Spiegel (the physician whose work is discussed earlier in this chapter and who owns up to having sustained a fair amount of discomfort by having a name readily confused with Siegel's): "Psychosocial interventions and cancer." *Advances* 8, 2. The Herbert Weiner quotation comes from his 1992 book, *Perturbing the Organism: The Biology of Stressful Experience* (Chicago: University of Chicago Press).

PAGE 159: The lapsarian in the Reagan administration: In an extraordinary episode, a top appointee in the Department of Education turned out to hold lapsarian views. "There is no injustice in the universe," she wrote. "As unfair as it may seem, a person's external circumstances do fit his level of inner spiritual development. . . . [The handicapped] falsely assume that the lottery of life has penalized them at random. This is not so. 'Nothing comes to an individual that he has not [at some point in his development] summoned.'" (Second set of brackets her own.) She extended this philosophy to explaining why James Brady, Reagan's press secretary, had been seriously wounded in John Hinckley's assassination attempt. Her policy advice included terminating any special educational programs for the handicapped. Fortunately, she lasted three days in her new position before being returned to the conservative fundamentalist think tank from which she had emerged.

Testimony by and about the woman, Eileen Gardner of the conservative Heritage Foundation, can be found in the Senate Hearings Before the Committee on Appropriations, 99th Congress, First Session, 1986, HR 3424, part 3, Appropriations Hearings for the Departments of Labor, HHS, and Education, pages 74 and 177. The fiery hearings were reported in newspapers throughout the country (for example, *The New York Times*, 17–19 April, 1985; *Washington Post*, 17 May, 1985). In the Senate she expressed her view that sometimes congenital illnesses are visited upon newborn infants not so much on account of their own sinfulness as because of the sinfulness of the parents — all the while apparently unaware that the Senator presiding over her hearings, Lowell Weicker of Connecticut, is the father of a congenitally retarded, institutionalized child and a passionate supporter of research into retardation and congenital abnormalities. Weicker, a veteran politician who probably is as knowledgeable as anyone can be about the corridors of power, described her testimony as "the most incredible thing I have read in my career in the United States Senate. I have never seen such callousness" (*The New York Times* 17 April, 1985).

P A G E 1 6 4 : The history of status thymicolymphaticus was originally published by me under the title "Poverty's remains." 1991. *The Sciences* (September/October), 8. The original observation of "enlarged" thymuses in SID infants was reported by Paltauf, A. 1889. *Plotzlicher Thymus Tod*. Wiener klin. Woechesucher, Berlin # 46 and 9. The supposed disease was named a few years later in Escherich, T. 1896. *Status thymico-lymphaticus*. Berlin klin. Woechesucher # 29. By the late 1920s it was in all the textbooks, complete with radiation advice (how much to administer, where to aim it, and so on). See, for example, Lucas, W. 1927. *Modern Practise of Pediatrics* (New York: Macmillan). Amid this generally grim story, I was amused to note that by the time of this textbook, the "disease" was so well established that the author now broke ground by describing the distinctive and striking behavioral features of infants who would later be found to have died of thymicolymphaticus. They were characterized as having "phleg-matic" dispositions—presumably because these were normal kids and thus were phlegmatic about their imaginary illnesses. It is a chilling experience to wander the dusty lower floor of a medical library, read-ing these forgotten texts and their confident discussions of this sup-posed disease. Page after page of errors. What similar mistakes are we making now?

Lost amid this consensus of the savants was a 1927 study by E. Boyd ("Growth of the thymus, its relation to status thymicolym-phaticus and thymic symptoms." *American Journal of Diseases of Chil-dren* 33, 867), which should have put the whole thing to rest. Boyd showed for the first time that a stressor (malnutrition, in this case) caused thymic shrinking. She demonstrated, moreover, that some chil-dren who died of accidents turned out, upon autopsy, to be "suffer-ing" from thymicolymphaticus, and suggested for the first time that the whole thing might be an artifact. It was not until the 1930s that the first of the pediatric textbooks began to voice the opinion that this conclusion might be correct; not until 1945 did the leading textbook in the field emphatically state that treating this "disease" was a disas-terous thing to do (Nelson, W. 1945. *Nelson's Textbook of Pediatrics*, 4th ed. Philadelphia: Saunders). In researching this subject, I had the pleasure to talk with the same Dr. Nelson, now in his nineties, still seeing inner-city children at the University of Pennsylvania Hospital every day and basking in the positive reviews of the recent edition of his classic textbook. He recalled how, by the early 1930s, the Young Turk pediatricians (one of whom he most surely was) were already contemptuous of the old guard for advocating something as crazy and outdated as radiating kids to prevent an imaginary disease. Despite that, the practice continued widely well into the 1950s.

CHAPTER 9: STRESS-INDUCED ANALGESIA

PAGE 165: The extended quotation comes from page 178 of Joseph Heller's *Catch-22* (New York: Simon and Schuster, 1955).

PAGE 166: Pain asymbolia (the inability to feel pain): Appenzeller, O., and Kornfeld, M. 1972. "Indifference to pain: A chronic peripheral neuropathy with mosaic Schwann cells." *Archives of Neurology* 27, 322; Murray, T. 1973. "Congenital sensory neuropathy." *Brain* 96,

387; Fox, J., Belvoir, F., and Huott, A. 1974. "Congenital hemihypertrophy with indifference to pain." *Archives of Neurology* 30, 490.

PAGE 169: The interactions of fast and slow pain fibers were first described in the classic paper by Melzack, R. and Wall, P. 1965. "Pain mechanisms: A new theory." *Science* 150, 971. They are elaborated in Wall, P. and Melzack, R. 1989. *Textbook of Pain*, 2nd ed. (Edinburgh: Churchill Livingstone).

PAGE 171: Pain medication requests by gallbladder surgery patients: Ulrich, R. 1984. "View through a window may influence recovery from surgery." *Science* 224, 420.

PAGE 172: Most clinicians concerned with chronic pain syndromes are anecdotally familiar with stress-induced analgesia, and many basic neurology, neuroscience, or physiological psychology texts cover the subject—for example, see the chapter on pain by Dennis Kelly in *Principles of Neural Science* by E. Kandel and J Schwartz. 1985. (New York: Elsevier). This also contains the famous description of the phenomenon by Dr. David Livingstone upon the occasion of his being mauled by a lion. Also see Fields, H. 1987. *Pain* (New York: McGraw-Hill).

Requests for morphine by soldiers versus civilians: Beecher, H. 1956. "Relationship of significance of wound to pain experienced." *Journal of the American Medical Association* 161, 17.

PAGE 173: Stress-induced analgesia in animals: Terman, G., Shavit, Y., Lewis, J., Cannon, J., and Liebeskind, J. 1984. "Intrinsic mechanisms of pain inhibition: Activation by stress." *Science* 226, 1270.

Opiates, opiate receptors, and opioids: For technical reviews on this subject, see Akil, H., Watson, S., Young, E., Lewis, M., Khachaturian, H., and Walker, J. 1984. "Endogenous opioids: Biology and function." *Annual Review of Neuroscience* 7, 223; Basbaum, A. and Fields, H. 1984. "Endogenous pain control systems: Brainstem spinal pathways and endorphin circuitry." *Annual Review of Neuroscience* 7, 309. For a surprisingly readable account of the history of this field, see Snyder, S. 1989. *Brainstorming: The Science and Politics of Opiate Research* (Cambridge: Harvard University Press). Snyder, one of the discoverers of the opiate receptor and a leading figure in the field, is an excellent nontechnical writer.

PAGE 175: The effects of acupuncture are mediated by opiate receptors: Mayer, D., Price, D., Barber, J., and Rafii, A. 1976. "Acupuncture analgesia: Evidence for activation of a pain inhibitory system as a mechanism of action." In *Advances in Pain Research and Therapy*, Vol. 1. Bonica, J. and Albe-Fessard, D. (eds.) (New York: Raven Press), 751; Mayer, D. and Hayes, R. 1975. "Stimulation-produced analgesia: Development of tolerance and cross-tolerance to morphine." *Science* 188, 941.

First demonstration of endorphin release during stress: Guillemin, R., Vargo, T., and Rossier, J. 1977. "Beta-endorphin and adrenocorticotropin are secreted concomitantly by pituitary gland." *Science* 197, 1367. Its stimulation by a variety of stressors: Colt, E., Wardlaw, S., and Frantz, A. 1981. "The effect of running on plasma beta-endorphin." *Life Sciences* 28, 1637; Cohen, M., Pickar, D., and Dubois, M. 1982. "Stress-induced plasma beta-endorphin immunoreactivity may predict postoperative morphine usage." *Psychiatry Research* 6, 7; Katz, E., Sharp, B., and Kellermann, J. 1982. "Beta-endorphin immunoreactivity and acute behavioral distress in children with leukemia." *Journal of Nervous and Mental Disease* 170, 72; Jungkunz, G., Engel, R., and King, U. 1983. "Endogenous opiates increase pain tolerance after stress in humans." *Psychiatry Research* 8, 13.

CHAPTER 10: WHY IS PSYCHOLOGICAL STRESS STRESSFUL?

PAGE 178: Teddy Roosevelt's childhood lament can be found in Morris, E. 1979. *The Rise of Theodore Roosevelt* (New York: Ballantine Books). For a history of the field of stress research, as well as the celebrated debate between Selye and Mason, see Selye, H. 1975. "Confusion and controversy in the stress field." *Journal of Human Stress* 1, 37; Mason, J. 1975. "A historical view of the stress field." *Journal of Human Stress* 1, 6. For a nontechnical review of Weiss's work, see Weiss, J. 1972. "Psychological factors in stress and disease." *Scientific American*, June, 226, 104.

PAGE 182: Outlets for frustration: The difference in the stress-response in patients depending on whether they expressed fear to their doctor: Greene, W., Conron, D., Schalch, S., and Schreiner, B. 1970. "Psychological correlates of growth hormone and adrenal secretory responses of patients undergoing cardiac catheterization." *Psychoso-*

matic Medicine 32, 599. The demonstration that social support networks are associated with lower glucocorticoid concentrations can be found in Ray, J. and Sapolsky, R. 1992. "Styles of male social behavior and their endocrine correlates among high-ranking wild baboons." *American Journal of Primatology* 28, 231.

PAGE 183: Social support and cardiovascular disease susceptibility: Williams, R., Barefoot, J., Califf, R., Haney, T., Saunders, W., Pryor, D., Hlatky, M., Siegler, I., and Mark, D. 1992. "Prognostic importance of social and economic resources among patients with angiographically documented coronary artery disease." *Journal of the American Medical Association* 267, 520.

PAGE 185: Predictability: An analysis similar to mine (a warning signal tells you when to worry and, even more importantly, when you can relax) has been termed the safety-signal hypothesis by psychologist Martin Seligman (*Helplessness: On Depression, Development and Death* (San Francisco: W. H. Freeman and Co., 1975).

PAGE 187: Ulcers and bombings in World War II: Stewart, D., and Winser, D. 1942. "Incidence of perforated peptic ulcer: Effect of heavy air-raids." *The Lancet* (28 February), 259.

Gary Gilmore and his execution were the subject of Norman Mailer's book, *The Executioner's Song* (Boston: Little, Brown and Company, 1979).

PAGE 188: Control: You don't need to actually exercise control in order to get its benefits: Glass, D. and Singer, J. 1972. *Urban Stress: Experiments on Noise and Social Stressors* (New York: Academic Press).

PAGE 189: The perception of things worsening or improving: Baboons rising or declining in the hierarchy: Sapolsky, R. 1992. "Cortisol concentrations and the social significance of rank instability among wild baboons." *Psychoneuroendocrinology*, 17, 701 (cortisol is glucocorticoid found in the bloodstream of primates and humans). Parents of children with cancer: Wolff, C., Friedman, S., Hofer, M., and Mason, J. 1964. "Relationship between psychological defenses and mean urinary 17-hydroxycorticosteroid excretion rates." *Psychosomatic Medicine* 26, 576 (17-hydroxycorticosteroids are the versions of glucocorticoids that humans excrete).

PAGE 194: Executive stress syndrome and ulcerating monkeys: Technical and nontechnical versions of the famous experiment with executive monkeys can be found, respectively, in Brady, J., Porter, R., Conrad, D., and Mason, J. 1958. "Avoidance behavior and the development of gastroduodenal ulcers." *Journal of the Experimental Analysis of Behavior* I, 69, and Brady, J. 1958. "Ulcers in 'executive' monkeys." *Scientific American,* 199, 95. Technical and nontechnical critiques by Weiss of this experiment can be found, respectively, in Weiss, J. 1968. "Effects of coping response on stress." *Journal of Comparative and Physiological Psychology* 65, 251, and Weiss, J. 1972. "Psychological Factors in Stress and Disease." *Scientific American* 226, 104. A technical critique is also offered by Natelson, B., Dubois, A., and Sodetz, F. 1977. "Effect of multiple stress procedures on monkey gastro-duodenal mucosa, serum gastrin and hydrogen ion kinetics." *American Journal of Digestive Diseases* 22, 888.

Many of the ideas in this chapter will be returned to in the final chapter on stress management, along with additional references.

CHAPTER 11: STRESS AND DEPRESSION

A masterful overview of the entire field can be found in Goodwin, F. and Jamison, K. 1990. *Manic-Depressive Illness* (New York: Oxford University Press).

PAGE 196: Five to 20 percent of the population will suffer from a major depression: Robins, L., Helzer, J., Weissman, M., Orvaschel, H., Gruenberg, E., Burke, J., and Regier, D. 1984. "Lifetime prevalence of specific psychiatric disorders in three sites." *Archives of General Psychiatry* 41, 949; Weissman, M. and Myers, J. 1978. "Rates and risks of depressive symptoms in a United States urban community." *Acta Psychiatr. Scand.* 57, 219; Helgason, T. 1979. "Epidemiological investigation concerning affective disorders." In Schor, M. and Stromgren, M. (eds.). *Origin, Presentation and Treatment of Affective Disorders* (London: Academic Press), 241.

PAGE 197: Good descriptions of the symptoms found in different depressive subtypes can be found in the bible on the subject, the *Diagnostic and Statistical Manual of Mental Disorders* (DSM-III-R), 3rd ed., revised. American Psychiatric Association, 1987, Washington, D.C. Also see Gold, P., Goodwin, F., and Chrousos, G. 1988. "Clinical and biochemical manifestations of depression. Relation to the neurobiology of stress." *New England Journal of Medicine*, 319, 348.

P A G E 2 0 0 : For the classic discussion of depression as a cognitive disorder, see Beck, A. 1976. *Cognitive Therapy and the Emotional Disorders* (New York: International Universities Press).

P A G E 2 0 1 : Vegetative symptoms: For the first report of sleep changes in many depressives: Diaz-Guerrero, R., Gottlieb, J., and Knott, J. 1946. "The sleep of patients with manic-depressive psychosis, depressive type: An electroencephalographic study." *Psychosomatic Medicine* 8, 399. Also see Coble, P., Foster, F., and Kupfer, D. 1976. "Electroencephalographic sleep diagnosis of primary depression." *Archives of General Psychiatry* 33, 1124; Gillin, J., Duncan, W., Pettigrew, K., Frankel, B., and Snyder, F. 1979. "Successful separation of depressed, normal and insomniac subjects by EEG sleep data." *Archives of General Psychiatry* 36, 85.

Cortisol (glucocorticoid) levels are elevated in many depressives: for an early demonstration of this, see Sacher, E. 1975. "Neuroendocrine abnormalities in depressive illness." In Sachar, E. (ed.). *Topics of Psychoendocrinology* (New York: Grune and Stratton), 135. For a more recent review, see Sapolsky, R. and Plotsky, P. 1990. "Hypercortisolism and its possible neural bases." *Biological Psychiatry* 27, 937.

P A G E 2 0 3 : Depressive symptomatology can follow cyclic patterns over time: A classic demonstration of this can be found in Richter, C. 1938. "Two-day cycles of alternating good and bad behavior in psychotic patients." *Archives of Neurology and Psychiatry* 39, 587.

For a good review of seasonal affective disorders, see Rosenthal, N., Sack, D., Gillin, C., Lewy, A., Goodwin, F., Davenport, Y., Mueller, P., Newsome, D., and Wehr, T. 1984. "Seasonal affective disorder." *Archives of General Psychiatry* 41, 72. For demonstrations of the use of light therapy for SADs, see Rosenthal, N., Sack, D., Carpenter, C., Parry, B., Mendelson, W., and Wehr, T. 1985. "Antidepressant effects of light in seasonal affective disorder." *American Journal of Psychiatry* 142, 163; Wehr, T., Jacobsen, F., Sack, D., Arendt, J., Tamarkin, L., and Rosenthal, N. 1986. "Phototherapy of seasonal affective disorder." *Archives of General Psychiatry* 43, 870.

An excellent and accessible introduction to the topic of neuro-transmitters can be found in Barondes, S. 1993. *Molecules and Mental Illness* (New York: Scientific American Library, W. H. Free-man).

PAGE 205: The neurochemistry of depression is a vast subject with a dizzying number of papers, many of them contradicting each other. For an authoritative and relatively accessible discussion of the current confusion about whether it is a neuroepinephrine or serotonin prob-lem, involving too much or too little of the neurotransmitter(s), or too much or too little of the receptor(s), see Kandel, E. 1991. "Disorders of mood." In Kandel, E., Schwartz, J., and Jessell, T. *Principles of Neural Sciences*, 3rd ed. (New York: Elsevier). Also see Barondes, S. 1993. *Molecules and Mental Illness* (New York: Scientific American Library, W. H. Freeman).

PAGE 206: Pleasure pathways in the brain: For a history of the start of this field by one of its two discoverers, see Milner, P. 1989. "The discovery of self-stimulation and other stories." *Neuroscience and Bio-behavioral Reviews* 13, 61. For another general overview of the field, see Routtenberg, A. 1978. "The reward system of the brain." *Scientific American* (November). For a demonstration that stimulation of these pathways can be more reinforcing than food, see Routtenberg, A. and Lindy, J. 1965. "Effects of the availability of rewarding septal and hypothalamic stimulation on bar pressing for food under conditions of deprivation." *Journal of Comparative and Physiological Psychology* 60, 158.

For an early study implicating norepinephrine in the pleasure pathway, see Stein, L. 1962. "Effects and interactions of imipramine, chlorpromzaine, reserpine, and amphetamine on self-stimulation: Pos-sible neurophysiological basis of depression." In Wortis, J. (ed.), *Recent Advances in Biological Psychiatry*, vol. 4 (New York: Plenum), 288. This study showed that norepinephrine depletion in the rat decreases self-stimulation of the pleasure pathways. In recent years, there has been a shift in this field away from considering norepinephrine to be the principal neurotransmitter of the pleasure pathways, much as there has been a shift away from considering it the sole culprit in depression. A neurotransmitter called dopamine is moving toward the forefront as the first neurotransmitter among equals involved in plea-sure signaling. This makes some sense, as cocaine works mostly on dopamine synapses. However, although norepinephrine is probably not the most important neurotransmitter of pleasure perception, a defect in norepinephrine regulation in that part of the brain still has a great deal of potential for wreaking havoc. In considering how multiple neurotransmitters are used in many synaptic steps in these pleasure pathways, an analogy might help: a long cable may be made of stronger and weaker materials at different points; nevertheless, severing the cable in any place causes problems, and the norepinephrine link might be where the severing occurs. This is reviewed in Milner, P. 1991. "Brain-stimulation reward: A review." *Canadian Journal of Psychology* 45, 1.

A review of the human literature regarding pleasure pathways and self-stimulation can be found in Heath, R. 1963. "Electrical self-stimulation of the brain in man." *American Journal of Psychiatry* 120, 571.

PAGE 209: A brief tirade about ECT: Few medical procedures of our time have a worse popular image. In the past, ECT involved sufficient amounts of electricity to cause brain damage and memory loss, and to induce convulsions, causing body injury. Far worse, ECT's use for all sorts of things besides intractable depression—behavior disorders, juvenile delinquency, and so on—smacked of medico-political control and punishment. However, ECT is now conducted very differently—far less electricity is used, and there is no evidence that the modern form of ECT causes brain damage or permanent memory loss. Moreover, people are now typically sedated during ECT sessions, which virtually eliminates the danger of physical injury from convulsing. Most important, when it is administered correctly, ECT can save lives. For people who have been through every type of psychotherapy, every known antidepressant, and every combination of the two, yet are still suicidally depressed, ECT may be the only known technique that will ever get them functioning again. It can be an extraordinarily helpful procedure, and many former depressives swear by it. For a discussion of the history of ECT and its rather safe record as currently used, see Fink, M. 1985. "Convulsive therapy: Fifty years of progress." *Convulsive Therapy* I, 204. Mechanisms of ECT action: some papers showing effects of ECT on numbers of receptors for norepinephrine and related neurotransmitters: Kellar, K. and Stockmeier, C. 1986. "Effects of electroconvulsive shock and serotonin axon lesions on beta-adrenergic and serotonin-2 receptors in rat brain." *Annals of the New York Academy of Sciences* 462, 76; Chiodo, L. and Antelman, S. 1980. "Electroconvulsive shock: Progressive dopamine autoreceptor subsensitivity independent of repeated treatment." *Science* 210, 799; Reches, A., Wagner, H., Barkai, A., Jackson, V., Yablonskaya-Alter, E., and Fahn, S. 1984. "Electroconvulsive treatment and haloperidol: Effects on pre- and postsynaptic dopamine receptors in rat brain." *Psychopharmacology* 83, 155.

PAGE 212: For a discussion of the cons and surprising number of pros concerning cingulotomy (and for a thoughtful discussion of psychosurgical controversies in general), see Konner, M. 1988. "Too desperate a cure?" Originally published in *The Sciences* (May), 6; reprinted in Konner, M. 1990. *Why the Reckless Survive* (New York: Viking Penguin). For a technical discussion of the outcome of cingulotomies, see Ballantine, H., Bouckoms, A., Thomas, E., and Giriunas, I. 1987. "Treatment of psychiatric illness by stereotactic cingulotomy." *Biological Psychiatry* 22, 807. For a history of psychosurgery and its accompanying controversies, see Valenstein, E. 1986. *Great and Desperate Cures: The Rise and Decline of Psychosurgery and Other Radical Treatments for Mental Illness* (New York: Basic Books). Interestingly, a recent paper supports the rough picture of "the cortex whispering too many depressing thoughts to the limbic system"; this paper demonstrates that depressed patients have enhanced metabolism (relative to nondepressed patients) in the prefrontal cortex and the amygdala: Drevets, W., Videen, T., Price, J., Preskorn, S., Carmichael, S., and Raichle, M. 1992. "A functional anatomical study of unipolar depression." *The Journal of Neuroscience* 12, 3628.

Thyroid hormone insufficiency can lead to depression: Denko, J. and Kaelbling, R. 1962. "Psychiatric aspects of hypoparathyroidism." *Acta Psychiatr. Scand.* (Suppl. 164) 38, 7; Whybrow, P., Prange, A., and Treadway, C. 1969. "Mental changes accompanying thyroid gland dysfunction." *Archives of General Psychiatry* 20, 47. One way in which this may occur comes with the finding that thyroid hormones influence norepinephrine processing in the brain: Prange, A., Meek, J., and Lipton, M. 1970. "Catecholamines: diminished rate of synthesis in rat brain and heart after thyroxine pretreatment." *Life Sciences* 9, 901. Many patients with depression turn out to have an underlying thyroid hormone deficiency: Lipton, M., Breese, G., Prange, A., Wilson, I., and Cooper, B. 1976. "Behavioral effects of hypothalamic polypeptide hormones in animals and man." In Sacher, E. (ed.). *Hormones, Behavior and Psychopathology* (New York: Raven Press), 15.

Melatonin and depression: For one example of this style of study, see Winton, F., Corn, T., Huson, L., Franey, C., Arendt, J., and Checkley, S. 1989. "Effects of light treatment upon mood and melatonin in patients with seasonal affective disorder." *Psychological Medicine* 19, 585.

PAGE 213: Higher rates of depression in women than in men: Murphy, M., Sobol, A., Neff, R., Olivier, D., and Leighton, A. 1984. "Stability of prevalence." *Archives of General Psychiatry* 41, 990.

Sex differences in the rates of depression: The best overview of some of the nonhormonal theories can be found in Nolen-Hoeksma, S. 1987. "Sex differences in depression: Theory and evidence." *Psychological Bulletin* 101, 259.

Hormonal aspects of sex differences in depression: Women have particularly high incidences of depression around the time of menstruation: Abramowitz, E., Baker, A., and Fleischer, S. 1982. "Onset of depressive psychiatric crises and the menstrual cycle." *American Journal of Psychiatry* 139, 475. The immediate post-parturition period is one of great risk for depression: Campbell, S. and Cohn, J. 1991. "Prevalence and correlates of postpartum depression in first-time mothers." *Journal of Abnormal Psychology* 100, 594; O'Hara, M., Schlechte, J., Lewis, D., and Wright, E. 1991. "Prospective study of postpartum blues. Biologic and psychosocial factors." *Archives of General Psychiatry* 48, 801. What is generally viewed to be a heretical idea was voiced in a recent study, namely that fathers have the same rate of postpartum depression as mothers do: Richman, J., Raskin, V., and Gaines, C. 1991. "Gender roles, social support, and postpartum depressive symptomatology." *Journal of Nervous and Mental Disease* 179, 139.

Estrogen and progesterone have effects on the brain: As just some examples of these, estrogen will change the electrical excitability of the brain (Teyler, T., Vardaris, R., Lewis, D., and Rawitch, A. 1980. "Gonadal steroids: Effects on excitability of hippocampal pyramidal cells." *Science* 209, 1017) and the number of receptors for some of the major neurotransmitters (Schumacher, M. 1990. "Rapid membrane effects of steroid hormones: An emerging concept in neuroendocrinology." *Trends in Neurosciences*, 13, 359; see also Weiland, N. 1990. "Sex steroids alter N-methyl-D-aspartate receptor binding in the hippocampus." *Society for Neuroscience Abstracts* 16, 959), as well as the number of receiving sites on dendrites ("dendritic spines") that form synapses with axon terminals. This last observation is particularly interesting, as it has been shown that the number of dendritic spines fluctuates in parts of the brain of the rat as a function of the reproductive cycle of the female (Woolley, C., Gould, E., Frankfurt, M., and McEwen, B. 1990. "Naturally occurring fluctuation in dendritic spine density on adult hippocampal pyramidal neurons." *Journal of Neuroscience* 10, 4035).

Progesterone also has effects, in that one of its breakdown products (metabolites) can bind to one of the main neurotransmitter receptor types in the brain and alter its functioning (Majewska, M., Harrison, N., Schwartz, R., Barker, J., and Paul, S. 1986. "Steroid hormone metabolites are barbiturate-like modulators of the GABA receptor." *Science* 232, 1004). This is particularly interesting for two reasons. First, the fact that the critical agent there is not progesterone but its metabolite (called "3-alpha-hydroxy-5-alpha-dihydroprogesterone" by its close friends) means that one must not only keep track of how much progesterone there is on the scene but how much of it gets converted to the latter. Of particular interest in terms of the menstrual cycle, progesterone, mood, and depression is the fact that these progesterone metabolites bind to the same receptor complex that binds the benzodiazepine tranquilizers (like those marketed as Valium and Librium) as well as barbiturate anesthetics ("downers"). Moreover, at proper doses, this progesterone metabolite can work as an anesthetic itself (such "steroid anesthetics" have even been used on humans during surgery). No one has quite sorted out the functional significance of this yet, but everyone assumes that something extremely interesting is going on.

Finally, for a way in which estrogen and progesterone can alter the action of antidepressant drugs in the brain, see Wilson, M., Dwuyer, K., and Roy, E. 1989. "Direct effects of ovarian hormones on antidepressant binding sites." *Brain Research Bulletin* 22, 181. For a demonstration that females break down antidepressant drugs in the bloodstream more slowly than males, so that more gets into the brain, see Biegon, A. and Samuel, D. 1979. "The in vivo distribution of an antidepressant drug (DMI) in male and female rats." *Psychopharmacology* 65, 259. For a fascinating discussion of the ways in which people of different ethnic backgrounds vary in their sensitivity to various psychoactive drugs, see Holden, C. 1991. "New center to study therapies and ethnicity." *Science* 251, 748.

PAGE 215: Freud's classic essay, "Mourning and melancholia," can be found in *The Collected Papers, Vol. IV* (New York: Basic Books, 1959).

PAGE 217: Psychological features of learned helplessness: The definitive book on the subject is by Martin Seligman (from which the various quotations are taken): *Helplessness: On Depression, Development and Death* (San Francisco: W. H. Freeman, 1975). This monumental (and quite readable) work is one of the most influential books ever published in psychology. The specific human experiments cited in this section are Hiroto, D. 1974. "Locus of control and learned helplessness." *Journal of Experimental Psychology* 102, 187 (uncontrollable noise induces helplessness with a noise-avoidance task); Hiroto, D. and Seligman, M. 1974. "Generality of learned helplessness in man." *Journal of Personality and Social Psychology* 31, 311 (uncontrollable noise disrupts learning of simple word puzzles, and unsolvable tasks induce helplessness); Seligman, 1975, p. 35 (unsolvable tasks induce social helplessness).

PAGE 219: For a discussion of learned helplessness as a cognitive/affective phenomenon, see Seligman, M. 1975. *Helplessness: On Depression, Development and Death* (San Francisco: W. H. Freeman). For a discussion of learned helplessness as a phenomenon of psychomotor retardation, see Weiss, J., Bailey, W., Goodman, P., Hoffman, L., Ambrose, M., Salman, S., and Charry, J. 1982. "A model for neurochemical study of depression." In Spiegelstein, M. and Levy, A. (eds.). *Behavioral Models and the Analysis of Drug Action* (Amsterdam: Elsevier).

"Learned laziness" in animals given noncontingent reward: The use of the term "spoiled brat" is cited by Seligman, 1975, p. 35. The published version of those findings can be found in Engberg, L., Hansen, G., Welker, R., and Thomas, D. 1973. "Acquisition of keypecking via autoshaping as a function of prior experience: 'Learned laziness?'" *Science* 178, 1002.

PAGE 220: Biological features of learned helplessness, where rats show altered grooming, social behavior, sexual behavior, feeding, plus many of the vegetative symptoms: Stone, E. 1978. "Possible grooming deficit in stressed rats." *Research Communication in Psychology, Psychiatry and Behavior* 3, 109; Weiss, J., Simson, P., Ambrose, M., Webster, A., and Hoffman, L. 1985. "Neurochemical basis of behavioral depression." In Katkin, E. and Manuck, S. (eds.). *Advances in Behavioral Medicine*, Vol. 1 (Greenwich, Conn.: JAI Press); Weiss, J., Goodman, P., Losito, P., Corrigan, S., Charry, J., and Bailey, W. 1981. "Behavioral depression produced by an uncontrolled stressor: Relation to norepinephrine, dopamine and serotonin levels in various regions of the rat brain." *Brain Research Reviews* 3, 167. For an explicit comparison between the symptoms of depression (DSM-III criteria) and learned helplessness, see Weiss, J., Bailey, W., Goodman, P., Hoffman, L., Ambrose, M., Salman, S., and Charry, J. 1982. "A model for neurochemical study of depression." In Spiegelstein, M. and Levy, A. (eds.). *Behavioral Models and the Analysis of Drug Action* (Amsterdam: Elsevier).

Learned helplessness can be lessened by antidepressants or ECT: Dorworth, T. and Overmier, J. 1977. "On learned helplessness: The therapeutic effects of electroconvulsive shocks." *Physiological Psychology* 5, 355; Leshner, A., Remler, H., Biegon, A., and Samuel, D. 1979. "Desmethylimipramine counteracts learned helplessness in rats." *Psychopharmacology* 66, 207; Petty, F. and Sherman, A. 1980. "Reversal of learned helplessness by imipramine." *Communications in Psychopharmacology* 3, 371; Sherman, A., Allers, G., Petty, F., and Henn, F. 1979. "A neuropharmacologically-relevant animal model of depression." *Neuropharmacology* 18, 891.

PAGE 222: Rozin, P., Poritsky, S., and Sotsky, R. 1971. "American children with reading problems can easily learn to read English represented by Chinese characters." *Science* 171, 1264.

Early parental loss increases the risk of adulthood depression: This subject is reviewed in Breier, A., Kelso, J., Kirwin, P., Beller, S., Wolkowitz, O., and Pickar, D. 1988. "Early parental loss and development of adult psychopathology." *Archives of General Psychiatry* 45, 987.

PAGE 223: Stress depletes parts of the brain of norepinephrine, while also increasing the activity of tyrosine hydroxylase: Stone, E. and McCarty, R. 1983. "Adaptation to stress: Tyrosine hydroxylase activity and catecholamine release." *Neuroscience and Biobehavioral Reviews* 7, 29. Glucocorticoids have something to do with this: Dunn, A., Gildersleeve, N., and Gray, H. 1978. "Mouse brain tyrosine hydroxylase and glutamic acid decarboxcylase following treatment with adrenocorticotropic hormone, vasopressin or corticosterone." *Journal of Neurochemistry* 31, 977. In addition, CRF may have something to do with this: Ahlers, S., Salander, M., Shurtleff, D., and Thomas, J. 1992. "Tyrosine pretreatment alleviates suppression of schedule-controlled responding produced by CRF in rats." *Brain Research Bulletin* 29, 567.

For broad discussions of the connections between stress and depression, see Gold, P., Goodwin, F., and Chrousos, G. 1988. "Clinical and biochemical manifestations of depression. Relation to the neurobiology of stress." *New England Journal of Medicine* 319, 348 (outlines a model, very similar to that proposed in this chapter, of the genetic defect in depression as a failure for stress to induce tyrosine hydroxylase); Zis, A. and Goodwin, F. 1979. "Major affective disorders as a recurrent illness: a critical review." *Archives of General Psychiatry* 36, 385; Anisman, H. and Zacharko, R. 1982. "Depression: The predisposing influence of stress." *Behavioral and Brain Science* 5, 89; Turner, R. and Beiser, M. 1990. "Major depression and depressive symptomatology among the physically disabled: Assessing the role of chronic stress." *Journal of Nervous and Mental Disease* 178, 343.

CHAPTER 12: AGING AND DEATH

PAGE 231: Functioning in old organisms is disrupted by stress more than in young ones: The classic studies on temperature dysregulation during aging can be found in Shock, N. 1977. "Systems integration." In Finch, C. and Hayflick, L. (eds.). *Handbook of the Biology of Aging*, 1st ed. (New York: Van Nostrand). A detailed discussion of all the ways in which the cardiovascular system functions similarly in young and old healthy subjects in the absence of stress can be found in Lakatta, E. 1990. "Heart and circulation." In Schneider, E. and Rowe, J. (eds.). *Handbook of the Biology of Aging*, 3rd ed. (New York: Academic Press). Decrease in maximal heart rate and work capacity with age: Gerstenblith, G., Lakatta, E., and Weisfeldt, M. 1976. "Age changes in myocardial function and exercise response." *Progress in Cardiovascular Disease* 19, 1. Decreased ejection volume during exercise with age: Rodeheffer, R., Gerstenblith, G., Becker, L., Fleg, J., Weisfeldt, M., and Lakatta, E. 1984. "Exercise cardiac output is maintained with advancing age in healthy human subjects: Cardiac dilatation and increased stroke volume compensate for diminished heart rate." *Circulation* 69, 203. Increased cardiac muscle stiffness with force as a function of age: Spurgeon, H., Thorne, P., Yin, F., Shock, N., and Weisfeldt, M. 1977. "Increased dynamic stiffness of tabeculae carneae from senescent rats." *American Journal of Physiology* 232, H373.

PAGE 233: The aged brain is slower in compensatory sprouting after an injury than is the young brain: Cotman, C. 1985. *Synaptic*

Plasticity (New York: Guilford). The effect of age on the vulnerability of cerebral metabolism to a metabolic stressor: Benzi, G., Pastoris, O., Vercesi, L., Gorini, A., Viganotti, C., and Villa, R. 1987. "Energetic state of aged brain during hypoxia." *Gerontology* 33, 207; Hoffman, W., Pelligrino, D., Miletich, D., and Albrecht, R. 1985. "Brain metabolic changes in young versus aged rats during hypoxia." *Stroke* 16, 860.

The effect of age on performance on intelligence tests: this vast subject is reviewed in a number of chapters in Birren, J. and Schaie, K. 1990. *Handbook of the Psychology of Aging*, 3rd ed. (New York: Van Nostrand): Cerella, J. "Aging and information-processing rate"; Kausler, D. "Motivation, human aging and cognitive performance"; Hultsch, D. and Dixson, R. "Learning and memory in aging." See also Katzman, R. and Terry, R. 1983. *The Neurology of Aging* (Philadelphia: Davis).

Elevated epinephrine and norepinephrine concentrations during exercise as a function of age: Fleg, J., Tzankoff, S., and Lakatta, E. 1985. "Age-related augmentation of plasma catecholamines during dynamic exercise in healthy males." *Journal of Applied Physiology* 59, 1033. Decreased cardiovascular sensitivity to adrenalin and noradrenalin with age: Lakatta, E. 1987. "Catecholamines and cardiovascular function in aging." *Endocrinology and Metabolism Clinics of North America* 16, 877.

PAGE 234: Slower epinephrine/norepinephrine recovery after the end of stress: McCarty, R. 1986. "Age-related alterations in sympathetic-adrenal medullary responses to stress." *Gerontology* 32, 172. Slower glucocorticoid recovery after the end of stress: Sapolsky, R, Krey, L., and McEwen, B. 1983. "The adrenocortical stress-response in the aged male rat: Impairment of recovery from stress." *Experimental Gerontology* 18, 55; Ida, Y., Tanaka, M., and Tsuda, A. 1984. "Recovery of stress-induced increases in noradrenaline turnover is delayed in specific brain regions of old rats." *Life Sciences* 34, 2357. The delayed glucocorticoid recovery may accelerate tumor growth: Sapolsky, R. and Donnelly, T. 1985. "Vulnerability to stress-induced tumor growth increases with age in the rat: Role of glucocorticoid hypersecretion." *Endocrinology* 117, 662.

Resting epinephrine and norepinephrine levels increase with age: Fleg, J., Tzankoff, S., and Lakatta, E. 1985. "Age-related augmentation of plasma catecholamines during dynamic exercise in healthy males." *Journal of Applied Physiology* 59, 1033; also Rowe, J. and Troen, B.

1980. "Sympathetic nervous system and aging in man." *Endocrine Reviews* I, 167. Resting glucocorticoid levels rise with age in the rat: reviewed in Sapolsky, R. 1991. "Do glucocorticoid concentrations rise with age in the rat?" *Neurobiology of Aging* 13, 171. In the aged human: reviewed in Sapolsky, R. 1990. "The adrenocortical axis." In Schneider, E. and Rowe, J. (eds.). *Handbook of the Biology of Aging*, 3rd ed. (New York: Academic Press). In the wild baboon: Sapolsky, R., and Altmann, J. 1991. "Incidences of hypercortisolism and dexamethasone resistance increase with age among wild baboons." *Biological Psychiatry*, 30, 1008.

The elevated epinephrine/enorepinephrine levels contribute to the elevated blood pressure: Lakatta, E. 1990. "Heart and circulation." In Schneider, E. and Rowe, J. (eds.). *Handbook of the Biology of Aging*, 3rd ed. (New York: Academic Press). Hypertension as the most common disease of the elderly: Kannel, W. and Vokonas, P. 1986. "Primary risk factors for coronary heart disease in the elderly. The Framingham study." In Wenger, N. and Furberg, C. (eds.). *Current Heart Disease in the Elderly* (London: Elsevier).

The elevated glucocorticoid levels disrupt the ability of the brain for sprouting after injury: Scheff, S. and Cotman, C. 1982. "Chronic glucocorticoid therapy alters axon sprouting in the hippocampal dentate gyrus." *Experimental Neurology* 76, 644; DeKosky, S., Scheff, S., and Cotman, C. 1984. "Elevated corticosterone levels: A possible cause of reduced axon sprouting in aged animals." *Neuroendocrinology* 38, 33.

PAGE 236: Can stress accelerate the aging process? For those who want to go straight to the horse's mouth (in German), there is Rubner, M. 1908. *Das problem der lebensdauer und seine beziehungen zun wachstum und ernahrun* (Munchen: Oldenbourg). Also see Pearl, R. 1928. *The Rate of Living* (New York: Knopf) for the most detailed exploration of rate of living hypotheses. For some of Selye's ideas about stress and aging, see Selye, H., and Tuchweber, B. 1976. "Stress in relation to aging and disease." In Everitt, A., and Burgess, J. (eds.). *Hypothalamus, Pituitary and Aging* (Springfield, Ill.: Charles C. Thomas). For a scholarly discussion of the whole topic by one of the wisest thinkers in gerontology, see chapter 5 ("Rates of living and dying: Correlations of lifespan with size, metabolic rates, and cellular and biochemical characteristics") in Finch, C. 1990. *Longevity, Senescence, and the Genome* (Chicago: University of Chicago Press).

PAGE 237: For a discussion of why programmed aging (and aging in general) may have evolved, see Sapolsky, R. and Finch, C. 1991. "On growing old: Not every creature ages, but most do. The question is why." *The Sciences* (March/April), 30. For the original demonstration of what goes wrong in the salmon, see Robertson, O. and Wexler, B. 1957. "Pituitary degeneration and adrenal tissue hyperplasia in spawning Pacific salmon." *Science* 125, 1295. For a comparison of the effects of salmon aging with the effects of glucocorticoid excess, see Wexler, B. 1976. "Comparative aspects of hyperadrenocorticism and aging." In Everitt, A. and Burgess, J. (eds.). *Hypothalamus, Pituitary and Aging* (Springfield Ill.: Thomas). For an introduction to the marsupial mouse aging literature, see McDonald, I., Lee, A., and Bradley, A. 1981. "Endocrine changes in dasyurid marsupials with differing mortality patterns." *General and Comparative Endocrinology* 44, 292, and McDonald, I., Lee, A., and Than, K. 1986. "Failure of glucocorticoid feedback in males of a population of small marsupials (*Antechinus swainsonii*) during the period of mating." *Journal of Endocrinology* 108, 63.

PAGE 238: A brief digression: what about those children who senesce incredibly rapidly and die of old age when they are twelve? Progeria, as the disease is called, is extremely rare. Those afflicted go bald, have bony chins, beaked noses, and dry, scratchy voices; they lose their hearing, get hardening of the arteries and heart disease (which is what usually kills them). When you try to grow some of their cells in a petri dish, you have as much trouble as you would with the cells of a seventy-year-old. Despite that, not everything about progeric kids is prematurely aged: they don't become demented, nor do they get cancer—two diseases typically linked with aging (although not necessary features of it, obviously). General consensus in the field is that progeria is a disease of some *facets* of aging being accelerated, rather than the entire aging process (which indirectly demonstrates that aging involves the ticking of multiple and independent clocks in the body). For a discussion of progeria and its relationship to aging, see Finch, C. 1991. *Longevity, Senescence and the Genome* (Chicago: University of Chicago Press); Mills, R. and Weiss, A. 1990. "Does progeria provide the best model of accelerated aging in humans?" *Gerontology* 36, 84.

PAGE 240: Old humans, primates, and rats tend to become dexamethasone resistant with age: reviewed in Sapolsky, R. 1990. "The adrenocortical axis." In Schneider, E. and Rowe, J. (eds.). *Handbook of the Biology of Aging*, 3rd ed. (New York: Academic Press). In the wild baboon: Sapolsky, R., and Altmann, J. 1991. "Incidences of hypercortisolism and dexamethasone resistance increase with age among wild baboons." *Biological Psychiatry*, 30, 1008.

Patterns of neuron loss during aging: for the definitive review, see Coleman, P. and Flood, D. 1987. "Neuron numbers and dendritic extent in normal aging and Alzheimer's disease." *Neurobiology of Aging* 8, 521.

The hippocampus plays a role in inhibiting glucocorticoid secretion: reviewed in Jacobson, L. and Sapolsky, R. 1991. "The role of the hippocampus in feedback regulation of the hypothalamic-pituitary-adrenocortical axis." *Endocrine Reviews* 12, 118.

PAGE 241: Glucocorticoids damage the hippocampus and accelerate its aging: Aus der Muhlen, D. and Ockenfels, H. 1969. "Morphologische veranderungen in diencephalon und Telencephalon nach Storgen des Regelkreises Adenohypophysenebennierenrinde. III. Ergebnisee beim Meerschweinchen nach Verabreichung von Cortison und Hydrocortison." *Z. Zellforsch.* 56, 395; Landfield, P., Baskin, R., and Pitler, T. 1981. "Brain aging correlates: Retardation by hormonal-pharmacological treatments." *Science* 214, 581; Sapolsky, R., Krey, L., and McEwen, B. 1985. "Prolonged glucocorticoid exposure reduces hippocampal neuron number: Implications for aging." *Journal of Neuroscience* 5, 1221; Meaney, M., Aitken, D., Bhatnager, S., van Bekel, C., and Sapolsky, R. 1988. "Effect of neonatal handling on age-related impairments associated with the hippocampus." *Science* 239, 766; Kerr, D., Campbell, L., Applegate, M., Brodish, A., and Landfield, P. 1991. "Chronic stress-induced acceleration of electrophysiologic and morphometric biomarkers of hippocampal aging." *Journal of Neuroscience* II, 1316.

The hippocampus is critical for certain types of learning: Squire, L. 1986. "Mechanisms of learning." *Science* 232, 1612.

The interaction between the effects of glucocorticoids on the hippocampus and the effects of the hippocampus upon glucocorticoid secretion: Sapolsky, R., Krey, L., and McEwen, B. 1986. "The neuroendocrinology of stress and aging: The glucocorticoid cascade hypothesis." *Endocrine Reviews* 7, 284.

Glucocorticoids make neurological insults to the hippocampus worse: Sapolsky, R. 1985. "A mechanism for glucocorticoid toxicity in the hippocampus: Increased neuronal vulnerability to metabolic insults." *Journal of Neuroscience* 5, 1228; Sapolsky, R. and Pulsinelli, W. 1985. "Glucocorticoids potentiate ischemic injury to neurons: therapeutic implications." *Science* 229, 1397; Morse, J. and Davis, J. 1990. "Regulation of ischemic hippocampal damage in the gerbil: adrenalectomy alters the rate of CA1 cell disappearance." *Experimental Neurology* 110, 86; Koide, T., Wieloch, T., and Siesjo, B. 1986. "Chronic dexamethasone pretreatment aggravates ischemic neuronal necrosis." *Journal of Cerebral Blood Flow and Metabolism* 6, 395.

Glucocorticoids make damage to individual neurons growing in a dish worse: Sapolsky, R., Packan, D., and Vale, W. 1988. "Glucocorticoid toxicity in the hippocampus: in vitro demonstration." *Brain Research* 453, 367. Tombaugh, G., Yang, S., Swanson, R., and Sapolsky, R. 1992. "Glucocorticoids exacerbate hypoxic and hypoglycemic hippocampal injury in vitro: Biochemical correlates and a role for astrocytes." *Journal of Neurochemistry* 59, 137.

PAGE 243: These various neurological insults constitute energy crises: Auer, R. and Siesjo, B. 1988. "Biological differences between ischemia, hypoglycemia, and epilepsy." *Annals of Neurology* 24, 699.

Glucocorticoids inhibit the movement of glucose into hippocampal neurons: Kadekaro, M., Ito, M., and Gross, P. 1988. "Local cerebral glucose utilization is increased in acutely adrenalectomized rats." *Neuroendocrinology* 47, 329; Horner, H., Packan, D., and Sapolsky, R. 1990. "Glucocorticoids inhibit glucose transport in cultured hippocampal neurons and glia." *Neuroendocrinology* 52, 57; Virgin, C., Ha, T., Packan, D., Tombaugh, G., Yang, S., Horner, H., and Sapolsky, R. 1991. "Glucocorticoids inhibit glucose transport and glutamate uptake in hippocampal astrocytes: implications for glucocorticoid neurotoxicity." *Journal of Neurochemistry* 57, 1422.

Additional energy buffers hippocampal neurons from the endangering effects of glucocorticoids: Sapolsky, R. 1986. "Glucocorticoid toxicity in the hippocampus: reversal by supplementation with brain fuels." *Journal of Neuroscience* 6, 2240; Sapolsky, R., Packan, D., and Vale, W. 1988. "Glucocorticoid toxicity in the hippocampus: in vitro demonstration." *Brain Research* 453, 367. Tombaugh, G., Yang, S., Swanson, R., and Sapolsky, R. 1992. "Glucocorticoids exacerbate hypoxic and hypoglycemic hippocampal injury in vitro: Biochemical correlates and a role for astrocytes." *Journal of Neurochemistry*, 59, 137.

PAGE 245: Drugs that reduce glucocorticoid secretion can protect the hippocampus from neurological damage: Stein, B. and Sapolsky,

R. 1988. "Chemical adrenalectomy reduces hippocampal damage induced by kainic acid." *Brain Research* 473, 175 (kainic acid is a drug that induces seizures); Morse, J., and Davis, J. 1989. "Chemical adrenalectomy protects hippocampal cells following ischemia." *Society for Neuroscience Abstracts* 15, 149.4.

PAGE 246: Glucocorticoids and stress can damage the primate hippocampus: Uno, H., Tarara, R., Else, J., Suleman, M., and Sapolsky, R. 1989. "Hippocampal damage associated with prolonged and fatal stress in primates." *Journal of Neuroscience* 9, 1705; Sapolsky, R., Uno, H., Rebert, C., and Finch, C. 1990. "Hippocampal damage associated with prolonged glucocorticoid exposure in primates." *Journal of Neuroscience* 10, 2897.

For a review of this entire topic in unreadably technical detail, the truly masochistic may want to buy a dozen copies of Sapolsky, R. 1992. *Stress, the Aging Brain and the Mechanisms of Neuron Death* (Cambridge: MIT Press). The final chapter is a detailed discussion of whether glucocorticoids and/or stress can damage the human brain, and the possible implications for aging, Alzheimer's disease, depression, and a number of neurological disorders.

CHAPTER 13: MANAGING STRESS

PAGE 248: A technical description of alopecia areata can be found in Rook, A. and Dawber, R. 1991. *Diseases of the Hair and Scalp*, 2nd ed. (Oxford: Blackwell Scientific Publications). In actuality, though, there is not really a change in hair color under those circumstances. Alopecia areata occurs in people who already have some degree of whitening or greying of their hair. With the onset of the trauma, hair that is not white or grey falls out, probably because the immune system attacks dark hair bulbs. Thus, all that is left is the white or grey hair. Various experts I've consulted suggest that the phenomenon represents a bit of media hype—it is extremely rare and usually takes weeks or months, rather than occurring in a single night.

A particularly amusing account of the history of the disorder and speculations about it can be found in Jelinek, J. 1972. "Sudden whitening of the hair." *Bulletin of the New York Academy of Medicine* 48, 1003. Jelinek, a professor of dermatology, recounts many tales over the centuries of people who, condemned to be executed by their king, turn white with terror the night before the scheduled execution. The now white-haired prisoner is brought before the king and assembled court for execution the next morning. Everyone is moved with wonder and pity at the transformation, and the poor wretch is pardoned. Numerous sources claim that the hair and beard of Sir Thomas More, who had fallen out of favor with King Henry VIII and was condemned to death, turned white the day before his execution. In contrast to the general pattern of these tales, Henry, unimpressed, still had him killed and his head parboiled and displayed on London Bridge. Over the course of her imprisonment prior to her execution, Marie Antoinette's hair was also reported to have turned grey. This may not have represented a true case of alopecia areata, however. "It has cynically been conjectured that the keepers of her dungeon neglected to furnish their guest's dressing table with hair dyes. The iconoclast respects nothing, not even the grey hairs of royalty," opined the mordant Dr. Jelinik.

PAGE 249: The tendency for variability to increase in aging populations is discussed in Rowe, J., Wang, S., and Elahi, D. 1990. "Design, conduct, and analysis of human aging research." In Schneider, E. and Rowe, J. *Handbook of the Biology of Aging,* 3rd ed. (San Diego: Academic Press) 63.

PAGE 251: The encouraging topic of successful aging is reviewed in Rowe, J. and Kahn, R. 1987. "Human aging: Usual and successful." Science 237, 143; Baltes, P. and Baltes, M. 1990. *Successful Aging* (Cambridge: Cambridge University Press).

PAGE 252: Cognitively unimpaired aged rats showed none of the usual degenerations: Issa, A., Rowe, W., Gauthier, S., and Meaney, M. 1991. "Hypothalamic-pituitary-adrenal activity in aged, cognitively impaired and cognitively unimpaired rats." *Journal of Neuroscience* 10, 3247. Neonatal handling produces similar protection in old age: Meaney, M., Aitken, D., Bhatnager, S., van Berkel, C., and Sapolsky, R. 1988. "Effect of neonatal handling on age-related impairments associated with the hippocampus." Science 239, 766; Meaney, M., Aitken, D., and Sapolsky, R. 1990. "Postnatal handling attenuates neuroendocrine, anatomical and cognitive dysfunctions associated with aging in female rats." *Neurobiology of Aging* 12, 31.

PAGE 254: Coping styles among parents of children with cancer: Wolff, C., Friedman, S., Hofer, M., and Mason, J. 1964. "Relationship between psychological defenses and mean urinary 17-hydroxycortico-steroid excretion rates. I. A predictive study of parents of fatally ill children." *Psychosomatic Medicine* 26, 576. The follow-up study later showing that the parents with the lowest glycocorticoid levels during the period of remission (associated with a high degree of denial) had the highest glucocorticoid levels once the child came out of remission and died: Hofer, M., Wolff, E., Friedman, S., and Mason, J. 1972. "A psychoendocrine study of bereavement, Parts I and II." *Psychosomatic Medicine* 34, 481.

PAGE 256: Resistance to learned helplessness is discussed in Seligman, M. 1992. *Helplessness,* 2nd ed. (New York: W. H. Freeman).

PAGE 257: A nontechnical summary of my baboon work can be found in Sapolsky, R. 1990. "Stress in the wild." *Scientific American* (January). A detailed review can be found in Sapolsky, R. 1992. "Endocrinology alfresco: Psychoendocrine studies of wild baboons." *Recent Progress in Hormone Research*, 48, 437. The personality studies can be found in Sapolsky, R., and Ray, J. 1989. "Styles of dominance and their physiological correlates among wild baboons." *American Journal of Primatology* 18, 1; Ray, J. and Sapolsky, R. 1992. "Styles of male social behavior and their endocrine correlates among high-ranking baboons." *American Journal of Primatology,* 28, 231.

PAGE 266: Change in cholesterol profiles in Type A individuals receiving counseling: Gill, J., Price, V., and Friedman, M. 1985. "Reduction in Type A behavior in healthy middle-aged American military officers." *American Heart Journal* 110, 503. Also see Thoresen, C., and Powell, L. 1993. "Type A behavior pattern: New perspectives on theory, assessment and intervention." *Journal of Consulting and Clinical Psychology,* in press.

Some papers showing the salutary effects of transcendental meditation on various physiological endpoints (resting glucocorticoid levels, oxygen consumption, heart rate, and so on): Wallace, R. 1970. "Physiological effects of transcendental meditation." *Science* 167, 1751; Wallace, R., and Benson, H. 1972. "The physiology of meditation." *Scientific American*, February, 84 (these two papers cover much the same material, but the latter is more accessible and gives more of an overview of the subject); Jevning, R., Wilson, A., and Davidson, J. 1978. "Adrenocortical activity during meditation." *Hormones and Behavior* 10, 54.

Changing of the stress-response over time among parachuting trainees: Ursin, H., Baade, E., and Levine, S. 1978. *Psychobiology of Stress* (San Diego: Academic Press).

PAGE 267: Self-medication among acute pain patients can be conducted safely: Norman, J., White, W., and Pearce, D. 1978. "New possibilities in analgesia: The demand analgesia computer. Round table on morphinomimetics." *5th European Congress of Anaesthesiology,* Paris; Jully, C. and Sibbald, A. 1981. "Control of postoperative pain by interactive demand analgesia." *British Journal of Anaesthesiology* 53, 385; Baumann, T., Bastenhorst, R., Graves, D., Foster, T., and Bennett, R. 1986. "Patient-controlled analgesia in the terminally ill cancer patient." *Drug Intell Clinical Pharmacology* 20, 297; Citron, M., Johnston-Early, A., Boyer, M., Krasnow, S., Hood, H., and Cohen, M. 1986. "Patient-controlled analgesia for severe cancer pain." *Archives of Internal Medicine* 146, 734. Such self-medication can be associated with an overall decrease in the amount of medication taken: Chapman, C. and Hill, H. 1989. "Prolonged morphine self-administration and addiction liability: Evaluation of two theories in a bone marrow transplant unit." *Cancer* 63, 1636; Chapman, C. 1989. "Giving the patient control of opioid analgesic administration." In Hill, C. and Fields, W. (eds.). *Advances in Pain Research and Therapy,* Vol. 11 (New York: Raven Press), 339; Chapman, C. and Hill, H. 1990. "Patient-controlled analgesia in a bone marrow transplant setting." In Foley, K. (ed.). *Advances in Pain Research and Therapy,* Vol. 16, 231.

PAGE 268: Coping styles differ between young and aged humans: Folkman, S., Lazarus, R., Pimley, S., and Novacek, J. 1987. "Age differences in stress and coping processes." *Psychology and Aging* 2, 171.

PAGE 269: Manipulating psychological variables in nursing home populations: This large literature is reviewed in Rodin, J. 1986. "Aging and health: Effects of the sense of control." *Science* 233, 1271; Rowe, J. and Kahn, R. 1987. "Human aging: Usual and successful." *Science* 237, 143. The particular study in which function declined below pre-experiment levels after the end of the study is reported in Schulz, J. 1976. "Effects of control and predictability on the physical and psychological well-being of the institutionalized aged." *Journal of Personality and Social Psychology* 33, 563; Schulz, R. and Hanusa, B. 1978. "Long-term effects of control and predictability-enhancing interventions: Findings and ethical issues." *Journal of Personality and Social Psychology* 36, 1194.

PAGE 272: Immune function tends to decline in rodents socially housed: Bohus, B. and Koolhaas, J. 1991. "Psychoimmunology of social factors in rodents and other subprimate vertebrates." In Ader, R., Felten, D., and Cohen, N. (eds.). *Psychoneuroimmunology,* 2nd ed. (San Diego: Academic Press), 807. Social housing tends to elevate glucocorticoid levels in rodents and primates: Levine, S., Wiener, S., and Coe, C. 1989. "The psychoneuroendocrinology of stress: A psychobiological perspective." In Levine, S. and Brush, F. (eds.). *Psychoendocrinology* (San Diego: Academic Press). This review also discusses the study showing that infant monkeys separated from their mothers are not necessarily comforted (that is, show lowered glucocorticoid secretion) merely by being put in a social group. Also see Clarke, A., Czekala, N., and Lindburg, D. "Behavioral and adrenocortical responses of male cynomolgus and lion-tailed macaques to social stimulation and group formation." *American Journal of Primatology,* submitted. Marital discord is associated with immune suppression: Kiecolt-Glaser, J., Fisher, L., Ogrocki, P., Stout, J., Speicher, C., and Glaser, R. 1987. "Marital quality, marital disruption, and immune function." *Psychosomatic Medicine* 49, 13; Kiecolt-Glaser, J., Kennedy, S., Malkoff, S., Fisher, L., Speicher, C., and Glaser, R. 1988. "Marital discord and immunity in males." *Psychosomatic Medicine* 50, 213.

PAGE 274: Cyril Radcliffe and his terrible footnote in history are discussed in Collins, L. and Lapierre, D. 1975. *Freedom at Midnight* (New York: Simon and Schuster). Radcliffe's bizarrely detached speech, "Thoughts on India as 'The page is turned'" can be found in Radcliffe, C. 1968. *Not in Feather Beds: Some Collected Papers* (London: Hamish Hamilton).

PAGE 277: The advantages of denial: Lazarus, R. 1983. "The costs and benefits of denial." In Breznitz, S. (ed.). *The Denial of Stress* (New York: International Universities Press), 1.

Warning against overloading aged individuals with too much control and responsibility: Rodin, J. 1986. "Aging and health: Effects of the sense of control." *Science* 233, 1271; Langer, E. 1983. *The Psychology of Control* (Beverly Hills, Calif.: Sage); Langer, E. 1989. *Mindfulness* (Reading, Mass.: Addison Wesley Publishing Co.).

The dangers of unrealistic anger: Williams, R. 1989. *The Trusting Heart: Great News About Type A Behavior* (New York: Random House). Also Williams, R. and Williams, V. 1993. *Anger Kills: Seventeen Strate-*

gies for Controlling the Hostility That Can Harm Your Health (New York: Times/Random House).

Spiegel, D. 1992. "Psychosocial interventions and cancer." *Advances* 8, no. 1, 3. The study he cited concerning types of beliefs in control in cancer patients: Watson, M., Greer, S., Pruyn, J., and van den Borne, B. 1990. "Locus of control and adjustment to cancer." *Psychological Reports* 66, 39. Also of interest should be Friedman, H. 1991. *The Self-Healing Personality* (Hutter Books).

The advantages of denial in the immediate aftermath of a medical disaster: Lazarus, R. 1983. "The costs and benefits of denial." In Breznitz, S. (ed.). *The Denial of Stress* (New York: International Universities Press), 1.

Seligman, M. 1991. *Learned Optimism* (New York: Knopf).

THE FAR SIDE   By GARY LARSON

SOURCES

PAGE 3
The National Archives

PAGE 6
Courtesy of Robert Longo and Metro Pictures

PAGES 20–21
Quote from D. H. Lawrence, 1929, *Lady Chatterley's Lover*, in *The Works of D. H. Lawrence*, Cambridge University Press, 1993; reprinted by permission of Laurence Pollinger Ltd. and the Estate of Frieda Lawrence Ravagli

PAGE 26
Merrilley Borell, 1976, *Bulletin of the History of Medicine, 50*, page 309, and Johns Hopkins Press, Baltimore, Maryland

PAGE 29
Robert Guillemin and Roger Burgus, 1972, "The Hormones of the Hypothalamus," *Scientific American*, (November) page 24; courtesy of Robert Guillemin, The Whittier Institute

PAGE 40
THE FAR SIDE © 1988 FarWorks, Inc. Distributed by UNIVERSAL PRESS SYNDICATE. Reprinted with permission. All rights reserved.

PAGE 43
Biophoto, Photo Researchers, Inc.

PAGE 45
Superstock Inc.

PAGE 47
Custom Medical Stock Photo, Inc.

PAGE 60
Drawing by R. Chast; © 1983 *The New Yorker* Magazine Inc.

PAGE 66
David M. Phillips, Science Source, Photo Researchers, Inc.

PAGE 71
J. James, Science Photo Library, Photo Researchers, Inc.

PAGE 80
Courtesy of Mark Daughetee

PAGE 88
P. Saenger et al., 1977, "Somatedin growth hormone in psychosocial dwarfism," *Padiatrie und Padologie, Supplement 5*, page 2; courtesy of Maria I. New, New York Hospital/ Cornell Medical Center

PAGE 90
E. M. Widdowson, 1951, "Mental contentment and physical growth," *The Lancet*, (16 June) page 1316; courtesy of E. M. Widdowson

PAGE 94
Data from P. Saenger et al., 1977, "Somatedin growth hormone in psychosocial dwarfism," *Padiatrie und Padologie, Supplement 5*, page 2

PAGE 96
M. Newman, Superstock Inc.

PAGE 106
Courtesy of Harlow Primate Laboratory, University of Wisconsin

PAGE 115
Courtesy of Laurance Frank, University of California, Berkeley

PAGE 121
Konner, Anthro-Photo

PAGE 138
Courtesy of Gilla Kaplan, The Rockefeller University

PAGE 144
Pushkin Museum, Moscow, Russia; Scala/Art Resource, NY (only a detail of the painting is used)

PAGES 156–160
Quotes from Bernie Siegel, 1986, *Love, Medicine, and Miracles*, Harper & Row, New York

PAGES 161–164
Material from Robert Sapolsky, 1991, "Poverty's Remains," *The Sciences*, (September/October); reprinted by permission of the New York Academy of Sciences

PAGES 165–166
Quote from Joseph Heller, 1955, *Catch-22*, Simon & Schuster, New York; reprinted by permission of Simon & Schuster, Inc. © 1955, 1961, 1989 Joseph Heller

PAGE 167
Philadelphia Museum of Art: SmithKline Beckman Corporation Fund

PAGE 176
Courtesy of Vic Boff

PAGE 180
Drawing by M. Stevens; © 1982 *The New Yorker* Magazine, Inc.

PAGE 184
Private collection; courtesy of George Tooker and Chameleon Books, Inc.

PAGE 186
Drawing by Roz Chast

PAGE 198
New Britain Museum of American Art, Gift of Olga H. Knoepke; courtesy of George Tooker and Chameleon Books, Inc.

PAGES 217–222
Quotes from Martin Seligman, 1975, 1992, *Helplessness: On Development, Depression & Death*, W. H. Freeman and Company, New York

PAGE 227
Courtesy of Morris Zlapo

PAGE 229
DeVore, Anthro-Photo

PAGE 230
Drawing by Anthony; © 1983 *The New Yorker* Magazine, Inc.

PAGE 237
Rick Blacklaws, Image West Photography

PAGE 249
Hermitage Museum, St. Petersburg, Russia; Scala Art Resource, New York; © 1993 Succession H. Matisse/ARS, New York

PAGE 254
Courtesy of Ed Spielman and E. Allen Becker and Son

PAGES 258 and 259
Courtesy of Robert Sapolsky, Stanford University

PAGE 275
Quote from W. H. Auden, 1966, "Partition," in Edward Mendelson, 1976, 1991, *W. H. Auden: Collected Poems*, Faber and Faber Limited, London, pages 803–804; reprinted by permission of Random House Inc., Faber and Faber Limited, and the Estate of W. H. Auden

PAGE 279
Drawing by Koren; © 1993 *The New Yorker* Magazine, Inc.

PAGE 281
Philadelphia Museum of Art: The Louise and Walter Arensberg Collection; © 1993 ARS, New York/ADAGP, Paris

PAGE 282
Courtesy of Sidney Janis Gallery, New York; © 1993 George Segal/VAGA, New York

PAGE 354
THE FAR SIDE cartoon by Gary Larson is reprinted by permission of Chronicle Features, San Francisco, California. All rights reserved.

INDEX